MODERN EUROPEAN
INTELLECTUAL HISTORY

MODERN EUROPEAN INTELLECTUAL HISTORY

INDIVIDUALS, GROUPS, AND TECHNOLOGICAL CHANGE, 1800–2000

David Galaty

BLOOMSBURY ACADEMIC
LONDON • NEW YORK • OXFORD • NEW DELHI • SYDNEY

BLOOMSBURY ACADEMIC
Bloomsbury Publishing Plc
50 Bedford Square, London, WC1B 3DP, UK
1385 Broadway, New York, NY 10018, USA
29 Earlsfort Terrace, Dublin 2, Ireland

BLOOMSBURY, BLOOMSBURY ACADEMIC and the Diana logo are trademarks
of Bloomsbury Publishing Plc

First published in Great Britain 2022

Cover design by Tjaša Krivec.
Photograph © Ilcho Trajkovski / Alamy Stock Photo

A catalogue record for this book is available from the British Library.

Library of Congress Cataloging-in-Publication Data
Names: Galaty, David H. (David Holt), 1942- author.
Title: Modern European intellectual history : individuals, groupings, and technological change,
1800-2000 / David Galaty.
Other titles: Individuals, groupings, and technological change, 1800-2000
Description: London; New York: Bloomsbury Academic, 2022. | Includes bibliographical
references and index.
Identifiers: LCCN 2021036450 (print) | LCCN 2021036451 (ebook) | ISBN 9781350105409 (hb) |
ISBN 9781350105393 (pb) | ISBN 9781350105416 (epdf) | ISBN 9781350105423 (ebook)
Subjects: LCSH: Europe–Civilization–19th century. | Europe–Civilization–20th century. |
Europe–Intellectual life–19th century. | Europe–Intellectual life–20th century. | Technology–Social
aspects–Europe–History.
Classification: LCC CB204 .G35 2022 (print) | LCC CB204 (ebook) | DDC 940.2/8–dc23
LC record available at https://lccn.loc.gov/2021036450
LC ebook record available at https://lccn.loc.gov/2021036451

ISBN: HB: 978-1-3501-0540-9
PB: 978-1-3501-0539-3
ePDF: 978-1-3501-0541-6
eBook: 978-1-3501-0542-3

Typeset by Deanta Global Publishing Services, Chennai, India
Printed and bound in Great Britain

To find out more about our authors and books visit www.bloomsbury.com and
sign up for our newsletters.

This book is dedicated to Mara and her sisters: Elise, Kassel, and Laurel.
My life would be impoverished without you.

CONTENTS

Contents

Contents

Contents

Contents

ILLUSTRATIONS

Figures

Maps

PREFACE AND ACKNOWLEDGMENTS

What Is Intellectual History

Until well past the middle of the twentieth century, the field of intellectual history was still known as the history of ideas. In the first decade of the Cold War, many mainline scholars in Western Europe and the United States were reticent to discuss too strongly a causal relationship between social structure and ideas. Marx had written that ideas and institutions were "superstructure" springing from the base, the economic form of the "means of production." To non-Marxists, however, ideas were discovered as part of the search for truth—the search for that which is eternally true beyond the apparent changes we observe in the world around us.

By the end of the 1960s, young scholars in the history of ideas and allied fields had begun to expand their research beyond the model of "ideas beget ideas." One did not have to be a Marxist to consider how social structures shaped the development and expression of ideas. Out of the developing research came the field of intellectual history as something distinct from the history of ideas. The "social construction of ideas" was an approach that informed, but that did not limit, intellectual history.

This textbook is written with an eye to all of the approaches implied in this too-brief description of the field. The text discusses important ideas in depth and in relation to the ideas that stimulated them. The text also makes a point of including scientific and technological ideas along with philosophical systems. The text thus seamlessly connects ideas to relevant political, social, economic, and technological events. This book can therefore be used in a wide variety of approaches and formats.

As an introduction to the field of intellectual history, the text is designed to be accessible to undergraduates and people who are not yet intellectual historians. It is also designed to discuss ideas and events accurately. To the end of both comprehensibility and accuracy, students and faculty from a variety of disciplines participated in vetting the manuscript in whole or in part.

Definitions and Clarifications

Three words in the title of this book need some clarification. First, the word "modern" denotes not just a recent era but also a process: the change from a primarily agricultural, feudal society to a globally expanding scientific and technological industrial and postindustrial society. The main task of intellectuals in the past quarter millennium has been to react to and understand this radically new way of being human. As we will see, some intellectuals fostered the changes while others opposed them.

The word "European," then, in the context of this book refers to those parts of Europe that were contributing to the discussions about the implications of this modern world. An emphasis on the process of becoming modern tilts the book toward Western Europe, especially the UK, France, and Germany, because those are the parts of Europe that were first concerned with this newly emerging context. But Eastern European thinkers, as well as those from some parts of the European colonial world, do play an important role in the conversation, and many make an appearance in this text. Intellectuals from the United States have been intentionally omitted, except for a few emigres from Europe.

"Intellectual history" is a term that means many things to different people. In this book, the term is used to broadly refer to the history of ideas as they are embedded in, and interact with, society. Often the same word or expression means different things in different eras and different places, and we have tried to pay close attention to the context of ideas. Scientific and technological ideas have often been downplayed in, or even omitted from, intellectual history, and this book is designed to correct that omission by centering science and technology in the discussion while framing the discussion in an accessible manner.

Historical research in general is driven by debate. The text tries to steer clear of extreme positions in the field (though at times it may fail) and to present each chapter in the light of generally accepted points of view. At the very least, every treatment in the text can be reasonably defended. If a teaching professor is convinced that another interpretation is more convincing, the text should serve as a backdrop against which alternate positions can be developed. Most of the thinkers and ideas usually taught in an introductory intellectual history course can be found in these pages, but many thinkers have been necessarily omitted for reasons of space.

One of the best ways to put students to sleep is to introduce a string of unfamiliar people in dialogue with one another about unfamiliar ideas. This text therefore omits the scholarly debates that inform our present-day understandings. That is, the text errs on the side of students new to the field as opposed to students or scholars who have made a commitment to the field. In a more advanced text, scholarly debate would figure heavily.

Thank You

I am deeply indebted to all the students and colleagues with whom I have interacted over the years. However, I wish to acknowledge a deep obligation to the following people:

Three scholars and friends who read every word and commented insightfully and fully, in alphabetical order:

Howard Aaron, MFA, Adjunct Professor of Creative Writing, Washington State University-Vancouver, who carefully read every page with red ink in hand. Our many walks helped crystalize many ill-formed ideas and showed that laughing is as important as thinking in attaining perspective.

Preface and Acknowledgments

John Galaty, PhD, Professor of Anthropology, McGill University, Montreal, who also read every page carefully and with great editorial acumen. His wide-ranging intellect informed my ideas not only in the social science sections but also throughout the entire book. Thanks for a lifetime of deep conversation.

Benjamin Westervelt, PhD, Associate Professor, Early Modern Intellectual History, Lewis & Clark College. My thanks not only for tirelessly reading and commenting but also for delightful and wide-ranging conversations for several years.

The student perspective from:

Emma Moorhead, BA, Lewis & Clark College, my research assistant, who carried out invaluable bibliographical research and who provided the invaluable perspective of the knowledgeable student.

Kassel Galaty, BA, MPhil, MD, who read and edited with great insight. She has become a close colleague in history and ideas. A talented artist, she also contributed four of the figures in the book.

And colleagues:

Jerry Harp, PhD, Professor of Literature, Lewis & Clark College. Thank you for reading and commenting, but also for an engaging friendship.

Kurt Fosso, PhD, Professor of Literature Lewis & Clark College. My thanks for important insights into romanticism and for good-natured discussion for many years.

I am also indebted to my coauthors and study group colleagues at the University of Wisconsin-Green Bay, with whom I spent a most delightful year teaching one another about our respective fields. *Revolution in Art and Ideas at the Turn of the Twentieth Century* emerged from our interaction. Thanks, Sid Bremer, Gary Greif, Mike Murphy, Gil Null, Jerry Rodesch, Irwin Sonenfield, and Louise Witherell. The entire exciting interdisciplinary intellectual atmosphere of the University of Wisconsin-Green Bay, especially in the early years, shaped me as a scholar.

I thank the National Endowment for the Humanities for the grant that allowed us all to work together.

I also thank Harris-Manchester College at Oxford for offering support and resources during the early stages of this book.

I thank Elise and Joachim Alpen and their wonderful children David and Anna, my Swedish family, for the generous loan of their beautiful home in Visby, Gotland, Sweden, where I spent many summer days writing this book. As always, we had many enjoyable animated discussions as the book took shape.

I greatly appreciate Laurel Galaty's joyful engagement and technical support. And thanks, Olivia Zhao and Max Rippe, for your enthusiasm for the project.

I am deeply grateful to the support of Lewis & Clark College for the time, money, and resources to enable me to complete this book. Thank you, Dean Bruce Suttmeier and Associate Dean Naiomi Cameron. Furthermore, Lewis & Clark College will always have a special place in my heart for their generous support during one of the most trying times of my life.

Laura Reeves and Rhodri Mogford supported and guided me through the process, and I thank them for that. This book could not have existed without their hard work.

And finally, my greatest thanks go to my wife Debra Galaty, teacher extraordinaire, whose misgivings about having me devote so much time to this project turned into unflagging support. I couldn't have done it without you.

TIMELINE

A Sampling of the Inventions, Theories, and Schools of Thought

——— AGRARIAN WORLD ———	INDUSTRIAL WORLD ———		POST-INDUSTRIAL WORLD	CYBER WORLD ———
1800-1850	**1850-1900**	**1900-1950**	**1950-2000**	

Technologies

1800-1850	1850-1900	1900-1950	1950-2000
● RAILROADS	● REFRIGERATION	● AUTO-MOBILES ● RADIO	● COMPUTERS ● INTERNET
● STEAM ENGINE	● TELEGRAPH ● TELEPHONE	● X-RAYS	● ATOMIC BOMB ● MRI/CT
● FACTORIES	● ANESTHESIA	● AIR-PLANES ● RESPI-RATORS	● JETS ● RADIO TELESCOPE
● ELECTRIC BATTERY	● ANTISEPSIS	● GERM THEORY	● ANTIBIOTICS ● GENETIC ENGINEERING

Scientific Theories

Field

1800-1850	1850-1900	1900-1950	1950-2000
△ ELECTROMAGNETISM	△ ELECTRIC FIELD	△ GENERAL RELATIVITY	△ INFLATIONARY UNIVERSE
△ WAVE LIGHT THEORY		△ EXPANDING UNIVERSE	

Atomic

1800-1850	1850-1900	1900-1950	1950-2000
△ CHEMICAL ATOMS	△ THERMODYNAMICS	△ RADIO-ACTIVITY △ QUANTUM THEORY	△ DNA STRUCTURE
	△ PERIODIC TABLE	△ SPECIAL RELATIVITY △ PARTICLE PHYSICS	△ STANDARD MODEL

Emphasizes

Groupings

1800-1850	1850-1900	1900-1950	1950-2000
OWENISM	MARXISM	LENINISM/STALINISM	
UTOPIAN SOCIALISM		SOCIOLOGY NAZISM	STRUCTURALISM
CONSERVATISM		FACISM	DEMOCRATIC SOCIALISM EUROPEAN UNION
GERMAN IDEALISM	SCIENTIFIC RACISM		
ROMANTICISM	NATIONALISM ZIONISM	CONTINENTAL PHILOSOPHY	KEYNESIAN ECONOMICS KUHN & THE STRONG PROGRAM
WOMEN'S RIGHTS	SOCIAL DARWINISM FREUDIANISM		COLONIAL INDEPENDENCE

Individuals

1800-1850	1850-1900	1900-1950	1950-2000
LIBERALISM		ANALYTIC PHILOSOPHY	NEOLIBERALISM
CLASSICAL ECONOMICS	MARGINAL ECONOMICS	EXISTENTIALISM	
UTILITARIANISM ANARCHISM	NIETZSCHE		POSTMODERNISM

PROLOGUE

Figure 0.1 The frontispiece to Thomas Hobbes's *Leviathan*, 1651. The king's body is made up of the people of his realm. An example of the primacy of the whole. © Wikimedia Commons (public domain).

Individuals and Groups, Units and Wholes

The frontispiece to Thomas Hobbes's seventeenth-century *Leviathan* showed a being, the monarch, made up of the individual members of his realm. These subjects were not freely acting individuals but were rather pieces of a grand organic whole. This idea of human beings designed to be members of a vast social "whole" contrasts with the ideas of Adam Smith in which "every individual . . . neither intends to promote the public interest, nor knows how much he is promoting it . . . he intends only his own gain, and he is in this, as in many other cases, led by an invisible hand to promote an end which was no part of his intention." For Smith, social order arises spontaneously from the free actions of selfish individuals. For Hobbes, the society, personified in the sovereign, is supreme, and individuals without a strong society will descend into chaos in which the life of individuals is "solitary, poor, nasty, brutish, and short."

Most of the ideas developed in the nineteenth and twentieth centuries and discussed in this book existed primarily within one of these two worldviews: (1) freely acting individual human beings define reality and society and (2) individuals can only be understood as parts of a transcendent organic whole. Most thinkers lived between the poles, but each had to grapple with the dilemmas found in the interaction between the autonomous individual actors and inescapable transcendent wholes. On the one hand, we see thinkers like John Stuart Mill arguing for individual liberty, an atomic theory of society, and on the other, we see thinkers like Hegel for whom individuals exist at the collective level: "the spiritual individual, the nation—insofar as it is internally differentiated so as to form an organic whole—is what we call the state." Both Mill and Hegel had their moments wrestling with the other side of the equation but without being able to move into the opposite camp.

And we will also see women struggle to cope with the difficulty of understanding themselves in a world in which they were required to play gender-defined roles outside of the public sphere while simultaneously experiencing themselves as individuals with talents and aspirations suited to the public sphere.

Similar poles also exist in science. Both physical and biological scientists moved between two apparently incompatible ways of depicting the parts of nature that they studied. In one view, the physical world was made up of atoms, and the interaction of these atoms to form molecules and larger structures eventually produced the physical world that we experience. In the other view, nature consisted of networks of forces that moved in concert to create the phenomena that we observe. The wave theory of light presented light as a wave, the motion of a continuous substance called, from the Greek, the *aether*. Atoms are things, nouns. Waves are motions, verbs. The grammar of the two seemed to be incompatible and difficult to resolve mathematically. Today physicists have found a resolution by giving up any intuitive visually oriented understanding of the natural world in favor of abstract mathematical descriptions. In this way, they have devised a combination of particles and fields: the quantum field theory. But still gravitational field theory resists incorporation into quantum theory.

In the mid-nineteenth-century biology, the units became cells, and in the twentieth century the units became genes. The alternate view can be seen most plainly in the early nineteenth century when organisms were seen as wholes that could not be understood by reductively breaking them down into smaller and smaller units. This vision was carried into the twentieth century in the work of some biologists who denied the existence of particle-like genes but, rather, saw the gene as the interaction of many parts of the organism. Today genes are understood as parts of complex interacting relationships.

Certainly, there are other cogent ways of organizing the intellectual output of the past two centuries, and in this sense, these categories are arbitrary. Nonetheless, if the reader keeps in mind that sometimes ideas work outside of these worldviews, the book's organization can be revealing. The polar ideas of "units versus wholes" are useful in understanding the dialogues that drove the development of not only social but also scientific theories. And both responded to changes in the technological world.

Technological Changes

At the midpoint of the nineteenth century, a nostalgic Thomas De Quincey bemoaned the changes in transportation he had seen in his adult life.

> The modern modes of traveling cannot compare with the mail-coach system in grandeur and power. They boast of more velocity, but not however as a consciousness, but as a fact of our lifeless knowledge. . . . We heard our speed, we saw it, we felt it as a thrilling . . . incarnated in the fiery eyeballs of an animal . . . and the trumpet that once announced from afar the laurelled mail . . . has now given way forever to the pot-wallopings of the boiler.

In fact, more than transportation had been changed by an accelerating technological revolution. Two years after De Quincey wrote these remarks, Prince Albert (and Queen Victoria) sponsored the privately funded Great "Crystal Palace" Exhibition of technology with an aim of encouraging technology and manufactures. Besides gaudy spectacle, visitors could see the new daguerreotypes, the first public toilets, the glass and iron wonder of the Crystal Palace itself, and more. But the most important contribution of the exhibition was symbolic. It highlighted changes in technology, manufacturing, and society that were already taking place and called for more.

By the end of the nineteenth century, De Quincey would have been astounded at the profusion of marvels. Besides railroads and telegraphs, an urban dweller in the industrialized West would have gone through gaslit streets to electric lights, telegraphs to telephones, steam locomotives to internally combusted automobiles, the phonograph, cinema, ocean-going steamships, agricultural machinery augmented by artificial fertilizers, public health and sanitation systems, and medical techniques that could, at times, actually promise cure; the list could continue for pages.

As we survey the 100 years of the nineteenth century, it is clear that industrial nations were well on the way toward shedding their rural base for an urban one. The changes already wrought, and the changes promised, altered the lives and imaginations of educated Europeans in both the urbanizing West and in the still peasant-based East. The differences between the exciting ideas of the seventeenth century and the breathtaking ideas of the nineteenth century reflect the differences between a rural, yet commercializing, culture and the ideas of an urban industrializing world.

Technology, then, provided a context within which intellectuals had to work. But technology did not itself provide answers. Modern intellectual history is the study of the dialogue between necessity and freedom, between the prose of new routines and the poetry of creativity.

Technology and Metaphor

The primary technological metaphors were inherited from the seventeenth and eighteenth centuries. First, *time* was seen not as an organic experience but as a substance that was measured by the machine known as a clock. Second, *space* was not seen as that which is experienced, but as that which is measured by tools like a ruler. A third, older metaphor was that this is a "mechanical, clockwork universe."

The next step was to use the mechanical, mathematical universe to convert a complex human society into a "free market" society. Once clocks, rulers, and equations become the main tools for understanding the universe, then money became the lever for assessing human wants, needs, and behaviors. The phrase "Time is money" was only possible after time had been mechanized.

The power of the mechanization and mathematization of the universe was seen in Pierre-Simon Laplace's reputed response to Napoleon after Napoleon had asked about Newton's description of God's action in fixing the orbits of the planets. Laplace replied, "Sire, I had no need of that hypothesis." The point was not that God does not exist, but that He is not needed to describe the mechanical universe. For those rationalists who did not incline toward atheism, God had become a clockmaker.

Enlightenment thinkers of the eighteenth century believed by using reason humans could construct of a better society. The idea of progress was linked with rationality. Many of the arguments against this rational project in the last two centuries have centered on the scientists' use of mechanical, mathematical metaphors to describe human, organic, experience. One only has to look at the power of the statement, "the mind is a computer," today to see the latest stage in the arc of technological metaphor. In this book, we will pay attention to the differing ways that technological invention changes modes of thinking in different eras. We will see that often the opponents of reason used organic metaphors. When one side spoke organically while the other spoke mathematically, understanding one another became problematic.

And technology has a partner: modern science. Since the time of Galileo, nonscientists have increasingly allocated an authority to scientists that was previously reserved for the Bible. To Galileo, nature was God's other book, written in mathematics. Today God's second book has virtually replaced the first; and the book has replaced its author. In the European twentieth century, no philosophy could be taken seriously if it was not framed with scientific knowledge in mind. We will thus discuss at some length the nature of that scientific knowledge as it developed.

Interacting Ideas

Most ideas were primarily worked out in one particular European language. If writers published in German, their initial readers and responders were German speakers.

Generally, only after ideas or intellectual systems proved interesting and resilient were they translated. Accurate translation was quite hard to accomplish, so often the ideas were subtly altered as they were introduced into a new intellectual community. Furthermore, thinkers in different cultures often concerned themselves with different problems using varying approaches. For a foreign idea to become compelling, it had to be adapted, if only slightly.

Thus, European intellectual culture can perhaps best be seen as a group of contiguous ecosystems. The plants in each ecosystem interacted symbiotically and slowly evolved in a mutual dance. Plants (ideas) from other ecosystems might be invasive species. They also might offer a new food source. At any rate, they inevitably became altered as they wriggled their way into a new environment.

This text is not designed to trace the routes of mutual influence as ideas cross from one language and one culture to another. But the reader should be alert to the notion that such translation happened throughout the nineteenth and twentieth centuries. German Darwinism is not the same as English Darwinism. Italian Marxism is not German Marxism. Freud in English reads differently than it does in German.

Darwin's *Origin of Species* ends with a description of a "tangled bank" teeming with different species. If we adapt this description metaphorically, the resulting image may be of help in understanding the interplay of ideas described in this text. Imagine that the river descends from mountains through deserts to meadows. In each ecosystem, the bank would support differing species. Some species would send seeds and shoots up and down the bank to a different environment. Some would become rooted. Others would die. Some species prey on one another, but others are symbiotic. In this conceit, each new ecosystem represents a different linguistic and cultural community, and each species represents a different set of ideas.

Sometimes outside influences—storms, droughts, machines—uproot whole species and doom others to slow extinction. Others rush in to take their place. We can't understand an ecosystem—and we can't understand intellectual endeavors—without considering the effects of a larger context.

Until very recently, the intellectual ecosystems across Europe were hostile to ideas expressed publicly by women. Social structures were highly gendered, and both public and private life were patriarchal. A woman of genius often could only participate in public discourse through a sympathetic male. She often adopted a male pen name. Numbers of brilliant women had no chance at an education. Many either never conceived of entering the public sphere or gave up trying. They expressed themselves in conversation, diaries, and private correspondence—or fell silent. Unfortunately, the scope of this book does not permit exploring these private conversations in the depth they deserve. But some women found ways to become valued members of public intellectual communities, and the ideas of such women play an important role in this book. There are necessarily many more male than female thinkers included, but for this reason most of the chapters in the book begin by highlighting the work of a female intellectual.

A textbook in intellectual history is not an encyclopedia, and thus can never be complete. You will not find in these pages an exhaustive discussion of important ideas.

What you will find are many brilliant thinkers in discussion with one another—even after they are dead. Think of this text as an eighteenth-century salon, hosted by the eminent savant, Madame de Staël. Ideas arc from one side of the room to the other and bounce back with a wicked spin. Your instructor is already in the salon. It is time for you to join.

CHAPTER 1
IMPORTANT IDEAS AND EVENTS AS SEEN IN 1800 CE

Figure 1.1 Frontispiece of Voltaire's book *Elemens de la philosophie de Newton*, 1738. Émilie du Châtelet is depicted as Voltaire's muse as she reflects the light of truth to Voltaire. © Wikimedia Commons (public domain).

Newton's Interpreter: Émilie du Châtelet

Émilie du Châtelet was a mathematical genius. She was also rich, noble, and beautiful. Her only piece of bad luck was being pregnant for the fourth time in the wrong century. She died in childbirth in 1749 at the age of forty-three.

In 1733 two aristocratic lovers invited du Châtelet to a chicken fricassee dinner at a tavern so that she might meet the handsome, charming, witty writer known as Voltaire. Voltaire and du Châtelet were both smitten. He later wrote of her as "a young woman who thought as I did, and who decided to spend several years in the country, cultivating her mind."

When du Châtelet was 18, a marriage had been arranged with a 34-year-old nobleman who luckily was quite understanding of his younger wife's need for love with other men. Voltaire had recently returned from exile in England and had written a laudatory Anglophilic book entitled *Lettres philosophiques* (*Letters on England*). Invidious comparisons of the French government with that of the English led the royal family to order the hangman to burn the book. An arrest warrant was issued. With the support of her understanding husband, du Châtelet invited Voltaire to live with them in their protected estate so that Voltaire could escape the possibly fatal wrath of the official censors. Perhaps the 40,000 francs Voltaire offered to help restore the estate aided the husband's understanding.

Du Châtelet and Voltaire waged a campaign in favor of the English physicist Isaac Newton's physics against the then predominant scientific approaches of René Descartes. Du Châtelet translated Newton's *Principia Mathematica* into French and handled the mathematical portions of the Voltaire-du Châtelet campaign, something that the literary-minded Voltaire could not have done. In fact, du Châtelet developed Newton's work to devise a much clearer understanding of what we today call "energy." By the time the two of them were finished, other French thinkers had rallied to their cause. As a result, the Enlightenment thought of the second half of the eighteenth century in France was largely founded on the ideas of Newton and Locke.

Chapter Map

In this chapter, we explore important ideas and events about which virtually every European intellectual in 1800 had opinions. We begin with the mechanical, clockwork universe that seemed to be supported by the mathematical physics of Isaac Newton as modified by his successors. The new physics could not have been invented without telescopes, air pumps, microscopes, thermometers, and other apparatus that served the needs of both businessmen and scientists. The new science stimulated an examination of the human mind and the nature of human knowledge. Immanuel Kant built a theory of mind in which mind was an active force in creating the world observed by the senses. The physical world outside of mind was not accessible to human thought.

While some intellectuals worked to build and critique a new science with a new method, others saw opportunities in the new commercial world to develop a new, more efficient way of manufacturing goods for sale, a factory system. By the end of the eighteenth century, especially in Great Britain, it was clear to most thinkers that a revolution within the economic side of society was taking place: an Industrial Revolution.

In France, where political arrangements were still feudal in form, intellectuals began an exchange of ideas known as the Enlightenment. At the end of the Enlightenment,

France erupted into revolution that resulted in the execution of the king, the abolishment of nobility, and an attempt to build a society in which the needs of all would be met.

Newton and the Mechanical Worldview

A scientifically minded European in 1800 would certainly have been aware of, and almost certainly have embraced, the mechanical worldview. A mechanical universe evoked the idea of a machine, and so the clockwork universe (the most precise machine being a well-made clock) was born. In science, mechanics is the study of matter in motion as it interacts with other matter. Thus, the mechanical worldview reflected the idea that the entire observable world was made of atoms interacting with one another in a regular fashion that could produce motions lasting for millennia, like the orbits of the planets. In 1800 the person seen as responsible for demonstrating the inner mechanism of the universal machine was Isaac Newton.

The Newton of 1800, lionized, interred in Westminster Abbey, and practically worshiped as God's messenger bore little resemblance to the Newton known to his

Figure 1.2 Engraving of Sir Isaac Newton. This was made in 1702 when Newton was master of the Mint and a revered national legend. © John Parrot/Stocktrek Images/Getty Images.

contemporaries. The Newton of 1800 is reflected in this epitaph by the great English poet, Alexander Pope:

> Nature and Nature's laws lay hid in night:
> God said, Let Newton be! and all was light.[1]

The Newton of the late seventeenth century was reclusive, secretive, and suspicious. It was said that he often lectured to an empty classroom when students shunned his classes. He was born on Christmas Day 1642, in Woolsthorpe Manor, about 150 kilometers north of London, sired by a father who died before his birth. Newton may have had an unconscious Christ complex according to at least one psychoanalytic biographer. When his mother remarried and went to live with her new husband, Newton remained with his grandmother and nursed a grudge against both his mother and stepfather. As he grew older, he had only a few friends. He kept his theories close and published only reluctantly or not at all. In 1666 Cambridge University was closed by a plague scare, and in the ensuing year of enforced quarantine at his home, Newton experienced his "miracle year" (annus mirabilis) in which he produced his theory of colors and optics, the law of universal gravitation, and the mathematical field of calculus. In 1669 Newton became Lucasian professor of mathematics when Isaac Barrow, the holder of that chair, resigned and handed it to Newton, his genius pupil. After 1690 Newton acted as warden of the Royal Mint, later master of the Mint, in which position he actually ferreted out counterfeiters by posing as a frequenter of bars and prostitutes to gather evidence. Newton secured the conviction of twenty-eight such counterfeiters, and saw them suffer the penalty of hanging, drawing, and quartering. Newton became president of the Royal Society of London for Improving Natural Knowledge (Royal Society) in 1703 and was knighted in 1705. He died in 1727.

The intellectual world shifted slowly but profoundly after the publication of Newton's *Principia Mathematica* in 1687. By the end of the eighteenth century, virtually all of educated Europe had in one way or another adopted some form of his insights. At the time of Newton, the idea of science as a set of disciplines distinct from the humanities had not yet been developed. The historian William Whewell first used the words "science" and "scientist" in this sense in the 1840s. Today we know Newton as a mathematical physicist who founded the modern science of mechanics, but in the late eighteenth century Newton was seen as a person who had established a convincing argument for the idea that all the phenomena of nature were products of pieces of matter moving and interacting with other pieces of matter.

Newton himself had thought no such thing. Newton was not a Newtonian. His mechanical system was in fact based on (1) three laws, (2) the assumption that a force of gravity acted between pieces of matter (with a specific mathematical form called an "inverse square"), and (3) the assumption of the existence of space and time. But although French mathematical physicists thought Newton's mechanics were Newton's theory, in fact Newton's philosophical system contained much more.

For Newton, who spent much of his life decoding the secrets of the biblical "Book of Revelations," absolute space and time were the "sensorium of God" (where a sensorium is that part of the mind that perceives sensory information). Newton distinguished our perception of space, time, and motion from absolute space, time, and motion. If I perceive that an hour has passed, I can be wrong: for instance, if my clock runs fast. In order for me to be wrong, however, there must be a true answer. That is, there must be an absolute, real time. This issue will come up again in this book when we discuss Albert Einstein's different approach in the early twentieth century.

One reason that absolute space and time were necessary was that Newton's first law, the law of inertia (a body in motion continues in motion in a straight line unless acted on by an external force), required it. Newton was aware that two ships sailing at the same speed next to one another were essentially standing still with respect to one another. If one of the ships pulled away from the other at one knot an hour, then the relative speed was one knot. In order to claim that a body in outer space (like a moon) had a tendency to continue moving at the same speed in a straight line, then one needed a reference system that was not itself tied to that moon. Since observable space (i.e., the distance between two reference bodies) was relative, to have an absolute law, like inertia, one needed an absolute reference system. Thus, absolute space.

Newton also did not have a mechanical explanation for the force of gravity, and famously said "*hypotheses non fingo*" (I do not feign hypotheses) when pushed on the question of the mechanism of gravity. The issue was that if the universe is mechanical in nature, then there is no room for a non-mechanical "force" to be involved. "Force" is a metaphorical term that suggests the effect of one physical body pushing or pulling on another body that it is in contact with. Used as a word connected to something non-physical, "force" is a metaphor. If I sit across the room from you and think that I want to force you to move, my thoughts can do nothing. If I connect to you with a rope or rod, then I can exert force on you and make you change position. Similarly, how could the sun exert a force on the earth if there were no physical connection between the two? Newton's space was part of the mind of God. The physical universe was contained within the mind of God but was not itself God (pantheism.). Newton's universe therefore contains a "mentalness" that has no place in a mechanical worldview. Perhaps gravity emerged from the thoughts of God? Newton did not comment.

But Newton did comment on the need and possibility of God's action in the world when he engaged in debate with the German philosopher and physicist Gottfried Wilhelm Leibniz. Leibniz had developed a philosophically consistent mechanical physics in which he answered the question, "How could a good and all-powerful God allow suffering and evil in the world?" (The answer to this question is called theodicy.) For Leibniz, God had created "the best of all possible worlds," and thus all that existed was necessary. If God were to ease the suffering of a child, then that action would cause the best of all worlds to change into a less than best world. For instance, the child's suffering might ease, but the child might grow up to be a mass murderer. Therefore, the universe was completely determined, and there was no room for choice.

Nonsense, said Newton, God is the King of the Universe, and a king must be able to act. In a famous exchange of letters between Samuel Clark (acting as the ostensible author of Newton's letters) and Leibniz, the two great scientists and philosophers battled the question of theodicy, the issue of the nature of the force of gravity and several others, to an inconclusive end.

By the middle of the eighteenth century, these problems were forgotten. "Force" was reified (the process of turning an abstraction into a concrete noun). That is, the metaphorical use of the word was forgotten, and force took its place alongside matter as a concrete entity. Similarly, absolute space and time were reified and removed from any connection with God. Clocks could still be wrong, but not because time was in the mind of God. Absolute time and space existed with no explanation. The Newtonian worldview, then, became a philosophically incoherent, yet strangely satisfying view. If everything is matter in motion, then where would laws of nature or other nonmaterial ideas (for instance, mathematics) be? One didn't have to answer, because the question was no longer apparent.

The reason that the philosophical issues were uninteresting was that the main developers of Newton's system were not physicists, but rather mathematicians, like the Frenchman Jean d'Alembert, the Italian-French astronomer Joseph-Louis Lagrange, or the Swiss mathematicians Leonhard Euler, Johann Bernoulli, and Daniel Bernoulli. They used an algebraic form of analysis in which abstract symbols stood for experimental concepts, like position, mass, distance, and time. They made no use of any theories concerning the structure of matter or possible mechanical processes that might be involved in forces like gravity. The result was to draw a picture of the universe that was essentially raw abstraction that could be tied to experiments and observations that yielded measurements. The Newtonian theory came to be seen as the use of abstract mathematical entities to relate actual observations. The connection between observation and mathematics required no studies of the actual components of matter and no discussion of those aspects of perception that were not tied directly to measurable entities. Philosophical misgivings had no utility in this version of "Newtonianism."

The new science of mechanics bore little resemblance to the world perceived by a human being. We see the sun. The theory sees a "point mass." We might care how the sun produces light. The mathematical theory has nothing to say on this topic. The distance between mechanics and the world of beauty and ugliness, of sights and smells, and of color and music was a vast gulf. Thus, there is an inherent paradox in the mechanical worldview as an explanation for the world of human experience.

Immanuel Kant and the Critique of Knowledge

John Locke, Bishop Berkeley, and David Hume

The Englishman John Locke (1632–1704) began to analyze human knowledge with what he saw as the source of human experience: sensory perception. His system was empirical: based on experience. For Locke, the mind was a *tabula rasa*, a blank slate, on which sense impressions are written. That is, a human being has no innate knowledge, but rather receives knowledge from the senses.

The Irish Bishop George Berkeley (1685–1753) agreed with Locke that perception was important, but for Berkeley perception was everything. The only two types of objects that could be said to exist were a perceiving being and something being perceived. For Berkeley, no assumption about organs of sense need be made. Perceptions arrived directly in the mind. We might perceive organs of sense, like eyes, but it overstepped our understanding to claim that eyes somehow created mental perceptions. When one stopped perceiving something, did it exist? Yes, said Berkeley, because the mind of God always actively perceived everything.

The Scottish philosopher David Hume (1711–76) seemed to drive a nail in the coffin of any attempt to show that the new science of Isaac Newton (and of course others) gave us an accurate idea of what the universe might consist of beyond our perceptions. Using the empiricist model, Hume challenged the validity of induction, which he defined as a statement of how the world works when it is not being observed or remembered. Induction had been a primary means of thinking about the scientific method and been painstakingly described by Francis Bacon. In induction a scientist looks at carefully accumulated and arranged data to reach conclusions about the more general laws of nature.

There is no way that we can claim that just because something has always happened in a certain way that it will continue in the future to happen that way, said Hume. This challenge to the possibility of induction also is a challenge to any claims that one thing causes another. Just because nature has behaved in a certain way in the past is no guarantee that it will behave that way in the future. Hume showed that from sense perception one could not infer laws of connection among sense impressions. For instance, one might notice that one impression followed another, but one could not with any reason say that one caused the other. Causation was an assumption not found in the data themselves. Hume's skepticism caused a number of philosophers to despair about the philosophical usefulness of the new approaches to natural philosophy that we today know as modern science.

Immanuel Kant

The debate about perception and knowledge that had involved thinkers from all parts of Great Britain and Ireland eventually reached the far shores of East Prussia. Immanuel Kant (1704–1804) was born in Königsberg, East Prussia, an area that is now part of Russia. Kant lived in Königsberg all his life, though for a few years he taught in the towns around that city. It was said that the neighbors could set their clocks by observing the time of his daily walks. As a young man, Kant was an active scientist, and he developed, among other ideas, the nebular theory of the formation of galaxies. Throughout his life, he pursued research in mathematics and science, even though his major lines of inquiry were philosophical. In 1804 he died, his last words being: "It is good."

Kant said that Hume's analysis brought him out of his "dogmatic slumber." Kant was a Newtonian, and causality was part and parcel of Newtonian science. For instance, the earth goes around the sun because of the counteraction of inertial and gravitational

Figure 1.3 Portrait of Immanuel Kant. © Hulton Archive/Stringer/Getty Images.

forces in a lawful manner that can be described precisely mathematically. Kant wanted to establish firm philosophical grounds to support the new, exciting scientific endeavor. Kant began by assuming that we have some objective knowledge of the world. But following Hume, he acknowledged that this objective knowledge couldn't come from the senses alone. For three years, he withdrew and pondered the conundrum. He emerged with a book in 1781, *Kritik der reinen Vernunft* (*The Critique of Pure Reason*).

Unlike Hume, Kant did not remain caught in skepticism. His solution was to interpose an active subject between the object and perception. This subject, the human conscious mind, provides the laws that allow us to organize and perceive sensory data. The human mind has categories, one of which is causality. It also has intuitions such as space and time. So, when a human mind perceives an event caused by a different event, that mind has interpreted the sensory data and combined it with mental structures in such a way that a perception of a series of events and causal relationships is perceived.

Thus, Kant said that all knowledge is a mental act and that the organization of the mind itself is a necessary and inescapable part of knowledge. He did not argue for innate ideas but, rather, for innate organizing principles. In his "Copernican revolution," Kant wrote that just as the earth moves around the sun rather than the sun moving around the earth, so rather than the mind depending on objective reality, objective reality depends on the mind.

How then could we know what nature is really like outside of the mind? Kant's surprising answer is that we cannot. Kant uses a Greek word, *noumena*, to stand for an objective world outside of mind, and says that the noumenal world is absolutely closed to us. In contrast, the world of *phenomena*, the world as it is perceived by the mind, is available to us. Thus, science can study phenomena, that is, objects in the mind, but it can say nothing meaningful about the world outside of itself, the "thing in itself," or the *ding an sich*.

This analysis leaves us with a secondary question: How can we know that Kant's analysis provides a coherent picture of the world that is valid for all knowing human beings? Kant's answer is to make "transcendental deductions." His argument is that we know we have certain mental impressions. He then asks what is necessary in order that we might have such impressions. That is, we start with our experience, which is clear to us in that it exists for us, and then asks how this experience can be possible.

This novel method also allowed Kant to affirm a similarity among human minds. If a subjective human has a set of experiences such as those discussed by Kant, then that person's subjective mind must have a structure similar to that discussed by Kant. And one of the characteristics of mind deduced by Kant is unity. He argues that a mind that can see unity among objects over time and that can also recognize many objects existing at the same time must itself be a unity. Consciousness must be a unity. Thus, this unified consciousness can pull many perceptions into "one experience." Essentially then, the unity of consciousness implies the experience of individual identity and ultimately the experience of human identity.

The essence of the Kantian Revolution in thought lies mostly in denying the primacy of the world outside of the mind and the establishment of the mental world as primary. He established the philosophical meaning and scope of natural science. But Kant was not willing at all to accept that all knowledge concerned the physical universe. Humans have a variety of forms of knowledge that are embraced in, for instance, ethics, aesthetics, and religion. None of these, said Kant, can be explained by reference to the physical world.

Kant's ethics is based on the concept of duty. Recognizing that other human beings are equally valuable, Kant demands that they always be treated as ends in and of themselves. They should never be treated merely as means to some other end, but always also as ends in themselves. He went on to say that people should always ask whether they would be willing to have their moral decision legislated to apply to all other people. But this duty to act appropriately is based not on obligation but rather on goodwill. Acting morally should be voluntary. For Kant, humans were autonomous beings. Thus, we can choose, will ourselves, to meet our obligations of duty. This is a free choice, unencumbered by outside pressures or influences.

Kant also decoupled religion and science. As we shall see in a later chapter, one of the main arguments for the existence of God in the world of the new science was the argument from design: only a rational Creator could have constructed such an interconnected and smoothly running universe. But Kant also feared that if religion was based on science, at some future time science could then be used to argue against religion. Kant denied that reason could justify God and argued against the many traditional rational arguments for the existence of God. In fact, he argued that the concept of God is meaningless, because we cannot accurately imagine something that is outside of the sensory world, or, rather perhaps, we can inaccurately imagine many possible ideas about what that world might

15

be. Thus, religious doctrines cannot be assessed for truth or falsity but rather only for internal consistency. For Kant, then, faith is the basis of religion. Faith comes not in the world of reason, but in the world of action. Faith leads us to live in a certain way. Faith comes from a free assent, but faith is discovered and discerned through practice rather than through belief. As Kant said, "I must not even say, 'It is morally certain that there is a God,' but rather 'I am morally certain.'"

The Industrial Revolution

But neither scientists nor businesspeople waited for the solution to the problem of knowledge. Most of them, in fact, were unaware of the issues. The eighteenth century was a time of commerce and production—making money. In 1707, in fact, Scottish commercial people, amenable to bribes, of course, decided to unify Scotland and Ireland in Great Britain in the certainty that this would promote commerce. Intellectually and technologically, the results were excellent.

By the end of the eighteenth century, observers began to notice that the British economy was in the process of transformation, "a revolution in manufactures." This revolution, it was recognized, took place almost entirely in the textile industries. By the mid-nineteenth century, the phrase "revolution in manufactures" had become "industrial revolution." This revolution depended on the rise of technology: in particular, machines for carding, spinning, and (ultimately) weaving fibers. Associated developments took place in the use of water mills to power the new factories, the invention of steam engines that began to replace water as power sources, and agricultural improvements that allowed more calories to be grown on the same amount of land, using less human power.

The first innovation was in weaving broadcloth. It took at least two and sometimes four weavers to weave a cloth that was wider than a person could reach across. In weaving, a shuttle carries weft threads through the warp threads. Then the warp threads are reversed, and the shuttle is pushed back through the warp. If one person could not reach the shuttle to pull it back, another operator was needed to push it in the opposite direction. By rearranging the loom and inventing an automatic shuttle that "flew" back through the warp (the flying shuttle), John Kay, in 1733, was able to halve the number of weavers needed to produce a piece of broadcloth, and also to reduce the amount of time needed. As this system was employed in more and more places, it exceeded the capacity of the spinners to produce enough thread. Eventually, the need for more thread led to the development of the modern factory system.

The ideas that made this technical revolution possible had mostly been around for centuries. Having workers in the same trade work in one building together was one idea. Using water wheels to power manufacturing processes (like sawmills or felting mills) was old hat. Hand-powered spinning wheels had long existed. The innovation was inventing a machine that could spin several spindles while maintaining exactly the proper tension: too loose and the yarn would be shoddy; too tight and the yarn would break. This machine, ultimately patented as the "water frame" in 1769, used ideas developed by at least four people. Using waterpower, it arranged several spindles in a row so one spinner could operate them. The machine, however, was too big and cumbersome to be used in a cottage. Arkwright put his machine in a mill and built housing in the surrounding village for the migrant workers he would employ. And thus, the proto-type modern factory was created.

Like ideas that are created and developed in an essay through writing and rewriting, ideas embodied in a machine are created and developed by building and rebuilding. Rarely does a machine work the way its inventor thinks it should, and so a laborious process of tweaking and remaking is necessary before the ideas, now perhaps changed considerably, emerge into the public sphere as material things. But the ideas expressed by a machine can be as eloquent as those expressed in a book. The modern factory, for instance, was an idea that responded to the need of having large machines housed somewhere outside of an individual workshop or cottage and having something other than humans or animals power it. The factory system was an elegant physical answer to a hard question. As we will see, the factory system's unintended human consequences impoverished the lives of the people who worked in it.

Machines then led to new economic and social conditions that called forth ideas to understand them. Medieval ideas might have been sufficient to deal with the medieval world, but they had scant relevance to the emerging technological, industrial, and urban world. If we look at the development of the steam engine, with textile machines, the iconic symbol of the Industrial Revolution, we can learn a great deal about the emergence of new ideas in technology.

Figure 1.4 Thomas Lombe's Silk Mill, Derby, *c.* 1860. At the site of one of the first factories. © Universal History Archive/Getty Images.

In the early eighteenth century, England's coalmines had a problem: they had moved below the water table. All mines needed pumps that worked day and night. As the mines got deeper, a series of pumps was needed, for a pump can only raise water to a height in which the column of water weighs the same as the imaginary column of air above it, about 33 feet (10.3 meters). These pumps were powered by draft animals, and these animals cost money involving feeding, cleaning, and eventually, in death, hauling away.

Experimental scientists in the seventeenth century had noted that when water turns into steam, the volume increases by 1,700 times. Several people had the idea of using this expansive power to do work, and ultimately Thomas Newcomen developed a steam pump in 1712. He heated water in the bottom of a cylinder, and as the steam expanded, it raised a piston up the cylinder. He realized that if he attached the piston to a balance beam, when steam pushed the piston up, the beam would tilt toward the other side, and that if that beam were attached to a pump, the pump handle would be depressed. Then, if the cylinder were cooled, the steam would turn to water and the piston would be pulled back down into the cylinder, thus raising the pump on the other side. All he needed to run the pump was water to turn into steam (and they had plenty of water) and coal to heat the water into steam (it was, after all, a coal mine).

And so matters stood until the Scotsman James Watt, an instrument repairer at the University of Glasgow, began to tinker with a model Newcomen engine. He realized in 1763 that the entire cylinder of the Newcomen engine did not have to be cooled, but

Figure 1.5 Chelsea Water Works with Watt engine as the pump, 1810. An example of the power of Watt's engine to transform society. © Science & Society Picture Library/Getty Images.

Figure 1.6 Portrait of James Watt, 1788. © Stock Montage/Getty Images.

that the steam could be drawn into the vacuum of a separate cylinder where it could be cooled (condensed). As Watt worked to make a more efficient engine, he realized that many improvements would make it better. Piece by piece he added ideas.

A major problem was boring a precise cylinder in a cast iron block; the borers tended to wobble a bit. Thus, it was hard to get a good fit with the piston. In the gap between piston and cylinder wall, a lot of steam could escape. John Wilkinson, a cannon maker, who had discovered an exact method of boring cylinders, solved this problem. He fixed the drill and turned the entire block of iron around it! When Watt and his new business partner and financer, Matthew Boulton, found out about the Wilkinson process, they were able to manufacture their first steam pumps and begin marketing them. They were able to make money by charging a percentage of the amount of coal saved in comparison with a Newcomen pump.

So far, we have seen a few characteristics of technological ideas. First, they usually embody the ideas of several people. Second, they take a lot of development, and, in the process, ideas are changed and invented. Third, often ideas come from associated processes that are not clearly related. A cannon maker provided a crucial idea for Watt's steam pump.

But perhaps the most striking is that so far no one had really figured out that a steam pump is a steam engine. Inventors do not necessarily know what they have invented! Very often someone who did not make the actual machine discovers the eventual use of a work of technology. An engine is a generalized power source. It can drive pumps, but it can also drive mills, boats, trains, and airplanes. The financier Boulton suggested that this engine could be used for multiple purposes. He persuaded Watt to develop a set of linkages that would transfer the reciprocal, up and down, motion of the piston to produce rotary motion that could imitate the motion of a water wheel and thus drive machines. In order to avoid paying patent fees to others, Watt invented a new kind of linkage, the sun and planet gear, to create the rotary motion. When it turned out that steam engines would explode when they ran faster and faster, Watt invented an ingenious "fly ball governor." As the engine ran faster, the rotating balls would move outwards, shutting down a steam valve. Less steam made the engine move slower, and as the balls slowed, they moved inward, opening the valve to make the engine run faster.

Until a machine was invented, the ultimate use of the invention remained undiscovered. When they were invented, the horseless carriage was not yet an automobile, and the wireless telegraph was not yet a radio. Only the embodiment of these ideas permitted them to be understood.

But with this new idea, that the machine was not just a pump but also an engine, the Industrial Revolution received a boost. Factories were no longer tied to streams, and in the nineteenth century steamboats and railroads transformed transportation. The new machines transformed society and intellectual life.

The Enlightenment

Newtonian science (along with its Continental rivals, Cartesian and Leibnizian science) also stimulated what by 1750 had become known as the Enlightenment. The Enlightenment was a philosophical movement in France that spread to other European countries, each of which tended to give unique characteristics to it. Enlightenment thinkers embraced the use of reason to solve or ameliorate social problems. They reasoned that if Newton could solve the motions of the planets, through the use of reason and observation, then humans should be able to use reason to make a better society. A twenty-first century correlate might be the question, "If we can put a man on the moon, why can't we solve the problem of hunger (or poverty, or criminality, etc.)?" It was a movement characterized by discussions and debate, especially at salons, meetings hosted by intellectual women who brought together groups of noted thinkers to engage in witty and informed conversation. The conversations also occurred at places as varied as coffee houses and scientific academies. And of course, the conversation was carried out in writing.

Two of the best-known Enlightenment thinkers were Voltaire (Francois-Marie Arouet) and Jean-Jacques Rousseau. Voltaire, the popularizer of Newton's ideas in France (along with Émilie du Châtelet, as we have seen) was an opponent of the Catholic Church and of religion in general. In *Candide* (1759), he poked fun at Leibniz's idea that "this is the best of all possible worlds." How could one reform society if God constructed it in the best way possible? The more pessimistic Rousseau saw civilization as a corrupting influence and sought to deduce what society would be like if it were based on the natural instincts of humans.

In *On the Social Contract; or Principles of Political Rights* (1762), the Swiss Jean-Jacques Rousseau (1712–78) defined a state of nature in which all people were born free—uncorrupted by society. But when society and government formed, those who owned property dominated. Both the property-owners and the property-less were unfree, separated from one another.

Rousseau imagined a society in which people could form a social compact, either explicitly or tacitly. Thus, a collective body could form that was bigger than an individual. All of the individual members would have common interests expressed by the collective, or general, will. However, Individuals may have an individual will opposed to the common will. For instance, some people may think taxes are good and necessary (common will) but not want to pay their own taxes (individual will). In that case, the general will would be supreme.

For Rousseau, who began his *Contract* with the phrase: "Man was born free, and everywhere he is in chains," inequality was the source of bondage, and freedom could only be obtained in a society in which the interests of all were considered. Pursuit of individual interest by more talented members of society produces unfreedom, and so the general will constantly works against individual will to restore the primacy of the general will. If individuals work against the general will, then the society has the duty to force them to obey. For Rousseau, they have to be "forced to be free."

In the most fortunate societies, the general will could be embodied in a far-seeing leader. Rousseau mentioned the ancient Spartan king Lycurgus and the sixteenth-century thinker John Calvin of Geneva. Since the true sovereign would be the entirety of the citizens, the leader would be a kind of commissioned agent. If the agent, an individual or a group, usurped power from the people, then that agent would not be acting in good faith and would threaten the integrity of the state.

Rousseau's social contract was thus quite different from that of Hobbes (or Locke) for it maintained the supremacy of the whole of the citizenry. As the French Revolution reached the period known as "the Terror," the Jacobin leader Maximilian Robespierre saw himself as the leader who could best express the general will.

Most Enlightenment thinkers were anti-church. Christian churches had, since the time of Constantine, aligned themselves with secular powers, and had often themselves been secular powers. To Enlightenment *philosophes*, or philosophers of the Enlightenment, progress was hindered as much by churches as by monarchs. But most Enlightenment thinkers were not atheists. Some intelligence must have created this unimaginably complex world and universe, they reasoned. Many were Deists. They believed in a creator God, but not in the complex theologies of Christian churches.

The idea of progress was one of the most important ideas developed by Enlightenment thinkers. Before the eighteenth century, the predominant European idea was that God had instituted a social structure that would last as long as the world did. Although not everyone thought that the Archbishop Ussher had correctly calculated the beginning of the world at 6:00 p.m. on October 23, 4004 BC (Julian calendar), most believed that his order of magnitude was correct. If the world were only about 6,000 years old, and if the end times were within a century or two, then there wasn't much time for society to significantly change, and if there were change, it would be for the worse. For an example of this static view of society, one can look at virtually any biblical painting of the Renaissance to see biblical figures anachronistically decked out in Renaissance dress, surrounded by Renaissance architecture. The word "progress" was used, as in John Bunyan's *Pilgrim's Progress* (1678), but it meant the progress of a soul in attaining heaven.

Nevertheless, the Enlightenment thinkers considered the possibility that society might progress, not to heaven but to a more humane structure. To make this case, Enlightenment thinkers often turned to history. Marie Jean Antoine Nicolas de Caritat, Marquis of Condorcet (known to most as Nicolas de Condorcet) for instance, developed a theory of history that saw upward progress through ten stages. In the first stage, "men united into hordes," and he outlined a progress from agriculture through the golden age of Greece, through the "decline of learning" in the Middle Ages, and up to the formation of the French Republic. His tenth stage was "The Future Progress of Mankind," which he saw as virtually unlimited. He considered that the human mind itself might be improved, and he claimed that the classes and species of both animals and plants are in a process of perfectibility or deterioration. We will continue to see this idea: that species themselves can change if their environment (natural and social) changes, again and again in this book.

The key to progress, thought Condorcet, along with his companion *philosophes*, was the use of reason in advancing the sciences. In fact, his ten stages are based on the progress of knowledge, of science (in which "science" is defined as knowledge generally). When knowledge declines, so does the welfare of humankind. Ironically, Condorcet wrote this book while hiding from the Jacobin, radical wing, of the revolutionary government who purported to put Enlightenment ideas into practice (see the following text). Condorcet, a moderate, had criticized their new constitution. He died in prison shortly thereafter, by suicide, by poison, or by murder.

Ideas of the French Revolution

The French Revolution is to ideas as salmon are to fish eggs: many are spawned but few are chosen. The French Revolution has been variously portrayed as the door to democracy, the gateway to totalitarianism, and the window through which can view the social wreckage of revolutionary action, to name but a few. Still, the French Revolution echoes in the twenty-first century as one of the iconic events of modern European history.

Before the French Revolution few Europeans thought that government based on democracy was a good idea. Fewer thought that universal adult suffrage had anything to recommend it. The American experiment, only a few years old, was too new to reveal anything. The philosophes of the Enlightenment thought they could see clearly that an enlightened monarch (or despot) would be needed to institute needed social reforms. Jean-Jacques Rousseau wrote of "the general will," but he did not depend on democracy to express it. General will, for Rousseau is not found by averaging the votes of individuals who may not understand in what way it is in their interest to express the needs of the entire community as they search for the common good. In fact, forcing an individual to obey a law that expresses the common good is forcing that individual to be free.

With the French Revolution, republicanism (government lacking a monarchy) became a conceivable possibility. But the founders of the revolution did not intend in any way to establish a republic. Their model was more likely to be the constitutional monarchy of Great Britain. How did these moderate aims produce a set of ideas that recommended regicide and a radical overturning of government that then led to the imperial rule of the oxymoronic democratic emperor Napoleon Bonaparte?

The Situation

In 1789 Louis XVI of France called together the Estates General (for the first time in 150 years) in order to gain support for raising taxes. The Estates General was based on the notion that there were three social/political classes of French subjects: clergy, nobles, and commoners. These Estates General were a medieval institution that gave advice to the king in problematic times. And these were problematic times. The king was broke.

Not only was the treasury bleeding money to pay off loans that had supported wars in the eighteenth century, but the monarchy had already given tax exemptions to much of the nobility and clergy. Commoners were overtaxed. The king hoped that the three houses, meeting together, could find sources to keep coins flowing into the royal coffers. The monarch's assumption, and that of the first two Estates, was that the three houses would each have one vote. The Third Estate, the commoners, demanded and received double the representation of the other two Estates. Thus, there were exactly as many representatives in the Third Estate as there were in the First and Second Estates combined. If each Estate had one vote, then it did not matter how many delegates each Estate had. If the first two Estates, the clergy and nobles, voted together, they could overcome the Third Estate. However, if all representatives voted separately, then the Third Estate could tie the other two Estates. One renegade noble or priest could tip the vote toward the Third Estate. The Third Estate, unsurprisingly, demanded that votes be taken by polling each individual representative.

These preliminary stages, then, were about taxes and who would have to pay. Just as in seventeenth-century England, the non-noble upper-middle class was desperate to find a way to participate in government. The world of Western Europe was changing, and medieval institutions were incapable of providing sufficient avenues for the expression of the interests of new and powerful citizens.

Nothing went as the king had hoped. Eventually, on June 17, 1789, the Third Estate voted to declare themselves the National Assembly, and Assembly of the People. Three days later, locked out of the meeting rooms, the Third Estate met on a nearby Tennis Court and swore to meet until they had produced a constitution.

Documents

The first major document of the French Revolution was the *Serment du Jeu de Paume* (*Tennis Court Oath*). But at the time it was written, no one conceived their actions as revolutionary. In the oath, they swore to "maintain the true principles of monarchy." They also claimed that they were summoned to write a constitution, even though the king had not intended any such thing, and they also said that nothing could stop them from deliberating. The Third Estate had not invented the idea of a National Assembly, but by declaring it for France, the new National Assemblymen had decided that France should be a constitutional monarchy, in some ways like Great Britain.

In August 1789, the National Assembly issued a *Déclaration des droits de l'homme et du citoyen* (*Declaration of the Rights of Man and Citizen*) in which they declared that "the ignorance, neglect, or contempt of the rights of man are the sole cause of public calamities and the corruption of governments."[2] That is a striking claim that moved far beyond the ideas of "general welfare" in Great Britain or the new United States. Guarantee rights, said the French, and you will have avoided calamity.

The next step, of course, was to enumerate human rights. The first article noted, "Men are born and remain free and equal in rights," but it went on to protect social distinctions necessary to the general good. It started with echoes of Rousseau ("Man is born free; and everywhere he is in chains") and essentially ended with a continuing socially stratified country.

The second article, echoing Locke and Jefferson, enumerated the rights of "liberty, property, security, and resistance to oppression." The rest of the Declaration of 1789 bears many similarities to the Bill of Rights of the US Constitution. Liberty is defined as the right to do anything that is not forbidden by law, which is to be established as an expression of the general will. Important differences from the American version are that taxation, determined by representative government, is a right; transparency in government decisions and actions is guaranteed; and freedom of speech may be modified by law. This is a radical, but not path-breaking, document.

This declaration became one of the foundations for the first Constitution, that of 1791. Perhaps just as important for the constitution, Baron Montesquieu's 1748 book *De l'esprit des loix* (*The Spirit of the Laws*) provided a template. Montesquieu argued that a separation of government powers into an executive, a legislative, and a judicial branch, all coequal but separate, was absolutely necessary to protect the nation from the human tendency to overreach in ambition. Montesquieu also thought that a monarch should rule alongside this non-monarchical part of government.

The ambitions of the first era of the Revolution, then, were to set up a government similar to that of Great Britain. It took several committees two years to work out a compromise, but in the end, votes went only to male taxpayers. The rest of the citizenry were "passive" citizens who had civil rights, but no franchise. The king maintained an important role, including a limited veto power over legislation. Importantly, the king had to swear allegiance to the Constitution and could lose his throne by leaving the country.

The version of the "Declaration of the Rights of Man and Citizen" written in 1793, however, is the most radical document promulgated by a government to that date. Following the execution of the king, and echoing Rousseau, it defined equality as a natural right and condition. It was up to the law then, to ensure that social or governmental arrangements did not upset the natural state of equality. In fact, in order to ensure this natural condition, the Declaration of 1793 guaranteed a number of secondary rights, like education, property, public relief, and so forth. The Declaration further guaranteed to the people the right of insurrection if the government violated their rights.

The iconic slogan of the French Revolution was "Liberté, egalité, fraternité" (Liberty, Equality, Fraternity). In the *Declaration of the Rights of Man and Citizen* of 1789, the first two terms were introduced. Liberty, in this document, was expansive. All was permitted that did not interfere with the liberty of others. This of course was a tricky proposition in practice, especially if it was meant to result in equality. Powerful or wealthy people would not tend to give up their advantage to the less wealthy or powerful without a struggle. And yet the document declared that all citizens should be equal before the law, eligible to hold office, and guaranteed to be employed anywhere, as long as they were qualified.

The first Constitution was written to protect liberty against too much equality. The second Constitution was written in 1793 to restore the primacy of equality. However, it was never enforced, because the Terror took precedence. In effect, the writers of the Constitution of 1793 decided that constitutional government was ineffective, and that terror should be the order of the day.

For Maximilian Robespierre (the architect of the phase of the revolution known as "the Terror"), he himself embodied the general will of the people as described by Rousseau. In his opinion, virtue could not exist without terror. The philosophy of terror in the interests of equality was certainly one of the legacies of the French Revolution, and various reformist totalitarian governments have used similar arguments in defense of their methods. Robespierre was a purist, and he did not see virtue in parliamentary debate seeking a compromise among competing interests. For Robespierre, the more moderate or conservative parliamentarians stood in the way of justice and should be eliminated.

While Robespierre and his Committees of Public Safety (or Public Prosperity) ran the government, Robespierre set out to reform the culture of France. The committee set up a state religion to replace the Catholic Church. They reformed the calendar and instituted the metric system to measure time, including a ten-day week and the ten-hour day. The idea was to create an environment in which true citizens should be shaped.

These radical reforms, most of which were eventually dropped, augmented earlier reforms that essentially ended the feudal system. Church tithes, feudal dues, tax farming, and other impediments to a more modern economy all disappeared. Although the monarchy was restored after Napoleon's defeat, it only lasted another three decades. The ideas of republicanism, equality under the law, and a government responsive to the people, firmly entered the European mind.

The possibility of universal adult suffrage was also introduced. Olympe de Gouge produced a "Declaration of the Rights of Women and the Female Citizen" in 1791 (see next chapter). Although she did not carry the day, and although female suffrage waited for the twentieth century, she firmly placed the idea in the conversation. During the Terror, she was executed for her challenges to male authority.

Once Robespierre himself was eliminated, the compromise was a weakened government in the form of a five-person executive, called the Directory, and a bicameral legislature. The election system did not support the participation of the lower classes, who clearly suffered from continued external wars and a weak economy.

Eventually, of course, Napoleon was able to maneuver his way into a dictatorship. He established many of the ideas of the revolution and began to export them to the rest of Europe. By 1800, however, he had barely gained power, and no one knew that as an emperor he would attempt to impose his will on all Europe. He overthrew the Directory on November 9, 1799. At that point he was First Consul, with two consultative Consuls appointed by him. On January 1, 1800, Europe awoke to a France led by a very successful general.

Conclusion: Looking Ahead

The exponential curve of population growth is familiar to most people today. Around 1800, that curve began its increasingly rapid climb. What is less familiar to most people is that this curve can be applied to much more than population. The growth of population is related to an increasing quality of life. Nutritious food production began a rapid increase. Cities grew exponentially. The number of books and journals increased continually. The nineteenth and twentieth centuries represented an increase in affluence for most Europeans that would have astounded any would-be prophets in 1800.

In fact, the world in 1900 would have been unthinkable to an astute observer in 1800. In 1800 no one had any idea that washing one's hands before performing surgery would have any perceptible effect on the outcome. There was no germ theory of disease. As a result, growing cities often dumped their waste directly upstream from the water intake. There was no sewage treatment. Electric current had not yet been observed, so there was no telegraph, telephone, or radio. Every adult parent had experienced the death of young children, either their own or a sibling's. By 1900, mortality from a wide variety of causes had been contained.

All of these changes, in technology and technique, presented new possibilities and imperatives for intellectuals. In the next two chapters, we will look at the early development of these two ways of seeing humans: as individuals (Chapter 2) or as members of groupings (Chapter 3). Out of these two opposing worldviews came a spate of ideas about ethics, human knowledge, scientific studies, aesthetics, economics, and more.

CHAPTER 2
INDIVIDUALS AND ATOMS
INDIVIDUALS AS SOURCE OF WEALTH, REASON, AND MORALITY

Figure 2.1 Photo of John Stuart Mill and his stepdaughter Helen Taylor, 1860. Reversing the traditional positions of men and women. Both Mill and his stepdaughter were strong proponents of women's rights. © London Stereoscopic Company/Stringer/Hulton Archive/Getty Images.

Information: A Technological Interlude

The Victorian era, according to John Stuart Mill, was "the age of newspapers, railways, and the electric telegraph." In fact, it is impossible to understand intellectual events in the nineteenth century without looking at their technological context. As the sheer number of printed materials expanded, the cost of these materials plummeted, bringing newspapers and pamphlets within easy reach of all Western Europeans. A printing press in 1800 could produce 480 sheets an hour. By 1812 that had increased to 800 sheets an hour, and by 1818 the Koenig press could produce 2,400 sheets. Printing technology developed rapidly. In 1814 the *London Times* announced that it was now using steam-powered presses. With the invention of the rotary steam-powered press in 1843, a press could produce millions of copies of a page in a single day.

The ubiquity of printed materials was augmented by the amount of information available from distant places. In 1800 an Italian, Alessandro Volta, discovered how to produce an electric current using a Voltaic pile or battery. By 1838 electric current was used to power a rudimentary telegraph. By 1852 national telegraph systems existed in most European countries, although they greatly lagged the United States. By 1858 America and Europe were connected by transatlantic cable, and information could be sent in a matter of minutes instead of the ten days or so it took a ship. By 1870 India was connected electronically to Great Britain.

Public education expanded at the same time in different countries in different ways. In 1800 literacy in England was approximately 60 percent for males and 40 percent for females. By 1870 in Great Britain literacy was up to 70 percent for males and 55 percent for females. As more people could read, more people became engaged in discussion of the issues of the day. Literacy for working people allowed them to become more conscious of their tenuous economic situation and more likely to use collective movements to pressure politicians. With feudal ideas disintegrating rapidly, the problem for intellectuals was to devise new analyses to social, economic, and political circumstances.

Chapter Map

This chapter describes an intellectual world based on the assumption that what counted were the actions and ideas of individuals. Individualism became a worldview that underlay a variety of apparently unrelated intellectual approaches.

We will examine the development of nineteenth-century liberalism in economic, political, and ethical theory. In almost all of the discussion about rights in the early nineteenth century, writers assumed that only free males would hold rights. In the wake of the French Revolution, women like Mary Wollstonecraft and Olympe de Gouge argued for women's rights. Others saw that human rights and slavery were incompatible.

Even science was affected by individualism. Matter could be seen as non-particulate, or it could be seen as made up of atoms or molecules. As early as the seventeenth century, some saw atomic theory as a challenge to social cohesion. In the early nineteenth century, the new chemistry was placed successfully on an atomic foundation, challenging earlier ideas about the structure of matter.

Individualism was well established well before 1800. The soil nourishing its roots was comprised of religion interspersed with philosophy. But as Europe became more commercial, new rootlets emerged that fed on money—sales and invention. Commerce also produced a weak hybrid form: egalitarianism. Sellers and buyers were not defined by social status but, rather, by transactions. Human beings began to be seen not as parts of a "stupendous whole," but as self-contained atoms of meaning. In this chapter, we will watch these rootlets grow. Spoiler alert: by the end of the book, individualism will have become the dominant root-form.

Essentially the theme underlying this chapter is the search for a new ideology that would support commercial elites as they battle with the old nobility—a nobility that had originated as a warrior class but by 1800 had largely become decadent. In the next chapter, we will look at the other side: ideas that saw individuals only in a larger context that provided meaning and value.

Theory of Liberalism

Meet the ideal economic liberals! They produced and they bought. They made decisions based on calculated assessments of costs and benefits. They maximized their self-interest, and their main fear was losing their money. Their actions could be measured in quantifiable amounts. They produced wealth for the nation, as long as governments did not interfere with them. The market for goods and services was omniscient. It acted as if it were a supercomputer that made sure that the sum of millions of transactions was always for the best. The economic liberals took care of their own business and assumed that others were doing the same.

Ideal political liberals were closely akin to ideal economic liberals. They read and debated as they searched for the truth or for the best answer. They tried as best they could to shed their prejudices while recognizing that others may not have done the same. They thought it was important that they both had the right to vote and exercised it, but they were reluctant to share that right to vote with anyone who did not have the education to make informed choices. They recognized that society had been unfair to many, and so they tended to advocate for the abolition of slavery and the education of women. When they became aware of exploitation, they were willing to enact laws to stop that exploitation, all in the interest of the expansion of individual empowerment. But they believed in the marketplace, and in the marketplace of ideas, so they were loath to use any government power to help individuals or groups, beyond ensuring that all had reasonable opportunities to create their lives.

These ideal figures were both descriptive and prescriptive. They represented the best attempts of a group of thinkers to understand how society works and how society should work. In fact, economic and political liberalism provided an intellectual context for the redesign of laws and institutions that fostered the increasingly wealthy and powerful Europe that emerged in the nineteenth century. Naturally, the opponents of liberalism noticed that important aspects of individual and social life were missing from liberal analysis. Those critiques will be discussed in the following chapters. But in this chapter, we focus on the power of individualism and individual analysis.

In Chapter 1, we saw how the idea of progress underlay Enlightenment social analysis and contributed to the French Revolution. In this section, we will discuss how the idea of progress was developed in an economic direction. Two key points stand out.

First, in what has come to be called "classical economics," the actions of individual actors were seen to be more important than the workings of larger social structures. The best society emerged smoothly from individual actions, as social structure was too complex for anyone to understand or control. With important exceptions, the best thing governments could do was get out of the way. Second, those individual actions would result in a division of labor that immensely increased efficiency and wealth.

Adam Smith

The immediate stimulus to economic progressive thinking occurred in Scotland where the moralist Adam Smith's book *An Inquiry into the Nature and Causes of the Wealth of Nations* (*The Wealth of Nations*), published in 1776, provided the impetus for the development of modern economic thought in the nineteenth century.

Adam Smith was a somewhat strange-looking figure with a speech impediment who once described himself as "a beau in nothing but my books." He was capable of getting so

Figure 2.2 Statue of Adam Smith in Edinburgh, Scotland. Seagulls enjoy perching on the head of the great economist. © Photograph by David Galaty.

lost in thought that he forgot where he was or what he was doing. He once sleepwalked for 15 miles in his nightshirt before church bells startled him into awareness and sent him scrambling home to Kirkaldy, just across the Firth of Forth from Edinburgh. But Smith traveled. After studying at Glasgow and Oxford and teaching moral philosophy at Edinburgh, Smith accepted a job as a private tutor to the son of the late Duke of Buccleuch. The terms were munificent: double his stipend, with expenses, with the salary guaranteed as a pension for life. In 1764, the tutor and pupil began to tour Europe, beginning in southern France, where the monolingual Smith reported being bored out of his mind. He began to learn French and to write on economics. By the time they got to Paris, Smith knew just enough French to communicate with the intellectuals there. One of his most interesting conversation companions was François Quesnay, a court physician to Louis XV.

Quesnay had developed a way of thinking about economics that compared the circulation of income in the economy to the circulation of blood in a human. He developed his model in a complex chart, perhaps as complex as a diagram of blood circulation. Quesnay's supporters were known as physiocrats, and they had begun to challenge the mercantilist assumptions on which French and other European economies were built.

The mercantilists used tariffs to maximize a country's positive balance of trade: they believed that a country could only increase wealth by exporting more than it imported. Essentially, then, the focus on wealth was on the amount of money (gold or silver) that a country had at hand. Mercantilists thought wealth came from maintaining a positive balance of trade.

The physiocrats, however, argued that wealth actually came from agricultural produce, not from trade. France was almost entirely an agricultural country, as were its colonies. The physiocrats saw the "Proprietary" class as landowners and the "Productive" class as agricultural workers. Artisans and merchants were part of the "Sterile" class. The only thing that France had of value was food, so food could be exported for goods from abroad. France should only foster manufacturing to meet local needs. The government, however, should do all it could to encourage agriculture.

As he thought about it, Smith agreed with the argument that money was not the source of wealth in a country. But suddenly Smith's time in France, where he had the chance to meet other thinkers, like Benjamin Franklin and Voltaire, soon came to an unexpected end. His tutee's younger brother, who was visiting Paris, fell ill, and even Quesnay could not save him. The entire entourage returned to England, and Smith's services as a tutor were no longer required. Smith went home to write.

As he put his book together, he drew on insights from as many sources as possible. The origins of most of the major points in *The Wealth of Nations* can be found in the work of others, but Smith sharpened and extended the arguments and drew it all into the masterpiece that continues to be read today. Smith saw himself in the Newtonian tradition of uncovering the natural laws behind economic and social activity.

Unlike agricultural France, manufacturing and trade increasingly supported Great Britain's economy. So as Smith thought about the discussions he had with Quesnay, he realized that Quesnay was right to emphasize production over gold and silver (money) as a source of wealth. He saw that the increase of precious metals that New World mines provided Spain in the sixteenth century did nothing but force prices up, in the absence of new production of things to buy. In Britain, industrial production was just as important to trade as agricultural production. Smith saw manufacturing as the source of a growing economy that could expand practically without limit. The chief engine of that growth was labor.

Before he went to France, Smith had written a very well-received and influential book on ethics entitled *The Theory of Moral Sentiments* (1759). Smith's subject in that book was explaining the origin of moral judgments, given that people are essentially self-interested. How can essentially selfish people make decisions that lead them to sacrifice something for the good of another person? Smith's answer was that human nature includes the capacity to imagine an "impartial spectator" who carefully advises them about the best course of action for all people involved. People are able to have sympathy for others, and on the basis of this sympathy (empathy) are able to make choices for the good of others. Morality is not based on reason but on our social nature. When others feel sad, we feel sad too. When others are happy, we feel happiness. Thus, empathy is the basis of justice and of altruism.

Smith brought this perspective into The *Wealth of Nations*. The book was not merely what we today would call an "economics" text. Smith was interested in what really motivated people and how they work, as well as in the best social structure. Today there are two main lines of thought seen to define Smith's primary argument: (1) the idea of the invisible hand and (2) the idea of the division of labor.

The idea of the "invisible hand" is found in the following passage where Smith discussed a person making investment decisions:

> He generally, indeed, neither intends to promote the public interest, not knows how much he is promoting it . . . he intends only his own gain, and he is, in this, as in many other cases, led by an invisible hand to promote an end which was no part of his intention. Nor is it always worse for society that it was no part of it. By pursuing his own interest he frequently promotes that of the society more effectually than when he really intends to promote it. I have never known much good done by those who affected to trade for the public good. It is an affectation, indeed, not very common among merchants, and very few words need be employed in dissuading them from it.[1]

Although this quotation is part of an analysis of why investments will tend to be made at home rather than abroad, it also applied to other aspects of business. In any industry, those competitors who make the best product at the lowest price will sell their products, and others, who make shoddier or more expensive products, will be unable to make the sale. They will be driven out of business. As they look for other means of livelihood, they will find their niche or perish. As a result, the best cobblers will make shoes, the best pinmakers will make pins, the best ditchdiggers will dig ditches, and everyone will be sorted as if an omniscient divine being (the invisible hand) had organized society.

No government should try to protect inefficient home industries by tariffs or other means. The result of, say, protecting the English shoe industry from competition from better, cheaper Italian shoes would be an England that is poorly shod for a high price. The English would spend money on shoes that could be better spent elsewhere. Why not, asked Smith, allow Italians to dominate the shoe industry so that the English can concentrate their investments on other industries, such as textiles, in which they excel. Where there is specialization, wealth grows and flourishes. And all springs from concern for one's self-interest. As Smith wrote,

> It is not from the benevolence of the butcher, the brewer, or the baker, that we expect our dinner, but from their regard to their own interest. We address ourselves, not to their humanity but to their self-love, and never talk to them of our own necessities but of their advantages.[2]

The social structure that allows for self-interest to promote the public good is competition in a free market in a society ruled by justice. All are necessary for Smith. He warned that businessmen have a natural tendency to want to band together to fix prices and otherwise undermine the beneficial results of competition. Governments have a tendency to favor one set of businessmen over another by selling monopolies, setting tariffs, and favoring their own interests. Therefore, Smith promoted laws that prevented business collusion but also a laissez-faire government that did not interfere in the market.

The first sentence of the first chapter of *The Wealth of Nations* described the second line of thought that has produced over two centuries of commentary: the importance of the division of labor.

> The greatest improvement in the productive powers of labour, and the greater part of the skill, dexterity, and judgment with which it is anywhere directed, or applied, seem to have been the effects of the division of labour.[3]

Smith immediately discussed the trade of the pinmaker, who, Smith claims "could scarce, perhaps, with his utmost industry, make one pin in a day, and certainly could not make twenty." But, Smith continued, if the eighteen distinct operations in making a pin were given over to separate workers, combined they could make 48,000 pins in a day, even if some of the workers did two or three of the operations together. That is, 10 people could make the equivalent of 4,800 pins each, immensely more than the maximum of 20 pins one of them could make alone. Why is this? First, because practice makes perfect, and continual repetition of the same task increases dexterity in performing that task. Second, time is saved in passing from one task to the other. Third, experts begin thinking of better ways of doing the work, and they tend to invent new machines and procedures. In fact, Smith essentially predicted continuing technological improvement.

As Smith considered the effects of the division of labor, he described it as "that universal opulence which extends itself to the lowest ranks of the people . . . and a general plenty diffuses itself through all the different ranks of society." Everyone is unwittingly engaged in providing for everyone else in a great interconnected, incomprehensible whole. When he thought of the leather coat worn by a worker, Smith wrote that the coat is

> the produce of the joint labor of a great multitude of workmen, the Shepherd, the sorter of the wool, the wool-comber or carder, the dyer, the scribbler, the spinner, the weaver, the fuller, the dresser . . . [and] how many merchants and carriers, besides, must have been employed in transporting the materials from some of these workmen to others who often live in a very distant part of the country! How much commerce and navigation in particular, how many ship-builders, sailors, sail-makers, rope-makers.[4]

Smith went on and on to show an interconnected industrial world in which everyone grows richer and richer so that "the accommodation of a European prince does not always so much exceed that of an industrious and frugal peasant, as the accommodation of the latter exceeds that of many an African king."

But Smith was not unaware of the cost of division of labor on workers who remain unprotected by government regulation.

> The man whose whole life is spent in performing a few simple operations . . . has no occasion to exert his understanding. . . . He naturally loses, therefore, the habit of exertion, and generally becomes as stupid and ignorant as it is possible for a human creature to become. . . . But in every improved and civilized society this is the state into which the labouring poor, that is, the great body of the people, must necessarily fall, unless government takes some pains to prevent it.[5]

In many places in the book, Smith considered in a clear manner the plight of the working poor. The book is not, as some suppose, a paean to unrestrained, free-market capitalism. It is instead an attempt, using the methods of the Newtonian revolution, to clearly understand the evidence and to find the laws that govern the economic side of society. Where Smith saw the need for government regulation and action, he recommended it. Where he saw the potential harm in action by a government influenced by the money of the powerful, he warned against that action.

David Ricardo

David Ricardo (1772–1823) was an iconoclast. He was a rationalist who followed the dictates of reason wherever they might lead. Brought up as a Sephardic Jew, he was unable to rationalize his family's faith, and he began to be attracted to Unitarianism, a church to which many intellectuals belonged. When he was twenty-one, he married a Quaker, Patricia Ann Wilkinson, and the two of them converted to Unitarianism. Both families were dismayed, and Ricardo was quickly disinherited. From the age of fourteen, he had worked closely with his father as a stockbroker, and although it must have been frightening to be cut financially adrift at such a young age, the well-trained Ricardo was quickly able to establish himself on the stock exchange.

Ricardo specialized in government bonds. The wars with France that would run off and on from 1792 until 1815 necessitated a great deal of government borrowing. No one quite understood the relationship between paper money and hard currency, although many thought they did. Ricardo was able to see how these different forms of money provided ways of buying and selling to make small profits. Bonds were offered competitively to different groups of investors who made sealed bids on how much interest they would require in order to loan the government the requested money. After Napoleon returned from Elba in 1815, the value of government bonds sank. The astute Ricardo bought them up, held them as the Battle of Waterloo approached and the bonds sank further, and continued to buy more. When Wellington was victorious, the value of the bonds soared, and Ricardo may have netted as much as a million pounds. He retired from business soon after. In 1818 he moved to a career as a politician as a Whig Member of Parliament, buying his seat. He died of an infection at the age of 51, worth about £675,000–750,000 (over £61 million in today's currency).

Ricardo's name as an economist is tied to his *Principles of Political Economy and Taxation* (1817). He began as an economic analyst after a close reading of Adam Smith's *Wealth of Nations*, and like Smith he saw the actions of individuals as the important determiners of a nation's wealth. He reformulated an old idea as he enunciated the labor theory of value (which we will see was embraced later by Karl Marx). For Ricardo, the value of a commodity depended on the quantity of labor that went into making it, and not, as he wrote, "the greater or less compensation which is paid for that labor." Value, then, would not be determined by price, which is a different concept (cf. the approach of Alfred Marshall, Chapter 8). There is a natural price of a commodity that may differ from the price it is sold for.

For Ricardo, wages were inevitably tied to the price of the necessities of life, because competition within an industry would penalize those who tried to raise wages above that level. Profits, then, depended on wages, and wages on the price of food. There was no escaping this somewhat brutal fact, for Ricardo. Workers were condemned to subsistence living. Thus, the optimism of Adam Smith, who thought that in a properly maintained free enterprise economy all would prosper, turned into a bleak pessimism for the future possibilities of workers. Economics became "the dismal science."

Like Smith, a free trader, Ricardo was opposed to the "corn laws." In Britain, "corn" refers to grain, not to "maize," as in the United States, so the Corn Laws were laws that protected British farm landlords by setting a tariff on imported grain. The Corn Laws, then, kept the price of grain high, which meant that the price of bread was also high. Industrialists had to pay their workers a living wage, or their workers would die. Industrialists, then, who usually supported the Whig party, wanted to abolish the Corn Laws. However, before the Reform Act of 1832 (which expanded voting to about one in five males), only one in ten British males could vote, and these were overwhelmingly rural landholders who tended to vote Tory. The Corn Laws were eventually only abolished in 1846 as a result of the Irish potato famine and the need for imported food.

Ricardo recognized that with protectionism, like the Corn Laws, most of the profits accrued to landowners rather than farmers. As the demand for grain increased, tenant farmers would begin to till less productive lands. Yet no matter if corn was raised on productive land or less productive land, the price of that corn per bushel remained the same. As prices for grain went up, so did rents. Therefore, property owners rather than producers benefited from protectionist legislation. Ricardo did not think that increasing rents provided very much benefit to society as a whole. The windfall went entirely to the property owners.

David Ricardo developed the theory of comparative advantage, a theory that supported his advocacy of free trade. Ricardo assumed a highly simplified world economy of two nations, England and Portugal, who produce two goods of identical quality. Portugal has lower labor costs, so they are able to produce both wine and cloth more cheaply than England. However, Ricardo was able to show that each country is best off if it specializes in the production of the thing at which it is most efficient and imports other goods from the other. In this case, England would export cloth and Portugal would specialize in wine. Each country has a comparative advantage, even if not an absolute advantage. And both countries have more of the products their consumers want. Free trade is better overall than trade protected by monopolies or tariffs.

But what if producers in England move production to Portugal to take advantage of the lower costs of labor? Both Ricardo and Smith's answers were similar. As Ricardo wrote: "most men of property are satisfied with a low rate of profits in their own country, rather than seek a more advantageous employment for their wealth in foreign nations." Investment capital in those times was not very mobile. As capital became more mobile, as it was less and less tied to the actual possession of precious metals, the problem of "off-shoring" became more and more real. This was a problem for future economists.

Thomas Malthus

David Ricardo's dear friend Thomas Malthus (1766–1834) was also a political-economist. The two often worked out their theories in conversation with one another. Malthus was born in Surrey. He graduated from Cambridge University (Jesus College) in 1787 with prizes and honors in both languages and mathematics. He was ordained in the Church of England in which he served in Surrey and Lincolnshire. He later held a position as professor of history and political economy for the East India Company's college in Hertfordshire. In 1818 he was appointed as a fellow of the Royal Society of London.

Malthus's first noted publication in 1798 dealt with what he claimed as an inevitable increase in population that would outstrip the food supply. These ideas will be discussed more fully in Chapter 6 (Darwin). However, he used these ideas to analyze a rise in the cost of food. He claimed that the increase in food prices was due to the Poor Laws that provided a living to the unemployed poor. But Malthus reached the conclusion that the Poor Laws were beneficial economically and morally.

Malthus and Ricardo disagreed about the issue of the possibility of an excess of production in a capitalist society. The Frenchman Jean-Baptiste Say had developed a theory in which production causes demand. For Say, there could be no glut because once something is produced, a demand for it will develop. Products will always be exchanged for other products, and if an apparent glut occurred, that could only be caused by the failure to produce enough of other, tradable products. Ricardo supported Say's Law, while Malthus thought that economic downturns could occur in response to a glut. The two men emphasized different analytic methods. Ricardo tended to try to find the essential points so that he could draw up a simple model that would have predictive value. Malthus saw complexity and was loath to simplify too much. For Malthus, the historical circumstances of the Napoleonic Wars and their aftermath showed that surpluses and gluts were certainly possible. For Ricardo, such gluts were anomalies that the market would soon straighten out. In the twentieth century, as we shall see (Chapter 10), John Maynard Keynes approached the issue in a relatively Malthusian manner.

The two men also debated about the Corn Laws. We have seen that Ricardo believed that free trade, without tariffs, would benefit Great Britain. In the end, Malthus tended to agree. But Malthus saw the dangers of Great Britain becoming dependent on foreign imports of corn. It might be possible for Britain's enemies to blackmail Britain by threatening to withhold food imports. Malthus therefore reserved the possibility of tariffs to enable Great Britain effectively to defend herself. Ricardo thought that the exporting enemies of Great Britain (mostly France, the main source of imported corn) would suffer greatly if they shut down the exporting parts of their agriculture sectors, and so Britain would be defended. In the end, Ricardo held that the increased "opulence" of free trade would always bolster Great Britain's defensive capabilities, while Malthus thought that defense might sometimes require some sacrifice of opulence.

The issue of using simplified models to predict complex real-life circumstances continues to bedevil economists. When, later in the nineteenth century, the marginal revolution in economics encouraged a turn toward mathematical models, the issue became acute for some economists.

Jeremy Bentham and Utilitarianism

Utilitarianism is best known for its catchphrase: the greatest good for the greatest number. Although like many ideas it has ancient roots, it is best seen as the brainchild of Jeremy Bentham (1748–1832), who emphasized the importance of happiness. Bentham was born in London in 1748 to a Tory family. He went to the best schools, obtained a master's degree, and was admitted to the bar in 1769. In the tumultuous years of the American and French revolutions, Bentham was involved with London intellectuals in important discussions and tract writing. He developed a theoretical plan for a penitentiary that he called the panopticon in which prisoners would be constantly monitored and visible from a central watchtower. His idea was that prisoners should learn discipline in order to gain the capability of returning to society as good citizens.

Bentham died in 1832, and controversial to the end, provided in his will that his body should be embalmed and displayed in what he called an "Auto-icon." After his body was used for dissection, it was mummified using the practices of indigenous people in New Zealand. This left the head dried out and stretched over the skull, so eventually the head was replaced by a wax likeness. The auto-icon is now the property of University College London, where it is usually displayed to the public.

Bentham's utilitarianism began with the idea that all people seek happiness. They avoid pain and seek pleasure. As a confirmed atheist, Bentham did not seek for insight into God's will for the actions of people. Instead, he looked at observable principles. As he studied pains and pleasures, he developed a "felicific calculus," otherwise known as the Hedonistic calculus. In his system, there were twelve pains and fourteen pleasures of various strengths. In order to measure the amount of pain or pleasure, Bentham suggested using the categories of intensity, duration, certainty, proximity, productiveness, purity, and extent. Thus, in framing a law, a legislative body could assess how much pain and how much pleasure the law would produce. As Bentham wrote, "it is the greatest happiness of the greatest number that is the measure of right and wrong."[6] While Adam Smith had viewed morality as founded in sentiment, for Bentham morality was founded in reason.

Figure 2.3 Photo of Jeremy Bentham auto-icon. Moral philosopher Jeremy Bentham had his body stuffed and displayed. The head is wax. © Hulton Archive/Stringer/Getty Images.

James Mill

The connecting link behind utilitarian and economic ideas was the Scotsman James Mill (1773–1836). Mill had grown up in a working-class family with the name of Milne. His mother made sure that her son got a first-rate education, and he eventually graduated from the University of Edinburgh after specializing in Greek. His mother also decided that the family should change its Scottish name to a more English sounding "Mill." Although James Mill became ordained in the Church of Scotland (Presbyterians), he soon lost his faith and moved to London where he edited the periodicals *Literary Journal* and *St. James Chronicle*. In London, he met Jeremy Bentham and became a convert to utilitarianism. He also became good friends with David Ricardo. As a prolific writer, editor, and intellectual, Mill was in a good position to influence the development of ideas early in the nineteenth century. He persuaded Bentham to become more democratic and to consider economics as he developed utilitarianism. He learned from Ricardo, and ultimately persuaded Ricardo to become a Member of Parliament. Mill was known as a great conversationalist and quick mind, and as such he became a fixture in the London intellectual scene. Eventually Mill became financially secure as an assistant examiner at the East India Company.

Although Mill's most massive book (over 4,000 pages) was *History of British India* (1818), a book that showed little respect for traditional Indian languages or traditions, his most influential work was *Essay on Government* (1820). In this work, he made a strong case for representative government. He saw this system as the best way to ensure that government works in the interest of the happiness of all the individuals of a society. He wrote that it is human nature to do as little work as possible while still enjoying happiness and that tendency led people to live off the labor of others if they could get away with it. Neither monarchs nor aristocrats would pursue the goal of the happiness of all. On the other hand, if all the people were to take part in government, say by becoming informed and voting on every measure, act, and bill, they would have no time to pursue their true interests or to engage in productive labor. Total democracy, then, is ineffective. The best form of government is to let citizens choose representatives who can represent their constituents' interests. In order to keep the representatives from taking care of their own interests to the exclusion of the interests of their constituents, Mill recommended term limits and frequent elections.

Some Whig aristocrats, like Edmund Burke, argued that one need not have a vote to be adequately represented. This "virtual representation" was the system that was said to protect the interests of the American colonists before the Revolutionary War of Independence. The Americans, famously, disagreed. Mill argued against virtual representation because he believed that only the individuals could decide what is in their best interest. In order to ensure that all the various interests of a diverse society were represented, Mill thought that voting should include as many people as practical and desirable. However, for Mill, not everyone was qualified to vote. He saw intellectuals, people that he called "the middle rank," as those who could best understand how to translate interests into policy. The working and laboring classes should look to their intellectual betters for guidance. Mill was careful to point out that aristocrats are not necessarily part of this middle rank. Education, not inherited privilege, leads to merit.

Mill was thus a democrat, but not a radical one, certainly not radical enough for his son, John Stuart Mill. James Mill recommended the franchise for male heads of household over the age of forty. The older male householders could adequately represent the interests of younger men, and of all women. John Stuart Mill, a radical proponent of women's rights, later castigated his father for his conservatism with respect to female suffrage.

John Stuart Mill

James Mill's first son, John Stuart Mill (1806–73), was the person who most effectively developed explained and pushed forward the philosophy of liberalism. James Mill made of his son a kind of educational experiment. James spent hours each day teaching his son, and at the age of three, John Stuart began studying Greek. He began Latin at eight, studied mathematics, and by ten could easily read Plato. In his memoirs, John Stuart Mill remembered an emotionless and difficult childhood. "I never was a boy," he later wrote. As far as John Stuart was concerned, his mother was emotionally absent, and his father was emotionally incapable. But by the age of twenty, John Stuart Mill had mastered utilitarian philosophy and modern economics, and had quite clear ideas about how he would reform society.

But then the twenty-year-old asked himself, if all his plans were realized, if society were overnight reformed to his specifications, whether this would be "a great joy and happiness" to him. Shockingly, he had to answer "no." Stunned, he decided he had nothing left to live for and fell into a deep depression. Fortunately, he eventually discovered the poetry of the romantics (see Chapter 3), especially Wordsworth, Coleridge, Carlyle, and Goethe, and began to realize that contrary to his upbringing there was more to life than just reason and the intellect. The Enlightenment philosophy, which until then had been his bread and butter, was only one side of the truth. He decided that his life work would be to reconcile the two sides, reason and passion.

Eventually love brought him around and enabled him to continue to think and write. Harriet Taylor was an intellectual who friends thought would enjoy John Stuart Mill's company. The two were introduced at a dinner party, and soon more than an intellectual interest began to develop. Unfortunately, Harriet was married to John Taylor. Nevertheless, John Stuart Mill and Harriet Taylor met more and more frequently, and although her husband was uncomfortable, he agreed that the two could meet when he was not present. For John Stuart, Harriet was the love of his life, the most brilliant mind he thought he had ever known. Harriet was conflicted. At times, she tried to stop their meetings, but the two always found a way to continue. As far as anyone can tell, the affair was never consummated physically until Harriet's husband died in 1849. Two years later, she married John Stuart. The marriage lasted seven more years until she died while the two traveled in France.

According to Mill, every book he wrote after they began their intimate friendship was coauthored, even though he was the one who wrote the words. Harriet Taylor discussed issues and edited manuscripts. In 1833 the two traded essays on marriage in which they raised several ethical questions. Taylor maintained that women were raised to marry and for nothing else. She argued that both men and women would get much more pleasure from physical affection if both were coequal. She distinguished higher and lower pleasures, the higher providing a greater degree of enjoyment. Years after his wife's death Mill advocated equality for women, including the vote.

Throughout his life, Mill wrote prodigiously, and although his ideas evolved, there was an internal consistency to them. He focused on the human individual and individual happiness. An individual was a sensory being. Nothing could be known that did not emerge from the senses. There were no self-evident principles and no rational basis for morals. Everything had to be induced, that is, constructed on the basis of experience. Essentially, he adopted the empirical ideas of an eighteenth-century thinker like David Hume. Utilitarianism, the greatest good for the greatest number, was not a self-evident principle. It was derived from his own experience of preferring pleasure to pain. He was aware that he lived in a society of other human beings, who gave all appearances of being like him. That meant that for them as well happiness was of the ultimate importance.

But true happiness could not be unique to an individual. There were some sources of happiness, like pleasure in viewing beautiful art, that were higher than others. He knew this because he himself found more happiness in higher-order experiences than in mere bodily pleasure, and other educated people reported the same. He realized that not all people saw things that way, but he reasoned that they would if they had the opportunity to do so. A person uneducated to be an intellectual and cultured person could not have the ability to choose to enjoy higher pleasures, but they would if they knew of them. What were these higher-order pleasures? Pleasures "of the intellect, the feelings and imagination, and of the moral sentiments." Pleasures derived from active engagement are greater than those that one derives from passivity.

Lack of education not only prevents one from understanding higher-order pleasures but also inhibits the ability to understand the truth of a situation. Since we cannot possibly experience everything possible, most of what we know we are taught from the testimony of others. Lack of education, then, makes it difficult for a person to understand political issues. But since Mill thought that in general all humans had the same intelligence, the uneducated could improve their comprehension. Therefore, the voting enfranchisement should be extended to anyone who could read, write, and do arithmetic. However, those with more understanding should be able to cast more votes.

We see in the political ideas of the utilitarians a wrestling with a major dilemma of their age: How can we have widespread representation when people have different abilities and capacities? Mill was the most democratic of the lot, but he felt it was unwise to offer political equality to all. Like his father, he believed in a meritocracy. Unlike his father, he was unwilling to leave anyone, especially women, out of the public system.

Perhaps Mill's best-known work was *On Liberty*. In it he made a persuasive argument that individuals should not be prevented from speaking or acting in any way they pleased, unless their speech or action infringed upon the rights of others. The government should have no interest in controlling individual behavior that harms no one but that individual. As a utilitarian, Mill framed the issue in terms of happiness. The problem, Mill recognized, was that almost all speech and action affects others, and some speech or action will reduce those others' happiness. The question, then, was how to discern which influences should be controlled and which should remain up to private actors. For instance, Mill recognized that in the marketplace competition intrinsic to a modern industrial economy, some competitors must lose, and their happiness will be reduced. One could make an argument that competition should be stifled, but for Mill the structure of society should (and could) not be altered by restricting an individual. Mill, of course, was a convinced proponent of the market-place economy and thought that any alternative that involved government intervention would be harmful.

But while Mill thought that government tyranny was bad, the "tyranny of the majority" was worse. The majority may not be correct, but its voice is the loudest, and it is almost impossible to protect oneself from it. One can fight a government, but public opinion overwhelms all defenses. The weak voice of a solitary individual may in fact be expressing the truth, but majority opinion can silence it. Mill believed that even if an individual is wrong, it is important to allow people to develop according to their own inner logic.

> Human nature is not a machine to be built after a model, and set to do exactly the work prescribed for it, but a tree, which requires to grow and develop itself on all sides, according to the tendency of the inward forces which make it a living thing.[7]

For Mill, the welfare of the individual is paramount. It is the job of government to foster the conditions necessary for individual development. For example, youths, not yet educated, are not yet ready for the full freedom of adults, and Mill suggests that they should be required to undergo required private education. Public schools would be amenable to inculcating uniformity of opinion. But requiring and funding private education for all is an appropriate government task. His goal is the creation of a moral community that will support the individual rights of all.

In applying his principles, Mill considered several hard cases. For instance, poison (and a product like alcohol) is harmful but it can be used for good. It should therefore not be prohibited, but the government could require warning labels. Taxing products in order to discourage their use is wrong, but raising taxes is necessary, and governments could choose to tax products they saw as dangerous. Suicide and divorce are undesirable on the social level, but individuals should be permitted to govern their own affairs in both cases.

By 1873, Mill, still stimulated by the ideas of his deceased wife Harriet, realized that liberalism alone was not sufficient to deal with the social problems of his day. He wrote in his *Autobiography*: "The social problem of the future we considered to be, how to unite the greatest individual liberty of action, with a common ownership in the raw material of the globe."[8] He looked forward to a day when the common good would be more compelling than individual profit. And he even realized that modern institutions foster "deep rooted selfishness." He died searching for the next step in individualism—and saw that step in a kind of socialism.

Women's Rights

The issue of rights for women was raised in the tumultuous times surrounding the French Revolution. Middle-class women in general had education, and most were interested readers. They reacted to the Enlightenment discussions surrounding human rights through the prism of their experience as women and the personal experiences of women around them. In both England and France, women had few legal rights that were not derived from their responsibilities to their fathers and husbands. The legal concept of coverture treated a marriage as a union, so the family was one person under the law. The legal representative of that family-person was the husband. The husband, then, made all the legal decisions concerning property, and the wife had no standing as a separate individual under the law. Since voting was restricted to those who owned property, women could not become eligible voters.

Of course, the legal system was only one of the sets of ideas that affected the lives of women. In Christian countries, the relationship of a man and a woman in matrimony was seen as analogous to the relationship of Christ with His church. Oliver Cromwell writing to his son Richard noted, "Though Marriage be no instituted Sacrament, yet where the undefiled bed is, and love, this union aptly resembles that of Christ and His Church." A whole literature around romantic love encouraged young men and women to follow their hearts. In the informal realm that existed beside the legal, women and men could and did have excellent relationships and experiences. A wise husband consulted his wife before making financial decisions. But when love faded and husbands became jaded, the lot of a woman could become onerous, and she had little recourse. Furthermore, childbirth in the case of difficult births could be quite dangerous, and many women died in the process. Such a one was Mary Wollstonecraft.

Mary Wollstonecraft

Mary Wollstonecraft was born in 1759 in London. Her father squandered money, beat his wife, and created a decidedly unpleasant home. By the age of nineteen, Mary left and took a position as a lady's companion. Wollstonecraft then opened a school, which failed. A writer, Wollstonecraft detailed all of these experiences in novels and essays. Finally, she decided to support herself on what she could make as an author and found a supportive publisher. She began to meet and associate with such literary figures as Samuel Johnson, Thomas Paine, and William Godwin. When the revolution broke out in Paris, she moved there to be part of the movement. She became famous for her book A *Vindication of the Rights of Men*, written in support of the revolution in response to the conservative Edmund Burke's critique of the same process. Two years later, she wrote her

Figure 2.4 Portrait of Mary Wollstonecraft. © Print Collector/Hulton Fine Art Collection/Getty Images.

A *Vindication of the Rights of Woman* (1792), her most influential work. She had an affair with an American, Gilbert Imlay, which resulted in the birth of her daughter Fanny. Imlay abandoned the two, though Wollstonecraft beseeched him, and twice attempted suicide because of the difficult financial circumstances she and her daughter were in. Eventually she rejoined her London circle and began a love affair with William Godwin, a relationship that deepened as it grew. They married just before the birth of their daughter Mary, of whom we will read in the next chapter. Unfortunately, Wollstonecraft died of childbed fever ten days after the birth.

In *A Vindication of the Rights of Woman*, Wollstonecraft argued for the education of women. She drew on John Locke's theory of the importance of the senses in causing the development of the mind (see Chapter 1). Women, said Wollstonecraft, are the educators of all the children in the realm. By not educating women, the nation is putting its future, seen in the children, at risk. She argued that women are not deficient in mind—but are rather deficient in the training of their minds. For Wollstonecraft, women are the moral equals of men. In fact, said Wollstonecraft, women could serve as fit companions to men if they were educated. Instead, uneducated aristocratic women become shallow pursuers of beauty. "Taught from their infancy that beauty is woman's sceptre, the mind shapes itself to the body, and, roaming round its gilt cage, only seeks to adorn its prison."[9] Yet Wollstonecraft claimed that she did not want to "invert the order of things" and become legally equal to men. She merely wanted to allow women to become the best of who they were.

Wollstonecraft grew intellectually as she kept company with literary figures and intellectuals, most of who inevitably were men. She realized that she was privileged in a way that few women were, and she also realized that her education and abilities as a writer opened doors that were closed to other women. At the end of *A Vindication of the Rights of Women*, Wollstonecraft outlined an educational plan in which she advocated for education as "a grand national concern." However, she also saw that English schools are "hot-beds of vice and folly" in which "boys become gluttons and slovens" as they are separated from their mothers and homes. At the same time, she noted, that at home children's study is undisciplined, and they themselves get an inflated idea of their own importance. Some compromise between homeschooling and boarding school is necessary. Best would be coeducational education in state-supported schools tempered by sufficient time at home. Both sexes develop bad habits when they are only around members of the same sex. But if they study in a setting that includes both sexes, each will learn from the other and develop new strengths and insights. In fact, in the early grades she advocates for a mixture of social classes, and all would be taught reading, writing, arithmetic, natural history, and simple experiments in natural philosophy (science). After the age of nine, "young people of similar abilities, or fortunes" could be separated so that the coeducational system would continue but emphasizing more academic subjects for the most able and the techniques of trades for the less able. For part of the day, girls could be separated from boys as each learned the trades particular to their sex. Wollstonecraft also thought that good marriages would eventually emerge from such a system as girls and boys got to know one another. Children should sleep at home so that they learned to love the domestic, but should mingle with one another, "for only by the jostlings of equality can we form a just opinion of ourselves."

Wollstonecraft, then, concentrated on the education of women to make them better. She argued that if middle- and upper-class women usually seem silly and vacuous, then that is because they have been educated to be so. Wollstonecraft believed that women indeed have a nature that is different from men in many important respects, but women are necessary to the continuation and improvement of the human species. Their traits and nature are also necessary and worth educating and investing in. In fact, if women were allowed, they were capable of taking on many of the virtues attributed at this time only to men. If women were brought up with men, and if each sex recognized the powers of the other and supported the other in the accomplishments of their goals, society and the nation would be all the better for it. But if women continued to be enslaved, "their duties vanish, for rights and duties are inseparable."

Olympe de Gouges

Meanwhile, across the Channel, Olympe de Gouges emphasized marriage rights. She was born in 1748 as Marie Gouze in a lower-middle-class family in Southwestern France. Forced into a marriage at the age of sixteen, at twenty-one her husband died, leaving her with a child. She later wrote of the repugnance she felt for her husband. For her, marriage was "the tomb of trust and love." She moved to Paris where she changed her identity, became a playwright, and found a wealthy lover who helped her establish a theater company. She often used her plays as outlets for social views that advocated human rights, and she became notorious for her play "The Slavery of the Blacks." After the revolution of 1789, she joined the Society of the Friends of Truth, an organization meant to discuss politics. In general, the Society followed the ideas of Jean-Jacques Rousseau (see Chapter 1) and, instead of direct democracy, argued for a popularly elected dictatorship that could be dismissed by vote of citizens.

But the Society also included many members who advocated rights for women. When the documents of the new government did not include equality for women, de Gouge wrote the *Déclaration des droits de la femme et de la citoyenne* (*Declaration of the Rights of Woman and the Female Citizen*), using the exact form of the "Declaration of the Rights of Man and the Citizen" (see Chapter 1). For instance, Article I of the Rights of Man begins, "Men are born and remain free and equal in rights. Social distinctions may be based only on common utility." De Gouges writes, "Woman is born free and remains equal to man in rights. Social distinctions may only be based on common utility."[10] As she followed each point, she changed "men" to "men and women." She also added material of direct relevance to women, such as ensuring that women can identify the father of their child. (Incidentally, she believed that she herself was illegitimate.) One of her more famous lines was, "Women have the right to mount the scaffold; they must also have the right to mount the speaker's rostrum."

De Gouges also developed a "Form for a Social Contract Between Man and Woman" (echoing Rousseau's *Social Contract*) in which she advocated a civil union, or agreement, in place of marriages affirmed by the church and state. In her contract, the man and the women are equal partners in all ways, and they affirm themselves as such in the contract. Children have a right to the names of both the husband and wife. They hold property in common and spend and save by agreement.

For de Gouges, the problems for women began with their legislated relationship to men in marriage. Free women from the constraints of an unequal marriage, affirm that women have the same rights that men do, and the lot of women would be improved. De Gouges saw differences between men and women, but none that would affect their ability to act as citizens.

The impact of the French Revolution on intellectuals' expectations for women's rights can be seen in two petitions, the first to the French king and the second to the National Assembly. An anonymous petition presented to the French king by women of the Third Estate in January 1789, before the meeting of the Estates General and the resulting revolution, emphasized the desire of women to become better educated and protected, but not to overturn the system of male authority. The petitioners did not ask for representation in the Estates General, but rather trusted the king to represent their interests. They noted that if they have no beauty, "they get married, without a dowry . . . and give birth to children they are incapable of raising." But if they have beauty, "they become the prey of the first seducer . . . and die victims of dissolute ways."[11]

They noted that poverty forces women into prostitution, or, if they are lucky, the convent. So, their request was that the king keep men from working in the trades that belonged to women (seamstress, embroiderer, millinery shopkeeper, etc.), and women would in turn promise "never to handle the compass or the square." That is, these women wanted the right and ability to work so that they would be respected by men and not forced by circumstance into prostitution. They also asked for free schools where they could learn language, religion, and ethics. They also wanted the opportunity to provide a similar education to their children.

This anonymous petition was unchallenging and circumspect. It probably represented the views of many women. But it is worth comparing it to a petition issued later in the year, after the establishment of the National Assembly and after the march of the women on Versailles. This petition to the National Assembly was accusatory in tone. The National Assembly had decreed rights for all individuals but had omitted women! The first article of this petition demanded abolition of all privileges of the male sex. In fact, in article three, it noted that "the masculine gender will no longer be regarded, even grammatically, as the more noble gender, given that all genders, all sexes, and all beings are equally noble."[12]

This petition was angry. It demanded radical equality, even in the church. All offices should be open to women. Unfortunately, this was not to be. Olympe de Gouges was sent to the guillotine, probably because she belonged to a Girondist organization when the Jacobins were in power, but also, one suspects, her crime was being an outspoken woman who made extreme demands. The official charge was that she was a royalist, and in fact she advocated a constitutional monarchy. When the revolution had turned into the dictatorship and Empire of Napoleon, women still had made no political gains.

Abolition of Slavery

Slavery has been a fixture of civilizations for thousands of years. Thus, it does not seem strange that European countries should have allowed it as they expanded throughout the world. What perhaps is strange is that European countries had eliminated all legal slavery by the end of the nineteenth century. What was so special about the nineteenth century? In this section, we will be more concerned with the arguments against slavery than with the political circumstances that led to the demise of that dehumanizing institution. Yet the arguments arose in particular circumstances, and both arguments and circumstances ultimately caused the victory of the abolitionist forces. In a nutshell, the new convincing arguments used individualist arguments as they had been developed in the new economics of free enterprise.

Slavery in England and France had been abolished in principle long before the nineteenth century. For a time, however, it appeared that slavery might be reestablished in the mother countries as slave-owners returned home accompanied by enslaved servants, until court cases in England established that slaves were free as soon as they set foot in England. Thus, the arguments concerning abolition mostly centered on slavery in the colonies.

The arguments for abolition that were developed in the eighteenth century centered on religious objections to slavery as well as the development of theories of human rights. In Great Britain especially, the dissenting religious denominations took a strong stand in favor of the equality of all humans in the sight of God. Quakers, in particular, led the fight for abolition. Unfortunately, God's view of equality did not convince slavery-supporting Europeans that individuals were not different and that some were equipped only to do hard, manual work. In France, the principles of human rights accompanied by the Enlightenment led many to argue against slavery.

The difference between the eighteenth-century arguments for individual rights and the nineteenth-century arguments was that the nineteenth-century arguments increasingly made use of the new individualistic economics initiated by Adam Smith. It was one thing to argue a moral principle; but another to argue self-interest. And the economic liberalism of the nineteenth century was founded on individual actors, all pursuing their self-interest.

Abolition movements in Great Britain and France were instituted in the late 1780s. In Great Britain, the Committee for the Abolition of the Slave Trade led the struggle; in France, the movement was led by the Society of the Friends of the Blacks. Ultimately, it was Great Britain that led the successful end of both the slave trade and slavery. Of course, as the more advanced industrial economy, their earlier success was not surprising. William Wilberforce, a Member of Parliament, made the legislative arguments that ended slavery in Great Britain and her empire. The first to go was the slave trade, in 1807. In 1838 slavery throughout the empire was ended. The path to abolition in France was more circuitous. Initially abolished in 1794, slavery was reinstated by Napoleon in 1802 and was not successfully abolished until 1848 and the Second Republic.

In Britain, Thomas Clarkson, an indefatigable researcher and speaker, developed the main arguments for abolition. Clarkson interviewed people involved in or affected by the slave trade, and he collected specimens of everything from instruments of torture to documents to specimens of goods that could be traded with Africa if only there weren't a slave trade. Thus, his arguments took several forms. First was the cruelty of slavery. It violated every humane instinct and took a physical and psychological toll not only on the slaves but also on those who transported and controlled them.

A second argument was that Africa had much more to offer than slaves, but the slave trade interfered with normal commercial relations. Clarkson collected palm nuts, cotton, tobacco, oils, waxes, and many other products. He used them to demonstrate that normal trade would be much more lucrative for the country as a whole than was slavery. He argued that slavery was expensive because it required military intervention to put down slave revolts. He argued that slave ships would be more valuable transporting more lucrative cargo.

But the more telling arguments were those based on the new economics. Great Britain was becoming an industrial nation, and efficiency was more important than ever. Free labor could be given incentives for performance. Slaves would always resentfully drag their feet. As the British had less and less use for slavery, it was not hard to convince them that slavery was not an economic use of human power. Yes, it was true that American cotton was needed for British textile mills, but would not the production of cotton actually become more efficient if free workers produced it? After all, Adam Smith had argued that free individuals acting in their self-interest promoted the general good. He had not been optimistic about the general good produced by slaves.

It is interesting that human rights were initially most successfully advanced in societies that embraced individualism and free enterprise. When individual actors are seen as the shapers of social realities, it is hard to maintain that these actors should be content to stay in their place in a preordained hierarchy. In the world of Adam Smith and David Ricardo, everyone competed, and in competing invented, and in inventing created a society that progressed by making human life better for all. Of course, when slaves are free, that freedom does not necessarily give them what they need to compete successfully with those who are more privileged. But that issue had to be addressed in other intellectual contexts, as we shall see in succeeding chapters.

Atomic-Molecular Theory

The idea that human beings are mirrors of the natural world, the microcosm of the human structurally resembling the macrocosm of the universe, is an ancient idea. The premise of Plato's *Republic* is constructed on this idea. So, when the ancient idea that the universe was nothing but atoms, especially as expressed in Lucretius's *Of New Things* (*De rerum naturae*), was reintroduced into Western culture, and when this atomism became one of the primary ways of understanding the mechanical world in the new science of the seventeenth century, it was natural that thinkers would begin to see a correspondence between human beings and atoms. In his 1610 poem "The First Anniversary," bemoaning the death of a young lady, John Donne presented the world as worsening age by age since the Fall from the Garden of Eden. Part of that decline in his own age was caused by atomic theory:

> And new philosophy calls all in doubt . . .
> And freely men confess that this world's spent,
> When in the planets and the firmament
> They seek so many new; they see that this
> Is crumbled out again to his atomies.
> 'Tis all in pieces, all coherence gone,
> All just supply, and all relation;
> Prince, subject, father, son, are things forgot,
> For every man alone thinks he hath got
> To be a phoenix, and that then can be
> None of that kind, of which he is, but he.[13]

For Donne, atomic theory leads to radical individualism, and this radical individualism leads to social dissolution and loss of coherence. That is, the new science implied that human individuals were social atoms in which all atoms were essentially the same. There was no longer any essential difference between the prince and the subject. If Donne had been alive during the French Revolution, he might have seen those events of proof of his thesis. Certainly, as we will see in the next chapter, Edmund Burke thought so. But for social radicals, the bright new age of republics and human equality was a dawning day.

However, scientists in the eighteenth century found little use for atomic (corpuscular) theory. Chemical theory, for example, relied on observable characteristics, not on unobservable little corpuscles. Much of the exciting eighteenth-century chemical work was done on gases, and chemists learned to measure things like weight, volume, pressure, and temperature and to find mathematical relationships among such quantities. Scientists researching electricity found fluid analogies (electricity is like a flowing current) much more useful than atomic theories. Although Isaac Newton had been a corpuscularian, and suggested that perhaps elementary corpuscles (atoms) that were all the same came together to create more complex bodies, he was unable to connect these ideas mathematically to observed phenomena. He was an alchemist, but he found no way to incorporate corpuscular theory into alchemy.

By the end of the eighteenth century, chemists, led by the Frenchman Antoine Lavoisier, had begun to define chemical elements in a way that is recognizable to us. For Lavoisier, an element was a chemical that could not be broken down into simpler parts. Lavoisier was part of the French Enlightenment that had tried to reform knowledge by reclassifying and clearly defining it. No longer were gases different aspects of "air." Now different gases were different elements. Interestingly enough, not even chemists were immune from the French Revolution. Lavoisier had invested in a firm that collected taxes for a profit and was guillotined during the terror for making a profit from the poor.

In the first decade of the nineteenth century, the meteorologist-cum-chemist John Dalton used Lavoisier's idea that there were several fundamental elements to create a new atomic theory. Dalton was born in Cumberland in 1766 to a Quaker family. He became a teacher, eventually moving to Manchester as a tutor at the New College. He joined the Manchester Literary and Philosophical Society in order to have access to a library. He began to keep a daily log of the weather, including wind velocity and barometric pressure. Fascinated by air pressure, he began to carry a barometer up mountains and logged the effects of altitude on pressure.

Still interested in air pressure, Dalton began to do research on gases, logging the differences in pressure and temperature of different sorts of gases, including steam. He studied the transformation of liquids into gases and back again. As he puzzled about all these phenomena, he tried to envision how they were taking place. Eventually he could see no alternative but to think of gases and air as made up of elementary particles, or atoms. He thought that every element had a different sort of atom, with a different weight, but that all atoms of the same element had exactly the same weight.

Dalton assumed that two different atoms combined in the simplest possible ratio: for instance, in the case of water, one hydrogen atom for one oxygen atom. By comparing the weights of the amounts of oxygen and hydrogen that went into water, with no oxygen or hydrogen left over, he could see that oxygen is seven times as heavy as hydrogen. From our perspective, this is wrong, of course (we think there are two hydrogen atoms for each oxygen atom), but the idea was basically sound. Using his atomic theory with a few basic assumptions, Dalton was able to derive several properties of atoms and molecules.

Dalton's ability to use atomic theory to explain chemical phenomena was based on his idea that all atoms are not alike. Scientists like to find simple explanations and principles in their search to explain the physical world. Modern science is based on the assumptions that there are laws of nature and simple, underlying structures that can be related to one another by the use of mathematics. But sometimes the basic structure of the world is a bit more complex than they hoped for.

Scientists like the Frenchman Joseph Louis Gay-Lussac remained unconvinced of the physical existence of atoms. It might be a useful hypothesis, but that did not mean that atoms really existed. In fact, Gay-Lussac and those who agreed with him thought the atomic theory was misleading. Suppose, for example, that one experiment yields a ratio of 1.98 to 1. Another experiment yields a ratio of 2.2 to 1. This variation could be proof that nature herself varies. On the other hand, the two rations are so close to 2:1 that the variation could be simply due to inevitable experimental error. Since one needed theory to interpret the experiment, the experiment could not be used to prove the theory.

As chemists did finer and finer experiments, it seemed clear to many that atoms always combined in ratios of simple whole numbers. For instance, if you combined nitrogen and oxygen, or copper and oxygen, or any other combinations of atoms, they

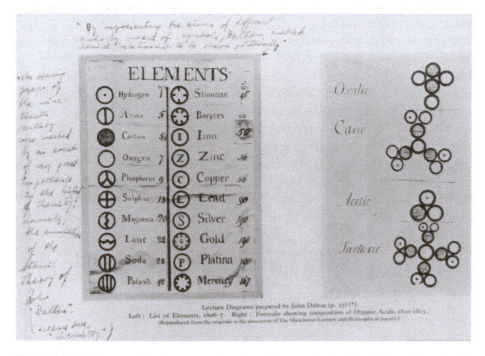

Figure 2.5 Lecture notes by the atomic theorist and meteorologist John Dalton. These display his symbols of the known elements and his ideas about how atoms may form molecules. © Hulton Archive/Stringer/Getty Images.

always joined in a 2:1, 3:1, 3:2, or other simple ratio. Such rations were never complex, such as 40.578: 31.662. It was easy to imagine that the simple ratios occurred because there were individual atoms combining together. If there had not been atoms, then any ratio might have worked, as different volumes of a fluid or gas joined together to produce a chemically distinct product, much like sugar or salt dissolving in water. In the case of a mixture like sugar and water, in which no new molecule is produced, any amount of sugar could be dissolved in any amount of water, up to the maximum reached at saturation.

Eventually many of the problems were worked out by two additional ideas: (1) there are equal numbers of molecules in equal volumes of gas and (2) some elements (like hydrogen) do not exist in simple form, but rather in combinations, in molecular form. When hydrogen is isolated without other elements, it joins to form two hydrogen atoms in one molecule of hydrogen. Some other elements behave the same way. With these additional assumptions, scientists could gradually work to determine atomic weights and the structure of chemical molecules. But still many scientists did not accept the atomic hypothesis. The controversy about the reality of atoms continued into the twentieth century. Why?

The existence of atoms could not be demonstrated by direct observation. Even with the strongest microscope, no one could see an atom or a molecule. Clearly, the theory of atoms was useful in solving certain kinds of chemical problems, but utility did not mean truth. The theory that the earth was still at the center of the universe was useful in solving navigation problems, but that utility did not mean that the earth actually was immovable. In short, the argument for the existence of atoms was circumstantial. There was no eyewitness testimony.

When they measured, chemists like Dalton focused on the weights of the atoms. Others, like the French chemist Gay-Lussac, focused on the volumes of the gases. Often neither side was totally clear about what was being measured. But what one looks at can make a difference. The great nineteenth-century Scottish physicist James Clerk Maxwell (of whom we will hear more in the next two chapters) wrote, "two modes of thinking . . . correspond to the two methods of regarding quantity—the arithmetical and the geometrical. To the atomist the true method of estimating the quantity of matter in a body is to count the atoms in it. The void spaces between the atoms count for nothing. To those who identify matter with extension, the volume of space occupied by a body is the only measure of the quantity of matter in it." The issue is whether we should look at the whole or at the parts when we attempt to understand nature. At the extreme, the question is whether discernable parts even exist or whether "all are but parts of one stupendous whole." But for the atomist, there is no whole except for the random arrangements of the truly existing atoms. An individualist would say the same of society.

Conclusion: The Engineer as Hero

The Scottish author and reformer Samuel Smiles (1812–1904) embodied the thoughtful individualism discussed in this chapter. As a reformer he supported universal suffrage, including women, free trade, and pay for members of parliament, among many issues.

Smiles watched his widowed mother work hard in order to support Smiles's studies and provide for his nine younger brothers and sisters. Eventually he gave up working for parliamentary reform in order to concentrate on what he saw as the one way that everyone could improve life: self-help. He preached a gospel of personal character and hard work to raise oneself in the world. For Smiles, no parliamentary reform could accomplish as much for the poor as their own dedication to removing themselves from the impoverished ranks. The answer, then, lay not in institutional reform but in individual achievement. The impact of this view on the poor, of course, was disastrous. Malthus saw the issues and recommended support for the unemployed and indigent. Smiles's point of view led to the socialist analyses that we will see in later chapters.

Smiles became a hagiographer of engineers. For Smiles, the successful engineers pulled society up by their individual efforts. They were indeed modern saints. He began his biographies with the inventors of the railway system, George and Robert Stephenson. Smiles showed how the Stephenson father and son had transformed Europe by allowing widespread trade and travel. He also showed their ingenuity in overcoming technical problem after technical problem to make rail travel so safe that you were more likely to die of being hit by lightning than of being in a railway accident.

Smiles went on to record the lives and accomplishments of several engineers, ending with the steam engine developers James Watt and Matthew Boulton. In these studies, Smiles did not just preach individualism. He illustrated it. Critics of the individualistic creed would point out the importance of institutions and social context for any inventions. But Smiles, writing in the tradition of Smith, Mill, and the others discussed in this chapter, was content to make his point by describing exemplary lives. For the thinkers discussed in this chapter, leaders of government were less important than individuals with dreams. For Smiles, the true hero was not the warrior or the statesman but the inventor and the technician. No institution could force their genius. For Smiles, and for many others, society was indeed created by the individual efforts of heroic people. In the next chapter, we will see a refutation of this position.

CHAPTER 3
TRANSCENDENCE: FROM COMMUNITY TO GOD
COLLECTIVE WISDOM AND REVOLUTIONARY TRANSFORMATION

Getting and spending, we lay waste our powers.

—William Wordsworth[1]

Figure 3.1 Portrait of Mary Shelley. © Hulton Archive/Stringer/Getty Images.

Victor Frankenstein Creates a Monster

On a literally cold and stormy night in 1816, caught in seemingly unceasing wet, dank, and chilly weather, a teenage Mary Godwin, later to become Mary Shelley (1797–1851), had a vision of a monster. Having run off with the young poet Percy Bysshe Shelley, Godwin found herself in Italy with a small group that included her lover Shelley and George Gordon Byron, Lord Byron. Byron proposed passing the forced indoor hours with a ghost story contest. The eighteen-year-old Godwin desperately tried to think of a story. Finally, after a late-night firelit discussion of the idea of electricity (galvanism) as the principle of life, a tossing-and-turning Mary had her vision:

> I saw the pale student of unhallowed arts kneeling beside the thing he had put together, I saw the hideous phantasm of a man stretched out, and then, on the working of some powerful engine, show signs of life, and stir with an uneasy, half vital motion. Frightful it must be; for supremely frightful would be the effect of any human endeavor to mock the stupendous mechanism of the Creator of the world.[2]

The ultimate result was *Frankenstein; or The Modern Prometheus* (1818). Mary Godwin herself had been haunted by the emergence of new life. She herself had been the unwitting cause of her mother, Mary Wollstonecraft's, death shortly after Wollstonecraft gave birth to her. She had guiltily faced Shelley's abandonment of his wife Harriet and their two children. She had been jealous of Percy's joy at the birth of his second son with Harriet. And Mary Godwin also lost a child, who was born prematurely.

So, Mary created a seemingly heroic individual protagonist, Victor Frankenstein, who successfully created life. But Frankenstein was not a hero. He had sacrificed everything to his ambition and had succeeded only in creating what he thought was a monster. Abandoned by its creator, the monster destroyed everything Victor Frankenstein valued his family, his best friend, his lifelong-love, and ultimately his community. *Frankenstein*, far from celebrating the power of the individual, exposed the shallowness of individual action in the service of self. *Frankenstein* is a cautionary tale that reveals what is meaningful beyond the individual and individual desire.

Chapter Map

This chapter presents the reply to the individualism described in the previous chapter. That is, this chapter outlines the dimensions of a worldview that emphasizes the significance of entities that are larger than human individuals.

Political and social conservatism were a set of approaches that lifted up community against the onslaught of individualism. To conservatives, human society was like an organism. Sudden change was almost never good for it.

The chapter continues with the search for the Absolute as a way of healing the rifts found in human thought. The Absolute mended the division between the phenomenal and the noumenal deduced by Kant (Chapter 1). The Absolute was then the totality of all, a truly universal being containing all.

Both German and British romanticism were movements that emphasized passionate emotion and spiritual experiences. Many romantics saw art as a nonrational route to a glimpse of the Absolute. German Idealism was a philosophical movement related to romanticism. It culminated with the philosophy of Hegel, an attempt to reconcile intellectual conflicts through an organic growth model of thought, society, and religion.

In both biology and physics, some scientists embraced the idea that nature and mind are one and that therefore we can study nature by studying ourselves. Throughout the nineteenth century, especially in physics, the idea that nature is a connected whole, rather than a set of individual atoms, proved extraordinarily fruitful. Theories of light, electricity, and magnetism all benefited by treating the phenomena as connected throughout space. Physics began to construct a non-Newtonian picture of the world. The chapter concludes by considering the vast technological changes that had occurred in the first half of the nineteenth century.

The opponents of individualism did not deny that individuals existed. In general, their point was that individuals can only be understood in a larger context. Just as a finger bone cannot be understood unless one knows that it once was attached to a human being, so an individual cannot be understood unless one recognizes that the individual participates in something greater.

Political Conservatism

Mary Shelley was not alone in her cautionary feeling about the glorification of the individual. Many others defended the status quo or created compelling visions of other transcendental contexts. It is to their arguments that we now turn.

In general, nineteenth-century conservatives responded negatively to the two revolutions discussed in Chapter 1: the Industrial Revolution and the French Revolution. They tended to criticize the Industrial Revolution because they felt it debased human beings by emphasizing wealth acquisition at the cost of exploiting workers and creating urban hellholes. They tended to disdain the French Revolution because in emphasizing the rights of individuals and promoting democracy it simultaneously rejected the essential human condition of participating in and being supported by a community—while also rejecting the evolutionary development of a strong community-based state. For conservatives, the rights of the community, which was made up of individuals of differing abilities and responsibilities, overrode the rights of separate individuals. For conservatives, individualism and democracy were likely to lead to fragmentation and divisive struggle ultimately leading to demagoguery and dictatorship.

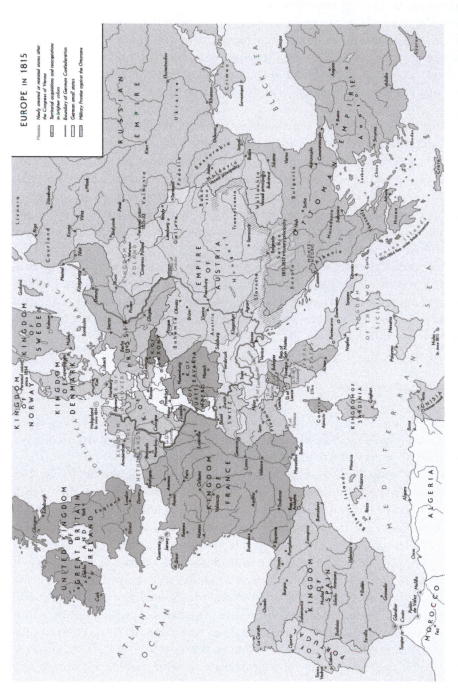

Map 1 Political map of Europe, 1815. Note the fragmentation of countries in Central Europe. Large states exist in the West. The Austrian, Russian, and Ottoman Empires are still Feudal, agrarian empires destined to disappear in the twentieth century.

Edmund Burke

The grandfather of nineteenth-century English conservatism was the unlikely Irish-born Member of Parliament (MP) Edmund Burke (1729–97). Burke moved from Dublin to London to study law, but eventually decided to pursue a living as a writer in an age that needed fuel to feed the growing hunger for good reading material. He began to associate with powerful politicians, two of whom he served as secretary, and he successfully entered the House of Commons in 1765. As an MP, Burke supported the American colonies in their complaints against the crown, as well as coming down on the side of free trade with Ireland and removing impediments to Catholic participation in official institutions.

At first, Burke watched with bemusement at "The French struggle for Liberty . . . not knowing whether to blame or applaud."[3] Eventually, he saw in the revolution a situation in which "the Elements which compose Human Society seem all to be dissolved, and a world of Monsters to be produced in place of it."[4] When finally he wrote *Reflections on the Revolution in France* (1790), he rejected the idea that any king, including the king of England, obtains his right to rule from the people. Kings had a right of inheritance stemming from long-established traditions. He compared the French Revolution with the English Civil War and the Glorious Revolution of 1688 in order to show that in neither English case did anyone claim that the people had a right to determine the monarch. Rather, Burke argued, a right of succession was reaffirmed in the face of extraordinary circumstances.

For Burke, change was necessary to the health of any society, but change should happen slowly, carefully, and for good reason. A society was an organism, and each society was a different kind of being. These complex entities developed according to their own inner logics, and what was right for one could not be said to apply to the others. There were no individual rights, except those that rose out of slow evolutionary changes over time.

Human reason was insufficient to comprehend the whole of which each individual mind was but a part. The French Revolution was founded on abstract principles, and thus was insufficient to deal with the practicalities of governing. For instance, the French intellectuals conflated liberty and equality, and these two concepts may, in fact, be opposed to one another. If the rich have liberty, they are unlikely to use their wealth to promote equality. Government should be of the heart rather than the head, and religion, especially Christian religion, was extremely important in guiding decisions of state.

Burke's influence only grew with time, and even today conservatives, especially social conservatives of a theoretical bent, often start with his ideas. In the nineteenth century, most conservative thought referred back to his writings. A large part of the appeal of Burke was his style. He turned phrases as easily as others turn pages. For instance, in his response to the French Revolution, he noted, "The effect of liberty to individuals is that they may do what they please: we ought to see what it will please them to do, before we risk congratulations."[5]

Thomas Carlyle

The Scotsman Thomas Carlyle (1795–1881) was the spokesperson of the next generation of conservatives. Like Burke, he wrote with flair. Raised a Calvinist, he died a Deist. Although he began his career as a mathematics teacher, he soon turned to writing. He was greatly influenced by German Idealism, and eventually developed a theory of history based on heroes, on great men. For Carlyle, a great man resembled Nietzsche's "Overman." The great man intuits the needs of the time and has a creative energy that can shape the creation of history. In a sense, the great man rises above all. Much like Rousseau's legislators who can intuit the general will, the great man embodies the Divine.

> Heroes are intrinsically of the same material; that given a great soul, open to the Divine Significance of Life, then there is given a man fit to speak of this, to sing of this, to fight and work for this, in a great, victorious, enduring manner; there is given a Hero—the outward shape of whom will depend on the time and the environment he finds himself in.[6]

Figure 3.2 Portrait of Thomas Carlyle. © Wikimedia Commons (public domain).

Carlyle's great men are not individuals but embodiments of God and community. Examples that Carlyle gives us span a great range: Mohammed, Napoleon, Shakespeare, Rousseau, and Martin Luther, to name but a few. Even the Norse god Odin makes his list.

Although Carlyle had been raised a Calvinist, he had a crisis of faith when he was at college in Edinburgh. His first successful book, *Sartor Resartus* (*The Tailor Retailored*, 1834), recounts the process of losing faith and eventually adopting a new, better one. Taufelsdröckh, a philosopher of clothes, refuses to accept the amount of pain and pettiness he sees in the world. He adopts a condition that the book describes as "The Everlasting No" in which he rejects everything and has nothing to replace it. From this condition, he enters into a kind of Buddhist-like "Centre of Indifference," from which he eventually emerges with an "Everlasting Yea."

The Yea that Carlyle adopted accepted the indifference of God to the pain of human beings, an indifference that can be seen every day in the world. Carlyle could not believe that God would create non-Christians and allow them to live and die, if they were destined to hell. But Carlyle could not give up the conviction that God was imminent in the world. He could not deny God, but he seemed to see this world as just a preparation for the next and God, then, as a mystery whose intentions we cannot really see.

Since Carlyle had to accept the cruelty of the world, he was able to see ideal leaders as having courage rather than love and as being able to accept cruelty as part of the world's condition. In fact, the heroic leader is someone that can be revered, much as God might have been revered. He advocates a new religion in which humanity is "the only divinity we can know." To Carlyle, Christ was not divine, but rather the best man that ever lived. In this, Christ is a model that we ourselves might emulate, at least in our best hours.

Joseph de Maistre and Louis de Bonald

On the continent, conservatism took a more reactionary line than in Great Britain. The French Revolution, and subsequent rise of Napoleon, who spent the first decade of the nineteenth century trying to conquer all of Europe, took its toll on many, but especially on the old aristocracy, who were displaced by the new democratic ideals. The leaders of the French conservative movement, like Joseph de Maistre and Louis de Bonald (both Counts), were supporters of the monarchy, most of whom fled France when it was clear that the revolution would be at least temporarily successful. Their arguments echoed the earlier defenders of the divine right of kings, but they brought new ideas to the table.

Maistre argued that the only legitimate authority came from God. Moses wrote the first constitution, and any attempts to change it are immoral. Over time, its true meaning unravels slowly. The only legitimate authorities in interpreting the current understanding of this ancient constitution are the monarch and the pope, the ultimate authorities. Maistre was an ardent Catholic. His family title, Count, had been bestowed by Piedmont-Sardinia, so when Maistre became an exile, he eventually moved to Piedmont-Sardinia for whom he served as ambassador to Russia.

For Maistre, the grievous French sin of listening to the *philosophes*, the thinkers of the Enlightenment, had to be punished. The *philosophes* were largely anti-Catholic, and they were also rationalists. They tried to use reason to improve society, and for Maistre their regard for reason over the word of God was offensive. Why then was there a French Revolution? Because Providence had decided to punish the monarch and aristocrats who had decided to take the *philosophes* seriously instead of promoting the general welfare under their rule and guidance. For Maistre, order requires a decisive authority to administer it. When that authority fails, God requires the blood of innocents to expiate the sins of the leaders and return the society to God. He supported capital punishment as the only way of maintaining order.

Count Louis de Bonald brought a different perspective on monarchical conservatism. Bonald had been a deputy to the Estates General, but he strongly objected to the ultimate decision to secularize the priesthood. During the Napoleonic years, he spent his exile in Heidelberg, and when he returned to France, he was active in the government of the restored monarchy.

Bonald argued that language had divine origins. The first language was able to express the words of God. But as language changed over time, it moved farther away from the expression of truth. He thought that words precede thought, so we speak before we think and then find out what we think as we listen to ourselves speak. The farther our language gets from the first language, the less able it is to express, or generate, true thought. This analysis negated the rationalist Enlightenment project, because thoughts that were developed with an impure language could not be accurate renditions of God's will.

For Bonald, all authority comes from the power of God, and this power is actualized in the works of government ministers whose works should improve the lives of the subjects of the kingdom. The same relationship exists in the family, where instead of God to minister to subject, the direction is father to mother to children. Once this idea is accepted, authoritarian power, stemming from God, comes naturally. What has the revolution produced? "Liberty ended by covering France with prisons, equality by multiplying titles and decorations, and fraternity by dividing us. Death alone prevailed."[7]

Prince Klemens von Metternich

Conservatism in German-speaking Austria and Prussia took two forms. One was the real-politik of Austrian chancellor Prince Klemens von Metternich. The second was the theoretical nationalism of young Germans like Johann Gottlieb Fichte and Johann Gottfried von Herder. Nationalism will be discussed in Chapter 7.

Metternich was the main designer of the peace agreed to in the Congress of Vienna after the fall of Napoleon. Metternich succeeded in engineering a balance of power among the five great powers of Europe: Austria, the United Kingdom of Great Britain and Ireland, Prussia, Russia, and France. Although both Russia and Prussia had aspirations to conquest, Metternich joined with France and Great Britain to resist such expansion. In general, the success of this treaty is credited for avoiding an all-European conflict until 1914 and the First World War.

Metternich argued that only two elements kept countries together: morality (both religious and social) and local needs. When societies ignore either one in an attempt to create new, reformed moralities or in an attempt to search for universal, transnational institutions, those societies are doomed to decay and dissolution. For Metternich, then, it was the duty of the monarchs to continually maintain justice and the rights of their subjects. It was up to wise and decisive rulers to keep their finances in order and to act diplomatically and militarily to put down the attacks on social order by misguided "reformers."

All of these conservative arguments seem strange to a twenty-first-century reader for whom "conservatism" connotes very different ideas. Nineteenth-century liberalism defended the status quo, and at that time the status quo was monarchical rule.

Search for the Absolute

In Chapter 1, we discussed the challenge to Newtonian science and the solution of Immanuel Kant. The challenge had pointed out that sensory perception had no necessary connection to a world external to the human mind. The external world outside of the mind seemed to depend on the existence of space, time, and causality, among other things, yet these categories could not be derived from sensory information. Kant's solution was to say that the categories were attributes of the human mind. Humans could only understand sensory data by organizing it into, for example, causal relationships. Internally, subjectively, humans experienced freedom and made choices. But the objective "external world," as experienced by a human, was subject to laws. The external world, as it might exist outside of a human consciousness, was unknowable. The "thing-in-itself" was a closed book.

The followers of Kant saw his approach as a tremendous advance that still left unanswered questions. For instance, how could the subjective world be at all affected by the unknowable external world? There seemed to be no connection, yet a human subject experienced the constraints of external events. The laws of nature bound human beings. For instance, no amount of wishing or imagining could allow a person to fall safely upward once the human had fallen off a cliff. But how could a subjective realm of free choice be constrained by a world of ironclad laws? How could one reconcile the human experience of an internal (mental) and an external (physical) world?

At the end of the eighteenth and beginnings of the nineteenth centuries, a number of German and then British thinkers began to conceive of subjective and objective, inner and external, as different aspects of a grand totality. Known as The Absolute, this grand totality encompassed mind and matter—as well as, perhaps, something more that is beyond the power of human beings to conceive. The Absolute was the grand totality, the universal being. Some were comfortable with conflating the Absolute with God, but for many of the thinkers and artists discussed in the following text, "God" was too anthropomorphic a term. "The Absolute" had no theological baggage.

The concept of the Absolute certainly solved the problem of two disjunctive yet interconnected worlds, but it left a gaping hole. How can one know and understand the Absolute? How can human beings reconcile their experience of the inner and outer worlds? How can we reconcile the simultaneous existence of determinism and freedom?

Romanticism

There were essentially four solutions: First, begin with the freedom found in the subjective and show that the apparent external world is actually a form of mind. This is the route taken by German Idealism. Second, begin with a law-based scientific approach and show that the subjective world is a product of the physical external world. This approach did not really blossom until the late twentieth century. Third, ignore the problem, do science, and create technology without worrying about basic philosophical problems. This was the approach of most European intellectuals. Fourth, recognize that the Absolute can never be comprehended rationally and that it can best be approached aesthetically, through art. This was the approach of the romantics.

German Romanticism: Art and the Absolute

The University of Jena in Thuringia was a swirl of ideas between 1798 and 1804. Young thinkers and artists like Friedrich Schlegel, Novalis (the pen name of George Philipp Friedrich von Hardenberg), and Friedrich Schelling, excited by the possibilities implied in the French Revolution and the Napoleonic era, worked to discover new approaches to old problems. Many of their answers became known as German romanticism.

Friedrich Wilhelm Joseph von Schelling (1775–1854) became one of the leaders of the Jena Romantics. Schelling grappled with the dualism of Kant (the knowable mind vs. the unknowable world beyond mind). Schelling suggested that the subjective world and the objective world were different aspects of the same thing. Nature was a productive subjective being that created the split between subjectivity and objectivity in order to know itself. The objective world that is represented in mind must have a structure similar to the world outside of mind. And whatever is outside of mind must also have a subjective nature.

The world before the split into subject and object was the Absolute. The processes by which the Absolute produced this split and produced the world of knowable nature are unconscious, at least to us. Human thought itself is produced by forces that are unknown to it. So how can we hope to reach an understanding of these unconscious processes of the Absolute? For Schelling, as for other thinkers in Jena at the time, art is a way to understand that which is beyond reason. Neither the production nor the appreciation of art can be accomplished by reason, although reason can reflect on the process.

In his "Introduction to Transcendental Philosophy," Friedrich Schlegel wrote in 1800, "If we abstract from all knowledge and will . . . we still find something more, that is *feeling* and *striving*. We want to see if we will perhaps find something here that is analogous to the consciousness of the infinite."[8] That is, the best way to the Absolute is through feeling, and we experience feeling when we create. And how do we discover this feeling? Through poetry. To a poet like Novalis, Schlegel's friend, poetry allows the "individual to live in the whole and the whole in the individual."[9]

A problem with approaching the Absolute through reason is that the Absolute includes all possible positions. It is necessity and freedom, subject and object. The attempt to found philosophy on first principles is thus bound to fail. Wherever you start, the opposite is also an alternative starting place. Like the epic, one has to start in the middle of the story. It neither begins nor ends. The literary form most suitable to embracing opposites is irony. To reach the same place we can start with the grand or with the mundane. As the British poet William Blake wrote (circa 1803):

> To see a world in a Grain of Sand
> And a Heaven in a Wild Flower
> Hold Infinity in the palm of your hand
> And Eternity in an hour.[10]

For romantics, irony is not merely a figure of speech, but rather a way of life.

The German romantics opposed the approaches to individualism described in the previous chapter, not because they were wrong, but because they were so limiting. The romantics have often been portrayed as the opponents of reason; but they were rather

Figure 3.3 Caspar David Friedrich, "Monk by the Sea," 1808–10. The monk is insignificant before a vast sky and sea, an example of the puniness of an individual confronted by transcending power. © DEA Picture Library/De Agostoni/Getty Images.

the opponents of *mere* reason. The romantics were advocates of reason combined with passion. Reason could only lead to the recognition that there was more beyond reason. For some, poetry was philosophy done properly.

The emphasis on artistic action to reach the Absolute focused attention on the arts, especially on painting and music. Artists like Caspar David Friedrich painted scenes of solitary individuals confronting infinite skies and indistinct seas. Mountain vistas figured prominently. If there were cities, they tend to be abandoned ruins from long ago. To the romantic artists, cities were places of philistine concerns with wealth and power accumulation. Nature was the locale of deep emotion and the chance to discover one's place in the vastness of the Absolute, while cities stimulated more mundane concerns and distractions.

British Romanticism: Poetry and Religion

British romanticism developed in the field of poetry. The poets William Wordsworth (1770–1850) and Samuel Taylor Coleridge (1772–1834) led the way with Wordsworth providing a theory of poetry and Coleridge providing philosophical, political, and theological analyses to complement both his and Wordsworth's literary ideas. A group of poets twenty years younger, George Gordon Byron Lord Byron (1788–1824, Percy Bysshe Shelley (1792–1822), and John Keats (1795–1821) further developed romantic poetry and provided two romantic examples of impetuous lives led carelessly. As part of the romantic critique of the modern world, there was also a turn, begun in the eighteenth century, toward medieval themes and the darkness of the Gothic.

Figure 3.4 William Wordsworth, 1819. © Hulton Archive/Stringer/Getty Images.

Behind British romanticism was the conviction that there were ways to knowledge besides perception and reason. Kant had recognized that perception and reason could not comprehend everything but had declared that whatever was beyond our consciousness was unknowable, noumenal. But Wordsworth boldly claimed, "The external World is fitted to the Mind."[11] To Wordsworth, the external world was comprehensible, if by "comprehension" we mean not just reason and perception but also an understanding that arises deep in our beings. The mind has an unconscious dimension that can experience the divine.

For Wordsworth, and for most romantics, the key was to shed the distractions and false ideas of the city and to find our natural selves in nature. To Wordsworth, poetry is "the spontaneous overflow of powerful feelings"[12] that can only be recalled in tranquility. These emotions eventually give rise to a desire to compose. Then true poetry can begin. But true poetry is best expressed as closely to the feelings as possible. That is, it should be expressed in the ordinary, straightforward language used by ordinary people who speak their minds directly, unadorned by literary devices and conceits.

Over 200 years ago, Wordsworth, sounding like a thoughtful critic of the internet and social media in the twenty-first century, was bemoaning the

increasing accumulation of men in cities, where the uniformity of their occupations produces a craving for extraordinary incident, which the rapid communication of intelligence hourly gratifies.[13]

The only way to connect with universal insight was occasionally to leave the urban bustle and return to nature.

For Wordsworth and the romantics, mathematical and observational science was indirectly satisfying to those who engaged in it, but many of them were missing

A motion and a spirit, that impels,
All thinking things, all objects of all thought,
And rolls through all things.[14]

The poet has a sense of spirit that is found in everything including the human mind. To miss communion with this underlying essence is to miss everything worthwhile.

Another reminder of the futility of the pursuit for wealth and power that is the increasing obsession of the capitalist, secular urban world is found in Shelley's sonnet "Ozymandias" (1818). A traveler reports that he has found "two vast and trunkless legs of stone" in the desert. Near them we see the head of this ancient sculpture, a head with sneering arrogance that depicts passions that can be recognized today. But the irony is found in the inscription on the pedestal: "My name is Ozymandias, King of Kings. Look on my works, ye Mighty, and despair!" It is ironic because

Nothing beside remains. Round the decay
Of that colossal Wreck, boundless and bare
The lone and level sands stretch far away.[15]

The reader is reminded that time is political, and the mundane, material world is ephemeral in the long run. Whatever is worth pursuing is not to be found there.

Keats shared this insight with German thinkers like Schelling: Art was a road to the Absolute. But there most of the British stopped. They were less interested in theorizing about poetry than in writing poetry. So, for instance, Keats expressed a kind of Platonic theory through images in his "Ode on a Grecian Urn" (1819). The narrator contemplates an urn on which is depicted a wedding banquet that seems to have taken the form of a bacchanalian revel. Through the poem, we see the time-traveling urn that has lasted thousands of years as a symbol standing for that which is truly eternal. The eternal is more beautiful than that which changes and dies. But while eternal ideas can be accessed by a human mind, they cannot depend on or reside in anything human, for humans themselves die. What is sweeter: actual musical sounds or the eternal idea of these sounds? Keats claims:

> Heard melodies are sweet, but those unheard
> Are sweeter.

And when he contemplates the frustration depicted in the form of a youth chasing a woman, he tells the youth not to grieve because

> She cannot fade, though thou hast not thy bliss,
> Forever wilt thou love, and she be fair.

What his advice to the young woman would be is not recorded. Is she playing coy or running for her life? Keats remains silent. But through the equally silent urn, we have a dialogue with time.

While Wordsworth found his inspiration in nature, Keats found his inspiration in art. Through true beauty, he was able to access eternal truths:

> Beauty is truth, truth beauty—that is all
> Ye know on earth, and all ye need to know.[16]

In a letter, Keats briefly described a Negative Capability: "when a man is capable of being in uncertainties, mysteries, doubts, without any irritable reaching after fact and reason." For Keats logical contradiction did not negate the insights that beauty gives us. Truth has to speak not only to one set of human capacities but to all capacities. He advocated an openness to the world, and implicitly to all cultures and ways of knowing.

By far the most philosophically competent thinker among the British romantics was Samuel Taylor Coleridge. Coleridge was born into a devoted Anglican family, flirted with Unitarianism, considered entering the ministry, and eventually returned to the Anglican Church as a theologian who used his romantic literary perspectives to make major contributions to nineteenth-century theology. As a Unitarian devoted to reason, he was attracted to the ideals of the French Revolution but was repelled by the Terror; he later became much more conservative in his political views. In 1797 Coleridge collaborated with Wordsworth in publishing *Lyrical Ballads*, the book that definitively declared the romantic break with old poetic forms. Shortly thereafter, he went to Germany where he learned German and enrolled in the University of Göttingen to study the philosophy of Kant and Fichte. That philosophy informed his theological and philosophical ideas.

Early in his life, Coleridge began to use opium to control discomforts, and soon became an addict. Some of his poems were shaped by opium dreams, and underneath his poetic images lay a world of writhing horrors. An example is "Kubla Khan" in which a river ran

Through caverns measureless to man
Down to a sunless sea . . .
A savage place! as holy and enchanted
As e'er beneath a waning moon was haunted
By woman wailing for her demon lover![17]

Eventually his opium addiction cost him his marriage, his friendship with Wordsworth, and his ability to write good poetry, but a Dr. James Gillman took him in and made sure that Coleridge's use of opium stayed under control. Coleridge turned to prose and both by writing and speaking became a leader of thought in Britain. James Stuart Mill called him along with Bentham the two most original thinkers of the early nineteenth century. Bentham was discussed in Chapter 2 on individual approaches. Coleridge provided the holistic counterpart.

He argued, along with other conservatives, that the rights of individuals grew out of communities, and that it was impossible to understand individual rights without understanding the communal structures that defined and supported them. To argue that individuals had rights against the institutions was to misunderstand the situation. Communities needed to be fostered and protected, and thus communal rights overrode merely individual rights.

The most important community was seen in the Christian Church. Coleridge set out to understand the church and its prescriptions for life. Coleridge saw the shortcomings of actual churches in his day but did not thus lose heart. Even if church leaders failed, the church as "Body of Christ," the community of Christians, could reform the institutions.

Coleridge viewed Christianity through two complementary lenses: (1) the insights of poetic diction informed by German Transcendental Philosophy and (2) the responses of German Idealism. To get to the bases of Christian ideas, Coleridge focused his poetic eye on the Bible as a work of literature, especially the letters of Paul and the Gospel of John, which he saw as related works. Ultimately, Coleridge saw the essence of Christianity in redemption. He wrote: "Christianity is not a Theory, or a Speculation; but a Life. Not a Philosophy of Life, but a Life and a living Process."[18] As Coleridge read the Bible, it contained truths expressed in analogy, metaphor, and allegory—all poetic ways of writing. The basic metaphors of redemption were stories of sacrifice, reconciliation, ransom (from slavery), and payment of debt to satisfy a creditor.

Coleridge had learned a great deal from German theologians, especially from Friedrich Schleiermacher, who in retrospect has been seen as the founder of modern hermeneutics, the study of how to read a text with understanding. To Schleiermacher, one had to pay attention to the language as used by a particular author at a particular time and to focus on the culture in which the work was written. The letters of Paul, says Coleridge, used Jewish metaphors to convince the Jews of his time that this was the new way to practice Judaism. Paul used concepts that were familiar to his audience to teach ideas that were unfamiliar. The reason that the language of sacrifice, blood, and atonement was used to explain nonmaterial ideas was that the world understood sacrifice, blood, and atonement. The world did not understand a spiritual renewal of a person's mind. The key to redemption is participation in a community of people trying to imitate the teachings of Christ. Blood sacrifice on the cross, then, is a way of showing people that together they should participate in drinking wine and eating bread together. Coleridge wants us not to think of the cross, but rather of the generative work of "the word" understood in community.

German Idealism

Kant left us with a world of mind, a world of phenomena, which we can understand. But he also left us with a world outside of mind, a noumenal world, which is inaccessible to our understanding. The "inner world" was a world of human freedom and choice. The "outer world" was a world of necessity and determinism. These two worlds, however, are interdependent. We experience a world beyond ourselves that is beyond our ability to control, but we also find ourselves able to affect that world in a variety of ways.

Reconciling freedom and necessity is not easy. Materialists chose to regard the mind as a product of a material world. The most succinct aphoristic way of describing materialistic determinism was, "Thoughts are to the brain as urine is to the kidneys." But that solved the problem by making a freedom an illusion. We will not develop the basis of materialism in this chapter, but rather explore its alternative. The other possibility was to use direct human experience as the starting point. We experience ourselves as knowers before we have any ideas about the material world of science. Perhaps it is the knower, and freedom, that is primary. The problem, then, is to derive the world of necessity from the world of the free human subject. To turn the materialist aphorism on its head, "Matter is a fairly good idea."

Johann Gottlieb Fichte

Fichte (1762–1814), the son of a poor and religious family, was born in 1762 in Lutheran Saxony. According to legend, a local landowner, late for church and sad to have missed the sermon, heard that a local boy could repeat the preaching word for word. The rich man decided to pay Fichte's tuition, which the nobleman did until his death in 1784. Fichte had to leave the University of Jena without a degree. He supported himself as a tutor and began to study Kant. Fichte took a trip to distant Königsberg, Kant's home, but his interaction was disappointing. Doggedly unwilling to give up on a fruitful recognition by Kant, he desperately wrote a book on divine revelation and Kant's philosophy. The book succeeded, and Kant lauded it, at least initially. Fichte was able to parlay his recognition by Kant into an associate professorship at Jena. As he developed his system of Transcendental Philosophy, he wrote prolifically. He seemed to use philosophy to define God and eventually to subsume God. Accused of atheism and nihilism, Fichte was dismissed from his professorship. The only German state that accepted him was Prussia, so Fichte moved to the University of Berlin in 1800. Napoleon's rise, the subsequent dissolution of the Holy Roman Empire as all of the Southern German states became part of the French Protectorship, and the German uprisings against Napoleon led Fichte to call off his lectures and urge his students to join the struggle. Fichte's philosophical work turned to German nationalism—a subject we will discuss in Chapter 7.

As he developed his philosophy in the aftermath of his meeting with Kant, Fichte endeavored to solve the noumenal/phenomenal dualism at the heart of Kant's approach. Fichte thought that in the Kantian system there was a tendency to see the "real" world as unknowable. This approach seemed to lead into skepticism and doubt. Instead, Fichte denied that consciousness is grounded in the "so-called real world." Instead, the phenomenal world of consciousness arises from the self-activity of consciousness. The "I" recognizes itself as it recognizes other freely acting beings. So, the activity of consciousness in thinking creates both human identity and human community. This thinking is not done by only one person, but rather by every person. The "I" recognizes itself only in a communal setting, that is, at least one other being must be involved. The freedom that the "I" experiences immediately finds a limit in its interaction with other freely acting beings. Eventually, as consciousness explores its own activity, it finds that other objects of consciousness are necessary to its own activity. Thus, it creates the world of phenomena from itself. No exterior noumenal world is necessary, because the observable objective world exists in consciousness.

Georg Wilhelm Friedrich Hegel

As we discussed Fichte, the figure of Napoleon loomed. It is difficult to discuss the development of any ideas in the late eighteenth and early nineteenth centuries without taking into account the threat, promise, and actuality of the ever-changing French Revolution and its eventual transformation into the Napoleonic Empire. Napoleon tried to maintain many of the democratic ideals (as he interpreted them) of the revolution for society at large, while maintaining firm dictatorial control at the very top of society. Throughout Europe, many were thrilled at the prospect of overthrowing monarchical families who viewed themselves as exclusive owners of the lands and peoples under their rule. They approved of the legal reforms of the Napoleonic code that abolished feudalism and many taxes. Others were appalled by the same radical transformation of society, especially the regicide of the Terror (Chapter 1).

Hegel (1770–1831) was a philosopher of his time. In an age of rapid change and challenge to old forms of society emerging from France, Hegel developed a philosophy of change. In an age in which Christianity itself was under scrutiny, Hegel the seminarian developed a radical understanding of the meaning of the incarnation and resurrection of Christ. As philosophy flowered in Germany, Hegel responded to the challenges of many, including Immanuel Kant, Johann Gottlieb Fichte, and Friedrich Schelling.

Hegel built the insights of Fichte and others into a coherent system of thought. Hegel maintained the futility of trying to find permanent truths. Truth was a process of development. Truth was thus also action as well as ideas. In any age there is an overarching way of thinking, like a shape. People move and interact within this shape, and it seems to be the way of the world. But each shape, or system of ideas, or cultural form, that seems at one time to be complete, is later seen to be insufficient to comprehend the conditions of a new age. Thinkers find an idea's insufficiency as they posit new ideas that challenge the original one. The new system focuses on the insufficiencies in the old idea. In that sense it is a refutation of the old system. But, in fact, the old idea contains true and useful elements. It worked in an earlier age. As the old ideas and the new ideas clash, they create an even newer idea that includes elements of both. They are sublated (in German *aufgehoben*) into the new synthesis. This interaction of ideas is called dialectic. One way it has been described (not by Hegel) is that a thesis calls forth its antithesis, and the two battle until they have become sublated into a synthesis. The synthesis becomes, in its turn, a new thesis. Let's consider a concrete example.

In Hegel's own day, the shape of society defined by Christian feudalism had been challenged by the French revolutionaries, building on English ideas that had been honed during the Enlightenment. A result was a radical democratic egalitarianism that resulted in the Terror and the execution of the king. As Hegel came of age and began to write his first works, Europe was in a battle with revolutionary France. But the French government after the Terror, the Directory, was weak. Eventually it ended in the dictatorship, and then emperorship, of Napoleon. Napoleon promoted the ideals of equality as he created a new law code and created egalitarian (in his terms) social structures, but he also provided a strong state. He created a society that allowed inequality in the sense that different people were supposed to have different abilities and functions—but was equal in that all male citizens were equal under the law. A way of viewing this through Hegel's lens is that the Feudal system became a thesis under attack by an antithesis egalitarianism that attacked Feudal contradictions. This egalitarian system itself produced the Terror. But out of the Terror arose a new system that combined important elements of both. Thus, the battle between feudalism and egalitarianism was sublated into Napoleonism. For Hegel, Napoleon almost unconsciously embodied the needs of his day. He was an instrument of history.

For Hegel, the process of history, the movement from one cultural shape to another, has a direction and a goal. That direction is toward greater and greater freedom. There is no way the progress of freedom can be thwarted. At times, a dictator tries to stifle freedom, but that attempt backfires. The dictator serves as an unwitting tool in the cause of freedom. Hegel refers to this as "the cunning of reason." Essentially the actions of power-hungry dictators' actions have unintended consequences that result in furthering the cause of freedom. Napoleon, for Hegel, was such an individual. Napoleon as a dictator expressed the democratic spirit of the age, even when he repressed German aspirations. Hegel referred to Napoleon as a "world soul."

But Hegel does not begin with society in his magnum opus, *Phenomenology of Spirit*. He begins with individuals. All that has been described so far at the social level also occurs as consciousness develops. Like Fichte, he denies the essential split between the knower (subject) and the known (object). There is no unknowable noumenal world outside of mind. Human beings at earlier stages of consciousness experience the world as outside of themselves and out of their control. Nature seems to be a force that can do great harm that is beyond the ability of individuals to affect. When a hurricane sweeps out of nowhere, all human beings can do is hunker down. Society is another force that seems beyond the ability of normal people to manage. And God also seems to be a non-worldly force that can determine our fates, and all we feel we can do is pray for mercy.

Ultimately, Hegel wants us to see that human beings at both the individual and social levels create this "outside" world. We have taken parts or aspects of ourselves and projected them into the world as alien existences. Starting with the senses, Hegel shows that all of our sensory experiences are shaped by our thought. There is no raw sensory experience that pertains to just this moment, because just to see a tree we have to see it as a member of the class of trees. The word is used universally to define many more sensory experiences than just the one. As we perceive the tree, we begin to understand that it is connected to soil, air, sun, and so forth. That is, we see anything in its relations to other things. Even the word "I" is an experience had by every person at all times.

As we understand that particular perceptions are always linked to others, we need to become conscious of ourselves. That is, we become self-conscious. Self-consciousness involves splitting the self into an acting self and an observing self. We watch ourselves think. As we become self-conscious, we also realize that there are other self-conscious beings. We engage in struggle, both in our own minds and in interaction with other minds. Out of this struggle, and only out of this struggle, we can reach increased awareness of our world and ourselves.

We see with language. Without thought, there are no objects of perception. Language, however, is a social system that an individual is born into. Although an individual may feel that his or her experience is unique, eventually the process of exploring this idea will reveal contradictions. The process of thinking moves dialectically (idea, anti-idea, synthetic idea) toward the recognition that the "individual" does not exist as a being separate from other individuals. Eventually the process of thinking will arrive at the conclusion that the division of the world into subject and object makes no sense.

As these ideas develop in consciousness, consciousness experiences itself as both subject and object. There is the knower (subject) and the known (object). But this division is seen as a product of the language we use to express the situation. In the grammar of our sentences, a subject acts on or recognizes an object. For instance, "Anna sees the big green ball," is a typical sentence in English. But the big green ball only exists in Anna's mind. We say that the ball "has" the characteristics of being green and big. Does the ball exist without these characteristics? The ball in this sentence exists as Anna sees it. So, the ball exists in relation to Anna and to its characteristics. Take those away, and we essentially take away the ball. The same is true of Anna. Anna in this sentence exists while she sees the ball. Anna may also exist in a large number of other situations in which she sees or acts. But what is Anna if we take all those sentences (all those situations) away? Essentially, we have an unanalyzed situation in which something is known. At this point, the distinction between subject and object collapses into consciousness that acts or recognizes. All is both subject and object. The truth is the whole, not the parts. Anna, green, big, and ball, all collapse into one.

The situation becomes more complex when we reflect that different languages express relationships differently. They divide the world in slightly different ways. Each of these languages reacts to a different cultural situation, and so the ideas expressed at any time in any language must be different. And each of these cultural situations is constantly changing in some way. The dialectic described earlier is different in each culture. The truth that all of these ideas seek is mistakenly seen to be an object of thought. In fact, the truth is thought itself. Truth is a process.

Humans exist in communities, and these communities have customs, rules, traditions, and laws. The individuals in these communities engage in a kind of "dance" of which they are unaware. That is, they interact, each playing a role without knowing that they are playing a role. The shape of the culture is unseen by most of them. The dance goes on; when individuals drop out (perhaps by dying), others take their place. Ultimately, the dance is what is important, not the individual moves.

Society develops as shapes of the "dance" become insufficient to encompass changing social structures. For instance, in ancient society the freedom of the monarch was the only freedom that was known. What the king said was the law. But as gods were added, people began to ask what the gods said. The battle for legitimacy between the monarch and the rules of religion formed the basis of many Greek tragedies. Eventually shapes of consciousness began to emerge that embraced universal laws of property. Nonetheless, laws and empires were experienced as alien despotic structures.

In Hegel's time, the Enlightenment saw itself as opposing reason to superstition, science to religion. Before the Enlightenment, to Hegel, faith was practically universal in Western Europe. There was no alternative. The idea that reason could provide an alternative to religion created a thesis-antithesis struggle. Religious people now began to accept the definition of faith as defined by the Enlightenment and to engage in the struggle. But something is lost in the Enlightenment definition. In the pre-Enlightenment era, says Hegel, faith involved a "beautiful unity of trust and immediate certainty." Faith became a kind of restless yearning. But we find that the Enlightenment has nothing to replace this faith other than new abstractions. In the first chapter, we saw that development of Newtonian science in the eighteenth century reified (artificially made real) concepts like gravity. In fact, "matter" itself is such a concept. The Enlightenment replaced God with scientific concepts, but these concepts are themselves as abstract as God is. The

Enlightenment replaced faith with "utility." That is, things and people are evaluated for their usefulness. A further synthesis is clearly needed.

For Hegel the unity of humankind in community is necessary for the emergence of spirit. Spirit is not something ethereal and heavenly (or heaven-bound). It is rather the unity of human consciousness that begins to recognize that the entire world is its creation. Humans (together, as spirit) make laws. Spirit creates language. Spirit creates the categories and methods of science. Out of this realization, that the human world is sufficient to embrace the entire universe, true, absolute freedom can emerge. We can only be free when we realize who we really are.

Freedom, however, is not abstract. It must be embodied. In fact, actual human beings carry out all philosophy, and thus all thought is embodied. Much of the time "God" is a misguided projection outward of human actions. As Hegel says, "One begins with the word 'God'. This by itself is a meaningless sound, a mere name; it is only the predicate that says, *what God is* gives Him content and meaning. Only at the end of the proposition does the empty become actual knowledge." Eventually we shall see that God is something that reflects on itself and is therefore a subject. God is not an object to be known, but rather is itself the knower. The Absolute is Spirit (*Geist*) as is the totality of humanity.

Hegel sees art, religion, and philosophy as different ways of communicating similar things. All three contain the Spirit, as that spirit is experienced in an age. Art deals almost entirely in images. Religion provides myths, that is, stories and images that give us insight when they are understood in their true form. Philosophy gives us concepts that reveal more clearly what the actual spirit is. But of course, none of these is in itself true, because truth lies not only in thinking but also in acting and living.

For example, in the story of the incarnation of Jesus Christ, God, the spirit, becomes fully embodied in a human being. Eventually, Jesus is crucified and dies; but he is resurrected. He rises again. As Hegel says, "[J]ust as formerly He rose up for consciousness as a sensuous existence [the incarnation], now He has risen in the spirit."[19] If we remember that Spirit is the totality of humanity, we see that God has ceased to exist as a spiritual concept but is now embodied in the entire Christian community. In a way, God has become unified in the Holy Spirit, which is the life of the community.

Later in his life, Hegel wrote about the form of this community in *Philosophy of Right*. For Hegel, community consists of the family, the civil (or economic) society, a "universal class" of well-educated bureaucrats, and a government of legislators, police and judges, and a monarch. Most of society is composed of economic actors, but these actors are responsible for acting morally. The government regulates their work. Laws can only be proposed by the universal class (the bureaucrats), but the laws are enacted (or not) by the legislature and signed by a practically figurehead monarch. It is a society of trust tempered by checks and balances.

By the 1820s, Hegel was perhaps the most prominent philosopher in Germany. He died suddenly of cholera in 1831, and others further developed his ideas. Politically, the followers of Hegel could be on the right and the left. Hegel continues to be influential today, even when philosophers refute his work. In future chapters, we will explore the ways his work was used, especially when we consider Karl Marx in Chapter 5.

Individualist Opponent: Søren Kierkegaard

Søren Kierkegaard (1813–55) opposed the approach of Hegel, other idealists, and romantics as misunderstandings of both God and humans. A wealthy Dane who lived as a freelance writer, Kierkegaard spent his life trying to live as a Christian. For Kierkegaard, God was an inaccessible infinite, transcendent being who was incomprehensible to finite humans. Thus, reason and logic had nothing to contribute to Christian understanding. Christianity was based, simply, on love. Kierkegaard thought that Christianity demanded deeds, not thought and not comprehension. The source of Christianity lay in individuals, not in groups and not in churches. Kierkegaard walked through the streets of Copenhagen talking with whomever he met. His idea was that at least one person would show interest in the lives and experiences of even the poorest inhabitant of the city.

Although humans cannot understand God's love, a Christian has to accept it. One of the sources of despair is failure to accept God's forgiveness. For some reason, God has decided to forgive the unforgiveable. But God also has demands. Sometimes, as in the case of God's demand that Abraham sacrifice his son Isaac, it is hard to see why God's will is so outside of normal practice. Individuals have to decide whether what seems a command of God really is one. There is no hope of sureness, for a command such as this is outside of all boundaries. We must make a decision and take responsibility for it. And this decision is sheer agony, made in "fear and trembling" (the title of Kierkegaard's book). In the biblical story, God lifts the decision from Abraham at the last moment, after both Abraham and Isaac have lived for days in terror. But there is no assurance that God will do the same in other situations. This story, says Kierkegaard, shows us the difference between the ethics of society and the ethics that springs from inside the individual and that cannot be part of a group experience. Thus, the emphasis of Christianity on the belonging to and attending a church is misplaced. Only individuals can experience divine grace.

This emphasis upon the terrible weight of decision experienced by Christian individuals has led several thinkers to refer to Kierkegaard as the predecessor of existentialism, a twentieth-century philosophy discussed in a Chapter 12.

Romantic Science

Schelling was not only a founder of German Romantic theory but also of a distinctly German approach to science. Since Schelling believed that the structure of the world was essentially the same as the structure of the knowing mind, and that therefore the structure of nature must be both subjective and objective, Schelling thought that the best way to understand nature was to reflect on the thinking process. This approach to science was known as *naturphilosophie*. "Thinking is not my thinking, and being is not my being, for everything is only of God or the totality."[20] For *naturphilosophie* the essence of nature was duality, starting with subject/object, but extending to male/female, or even positive/negative, as in electricity.

Romantic Biology

By 1800 there were two ways of viewing nature: nature is like a machine and nature is like an organism. *Naturphilosophie* lies squarely in the organism camp. We can understand a machine by taking it apart, analyzing the structure of the parts and the ways they interact, and then by building it back up through a process of synthesis to make sure we have analyzed it properly. An organism, however, is not equal to the sum of its parts. We have to understand it as a totality. Furthermore, organisms grow and develop, whereas machines stay the same. Nature itself was undoubtedly in a process of growth and development.

The future of all the sciences, including biology, as we shall see, lay in analysis and synthesis, of treating even organisms like machines. But there are areas of biology, like embryology, where the study of organic growth and development is important, in which *naturphilosophical* approaches were effective. In general, though, the verdict of experimental biologists in the later nineteenth century was that *naturphilosophie* had stunted the growth of biology by its tendency to be too speculative and its attempts to prematurely interpret the small scale in terms of the large. By the late 1830s, the future of experimental biology lay in microscopes, not in grand syntheses.

Romantic Physics: Light

By about 1825, physicists were aware that space was probably filled everywhere with an ethereal substance that was somewhat sticky. This substance was needed to support the kind of waves that made up light (transverse waves, in which the oscillating motion is perpendicular to the direction the wave is moving). Physicists were also aware that if planets moved through a sticky substance, they would slow down and soon spiral into the sun. The substance, named aether, had to not interact with matter but be sticky enough to support transverse waves when stimulated by a light source, like the distant stars. The most fundamental problem in nineteenth-century physics was finding a mathematical description of the aether that fit the requirements. This problem essentially remained unsolved.

The prevailing Newtonian approach (discussed in Chapter 1) assumed that space was empty and that light was a kind of particle that passed through space. This approach solved the problem of planetary slowing down and seemed to be sufficient. However, no one could figure out just how particles could produce transverse waves. By 1825 the evidence that light was made up of transverse waves was persuasive. Since we can see the stars, the evidence that all space is filled with whatever it was that was waving was also persuasive. Since planets stay in orbit century after century, the evidence that they were not slowing down was also persuasive.

Particles and waves are very different kinds of things, as different as nouns and verbs. A particle is a thing, located at a particular time in a particular space. A wave is a motion, located throughout an extended area in some amount of time. One could imagine capturing a particle in a photograph. To see a wave motion, one would need to imagine a movie. Mathematicians used very different techniques to describe a space full of particles and a space full of waves. In short, if light was a particle, it was not a wave; and if it was a wave, it was not a particle. By 1825 physicists were convinced that light was a transverse wave. They just had no idea what was waving.

Romantic Physics: Electricity

With the invention of the battery by the Italian Allesandro Volta in 1800, electricity in current form was available for the first time. The very word "current" is based on a metaphor: electricity is a fluid that flows. The Newtonian approach suggested that electricity should be made up of particles, so electric current would be a flow of electrical particles through a wire. Since many of the mathematical issues involved in water flow had been solved, a ready-made theory could be adapted to fit the electrical case. The only difference was that whereas water was made up of one kind of matter, electricity could come in a positive or a negative form. Therefore, attractive and repulsive forces had to be involved.

Soon after its invention, the battery was used industrially. Scientists found that they could dissociate many chemicals by running electricity through them. For instance, water could be dissociated into oxygen and hydrogen. They also discovered that they could use electricity to join elements in, say, the electroplating of metals. Some chemicals gathered at the positive pole of a battery and different ones at the negative pole. It seemed clear that matter involved electrical polarity, and this fits nicely into the views of the German *naturphilosophes*.

The Danish physicist Hans Christian Oersted (1777–1851) had studied in Germany and became friends with the *naturphilosophe* physicist Johann Wilhelm Ritter. Oersted was quite attracted to the ideas of Friedrich Schelling, in particular. As a result, Oersted was convinced that there was a unity among all the forces in nature. Electricity was a polar kind of phenomenon. Another polar phenomenon involved magnetism. Shouldn't there be, then, Oersted asked himself, a basic connection between electricity and magnetism? He was not the only person to have had this idea, but no one had been able to establish such a connection. Physicists were looking for a way that electrical particles, in either attracting or repelling, might create a magnetic effect. No one could find it.

One day in 1820, Oersted was setting up some equipment for an experimental demonstration of electricity to his university class. He noticed that a compass needle near a current carrying wire was deflected. Strangely, the needle was neither attracted to nor repelled by the wire. Whatever force was involved seemed to move in a circle around the wire. When he reported his findings, Oersted used the terminology of naturphilosophie, speaking of contending powers and conflict. Ultimately, he claimed that the conflict acted in a circle.

For Oersted, as for the *naturphilosophes*, the World Spirit lay behind the polar conflicts in nature. The entire universe was unified in an Absolute mind. The findings of Oersted represent one of the highest triumphs of Romantic Science. But if electricity could produce magnetism, the opposite should be possible. However he might arrange the magnets, Oersted could not show any evidence of electric current. But in the 1820s, electromagnets and even an experimental magnetic engine capable of moving began to be used industrially.

The English Michael Faraday (1791–1867), born in poverty, had to educate himself. An apprentice to a bookbinder, Faraday read incessantly, if a bit sporadically. He attended the lectures of Humphrey Davy at the Royal Institution, which was founded to promote research and education. Faraday showed Davy a 300-page book based on his notes on Davy's lectures (and bound by Faraday himself). Davy soon employed Faraday as an assistant, and Faraday proved to be a genius at scientific experiment. He had little mathematical training, but he could visualize the effects of his experiments as if he could see into the heart of nature. Throughout the 1820s, Faraday worked on electromagnetism and made several important discoveries.

In 1831 Faraday had set up an apparatus consisting of a coil of wire connected to a galvanometer (a way of measuring electricity). When he moved to insert a magnet into the coil, the galvanometer twitched. When he removed the magnet, the galvanometer twitched in the opposite direction. In short, magnetism could produce electricity, but only by moving. If one reflects that electric current was seen as moving particles of electricity, the idea that electricity produces magnetism is not accurate. Moving electricity produces magnetism, and moving magnetism produces electricity. In short, electricity and magnetism are examples of the same underlying process.

Faraday was not a *naturphilosophe*, but he was a Sandemanian, a fundamentalist Christian group that stemmed from the Church of Scotland. Sandemanians believed that all nature reflects the existence of God. Because God is one, nature is one. Faraday and Oersted arrived at their conviction of the fundamental unity of all nature from different directions, but they coincided in their approach to developing a theory of the physical world. The ideas of God are not obvious, so careful experiment must be used to discover them. This reliance on careful observation distinguishes romantic physics from romantic biology.

As Faraday imagined electromagnetism, he envisioned lines of forces stretching and curving across the universe. His forces were not the push-pull forces of Newtonian physics, but Faraday did not know enough mathematics to notice. Mathematical physicists saw these lines of force as indicative of Faraday's mathematical ignorance. They could appreciate his experiments, but not his visualizations. It would take a new branch of mathematics and a similarly creative mind to make use of Faraday's ideas, in the process uniting the sciences of optics and electromagnetism. And that story will be told in the next chapter.

Figure 3.5 Lines of force demonstrated by iron filings in a magnetic field. The forces seem to curve and fill all space, unlike the straight-line forces of Newtonian physics. © Getty Images.

What we are seeing here is the reluctant construction of a non-Newtonian view of nature. Newton's work was entirely consistent with the individualism discussed in Chapter 2. For Newton, particles endowed with various forces acted on one another across space. The totality of nature could be described in terms of the interactions of individual particles. Newtonian determinism was founded on the idea that if an infinite mind knew the positions and velocities of every particle in the universe, that infinite mind would be able to calculate all that had ever been and all that would ever be. All groupings in the universe could be seen as a result of the actions of individual particles.

The newly emerging physics emphasized, haltingly, connections. Aether connected everything. Aether was not constrained to only push and pull, because aether could whirl. Slowly the idea of the *field* was emerging. The physics of the whole had not yet been constructed, but we can see at this point that something different is emerging. Interestingly enough, that new something is tied to a worldview that is consistent with certain versions of the worldview of idealism and romanticism.

Conclusion

This chapter has shown the reasoned reactions of thinkers who were appalled and frightened by the new industrial-commercial-scientific-individualistic society that was springing up around them. The technological/commercial changes seemed out of control and likely to create a much worse human world. In particular, what romantics, idealists, and conservatives saw in the new individualism was a despiritualized culture that worshipped reason, a deity that could understand machines, but not people, certainly not a community, and absolutely not the Divine. In place of commercial and scientific calculation, the conservatives imagined a world built on love and justice, as they conceived it.

Another way of thinking about their repulsion is that the alternative approach concentrated on individuals as ends in themselves. Conservatives and romantics did not all think that individualists were atheists, but they all certainly thought that the thinkers discussed in the previous chapter concentrated on trees instead of the forest. Many scientists also realized that the atomistic approach of Newton and Dalton was insufficient to grasp the nature of forces and phenomena that stretched out in space. Oersted and Faraday followed Schelling in seeing all of space as an interconnected whole. Space was not empty, and atoms did not make up space. Atoms were part of space and drew their nature from participating in the universal whole.

In the next chapter, we shall examine the state of technology and science in the earlier part of the nineteenth century, and we shall see how Faraday's conception became the idea of the electromagnetic field.

CHAPTER 4
MECHANIZING THE HUMAN WORLD

Figure 4.1 Portrait of Mary Somerville painted by Mary Fairfax, 1834. © National Galleries of Scotland/Hulton Fine Art Collection / Getty Images.

The Woman Who Made Science Popular

In 1834, William Whewell, polymath, Cambridge professor, and early historian of science, had just finished reading Mary Somerville's (1780–1872) new book, *On the Connection of the Physical Sciences*. Whewell recognized the creative power of this remarkable synthesis of ideas and began writing a review for the *Quarterly Review*. How could he describe the author? Had she merely written about theories of the planets and stars, she could have been called an astronomer. But she wrote about all the physical sciences and their interconnections. The only phrase that was then available in English was "man of science," but obviously, that did not fit a woman who had mastered physics, mathematics, astronomy, and geology (among others). Whewell, recognizing a kindred spirit, finally coined the word "scientist."

The Scotswoman Mary Somerville (born Fairfax) was born into an illustrious family in 1780. She remembered that her mother wanted to restrict her education to "write well and keep accounts, which was all a woman was expected to know." When she was twenty-eight, however, her first husband died, leaving her a comfortable inheritance, and Mary, guided by some of the leading intellectuals of Scotland, turned to the study of mathematics. Among the books she mastered was Newton's *Principia* (see Chapter 1), but when she read the French physicist/mathematician Pierre-Simon Laplace, she realized just how archaic the calculations of Newton were. She later wrote that English mathematical physics had been held back by not using the advancements in calculus initiated by Leibniz and developed by the French.

As one of the few English who could understand Laplace's *Méchanique Céleste* (*Celestial Mechanics*), she was encouraged to translate the book. Instead, Mary Somerville explained the book, using clear mathematical diagrams and expositions, saying later, "I translated Laplace's work from algebra into plain language."[1] Her book was published in 1831 as *The Mechanism of the Heavens*. It was reviewed by one author as the greatest intellectual achievement since the *Principia*, and soon became a textbook for undergraduates at the University of Cambridge. She followed this work with *On the Connection of the Physical Sciences*, which cemented her reputation. In 1835, Mary Somerville and Caroline Herschel were chosen as the first female members of the Royal Astronomical Society.

Later in her life, Mary Somerville, remembering some of the original mathematical discoveries she made, wondered whether she should have focused her efforts on mathematics rather than writing popular books. But as a science popularizer, she was a pioneer. The eighteenth and nineteenth centuries saw the development of numerous opportunities for average people to learn about the fields of science. There were public lectures, private talks, institutes, articles in periodicals, and books. One of the reasons that scientific ideas had such an impact on the world of ideas in general was that almost every new scientific idea was promptly turned into fodder for a public eager for novelty.

Mary Somerville was the first popularizer to emphasize connections in nature. As she wrote in her second book, "we perceive the operation of a force which is mixed up with everything that exists in the heavens or on earth; which pervades every atom, rules the motions of animate and inanimate beings."[2] James Clerk Maxwell, the great Scottish scientist of whom we will read a great deal in this chapter, remarked that the same insight that motivated Somerville motivated the search that resulted in the first law of thermodynamics: in a closed system, energy cannot be created or destroyed. (However, it can be transformed, and therefore is the great connector of all physical processes.)

Chapter Map

This chapter surveys technology and science from a mid-century perspective as a problem in intellectual history. Technology, always a part of culture, had begun to inform European daily experience. Stimulated by technology, a new set of intellectual roots, scientific ideas, and methods spread beneath the forest, mostly ignoring the old root systems. The old roots often grafted themselves onto the new as ideas became more secular and individualistic.

At first, we focus on the development of railroads and telegraph systems and then move to the ideas behind weather prediction. The chapter then turns to biology. The idea of organisms as machines was old by the middle of the nineteenth century, but experimental biologists and physicians at this point challenged that metaphor. Some scientists, like Claude Bernard, avoided theories in favor of clear observations. In the absence of comprehensive theoretical commitments, scientists were able to find unexpected connections.

In physics, the inability to explain the science behind steam engines led to the development of a whole new branch of physics: thermodynamics. The concepts of energy and entropy had to be invented and put into mathematical form. Ultimately, energy was seen as more fundamental than matter. Thermodynamics not only was useful in physics, but it seemed to suggest new ways of thinking about the universe that were available to nonscientists.

While physicists worked on thermodynamic theory, one of them, James Clerk Maxwell, decided to apply new mathematical discoveries to a qualitative theory of Michael Faraday, known as "lines of force." Maxwell built a field theory, that is, a view of forces acting at every point in space, uniting electricity, magnetism, and optics. Maxwell's theory made possible the invention of the radio.

In chemistry, scientists had worked with an atomic theory for decades. But no one could figure out how to arrange these atoms into a classification system. A Russian chemist working on a textbook, Dmitri Mendeleev, developed a table of elements that not only organized current knowledge but also made predictions leading to new discoveries.

The chapter ends with the invention of the idea of the computer in the work of Charles Babbage and Ada Lovelace. The twentieth century beckoned.

The Idea of Technological Progress

By the middle of the nineteenth century, thanks in part to the work of people like Mary Somerville, the European populace increasingly viewed with awe both the use of machinery to accomplish human purposes and the complex methods of scientific investigation to satisfy human knowledge. The two increasingly were seen as complementary processes. Karl Marx was no fan of capitalism, but he was an admirer of the technological accomplishments that so far had been fostered uniquely by capitalists:

> The bourgeoisie, during its rule of scarce one hundred years, has created more massive and more colossal productive forces than have all preceding generations together. Subjection of Nature's forces to man, machinery, application of chemistry to industry and agriculture, steam-navigation, railways, electric telegraphs, clearing

of whole continents for cultivation, canalisation of rivers, whole populations conjured out of the ground. (*The Communist Manifesto*)

In 1851, three years after the publication of the *Manifesto*, Great Britain sponsored the Crystal Palace Exhibition (officially known as the Great Exhibition of the Works of Industry of All Nations), the first worldwide trade fair. The popular name of the Exhibition was taken from the gigantic glass hall that displayed the architectural possibilities inherent in steel support beams. Essentially a giant greenhouse, the hall was 1,848 by 454 feet and 135 feet tall. Throughout, the hall was filled with trees that demonstrated human power over nature.

By the mid-nineteenth century, Western Europe was on the verge of being transformed by two great inventions in transportation and communication: the railroad and the telegraph. Although we tend to see each of these as a single invention, in fact, they consist of multitudes of inventions. That is, the railroad is a system of ideas, even if it consists of only one engine on one short length of track. Today, if we read "railroad system," we tend to think of crisscrossing tracks connecting multiple destinations with several railroad companies interacting. But in fact, underneath such a macro-system lies a micro-system of inventions that make up just one machine.

Figure 4.2 The Crystal Palace, 1851. The hall holding the first exhibition of technology—the building itself, made of glass and iron, was a prime example of technological possibility. © The Universal Images Group/Getty Images.

This systemic view of invention implies that once someone gets an idea, like the railroad or the telegraph, it is quite difficult to put the pieces together to make a socially useful apparatus. The idea of using a steam engine to drive a vehicle had existed since the eighteenth century. Unfortunately, building a steam engine with sufficiently high pressure to power such a vehicle was difficult. The cylinder within which a piston moved up and down never quite fit the size of the piston. Once high pressure was achieved, the engine was still too heavy. Without going through the hundreds of problems that needed to be solved by ingenious invention, one can see the difficulties. On the other side, the rails had to be properly shaped and a way to anchor them firmly to the ground had to be devised.

In fact, understanding the intricacies of any invention is at least as complex and arduous as understanding a system of philosophy, like that of Kant or Hegel (see Chapter 3). Generally, knowledge is compartmentalized, and any one compartment is the purview of specialists. We understand this, and so are impressed by the wide-ranging expertise of a Mary Somerville or a William Whewell. Words like "polymath" (a master of multiple branches of knowledge) or polyglot (a master of multiple languages) are properly used to describe a small number of people.

Of course, the mind-breaking set of ideas involved in inventions like the telegraph or the railroad are not needed for the employment of these technological marvels. One can be trained to be a telegraph operator or a railroad engineer. Once the inventions are in use, one can also be trained to repair and maintain them. And with future technological development, the use of these systems becomes more "user-friendly." Thus, technology

LOCOMOTIVE ENGINE—DUBLIN AND KINSTOWN RAILWAY.

Figure 4.3 The Hibernia, early locomotive, 1834. An illustration for the eager public in *The Dublin Penny Journal.* © Wikimedia Commons (public domain).

can seem routine to mechanics, even more so to users, but still remain devilishly difficult to inventors.

The railroad was first developed in Great Britain in 1828, and soon after German states and France began to develop their own systems. By 1850 railroads had routes throughout England and Scotland (up to Glasgow). Prussia had railroads connecting west to east, and many of the German states had railroads between major cities. France had railroad lines in the industrial north and only a few in the south. Even Spain and Italy had railroads connecting some major cities. The potential was clear to most of the leaders of those countries, and significant support for rapid expansion emerged throughout industrial Europe. Especially in Germany, leaders who sought German unity saw clearly that railroads would enable effective connections of the various Germanys.

Similarly, the telegraph was an invention that was on the edge of rapid expansion. Two electrical systems existed, the Cooke-Wheatstone system in England and the Morse system in the United States. France had an optical system of signaling that was cumbersome in comparison to the electrical systems. The advantage of the Morse system was that it only required one wire. The Cooke-Wheatstone system required more two or more wires. In the 1850s the countries of continental Europe agreed to adopt the Morse system with a modified code, while Great Britain continued to use the Cooke-Wheatstone system. But by the 1860s agreements were reached to allow messages to be sent from one system to the other.

The problem of standardization threatened to hinder the utility of both railroads and telegraphs. For instance, if the gauge, the distance between the two tracks, differed from company to company, the rail cars would only fit on one company's tracks. This problem could be, and was, solved by national governments mandating standards. The issue of moving on the same train between countries was more bedeviling. Passengers and freight often had to move on the ground from one system to another. Still today, there are differing track gauges in several different countries. The fix today is often technological, with sliding wheels or more than one set of tracks.

Nevertheless, the advantages of efficient transportation and communication within a country were apparent to leaders in all the countries of Europe. Miles of track and telegraph line expanded rapidly in the second half of the nineteenth century. And as countries became connected so rapidly, a person could see the changes in the course of a few decades. The entire structure of European societies and economies shifted rapidly. From one point of view, the enlightenment idea of progress was being realized in the technical, and scientific, spheres. From another point of view, the stresses of population shifts to urban areas and the needs to learn new job skills and ways of life signaled to some that technological change threatened human well-being.

Weather Prediction and Meteorology: A Case Study

Weather was for many a proof of the existence of divine forces. Weather was immediately changeable, often to the detriment of human life and fortune. Droughts, floods, and tornados all brought misfortune to someone. Even today, insurers still refer to "acts of God" when they exempt themselves from paying for a customer's losses. The problem with weather was that it could not be predicted. In a world without radio and few good roads, the weather outran the messenger. People were reduced to looking for omens in the sky (red sky in morning, sailors take warning; red sky at night, sailors' delight) or the arthritic pains that signaled falling pressure or increased humidity.

Weather prediction and an associated science, meteorology, awaited the new technologies of rail and telegraph and the new sciences of chemistry, thermodynamics, and fluid mechanics. The idea of prediction was old (compare the Book of Genesis story of Joseph's dreams of seven years of plenty followed by seven lean years), but prescient dreams aside, without a complex ingenious design, the idea could not have been realized.

One of the most important ideas, obvious only in hindsight, was that prognosticators would need some way consistently to compare weather events. In 1805 the British naval officer Francis Beaufort developed a scale of wind speed from zero to twelve, twelve representing a hurricane force wind in which "sea is completely white with foam and spray; considerable and widespread damage to vegetation." At about the same time, scientists began to develop cloud names. By observing the world around them, observers could be expected accurately to rate a wind. Instruments like thermometers of various scales, barometers, and hygrometers allowed observers to objectively assign numbers to weather observations, another important idea.

The final idea that shaped the key to prediction was to establish weather observation stations throughout a country—and eventually throughout the world. This happened in Great Britain, the United States, and France around the middle of the nineteenth century. In 1854 Admiral Robert Fitzroy (the same Fitzroy who captained the ship Beagle with Charles Darwin playing the role of naturalist) set up the UK Meteorological Office. Fitzroy insured that observations were regularly made at sea as well as on land. Using the telegraph, the weather service could draw weather maps of the entire country. By 1860 Fitzroy's office was publishing weather forecasts in *The Times*. Of course, the development of radio in the twentieth century allowed immediate transmission of observations made at sea, thus heightening the accuracy of forecasts.

Meteorology grew up alongside the development of the various sciences. The more chemistry developed, the more meteorologists could theorize about atmospheric composition. The more we understood the behavior of fluids, the more accurately meteorologists could analyze the movement of air and its interaction with the oceans. By the twentieth century, science could be used to make numeric weather predictions with some accuracy. The advent of computers, as we will see, allowed the use of massive amounts of data points to make accurate statistical predictions.

The development of meteorology and weather prediction not only had salubrious effects on commerce and agriculture, but it also challenged theologies. No longer could one say, "God only knows," when asked about future weather. Perhaps God knew, but so did we.

Biology and Medicine: The Machine Organism Reconsidered

The idea of the "clockwork universe" or the mechanical worldview was two centuries old by the middle of the nineteenth century. This worldview saw the universe not only as material but also as an organized mechanism: a machine, a special case of materialism. The idea of the machine-universe emphasized predictability and regularity, and had been expressed by Laplace in the aphorism: if there were an infinite mind that knew the position and velocity of every particle in the universe, that infinite mind would be able to calculate everything that had ever been and everything that would ever be. However, since human minds are not infinite, Laplace showed, we have to rely on statistics. Determinism can be a creed, but not a human accomplishment.

In biology, the metaphor of the human machine had early results. In the seventeenth century, the heart was seen as a pump and the motion of limbs could be analyzed using concepts of the lever. Nevertheless, the mechanical worldview foundered when analyzing reproduction. Anton van Leeuwenhoek identified sperm in 1677. How sperm might grow to produce a complex human being puzzled biologists. Mechanists could only imagine that inside each sperm resided a tiny fully formed human being. This "preformationist" view seemed absurd. Where did the previous generation come from? Did each tiny being living in a sperm include testes with even tinier sperm with minute human beings contained in them—getting tinier all the way back to Adam? The alternative, "epigenesis," was equally unsatisfactory. To epigeneticists, the material in the sperm somehow combined with as-yet-undiscovered material from a female, and out of this combination somehow human beings grew. The problem with epigenesis was that it relied on unknown processes. It seemed unscientific, a statement that "stuff happens." Of course, today epigenesis is much closer to the scientific view of reproduction arising from the actions of DNA than is preformation.

In the previous chapter, we saw that German Idealism rejected determinism in the human world. Human beings lived in an ethical world and were capable of making choices. In fact, even in the more general realm of biology, the study of life, it was hard to make a case for a mechanical system. It seemed that there was a special kind of force, a "vital force," that did not obey the laws of Newtonian physics. Romantic biology sought to look inward into the workings of the mind to see the laws of nature as experienced by humans. For instance, we experience polar opposites: male/female, positive/negative electricity, south/north magnetic poles. Polar opposites must be used to understand the world of life, the vital world. The mechanical worldview foundered on the problem of life.

But symbolically around the time of the death of Hegel in 1831, young biologists found that by using newly engineered microscopes that carefully combined different kinds of glass, they could eliminate the blurriness that seemed to inevitably accompany microscopic magnification. Both spherical and chromatic aberrations were greatly reduced. They could eschew the deductive biology of romantic science and meticulously record what they saw, carefully theorizing only on the basis of observation. Inductive biology was back in business.

Figure 4.4 Preformation (homunculus in sperm), 1694. Drawing from observation and imagination by Nicholas Hartsoeker in *Essai de Dioptrique*, 1694. An example of theory-driven observation—Hartsoeker showed what must be there if humans were preformed. © Wikimedia Commons (public domain).

Inductive science is much more akin to technological invention than it is to philosophy. Inventors get an idea, but then they try it out. No one can deduce how to make a machine, both because machines are too complex to anticipate how all the parts will work together and because there are many conceivable ways to accomplish whatever human purpose the invention is designed to accomplish. Both technology and science have a deductive and an inductive side, and the interplay of deduction and induction works variously in different cases.

By the end of the 1830s, the German microscopists Matthias Jakob Schleiden, professor of botany at the University of Jena, and Theodor Schwann, working as a laboratory assistant for the noted Johannes Mueller at the University of Berlin, formulated the theory that all life was composed of cells. Cells were seen as complete in themselves as living entities and also the building blocks of all more complex organisms. The theory of cells is an essential part of modern biology and modern medicine. Without cell theory, the biological and medical achievements of the later nineteenth century would have been insurmountable.

Schwann was seen by others of his generation as a first-rate experimenter, and he worked on the chemistry of living processes as well as microscopy. He isolated the digestive enzyme pepsin and showed that it could break foods into smaller units (peptones from albumin, for instance). Schwann claimed that such careful analysis, moving deeper and deeper into the smallest parts of the organism, would eventually be able to "explain the whole development of life." Although some of his older teachers thought his ideas might lead to a return to vitalism (because he emphasized life processes without showing they were mechanical), eventually his work became one of the foundations of a viable nonvitalistic view.

In the next few decades, a new biology was worked out that was neither mechanical nor vitalistic. The French scientist Claude Bernard (1813–78) described its principles in 1865 in his masterpiece of clear, nontechnical prose, *An Introduction to the Study of Experimental Medicine*.

Claude Bernard was born in a village in the Rhone Department and originally set out to be a playwright, at which he had moderate success. However, he turned to physiology and worked for the noted physiologist François Magendie. Both Bernard and Magendie were notorious for their vivisections, surgically experimenting on live, unsedated animals. Both of them defended the practice by citing the worth of the information they obtained in this way. Uninvolved objectivity was important to both as they strove for knowledge based on value-free observations. Bernard's wife divorced him over his acts of vivisection, and she and their daughters carried out a campaign against the practice. In fact, it is possible that the opposition of people who observed Magendie and Bernard's experiments furthered the anti-vivisection movement more than any rational arguments. Bernard made important discoveries in physiology, but perhaps his most notable achievement was describing and establishing the scientific method in physiology and medicine.

Bernard argued against vitalism because it pretended to be an explanation, and, in doing so, halted the process of experimental science. He also argued against mechanism because it was a system that did not allow itself to be examined experimentally. Systems, wrote Bernard, "are not found in nature, but only in the mind of man." His message was that experimental medicine is not a new system, but rather is the "negation of all systems."

Bernard argued against belief in any theory, since such beliefs hindered correct interpretation of clear observations. On the other hand, he noted that observations made with no idea behind them were unusable. They could only wait for someone to ask a question before they could be used. For Bernard, the idea preceded the observation, which was undertaken to test the idea. He told a story of how he had done an experiment and seen the effect he expected. But when he tried to repeat the experiment, he failed to see the effect. He thought hard about how the conditions might have changed from one experiment to the next, and eventually was able to repeat the experiment exactly as he had done it the first time, observing the first result.

From this experience, Bernard decided that no experiment could disprove an idea, because it is impossible to know if the idea would be correct if the conditions of the experiment were slightly altered. Science consisted neither in falsification nor in confirmation of ideas. The ideas were there in order to guide the experimental observations. The best that science could accomplish was to find the causal relationships among phenomena. But as science progressed, new phenomena were discovered and new relationships were established, so no theory was valid forever, no matter how well it was established. All theories must be continually exposed to "verification and criticism."

Bernard was opposed to the use of statistics in experimental medicine because while they showed some sort of relationship, they explained nothing. He called statistical medicine "conjectural medicine," because it compared roughly analogous cases without exploring the various conditions by which the cases may differ. If, says Bernard, we find that a certain medical procedure results in the death of a patient two out of five times, we should study each of the cases of death and survival to find out what the cause of the death really was. Saying that the procedure results in death 40 percent of the time tells us nothing useful. We shall see the same kinds of concerns about the use of statistics when we later examine physical theories.

The experimental mindset described and advocated by Bernard enabled other scientists to make significant medical advances. For instance, in 1854 John Snow was able to show the cause of cholera in London was waterborne, stimulating reform in the water supply and sewer systems of cities throughout Europe. Joseph Lister's 1867 book *Antiseptic Principle of the Practice of Surgery* described his experiments in sterilizing operating rooms and wounds to tremendously reduce the number of infections. Before Lister, surgeons reveled in the "surgical stink" of an unclean operating room and took the same pride in their bloodstained operating gowns as a football player today takes in a grass-stained uniform. In the 1840s, ether and chloroform were used successfully in operating rooms, and in 1853 their reliability had been well-enough established that Queen Victoria agreed to have John Snow anesthetize her for the birth of her eighth child.

By 1862 Louis Pasteur had shown that fermentation in wine only occurred when microorganisms were present and that he could stop fermentation by exposing a fermenting wine to heat, thus "pasteurizing" it. He ultimately became convinced that microorganisms caused disease. He experimented by injecting chickens with live cholera bacilli, infecting them, and then giving chickens heated bacilli, in which case they did not become infected. In 1879 Robert Koch described the correct series of procedure for establishing that a certain microorganism caused a certain disease.

This brief list of medical breakthroughs might help us see the power of experimental medicine and the striking effects medicine had on the public. To the layperson, it seemed science was explaining all. Imagine the difference of suffering from, say, a burst appendix in 1840, before antisepsis and anesthesia, and being able to have a relatively safe and comfortable appendectomy in 1870. Clearly, the idea of progress described what was happening in technology and medicine.

Understanding the Steam Engine: Thermodynamics

In the early nineteenth century, physicists were somewhat abashed to be unable to clearly explain the scientific theory behind the workings of a steam engine. Even as steam engines were transforming economic and social life in Great Britain, France, Belgium, Holland, and Germany, scientists were unable to clearly explain how they operated. The best idea lay in the metaphor "heat is a fluid substance" (known as caloric), an idea developed by the French scientist Sadi Carnot. The metaphor allowed physicists to use the science of water flow to understand how heat flow might cause a steam engine to work, much as a waterfall could cause a mill wheel to spin. Caloric could be said to flow from a high temperature to a lower temperature, just as water falls from a greater height to a lower height.

Nicolas Léonard Sadi Carnot (1796–1832) was known by his third name, given to him by his father in appreciation of the thirteenth-century Persian poet Sadi, whose poetic works used worldly images to attain spiritual insight. Sadi had been translated and widely distributed in Europe. Sadi Carnot's father was a leader of the French Revolution, and Carnot himself studied at the illustrious engineering school École Polytechnique and served in Napoleon's army. A committed republican (opponent of monarchy), Carnot found his career stifled after the fall of Napoleon and the restoration of the king. He eventually spent the rest of his short life working privately on scientific ideas. His 1824 book *Réflexions sur la puissance motrice du feu et sur les machines propres à développer cette puissance* (*Reflections on the Motive Power of Fire*) initiated a series of theories that resulted in what we today call thermodynamics.

Carnot's problem was to see if steam engines could be made more efficient, perhaps by using a substance other than steam. Carnot thought what made the steam engine go was caloric carried in the steam, not the steam itself. The steam was important only as a vehicle for caloric. As caloric fell from a higher to a lower temperature, no caloric was used up, just as no water is used up as a mill wheel is turned. Carnot was able to show that the power of the heat depends solely on the temperature difference, and not on the substance that carries the caloric. Thus, no caloric is lost in the process of steam engine operation.

In the eighteenth century, several people had tried to design a "perpetual motion machine" in which, for example, a water wheel turns a pump that pumps the water back up to the top so it can fall again, turning a pump that pumps it back, perpetually. No one had been able to achieve such a machine, and by the nineteenth century scientists accepted that perpetual motion was impossible. Although practically knowledgeable people stopped considering perpetual motion, no one knew quite why it was impossible. Why couldn't the ideal engine of Carnot send the caloric back to a higher temperature? The answer came from the following considerations.

As we saw in the previous chapter, the development of electricity and magnetism made possible other kinds of motion. After Faraday discovered how to create electricity from magnetism, he was able to invent an electric engine. By the 1830s, several scientists were examining the ways different motive forces could be used to create one another. The brewer James Joule found that as he stirred large vats with paddles driven by gradually falling weights, heat was produced. Gravitational force that made the weights fall seemed to be transformed into heat by the paddles. Electricity seemed to hold chemical molecules together and was also capable of breaking them apart.

In a striking case of simultaneous discovery, several scientists came up with the idea of the conservation of energy (although "energy" was called different things by each of them). In Germany, the young physician/physiologist/physicist Hermann Helmholtz wrote an 1847 paper "Über die Erhaltung der Kraft" ("On the Conservation of Force") in which he made the case that mechanical force of any kind (gravitational, bouncing springs waves), heat (including bodily heat), electromagnetism, and any other form of motion were equivalent forms of the same thing. They could be turned into one another without any "force" being lost (or created) in the process. He cited studies that showed that the amount of heat produced by an animal using food was the same as the amount of heat obtained in burning the food.

James Joule came up with similar ideas. For Joule, who was an ardent Christian, the interconvertibility of force suggested the providence of God who had created just enough force to allow all the processes of nature to work essentially forever. Only God could create or destroy matter or force. If force seemed to be lost, it was only because it had been converted into a different kind of force, like heat.

The Scot William Thomson (1824–1907) became Baron Kelvin of Largs in 1882, and he is today referred to mostly as Kelvin. Kelvin was an example of the excellent mathematicians who transformed British physics in the later part of the nineteenth century. Thomson's own father was a mathematics professor in Belfast, and Thomson won honors at Cambridge for his mathematical abilities. By the age of twenty-two, he was a professor at the University of Glasgow. As he and his colleagues transformed physics, Kelvin also became an inventor and consultant on industrial scientific projects. For instance, he played an important role in designing the transatlantic telegraph cable in the mid-1860s.

In the late 1840s, Thomson began to study the work of Carnot and Joule in order to develop a mathematical treatment of heat. Eventually he decided that heat could not be a material substance and that it probably was something else: energy. From 1851 to 1855, he summarized his findings in "On the Dynamical Theory of Heat." Nature provided two laws. The first, the law of conservation of energy, stated that energy (whatever it was) could not be created or destroyed. The second said that most engines could not be the perfect engine studied by Carnot, and that heat would be dissipated through processes like friction. There was, said Kelvin, an absolute loss of energy that was available for human use. This second law, the maximization of entropy, said that although energy was not destroyed in a machine, the remaining energy was unavailable for further work.

Kelvin quickly saw that the second law provided a way to conceive of time. The second law implied that all physical processes happened in one direction. Entropy always increased, never decreased. Up until the enunciation of the law of maximization of entropy, all physical theories described reversible processes. Newton's laws could describe processes that in principle could go backward. For instance, if two billiard balls collided, one could imagine them going in the other direction: leaving their ending positions, colliding in the reverse direction, and ending up where they had started. But if one added the second law of thermodynamics, heat would be dissipated in the collision, and there would not be enough energy to send them back exactly on the original path.

One can make a film of an egg breaking and run it backward to see the shattered egg come back together, but that can never happen in nature. One way of thinking of time, then, was to think of it as a result of the second law of thermodynamics. Time was the direction all physical processes had to go in: the direction of increasing entropy.

A further implication was that the universe itself would ultimately run down, as entropy was maximized everywhere. Would the world end finally in a "heat death" as energy was unavailable for human use and we all froze to death? Scientists were widely quoted in the popular press as the possibilities inherent in the second law fueled apocalyptic speculations.

Mathematics was an important ingredient in Kelvin's treatment of thermodynamic theory. In fact, several developments in theoretical mathematics in the nineteenth century made algebra and calculus much more powerful. One advance involved finding new ways to describe motions that occurred in a periodic pattern, repeating themselves after an interval of time: like waves. A problem faced by physicists was that the numbers used to describe motions included directions as well as the three numbers used to describe a three-dimensional space. A number with a direction is called a vector. Handling vectors was tricky, but in 1843 the Irish mathematician/physicist William Rowan Hamilton (1805–65) had a breakthrough. He realized that he could use complex numbers (a number that has both a real part and an imaginary part) to describe vectors and that if he imagined these complex numbers in four dimensions rather than three dimensions, he could work out a system for combining vectors. His system, called quaternions, enabled physicists to treat complex flows of particles, including swirls and eddies.

Kelvin teamed with his Scottish colleague Peter Tait (1831–1901) to establish all physics on the mathematics of thermodynamics. The beauty of using energy as the basic concept was that one could reach mathematical deductions without knowing exactly what the physics of a system were. The laws of thermodynamics worked whether a physical system was made up of discrete molecules or continuous sheets. A physicist didn't have to know exactly what was in the steam in order to work out the dynamics of a steam engine.

Another approach to understanding the laws of thermodynamics was found in the field of statistics applied to the kinetic theory of gas. We have already seen Claude Bernard's suspicion of statistical analysis in medicine and allied sciences. Physicists were equally leery. However, Adolphe Quetelet (1796–1874), a Belgian astronomer who turned to the study of society, successfully showed statistical correlations and distributions having to do with criminality and human physical characteristics, among other subjects. In his 1835 *Treatise on Man*, Quetelet announced a new science, social physics, and, in order to do so, used old and new statistical techniques to unravel the complexities inherent in the study of millions of individuals. Other social scientists, like August Comte (see next chapter) opposed Quetelet's approach. Nevertheless, Quetelet's data were too useful to be ignored.

James Clerk Maxwell explicitly cited Quetelet's work as he developed his own analysis of gases as collections of vast numbers of molecules. Quetelet had noted that statistics were only useful when dealing with very large numbers, thus implicitly confirming Bernard's reservations. But Maxwell realized that the number of molecules in a gas met the criterion of large numbers. The work of Maxwell, and the later work of Ludwig

Boltzmann, showed that thermodynamic results could be understood as statistical averages of huge numbers of molecules. For instance, heat could be understood as the energy of molecules, and even though some molecules went faster and some slower, the average speed represented the total amount of energy (heat) in the system.

Entropy could be understood as the total amount of disorganization in the system. A system in which all the fast molecules were on the left side of the container while all the slow molecules were on the right, would be a highly organized system. It would also be highly unlikely. If the molecules were allowed to mix, they would soon be equally distributed in the container. Thus, the amount of order had decreased, while the amount of disorder increased. Imagine, for instance, turning on your kitchen oven. Inside the oven, the air molecules would be very hot, meaning moving very fast. Outside the oven, the slower molecules would dominate. But if you turned off the oven and opened the door, in an hour the temperature in the room would be the same all over the kitchen. This is the most likely distribution of energy. Entropy would have increased to a maximum.

But if the second law of thermodynamics, the maximization of entropy, was only based on statistics, then perhaps it was not a true law of nature. After all, it is highly unlikely that all the molecules in a room would cluster in a corner, but it is not impossible. Perhaps once in trillions of years, such an event could happen. In this case, if entropy represented time's arrow, time would have gone backward.

A school of philosophy of science, phenomenology, was dominated by Ernst Mach (1838–1916). Mach was clear that the task of physics was to use mathematics to describe phenomena, that is, events as they appear in our minds (see the discussion of Kant in Chapter 1). The phenomenological school was opposed to any attempt to make statements about what the world really was when it was not being known (Kant had noted that the noumenal world is unknowable). Atomic theory, or molecular theory, made statements about that which could not be observed—so the phenomenological school saw atomic-molecular theories as unscientific. The phenomenologists dominated physics as the nineteenth century drew to a close, and it seemed that molecular theories were doomed to go the way of many old, discarded physical concepts, like caloric. The German physicist Ludwig Boltzmann despaired that his life work would be rendered meaningless.

The case has been made that starting with thermodynamics mathematical physics slowly became a discipline. Physicists still imagined some structure to matter as they worked out their physical theories, and they believed that ultimately the true structure of the material universe would be found, but they were willing to use models of material structure that were probably not exact in order to derive accurate mathematical treatments. An example is the theory of electromagnetism worked out by the great Scottish physicist James Clerk Maxwell in the 1860s.

Maxwell and Electromagnetism

James Clerk Maxwell (1831–79) was born in Edinburgh and was educated at Cambridge where he came in second in the mathematical tripos competition. At Cambridge,

Maxwell strengthened his Christian faith as he devoted himself to a rigorous intellectual examination of all parts of it. He eventually rejected everything about Christianity except for the idea that God became human and is at work through the Holy Spirit. Soon after, in 1856, he was appointed professor of Natural Philosophy at Marischal College in Aberdeen, Scotland, fifteen years younger than any other professors. In 1858 he married Katherine, the daughter of the principal of Marischal. In 1860 he moved to Kings College, London. In 1865 Maxwell resigned to move to his home in Glenlair, but he returned to academia when, in 1879 Cambridge asked him to become the Cavendish professor of physics and to develop the Cavendish Laboratory. He died at age forty-eight of abdominal cancer. His mother had died of the same disease at the same age.

Maxwell wanted to mathematize Faraday's idea that there was no empty space, but that all space was filled with lines of force. To do this, he wanted to use Hamilton's quaternions to describe the way the lines of force worked, and he wanted to utilize Kelvin's concept of energy as the power underlying all physical phenomena. He gathered together all the work that had been done in the fields of electricity and magnetism and summarized them with twenty differential equations (later simplified to four equations). He could combine these equations in different ways to get a fuller picture of electromagnetism. The picture of a space filled with lines of force, with no empty space in between, is often called a "field" picture. An electric field is conceptually quite different from an electric force. An electric particle with an electric force works in a straight line across empty space to attract or repel another particle. An electric particle in a field changes the shape of the field as the particle moves and the other particle reacts to the changes in the field. Maxwell imagined that magnetism consisted of long rotating tubes and that electricity consisted of particles between the tubes. If the electric particles moved, they started the magnetic tubes rolling. If the tubes began rotating, they started the electric particles moving. Thus, an electric current could cause changes in the magnetic field and a moving magnet could initiate an electric current. Although Maxwell explicitly denied that he thought the actual shape of space had this form, he did believe there had to be something in space that could support light waves: ether. He just did not know what the structure of ether was. Of course, the beauty of the new mathematical physics based on energy was that one did not have to know what the physical world was to make predictions about it. Physicists became more and more comfortable with ad hoc pictures of matter, pictures that were helpful in finding the right equations, but that did not have to conform to what was really there.

Maxwell solved his equations and found that a moving electric charge or moving magnet would cause undulations in the electromagnetic field. These undulations, or waves, moved at the speed of light. He therefore concluded that light was an electromagnetic wave. In one stroke, he had unified the fields of optics and of electromagnetism.

Other physicists did not know quite what to make of Maxwell's system. The German Heinrich Hertz (1857–94) studied in Berlin under Hermann Helmholtz. Helmholtz suggested that his pupil write a doctoral dissertation on testing Maxwell's theory with an experiment. Hertz couldn't figure out how to devise such an experiment, but a few years later it came to him. He set up a metal ring with a small gap across which

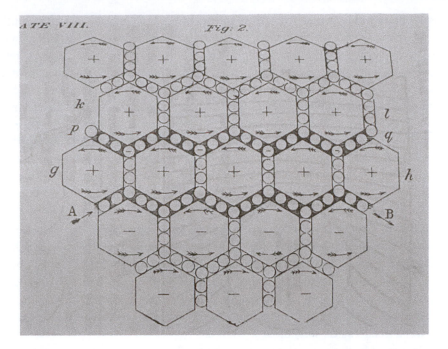

Figure 4.5 Diagram of Maxwell's lines of force. Drawing by James Clerk Maxwell. It is a cross section of an aether in which tubes of magnetic force and little electronically charged balls rotate together. The tubes rotate in the opposite direction from the balls, and thus all tubes rotate in the same direction. Maxwell used this model to derive his equations. He made no claims that the model had physical significance. © Photograph by David Galaty.

he could make sparks jump. On the other side of his laboratory, he set up a similar ring that was not connected to an electric source. When he set sparks oscillating rapidly back and forth across the gap, sparks began to jump in the apparatus on the other side of the lab. He had found electromagnetic waves moving at frequencies well below the frequency of light waves. Maxwell's theory predicted not only the existence of light waves but also the existence of a wide spectrum of waves at any imaginable frequency.

This idea was astounding, although it took a few years for anyone to realize just how astounding. As long as humans had existed, they had been surrounded with a light they could not see. No one suspected such a possibility. The power of Maxwell's theory was that it predicted waves no one had anticipated.

Hertz saw no utility in this discovery other than its demonstration that Maxwell was right. But in Italy young Guglielmo Marconi (1874–1937) saw a new industry in his imagination. Marconi was born into the Italian nobility of an Irish/Scot mother, and she educated him at home. Part of his early childhood was spent in England, so he spoke English and Italian fluently. The wealthy Marconi had the best tutors, and at age eighteen he began attending university lectures. One of his tutors had studied with Hertz in Germany, and Marconi soon learned about Hertz's experiment. Marconi began to conduct his own Hertzian experiments in his attic with the help of his butler. Several other scientists were conducting experiments on these new waves, and Marconi followed their experiments avidly. Eventually Marconi was able to invent a basic wireless telegraph. It could send the electricity from a telegraph key, and these messages could be received as the waves activated another telegraph key. When Marconi raised the height of his antennas and grounded his equipment, he was able to send signals much farther. By 1895 he had reached 2 miles and could see his way to more improvement. As he discussed his work in Italy, Marconi could find little interest and no funding offers. When Marconi was twenty-one, he and his mother went to England to demonstrate his apparatus. He showed that he could send radio signals over water, and in 1896 Marconi sent a message across the English Channel. Support began to gather. By 1902 Marconi had sent a transatlantic message.

The story of the wireless telegraph, the wireless telephone, and the radio belong properly to the twentieth century. But the nineteenth-century part of the story shows just how powerful mathematical science and its wedding with technology was. Physics had predicted unsuspected phenomena and these phenomena had been harnessed technologically ultimately to change the structure of human society. Inventors were becoming heroes, and by the end of the century few doubted that to most problems there was a technological solution.

Chemical Atoms

Although today chemistry and physics seem like allied sciences, in the nineteenth century they largely developed around different problems. For instance, by 1850 most chemists were quite comfortable with the notion that chemicals were made up of molecules (i.e., combinations of atoms), but physicists could still debate whether matter was molecular or not. A way of understanding this difference is to say that a chemical molecule was different from a physical molecule. As we saw in Chapter 2, the evidence that the substances studied by chemists were molecular lay in the laws of combination. For instance, combining two parts of hydrogen with one part of oxygen produced water. More than two parts of hydrogen rendered water plus hydrogen, and not just water. It was hard to see why substances would combine in definite proportions in which the proportions were almost always small whole numbers, if the substances were not atomic. But if one oxygen atom always united with two hydrogen atoms, and if there were an equal number of atoms of any substance in equal volumes of a gas, then the numbers all made sense.

To a chemist, all compounds consisted of atoms of different elements stuck together. A chemical element was a single atom that could not be dissociated—no matter what one did to it. A compound was a combination of atoms that could be sundered by a variety of means, including electricity. Since chemists were convinced that in gases the number of atoms of any element equaled the number of atoms of any other element, it was easy to find the relative weights of elements. Just weigh equal volumes of a gas of each element and divide one by the other. Since hydrogen is the lightest element, the weight of each atom could be expressed as a multiple of the weight of hydrogen. This idea is much more complex than expressed here, in part because many elements exist in a molecular form of two atoms forming the elementary unit. Nevertheless, as the second half of the century wore on, the problem of atomic weights began to be worked out, and new elements were discovered almost yearly.

The question for chemists was how to classify the atoms in ways that grouped them according to their chemical properties. The answer was found by the Russian Dmitri Mendeleev (1834–1907). Mendeleev was born in Siberia, but after a series of family financial mishaps, his mother brought him to St. Petersburg, where Mendeleev was able to go to college. In 1855 Mendeleev moved to the healthier Black Sea area because he was diagnosed with tuberculosis, but by 1857 his health was restored, and he moved back to St. Petersburg, where he built an up-to-date chemistry research laboratory at the University of St. Petersburg. In 1867 Mendeleev set about writing a chemistry textbook, and as he was organizing the material on each element, his main idea struck. He later wrote that it came to him in a dream that he immediately recorded upon awakening. He noticed that when he organized the elements according to their atomic weight, similar chemical characteristics occurred periodically as the weights increased. He arranged the elements by weight in rows and by similarity of property in columns. So, for instance, alkali metal elements all went in one column, elements that combined with oxygen in a 2:1 ratio went in another column, and so forth. Today we know Mendeleev's organization as the Periodic Table of the Elements.

The power of Mendeleev's arrangement was that he could see gaps in his table. He could therefore predict that an element of a certain weight with certain characteristics had yet to be discovered. When these predictions began to prove true in the coming years, Mendeleev's system gained a great deal of credence. No one knew why the chemical elements had such an arrangement; it would take the quantum mechanical theory of the atom to establish a plausible explanation. But the Mendeleev periodic of the elements did work to chemists' satisfaction.

The Nature of Science at the End of the Century

Successful prediction of previously unobserved phenomena is scientific gold. Mendeleev had hit the mother lode. The issue of whether or not a scientific concept can ever be verified or falsified will come up several times in this book. Claude Bernard had little use for either process, for instance—but Bernard did think that connections among phenomena could be established whether or not the overarching theory continued to work when later connections were established.

In physics, scientists wrestled with the same issues. Maxwell's theory worked, even if no one knew what either matter or the ether was. When Kelvin complained that he could not imagine a reasonable model that worked as Maxwell's theory demanded, Hertz responded: Maxwell's theory is Maxwell's equations. Mathematics could exist as a fundamental bedrock in science, even if no one knew what the mathematical equations were describing. This is a relatively new idea in science. Galileo had thought that God designed the world using the language of mathematics, but he did not think that the physical world was only mathematics. Of course, none of the scientists discussed so far thought that either, but they were frank in their inability to define the physical world in any other terms.

Clearly, if space were full of ether, Newtonian models of hard chunks of matter possessing forces (like gravity or electricity) and reaching with those forces across empty space was not tenable. What could matter be? Some thought it might consist of "knots" in the ether. Perhaps it was a vortex (whirlpool) in the ether. In 1858 Helmholtz worked out the theory of vortices in theoretical ideal fluids (fluids without frictional forces) and found that such vortices would never wear down. Perhaps that was what matter was. Other scientists used smoke rings to obtain a visual idea of how collisions of vortices might work. Another idea was that matter was an electrical effect. No physicist was quite sure.

Conclusion: Ada Lovelace's Futuristic Idea

In 1833 Mary Somerville introduced her student Ada Byron to Charles Babbage. Ada Byron was Lord Byron's (see Chapter 3) only legitimate child, but her father abandoned her and her mother when Ada was one month old. Her mother, nicknamed Annabelle, was understandably bitter, but she realized, as Byron's mistress Caroline Lamb unforgettably described him, that Byron was "mad, bad, and dangerous to know." Afraid that her daughter would be susceptible to Byron's madness, Annabelle made sure that her daughter was steered in a mathematical direction and away from Byron's proclivities. Ada never saw the family portrait of her father until she was twenty. Nevertheless, Ada, like her father, was attracted to a variety of sexual partners, perhaps beginning with one of her tutors with whom she had an affair as a teenager.

Given her position in society, Ada had the chance to meet the top mathematicians and scientists of Great Britain, which is why she found herself being tutored and befriended by the great Mary Somerville. Charles Babbage was the multitalented Lucasian professor of mathematics at Cambridge. Today he is best noted for having invented one of the earliest computers, his so-called difference engine and later his "analytic engine." His engines were to be mechanical and steam-powered, although for funding reasons he never was able to complete one. In an age before electricity, his computers would have been slow and clunky in comparison with those of the later twentieth century, but they would have streamlined calculations for an industrial age that increasingly needed numbers correct to several decimal places. One of the many subjects Babbage tackled was efficiency in factories. He realized that giving routine tasks to the less trained workers and assigning highly trained workers jobs that fit their skills could increase profits. One day he was looking at a table of logarithms and realized that these could all be calculated by repeated addition and subtraction. He had the idea that a machine could be invented to carry out these routine arithmetic tasks and that the machine would never make the errors to which human beings were prone. Thus, the idea for the difference engine was born.

Figure 4.6 Ada Lovelace, 1840. © Science & Society Picture Library/Getty Images.

Ada Byron was soon to marry and become a countess, thus changing her name to Lady Lovelace. We know her today as Lady Ada Lovelace. When Ada Lovelace saw Babbage's ideas, she was excited by the possibilities. She began to visit Babbage as often as possible. Although Babbage's first design, the difference engine, was a calculator, his analytic engine was a computer, with a memory, a processing unit, an input system (punched cards), and an output mechanism (printing). Lovelace quickly saw the possibilities. She may have written the first program, a way to calculate Bernoulli numbers (a special kind of mathematical number). Babbage was, of course, also exploring programming possibilities.

What Lovelace seems to have seen that no one, including Babbage, had seen, was that the engine could possibly explore relationships other than numbers, as long as those relationships could be expressed in a logical sequence. For instance, she wrote that the relationships among musical notes could be so expressed, and the engine could then compose pieces of music. Her insight was that numbers could represent things other than numbers. Even Babbage had not written of that possibility. But Lovelace also argued that the analytic engine could not have an original thought. It could only do the tasks for which it was programmed.

Figure 4.7 The remains of Babbage's difference engine. Oxford Science Museum © Photograph by David Galaty.

The analytical engine went nowhere, and computing had to wait for the twentieth century and electronics. Ada Lovelace herself died of uterine cancer at age thirty-six, leaving three children. Babbage had a long, illustrious career in which he made a contribution to several fields of inquiry, including economics. But Babbage and Lovelace captured the spirit of their age to see far into the future. The future belonged to technology and science, and human thought would have to adjust to include them.

CHAPTER 5
SOCIALISMS AND MARXISM

Figure 5.1 Women and children coal putters, 1848. This is an accurate depiction of the hard life in the mines. © Print Collector/Hulton Archive/Getty Images.

The Woman Who Worked Beside Marx

On June 25, 1867, Harriet Law (1831–97) joined the General Council of the International Workingmen's Association (IWA), also known as the First International, an organization that had five to eight million members at its peak. Although founded in 1864 to represent all workers, not until a year later did members vote to include women, and not until 1867 did the first and only woman, Harriet Law, begin to attend meetings. Law remained on the Council until it broke apart in 1872.

The anomalous lack of women in the main international workers' association in the later nineteenth century highlights the different ideas that both women and men struggled with as they tried to come to terms with the effects of the Industrial Revolution on the lower classes. Karl Marx, who eventually designed the structure of the IWA, recognized the need for women's participation in the labor movement and welcomed Law when she joined the Council. But other women did not follow. Women interested in gaining more rights for women were more likely to form their own associations than to join those dominated by men. Women who saw themselves primarily as workers were more likely to offer support to their male coworkers than to formulate a feminist agenda as a prerequisite to their participation. Men tended to agree that the onus for obtaining workers' rights fell on them, but they welcomed the support of women. And then there was the class issue. Leaders of women's movements tended to be middle-class, educated women. They had little interest in ceding leadership to poor and undereducated women.

The lower-class Law was born on a farm and brought up in a religious Baptist household. She actively proselytized until she lost her faith. She replaced that faith with belief in atheism, women's rights, and the cooperative approaches promoted by Robert Owen (see Owenism). She married Edward Law in 1855, and eventually had four children with him.

In 1859 she became a paid lecturer for the Secular, or Freethought, movement, which was composed mostly of workers. The society included some workingwomen in part because many of its members condemned treating women as commodities, and, instead of marriage (just another form of prostitution, they said), advocated joining women and men together in free love unions. These radical women further argued for collective childcare and housework, enabling women to have a full, public life. Although not all members were so radical, the Secular movement provided a home for ideas of all sorts.

Law's speeches often took place in the back rooms of pubs, and the audiences were often small. Sometimes she drew a crowd at a street corner. But sometimes she had a chance to speak to large crowds. Middle-class and Christian women's organizations refused to associate with the lower-class atheist that Law had become. She was physically attacked more than once. One of her lectures, "How I became a freethinker and why I remain one," became known as "the infidel lecture."[1] But her reputation grew, and in 1876 the Lancashire Secular Society hired her to give ten lectures, each of which was attended by 5,000 people.

So, when Law agreed to join the Council of the IWA, she did so as a woman who was shunned by many other women as a lower-class atheist and radical. As a board member of the First International, she advocated giving financial aid to striking women, most notably the silk workers of Lyon, France. During the meeting in which the French female silk workers were accepted into the IWA, Law pulled out her purse and made a donation there and then. Although many of the international's members opposed the use of machinery in factories, in order to save jobs for workers, Law argued that machinery equaled the playing field and reduced the dependence of women on men. Karl Marx had been her first supporter and had written the letter offering her a position on the board, but when he opposed turning the IWA into a "debating club," Law, the debater, argued against him.

She reserved one of her longest speeches at the board meetings for the discussion of education. Law advocated secularizing the property of the Church of England, or any other Established Church, and using it to build and support schools. She asked for fewer parsons and more schoolmasters. For Law, education should include everything that would improve a human being. She noted that if children had been taught what their labor was worth, they would not work so many hours.

When the First International splintered, Law pursued her advocacy role by buying the magazine, *Secular Chronicle*, in 1876. She lost £1,000 before she sold it in 1879. At that point, she retired from public life, only occasionally venturing out to speak. She died of a heart attack in 1897.

Chapter Map

The collectivism described in Chapter 3 was a collectivism of elites. As a new social class, factory workers, grew larger, it found no support from either elite individualists or elite collectivists. The forest-clearing operation that was the Industrial Revolution had unwittingly brought an invasive species, the proletariat, along with it. Socialism and Communism began to grow roots that grafted onto collective ideals but fed on the economic doctrines of classical economics.

In Chapter 5, we begin with several ideas about how to organize a humane society. Robert Owen, Charles Fourier, Henri de Saint-Simon, Auguste Comte, and Pierre-Joseph Proudhon all had ideas about the necessary steps. Meanwhile, developments in the arts and in technology focused public attention on the plight of the working poor. The radical ideas of Karl Marx and Friedrich Engels took shape as Europe exploded into unsuccessful revolution. Marx and Engels wanted to end capitalism in order to found society on a dictatorship of the proletariat. Eventually, representatives of the working classes founded a socialist movement with a governing body.

In this chapter then, we see several socialist ideas that grapple to redefine human needs and the consequent restructuring of society. The focus is on groupings: capitalists and workers, not on the heroic acts of individuals.

Owenism

The first person not only to think about the problem of the workers but also to begin to act on a solution was the Welsh industrialist Robert Owen (1781–1858). In the light of the past 200 years of socialist experience, it seems somewhat ironic that Owen's theories remained rooted in a capitalist system. For Owen, taking care of workers was good trade. Not taking care of workers was akin to refusing to oil your new Watt engine. One could continue to buy new engines or to hire new workers, but as the old ones broke down, production would become more costly. So, Owen developed a factory management system based on humanitarian principles combined with good business practices. Later in his life, his humanitarian ideas began to dominate, but his early experiments were clearly mostly derived from good management practice.

Owen was born in Newtown, Wales, in 1771, so he very likely was bilingual in Welsh and English. His father was a saddler, a postmaster, and a churchwarden, and his mother was a farmer. Robert was chosen to be an aid to his teacher in elementary school and seemed to have a knack for leadership. The Newtown school was built on the latest educational theory in which the best students in the upper grades taught the younger children in rote learning. By the age of ten, Owen left Newtown for Stamford and was apprenticed to a cloth merchant.

He spent his early teen years in the cloth business, learning all sides of the business. By his late teens, he had moved to Manchester and began to find investment partners, first selling spinning machinery and then actually spinning yarn. By the age of twenty-one, the precocious Owen was the manager of a large mill that used a Boulton and Watt engine. He was the overseer of 500 workers and was paid a large middle-class salary. He soon moved to a larger mill with wider customer and investor connections. Owen had become one of the industrial elites of Manchester.

An autodidact, Owen joined the Manchester Literary and Philosophical Society and the Board of Health where members gave papers and led discussions on a wide variety of topics of interest to educated men in general and those in the cloth trade in particular. Among its members was the chemist and meteorologist John Dalton. Newly exposed to Enlightenment ideas, Owen developed ideas about social reform.

As a manager of a mill, Owen quickly realized that one of his primary problems was that workers did not possess the values necessary to do good work. Workers tended to be drawn from the bottom of society, and many of them came to work drunk or avoided showing up altogether. They felt no inner drive to do a good job, so their work was often shoddy. The common management practice at the time was beating, withholding wages, or some other form of punishment. Most people thought that one was responsible for one's character, so bad behavior was the fault of individuals.

Owen, however, had become convinced that environments form people. Workers acted badly because they had been trained to do so. For instance, they may have grown up in circumstances that trained them to be lazy, to steal whenever possible, or to drink in order to ease their psychic pains. They were no more responsible for their behavior than was a stone responsible for falling. For Owen, there were laws of society (some known, others yet to be even suspected) that were as binding on human beings as were the laws of physics. Owen therefore began to manage his mill consonant with these insights. He rewarded good behavior and did everything he could to extinguish undesirable behavior.

Part of Owen's job was visiting with customers, and so he found his way to the mill in New Lanark, Scotland, owned by Peter Dale. Dale had been attracted to the location by the possibility of using the powerful and picturesque Falls of Clyde as a source of power. Unfortunately, the area near the falls was not easily accessed. The people who lived in the neighborhood were farmers uninterested in the dull, debilitating work of the factory system, so Dale had to build a village and find people willing to move there. Getting the New Lanarck mill going involved major capital expense. And Dale had a hard time finding people who wanted to relocate to a home far from anything they knew. As a result, according to Owen, those that came were particularly ill suited to the disciplined life of a factory worker. Dale ended up recruiting children from orphanages, and by the time Owen got there, half of New Lanark's 2,000 inhabitants were children or teenagers. To Owen's experienced eye, the new mill gave a manager the chance to create an environment that could produce a higher sort of worker.

On one of his visits to Scotland, Owen fell in love with Dale's daughter Caroline, and when he was twenty-eight, he married her. An aging Dale was eager to begin to shed some of his responsibilities. In 1799 Owen arranged for his Manchester plant to buy Caroline's father's mill in New Lanark, Scotland, and became the manager. He hoped to use the managerial experience he had gained in Manchester in order to create a humane workplace for his 2,000 employees, 500 of which were children. He was convinced that if he built a humane environment, he could ensure an absence of vice in his workers.

The first step for Owen was to build a playground for preschool-age children. He noted that basic habits are formed early in life, and he hoped that supervised play would instill

Figure 5.2 Overview of town of New Lanark with Robert Owen's model factory. © Getty Images.

cooperative and respectful habits. For instance, on entering the playground children were told to remember not to harm others but to help them. Eventually Owen built a school that was operated on cooperative theories he himself experienced as a child. The older children helped monitor and teach the younger ones. Children thus experienced sharing environments and would develop characters conducive to performing well in social settings. By the time his educational system fully matured, Owen had decided not to employ children under the age of ten in his mill. Younger children were to attend school. He also stopped recruiting children who had been brought up in unfavorable environments—like orphanages. He had found their characters too fixed to be easily changed.

He also planned to build a storehouse for food, a large kitchen, and a dining hall where nutritious food could be prepared and shared at a cost that was lower than individual families could afford. He began to develop cooperative ideas in which all the inhabitants of his industrial village would share in the profits. By the end of his life, he had become one of the inventors of the cooperative movement.

As a rich man, Owen had the wherewithal to promote his ideas widely. Between 1812 and 1814, Owen composed a set of essays in which he laid out the theories and practices of the New Lanark mill. He was an interested participant in discussions among intellectuals in Glasgow and London. James Mill convinced Jeremy Bentham to become an investor in New Lanark, and Owen began to use the language of utilitarianism (see Chapter 2), emphasizing the greatest happiness for the greatest number. Owen befriended William Godwin and frequently visited with his new friend. It is unclear whether Owen ever read

Godwin, but he certainly began to use the Englishman's ideas. Eventually Owen began to think about reforming all of Great Britain.

For Owen, it made little sense to employ young children in millwork before they had a basic education. He thought there should be a system of required basic education at the national level. All workers should have access to education, and such a system would pay back manyfold as educated workers were able to produce more efficiently than uneducated children. Similarly, Owen wrote that full employment in all of England made a great deal of sense. Instead of having roving families moving from place to place looking for work, it would be better for the government to give them public works employment during economic downturns. As long as public salaries were lower than private ones, people would readily move back to the private sector when the economy boomed and employees were needed. Meanwhile, by improving roads, building bridges, and maintaining canals, the laborers would be engaged in infrastructure rebuilding and thereby strengthening England's ability to support a strong economy.

Owen appealed to the elite of England. His ideas were couched in the language of economic good rather than humane treatment. As a result, he often failed to connect with social reformers, people who should have been his natural allies. They saw too much self-promotion, too much appealing to the wealthy owners of British society. The wealthy, on the other hand, often saw Owen as a pie-in-the-sky dreamer who promoted costly ideas without showing how they would increase profits. But the New Lanark mills brought in visitors galore who were also attracted to the spectacular Falls of Clyde. The whole region became interesting to tourists. But when they got to the mills, they were not invited to see everything. There were proprietary secrets that were not for the public to see. As Owen displayed his successes, some were left wondering what failures they were not allowed to witness.

Eventually Owen put the mills in the hands of his sons and partners and set off for America, where he hoped to be able to implement his ideas in a pristine social setting. He invested in the community of New Harmony, Indiana, where he hoped to build a new community where nothing had existed. New Harmony attracted a wide variety of people, all of whom had different ideas of what they wanted. Owen hoped to set up a cooperative structure in which all would participate. The experiment lasted two years and was never economically successful. Owen soon departed, leaving the community in the hands of one of his sons. The consensus among those who were there and who commented seemed to be that a parasitic part of the community hoped to profit from the work of others, thus dooming the enterprise. Nevertheless, the community continued to exist, and it stimulated several emulators in other states. The cooperative movement evolved from Owen's ideas, and still exists in one form or another today.

Fourierism

Imagine the best dinner party you have ever attended. People laughed, drank, flirted, made excellent conversation, and delighted in one another's different points of view. The food was excellent, and the company more so. That was Charles Fourier's (1772–1837) metaphor for the best possible society. For Fourier, life should be lived with passion in the company of other passionate people. Individuals needed the company of others in order to flourish, but the company could only flourish if all participants were free to express their own individualities.

Fourier's father was engaged in small business, and upon his death in 1781 Charles received a small fortune that eventually enabled him to travel widely. As he settled down, he worked for a salary and was appalled at what such work did to him. He found himself violating his own principles at the behest of his employer. Eventually he quit to become a writer, and his first book, *Theory of the Four Movements*, an initial failure, was published in 1808. He continued writing and tried again to publish *The New World of Love*, in 1822. No one was interested. But after his death in 1837, his books were brought out again with great success. Communities all over France and the United States attempted to form according to his principles.

According to Fourier, each person has different passions and abilities. The key to a thriving community and individual happiness was to find ways that all people could pursue their passions and exercise their abilities in concert with others of different passions and abilities. Since people have limited attention spans, after a few hours the groups would reform around different tasks. No one would try to coerce others to behave in ways other than their personalities desired.

Fourier believed that there were 810 distinct personality types, so work would be organized in phalanxes that included two of each, for a total of 1,620 people per phalanx. Each phalanx would live in a grand four-story hotel (remember there were as yet no elevators, so four floors was about the maximum height possible). Not everyone would be paid the same amount, but all would receive more than the minimum wage needed to lead a decent life. No one would be exempt from work except for those who were unable to work for some good reason. Even those unable to work would receive enough to lead a good life. Fourier believed that poverty, not inequality, was the source of disorder. Fourier advocated the equal treatment of women and men, and he seems to have been the first to use the term "feminism" in 1822. He believed all women should be able to work at any task, depending on ability and interest.

Fourier was concerned that any passions should not be bottled up, including sexual passions. Therefore, some people would tend to the sexual needs of those who for whatever reason had difficulty. People would be able to consult a card index of personality types in order to find partners suitable for recreational liaisons. Homosexuality was a preference of some, and Fourier approved. In fact, Fourier thought that people in general were androgynous and that their preferences may change over the course of a lifetime. He opposed marriage as an institution that oppressed women, although monogamous lifetime liaisons would be the choice of many.

Since he was trying to achieve the liberation of all, he thought education was very important, and he wrote about how to help learning take place from early ages on up. He thought children should be encouraged to pursue their natural curiosity according to their age. He recognized that imitation was important, as was a kind of natural social hierarchy in which the weak were attracted to the strong.

Fourier was one of those thinkers who was pejoratively classified as a "utopian socialist" by those who thought of themselves as "scientific socialists" (like Marx and Engels). The term has stuck.

Saint-Simonism

Henri de Saint-Simon (1760–1825) was a social theorist who developed unusual ideas about the classes of industrial society. He was also the initial mentor of Auguste Comte, one of the founders of sociology, who we will discuss in the next section. Saint-Simon was formally named Claude Henri de Rouvroy, Comte de Saint-Simon, and as a young man he fought under George Washington in the American Revolutionary War. Convinced that democracy was the future, he quickly endorsed the ideological goals of the French Revolution and set out to make a lot of money through land speculation in order to found a scientific school of improvement. He and the notorious Charles Talleyrand (a former Catholic Bishop) tried to capitalize on the anti-church sentiments prominent during the Terror and decided to buy Notre Dame in order to sell the metal in the roof for scrap. He went to prison on suspicion of "counter-revolutionary activities," but he was released in 1794 at the end of the Terror. He made a killing as the franc depreciated. Unfortunately, he ran through his funds quickly, so Saint-Simon found himself poor. Eventually he decided to devote his life to study and research. For the rest of his life, he mostly depended on friends and family for financial support.

Saint-Simon saw that the world would soon shift from an agriculture/warrior world into a scientific and industrial society. He believed that science would produce answers to most of the world's problems, and he advocated for a state run by scientists and industrialists. He thought that people's spiritual and religious needs should be left in the hands of scientists and engineers and that religion would become scientific—with Newton as a saint. He predicted the industrialization of the world and a reign of peace and harmony (a prediction that unfortunately did not prove true).

Saint-Simon did not base his analysis on class or oppression. He saw the industrialists as one class with scientists and financiers at the top followed by managers, bankers, and eventually workers. The threat to the order and prosperity produced by the industrial class was the class of idlers who avoided work. These idlers could be the inheritors of wealth, like the aristocrats, or they could be poor people who refused to work. In either case, they represented a threat to the newly emerging society, and Saint-Simon thought the government should force these idlers to work. The other task of government was to ensure circumstances necessary for a productive society. All other governmental activities, Saint-Simon believed, would reduce prosperity and lead to tyranny. Essentially Saint-Simon supported a meritocracy in which those most able would be able to rise to a level where they could best contribute.

Essentially Saint-Simon supported the classical economics of Adam Smith, who he saw as a true visionary. But he also cared for the poor, and as he grew older, he placed their needs at the top of his religion of scientists and engineers. This new emphasis on the poor caused a rift with his secretary, Auguste Comte. As with Fourier, Saint-Simon's influence was highest after his death.

Positivism

Auguste Comte (1798–1857) was raised in a Catholic and monarchist family with which he disagreed and which he left at the age of nineteen to go to Paris. He became the secretary to Henri Saint-Simon but split from Saint-Simon in 1824 when his employer began to develop a theory for a new Christianity. In 1822 Comte published *Plan of scientific studies necessary for the reorganization of society*, in which he advocated a reform of society designed by scientists. The book is also called *First System of Positive Polity*, and so Comte introduced the idea of "positivism" early in his writings. Science is seen not as an autonomous entity, but one that is embedded in politics. He also advocated for the act of love as the fundamental principle of both society and science. After love followed order and progress.

After his break with Saint-Simon, Comte married Carolyn Massin and began teaching his "Course in Positive Philosophy." The title of the course became the title of several volumes of books. In his positive philosophy, Comte categorized in order to understand. He taught that classification is what makes technology possible. First, he saw three stages in the development of human thought: the theological, the metaphysical, and the positive.

In the first, theological stage, people ask why things happen in nature. For instance, why are there storms? The answer comes in the form of anthropomorphized supernatural beings. These gods have purposes, and they work these purposes on earth. The social structure that corresponds to the theological stage is a warrior culture. In the second, metaphysical stage, people continue to ask why things happen in nature, but the answers come in the form of abstractions, like laws of nature. Ideas replace the gods. The corresponding social structure is legal. The lawyers and jurists begin to replace the warriors. In the third, positive stage, people begin to realize that they can find relationships among phenomena, but they stop asking why things happen. This is an industrial stage. The inventor or engineer tries to find out how to accomplish a human purpose, but the question of the existence of deep-seated natural abstractions is uninteresting. The question is how to make something work.

Comte also saw a structure to all of the sciences. The most basic was mathematics. Then came astronomy, physics, and chemistry. The organic world was of a different type, but it was built out of chemistry. In this stage, one finds biology and then sociology. Every one of these branches of science had a different method, but the two most fundamental were astronomy and biology. The list just mentioned, that is, mathematics, astronomy, physics, chemistry, biology, and sociology, is both a chronological and a historical list, since each of these sciences took its modern methodological form at different times. It was also an order of dependence. Each depends on the ones lower on the list, but the next stage cannot be derived only from the methods of the lower. As much as one knows about physics, it is impossible to derive chemistry from physics (or biology from chemistry).

Comte said that the higher depends on the lower but is not its result. Mathematics was an aid to all of the sciences as they used it to find the connections among phenomena.

For Comte, the highest science was sociology, and it was still in the process of formation. But sociology represents a double opportunity. Until his day, thinkers had distinguished moral philosophy (in German, the *Geisteswissenschaften*) from natural philosophy. Natural philosophy used objective methods, while the human sciences used subjective methods. But Comte said that with the development of sociology we could invert the process and derive natural processes using subjective methods. Sociology should be the coordinating science of all the others. In Comte's course, then, one first studied the nature and methods of each science before tackling sociology. There was no way to understand sociology without knowing something of biology.

When Comte's wife died, in 1846, he turned to an emotion, love, as the essential basis for all. Positivism came to be a kind of religion, but soon Comte began to write that art was even higher than science. Eventually he developed a religion of humanity that worships the power of humanity as a whole. As he continued in this vein, supporters and friends such as John Stuart Mill began to criticize him.

Comte was one of the first "sociologists" (he coined the term; see Chapter 8 for the further development of sociology) and one of the first philosophers of science. Although his system was criticized as he built it, its influence was profound.

Property Is Theft!

Pierre-Joseph Proudhon (1809–65) was known for developing a social philosophy of mutualism and for coining the phrase "Property is theft." It is hard to understand today why property could be considered theft until one reflects that individuals did not own most land until the commercial era of the seventeenth and the eighteenth century. Peasants had the right to use property, and warriors controlled the use of large-scale property, but a baron could not properly sell the land he had rights to. Only with the rise of commercial elites and the various wars that led to their eventual control of governments did the idea of property as a commodity become widespread and enacted into law. In fact, Adam Smith (see Chapter 2) had argued that the form of property must vary with the form of government. Property, to Smith, was an acquired rather than a natural right.

Proudhon's father was a brewer and cooper, and the family was far from wealthy. Proudhon was taught to read by his mother, who later cobbled together tuition for school. But Proudhon could not afford books or shoes, and was uncomfortable mingling with others who had more than he. He was most comfortable reading on his own. He became an apprentice in a printing shop, and over the years learned the various aspects of the trade. As a compositor he had the opportunity to work closely with authors, and had many interesting discussions with, for example, Charles Fourier (see earlier text). He began to write, and his first book *What Is Property* came out in 1840.

Eventually Proudhon developed a theory by which workers could form mutual cooperatives in which they shared the money made by their labor. He envisioned a

National Bank that would provide loans to workers and also a currency that was based on bank notes rather than gold. He thought that by this system he could end the rule of capitalists, who controlled money, essentially investment capital, but otherwise provided no useful service to the workers.

Proudhon called himself an "anarchist," inventing the term. As such, future anarchists saw him as their father of origin. He was a friend of Karl Marx, but the two differed on the causes of capitalism and its cure. In the next chapter, in which we discuss ideas that revolve around the ideas of Charles Darwin, we will meet Peter Kropotkin, who developed a theory of anarchy based on evolution.

Increasing Public Awareness

Written Accounts

Since the Industrial Revolution began in Great Britain, the problems of the new working class and their children first became apparent there. Beginning in the 1820s, a variety of studies and official reports on mill life focused public attention on the oppressive conditions found in mills. In 1833 Parliament passed a bill limiting the hours of children in factories and setting up an enforcement group to regularly investigate mill conditions. Combined with the 1832 reform act that gave the vote to people in cities (in place of some of the rural "rotten boroughs"), the stage was set for continuing legislation during the rest of the century.

Reports like those of the Sadler commission made for shocking reading as children detailed millwork that began before dawn and ended after dusk. They reported whippings, child rape, and in general a reduction of human beings to bestiality. Increasingly the public was outraged. Mill owners began to make changes on their own to avoid unpleasant legislation.

Perhaps more important were the novels of writers like Charles Dickens who, beginning in the 1830s and lasting through the 1860s, wrote gripping serialized stories of children and adults caught in an underworld of vice and degradation. His large readership eagerly awaited the next issue of whichever journal was running the latest story by Dickens. In France, a little later in the century Emile Zola wrote exposés of industries like the coal industry in *Germinal* (1885) in which he brought workers, small investors, and representatives of absentee cartels together. By the end of *Germinal*, it is clear that social reform is coming. We have already examined the impact of printing technology and increasing literacy (see Chapter 2) on the information consumed by Western Europeans. The realistic novel was another example.

Photography's Revealing Lens

Although Niécphore Niépce captured the first image in 1819, he was unable to create a practical photographic process. His partner, Louis Daguerre, publicly announced that he had invented a way to take permanent photographs in 1839. The main technical problem had been not just to find a chemical that changed when exposed to light but also to

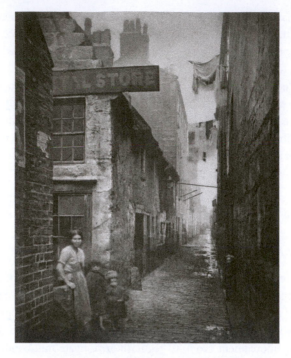

Figure 5.3 Thomas Annan, *Old Vennel Off High Street* in Glasgow, Scotland, 1868. Annan's photographs exposed the poorer sections of Glasgow. © Wikimedia Commons (public domain).

stop that chemical from continuing to change in light: that is, fixing the photograph. By 1839 Daguerre had reduced the exposure time to a few minutes. In 1838 he took a picture through a window, and although the passing traffic moved too quickly to affect the photo, it turned out that two men engaged in a shoeshine had remained still long enough to be photographed. This unplanned event is probably the first photograph of human beings. Soon, however, others began to improve the time of exposure and the methods of fixing the picture, and by 1850 photography was becoming commonplace. The main use was portraiture, but some photographers began to use scenes of battle and other destructive human activities as subjects worthy of photographing.

Thomas Annan visited Scottish slums and mills to photograph the lives of the poor. All of these subjects changed common perceptions. The exposure time was still too great to catch action, so actual battle scenes could not be captured, but the aftermath of dead and disfigured bodies was portrayed in nonglorious realism. Modern war was more and more seen as horrific. The same can be said of the slums. It is one thing to state that life is hard and brutal; it is another to see a brutalized child immortalized by the camera.

Artistic Realism

In 1850 the French artist Gustave Courbet (1819–77) saw two stonebreakers by the side of the road. He later said: "It is not often that one encounters so complete an expression of poverty and so, right then and there I got the idea for a painting. I told them to come to my studio the next morning." With this painting, he instituted the school of photographic realism. This school dominated avant-garde French painting for twenty years until it was displaced by impressionism (see Chapter 9). The realists dedicating themselves to painting life as it was, with emphasis on the until-now rarely noticed lower classes.

Courbet was lucky in that he had the full support of a wealthy father. When Courbet, therefore, decided to paint lower-class life, he did not have to worry about where he would sell the paintings. But the art world had slowly been changing, thereby allowing painters without an indulgent wealthy father remain solvent while breaking away from the strictures of official academies. Great Britain led the way with dealers in art who bought the art in order to sell it. Along with dealers and dealers' galleries came critics who could guide the public toward satisfying purchases. As art became a commodity, excellent artists had a freedom that they did not have when patrons paid for art. Furthermore, the 1841 invention of metal tubes to hold paint in a way that kept the paint from drying out, coupled with the increasing availability of fast-moving railroads, meant that artists could range far and wide as they looked for subjects.

The impact of artistic realism, combined with socially conscious photographs, combined with well-written novels of exposé, combined with parliamentary inquiries and published results, all led to a better-informed and increasingly outraged public. The worker question grew in importance as the nineteenth century wore on.

1848: Revolutions!

After the fall of Napoleon and the Congress of Vienna Accords of 1815, continental Europe had lapsed back into monarchical conservatism. But no accords could halt the expansion of industry and the growth of the Industrial Revolution in the Western part of the continent. Entrepreneurs chafed under the rule of kings who had little notion of what businesses needed. They built enterprises that hired workers who suffered under terrible conditions in factories. The quick French Revolution of 1832 put the "bourgeois monarch" Louis-Philippe on the throne, but entrepreneurial pressure continued to build for extension of the franchise and a parliamentary government, and workers increasingly demanded programs that would protect them. The pressure built up until the urban streets exploded in 1848. Starting in Sicily and moving on to France, Belgium, Germany, and Italy, popular revolts began to topple monarchs.

But the revolts fizzled. Armies remained loyal to hereditary leaders, and the innocent new parliamentarians' governments wasted time in debates about constitutions rather than consolidating power. In France, the king was gone, but soon the people, exercising their newly won right to vote, voted for the name they recognized best, Napoleon Bonaparte, nephew of the first Napoleon. When the new constitution did not provide for his reelection, he followed in his uncle's footsteps and made himself emperor, Napoleon III. In Austria, the emperor reneged on his pledge to establish parliamentary government, and the only real outcome was that the Hungarian part of the empire became autonomous.

But the revolutions showed everyone that if steps weren't taken, another revolution lay in wait. Socialists were heartened, and they continued to organize workers and to pressure governments for worker relief. The Conservative Otto von Bismarck (1815–98), the minister president and foreign minister of the Kingdom of Prussia and later chancellor of Germany, understood the threat. After engineering the unification of Germany in 1871, by 1880 he had outlawed socialism and passed the most extensive social legislation in Europe in order to wed the workers to the crown and undercut the socialists.

The developments briefly discussed in this section helped change the socialist discussions. No longer was socialism only a subject for individual theorists discussing the best possible organization of society, but socialism increasingly became the theory behind activist political forces whose proponents continued to argue about goals and means, but also undertook grand actions to accomplish the emancipation of the workers. The revolutions of 1848 occurred in the same year that Marx and Engels's *Communist Manifesto* was published.

Marxism

Karl Marx (1818–83) was a professional intellectual and writer who used the insights of many of the thinkers we have so far studied in this book to develop a radical theory of industrial/capitalist society and social revolution. His theory ultimately combined Hegel's analysis, the insights of the French utopian socialists, and the classical economics developed in Great Britain. He was born to a Jewish family in Trier, in the Rhineland, that before his birth had converted to Protestantism after Napoleon's emancipation of Jews was overturned. Karl Marx's father Heinrich (formerly Herschel) taught his son at home until Karl was ready for gymnasium. Karl ultimately attended the universities of Bonn and then Berlin to study law. However, he became interested in philosophy, particularly that of Hegel, and he joined the growing group of young Hegelians who used Hegel's dialectic while discarding his metaphysics. Eventually he wrote a doctoral dissertation on the difference between two ancient materialist and atomistic philosophies of nature. The University of Jena awarded him doctorate in 1841.

Marx and a baroness, Jenny von Westphalen, fell in love, and Marx was able to befriend her father, to whom Marx dedicated his doctoral thesis. In 1843 they were married, seven years after their engagement. In the succeeding years, Marx made a living as a journalist, preferring to write for radical papers. Conservative monarchs who were afraid of revolution ruled most of the countries of Europe, and so censorship made radical journalism a precarious living. Karl and Jenny Marx were forced to move around Europe as newspapers were closed—occasionally, Marx was exiled.

In 1842 Marx met Friedrich Engels (1820–95), whose industrialist father owned mills in England and Prussia, and in 1844 they befriended each other for life. Engels had

Figure 5.4 Friedrich Engels, Karl Marx, and Marx's daughters: Jenny Caroline, Jenny Julia Eleanor, and Jenny Laura. Photograph, author unknown, date approximately in 1860s. © Heritage Images/Hulton Archive/Getty Images.

been sent to England by his father to engage in management at one of his father's mills. His father hoped that managerial experience would temper his son's radicalism. Instead, Engels had been horrified at the conditions of workers in the mill and wrote a book, *The Condition of the Working Class in England* (1845). In 1844 he showed the manuscript to Marx and convinced his new friend that the working class was ready for revolt. Marx focused his studies on socialism and economic theory as he prepared theoretical system to account for Engels's findings. By 1844 or 1845, Marx seems to have worked out much of his system, as can be seen in a number of manuscripts (the early manuscripts) that were unpublished in Western Europe until after the Second World War.

Eventually Marx and Engels joined the underground Communist League and began to prepare a pamphlet describing the League's aims. This became *The Communist Manifesto* (1848). The two eventually ended up in England, Marx having become a stateless person, with Engels continuing to work in the family business to support the work and writings of Marx. In the 1840s, the two had collaborated on the unpublished *The German Ideology* and continued to work on several other articles. Marx became a correspondent for newspapers in New York published by Charles Dana (*The New York Daily Tribune* and

The New York Sun). In 1867 Marx published the first volume of *Das Kapital* (*Capital*). Volumes two and three were edited and published by Engels after Marx's death in 1883.

By reading the variety of Marx's manuscripts and books that were unpublished until the twentieth century, we can see Marx's system included a theory of human nature and a conception of society that supported his economic analysis. Marx saw the dominating bourgeois investor class and the consequent development of factory working class through the lens of a history dominated by opposing forces of economic production—forces underlying the political, legal, and intellectual shape of every tier of society. By "workers," or "the proletariat," Marx meant those people who labored in mills and factories. Certainly, people had been working before the Industrial Revolution, but agricultural labor or domestic services, or in fact any of the jobs held by the nonwealthy and non-nobles, were different in kind from the new factory work. Thus, the proletariat was a new phenomenon in history.

To Marx, every age had a dominant productive system. This system produced laws and ideas that represented the interests of those in power. This productive system, however, was insufficient to encompass all the creative energies of the population, and so counterforces began to gather. The struggle between the dominant forces and the counterforces is similar to Hegel's system of history. As the dominant productive system developed, and as new productive possibilities emerged, eventually a revolution in favor of the counterforces (but including elements of the previously dominant powers) created a new kind of society, the synthesis. The most recent productive system was capitalism. But capitalism depended on workers for the factories, and thus a new counterforce, the proletariat, was developing.

The bourgeoisie, Marx and Engels wrote in *The Communist Manifesto*, had been extraordinarily productive. Unfortunately, in order to achieve this development, they had exploited workers. For Marx, history would develop in such a way that soon workers would overthrow the bourgeoisie while keeping the possibilities for economic development discovered by their oppressors.

The trouble with the bourgeoisie from the viewpoint of workers (the proletariat) was that these factory owners had stolen the creative powers of the workers. The main trait that distinguishes human beings from animals is the ability to create new technology. For instance, our fingernails are not helpful in confronting the claws of an animal, but we have created weapons—much more powerful than claws. If workers were in their own workshops, they would be able to create whatever they wanted and feel a part of their creations. But in a capitalist society, workers were in factories. They were told what to do, and when, and because of the division of labor, each only played a very small role in whatever was made. They could feel no connection to their product. Even worse, from the viewpoint of the owners, the workers were just another cost of business. They were necessary to the business, but no particular worker was essential. They were interchangeable parts.

A way of thinking about this is to say that workers are themselves commodities. After a while they themselves start feeling like commodities. They are alienated from their humanness; they are alienated, then, from themselves. The only way they know to heal their self-alienation; the only way they have in a capitalist system is to acquire commodities. But, of course, this acquisition does not work, and they continue to feel alienated. For Marx, the only real cure is to stop selling themselves as commodities to the bourgeoisie. But this is not an option if they want to live. They need jobs to buy bread.

For Marx, even a beneficent employer cannot change the lives of workers. Robert Owen, the industrialist-turned-socialist, was ultimately unsuccessful. Why cannot a multitude of good-hearted employers turn the system around? Because the system is based on competition. In a competitive system, every factory owner competes with every other. They strive to cut costs so they can cut prices and still have some surplus capital to reinvest. The bourgeois owner that raises worker salary, the employer that cuts work hours, the investor that abolishes division of labor—these people are bound to be forced out of business. The system, not the individuals, is at fault. Both proletariat and bourgeoisie are caught in the system. They have to play their roles or perish.

Where does capital come from? Marx answers this question by developing the "labor theory of value" of the classical economists. For Marx, value comes only from labor. For a tree to become lumber, someone has to cut the tree down and others have to saw the tree into usable parts. Lumber is worth more than an uncut tree. But the only economic difference between an uncut tree and lumber is the labor of the lumberjacks and sawyers. These workers, however, do not get the total value of the lumber. They are paid wages, and these wages are always less than the price of the lumber minus the cost of the tree. The value comes from the labor, but labor only receives a wage. The owner of the tools and machinery keeps the rest, the surplus value. The investor then uses the surplus value created by workers to invest in other enterprises.

Why is the moneyed investor necessary? Marx thinks such people are unnecessary. If the workers collectively owned the enterprise, then the group of workers would include managers and financial experts. The workers collectively could decide how to shape their work lives. Everyone should be a worker. No one should be able to live from rents on property.

What might the workers decide? Well, for Marx, they could decide to give up the division of labor for individual workers. The work of the enterprise might be divided, but different workers could take turns doing it.

For as soon as the distribution of labour comes into being, each man has a particular, exclusive sphere of activity, which is forced upon him and from which he cannot escape. He is a hunter, a fisherman, a herdsman, or a critic, and must remain so if he does not want to lose his means of livelihood; while in communist society, where nobody has one exclusive sphere of activity but each can become accomplished in any branch he wishes, society regulates the general production and thus makes it possible for me to do one thing today and another tomorrow, to hunt in the morning, fish in the afternoon, rear cattle in the evening, criticise after dinner, just as I have a mind, without ever becoming hunter, fisherman, herdsman or critic.[2]

121

This paragraph reflects an unalienated existence for Marx. Workers are in control of their own productive lives.

But Marx sees this as only possible at a group level. The individual workers in a communist society cannot make this decision apart from the other workers. The collectivity of all workers owns and controls the productive forces of the society. Just as with Hegel, we can only be free in the context of the whole. What does this idea imply for liberal democracy? Marx has no confidence that individual workers have the capability of voting in their own best interest, especially since they have been conditioned by living in a capitalist society. If "capitalism" (a term not often used by Marx) were destroyed today, tomorrow everyone's values would still take a capitalist form. They might well choose to pay themselves a higher wage instead of choosing a more humane existence. Only after a few generations will people be able to understand the humane possibilities inherent in a communist system.

To understand this point better, consider Marx's distinction between the base and the superstructure. For Marx, every aspect of society springs from the form of the productive forces. Ideas, values, theories, schools, laws, and institutions in general—all reflect the interests of the ruling class, the elite of a society. The ideas and institutions are superstructures built upon, in this case, the capitalist form of production. As a society becomes communist, the superstructure cannot change overnight. People after the revolution will still have a set of values that are formed to further the cause of the bourgeoisie.

The implication is that the bourgeoisie and their representatives form all the laws and the declarations of rights. Voting for governors by individuals grew out of the needs of moneyed elites to have a say over what the monarchs decreed. In England, the Civil War and the Glorious Revolution established the power of a parliament that only included propertied men. The rights of free speech were designed to allow powerful men to create a strong commercial/industrial society. The theories and laws of property were constructed to protect the holdings of propertied men.

Thus, it is impossible to say that all these can be protected while capitalism (ownership of the means of production by a few) becomes communism (ownership of the means of production by all). In fact, only trained communists are capable initially of understanding just how pervasive the values of capitalism are. Workers may hope to become capitalists themselves, or they might be convinced by eloquent arguments that capitalists are necessary to worker well-being. Therefore, workers can only have a hope of living in an unalienated, humane society by trusting those who understand. After capitalism, government will still be necessary, but a government run by a benevolent dictatorship of the proletariat. Only after the children and grandchildren of the workers of today have been educated in schools designed by communists may the obsolescence of the state be seen and the state begin to wither away.

How should this future society be structured? Marx is vague and unspecific. He and Engels did list a set of initial objectives in *The Communist Manifesto*, including free education, graduated income tax, appropriation of land, and so forth, but these objectives were designed only for the initial stages of moving from capitalism to a dictatorship of the proletariat. Marx was less concerned about creating the blueprint for utopia than he was about understanding just how the capitalist system worked and what its weak points were. Only with such understanding could it be changed. In his polemic against many of the ideas of his old friend Ludwig Feuerbach (1804–72), *Theses on Feuerbach* (1845) Marx noted that "The philosophers have only interpreted the world in various ways; the point, however, is to change it."[3] And so while in his writings Marx attempted to understand the world, he also was an activist among socialists as they met and planned a variety of revolutionary actions. He was opposed to moderate socialists who demanded suffrage for workers, because he feared that workers would learn to settle for better salaries and benefits without ever trying to create the humane world he envisioned. But he was also opposed to anarchists who wanted to blow up the power structures before the revolution was ready.

Marx often lived a life of abject poverty, and it was evident in the health of his family. He and Jenny had seven children, but only three survived into adulthood. His wife Jenny passed away at the age of 67 in 1881. Marx lived his last years in ill health and died in 1883. Friedrich Engels died in 1895 and left Marx's two surviving daughters a generous portion of his estate.

The Socialist Movement

By 1848 most of the basic socialist positions had been published. After the revolutions and the failure of radicals to achieve most of their aims, many socialists decided to band together in an organization to continue to push for their goals. Although the first half of the century had seen the formation of various groups, like the Communist League, the only wide-scale movement had been the Chartist movement in Great Britain. After the Reform Bill of 1832 that had extended the franchise to propertied males only, the Chartists formed to force the government to enable all adult males to vote, to maintain a secret ballot, and to pay legislators in order that workers could afford to stand for Parliament. Although the movement was widespread, it eventually failed and ended in 1857. Eventually, in the twentieth century, all of the Chartist demands were made law.

As we saw earlier, in 1864 in London an international meeting of socialist groups took place under the aegis of a new international group, popularly known as the First International. Karl Marx represented German socialism, and he was one of the mainstays of the First International until it ended. Eventually, the First International housed several competing groups with different ideas about how to achieve a truly just society. The Marxists, as we have seen, advocated a dictatorship of the proletariat to oversee the radical reorientation of society. Anarchists, led by Mikhail Bakunin, advocated immediate revolution in order to move as quickly as possible to government by small groups of mutually and voluntarily acting citizens. The trade union movement, connected to the now defunct Chartist movement, occurred mostly in Great Britain and consisted at that time of skilled tradesmen who were not interested in including unskilled workers in their associations. The British workers were not concerned with the total reformation of society but rather wanted to work to make sure workers were well treated within the existing capitalist society. They formed the heart of twentieth-century labor parties across Western Europe.

In 1871, after the defeat of the French by Germany (and the creation of the German state), a group of socialists took over the government of Paris to form the Commune. This was a two-month triumph that was soon overcome by the new French government, the Third Republic (1870–1940). To socialists and radicals in general, the Commune represented a mythic entity that showed in brief what a socialist state would look like. Following are some of the more important ideas that were actually enacted: (1) to run public affairs by committee, without an executive head, (2) to separate church and state and confiscate church property, (3) to remit rents and return workers' tools pawned during the siege of Paris, (4) to allow employees to take over and run a business if the owner abandoned it, (5) to prohibit fines by employers against their employees, (6) to abolish interest on commercial debts, and (7) to abolish child labor and night work in bakeries. The Commune set up orphanages and schools and provided free food and clothing to children. But the Commune was riven by factions, including radical anarchism. Some radical women set up feminist organizations that sought wage equality, rights to divorce, and professional education for girls. What the Commune might have become is unclear, because the army of the Third Republic broke it up shortly after it began. Numbers of leftists, including both Marx and Engels, debated why the Commune was unable to hold its own.

With the fall of the Commune and the subsequent trials and executions, the socialist movement was seriously weakened. But by 1889, it was strong enough to organize a new international organization, the Second International. This organization eventually excluded liberal trade union groups (who organized themselves as the "Possibilists"— emphasizing what was possible under the circumstances) and anarcho-syndicalists, (who emphasized using violence to abolish the state in favor of workers' associations). The Second International emphasized working with organized national workers' groups and wavered on the issue of parliamentary democracy. Marxists in Germany merged with more centrist parties to form the Democratic Socialist Party (SPD) that still exists today. More radical Marxists, of course, eventually found their opportunity in Russia at the end of the First World War (see Chapter 10).

Early in the twentieth century, the Second International bent its influence to avoiding a European war, since they thought wars were a capitalist endeavor. It demanded that its members pledge not to go to war but rather to use any war to hasten the demise of capitalism. The First World War showed that nationalism was a more persuasive force than international workers' solidarity. We will discuss nationalism in Chapter 7.

Conclusion

In 1800 few Germans would have predicted that factory workers would grow to be one of the most significant political forces in Western Europe by the end of the nineteenth century. Yet in 1903, the German party that won the most votes for the Reichstag (parliament) was the Social Democratic Party (the SPD), with 31.7 percent and 81 seats. The next party, the Catholic Center Party (*Zentrum*), won 19.8 percent of the vote, but 100 seats (more than the socialists because of the organization of the electorate). However, in the election of 1912, the SPD broke through with 34.8 percent of the vote and 110 seats to *Zentrum*'s 16.4 percent and 91 seats. For the first time, a worker's party was the majority party in the lower house in Germany, which remained under the rule of the emperor (Kaiser) until the end of the First World War. By the end of the Second World War, a workers' party led the governments of virtually every major country in Europe.

Balancing the wealth-generating power of capitalism with the need for a distribution of that wealth to all of the citizens of a country became the most pressing domestic issue in most industrial countries. The ideas discussed in this chapter formed the base that supported the various proposals for creating a just society that emerged in the later nineteenth and twentieth centuries. Socialist thinkers emphasized the impact of society on individuals. Real change could only be social, group, change.

And yet, socialists were not the only active intellectuals in the political realm. The biologist Charles Darwin, by emphasizing the power of changing individual organisms to alter an entire species, created a set of ideas that changed the entirety of European intellectual life. It is to the impact of Darwinians that we now turn.

CHAPTER 6
FROM GOD'S PLAN TO
MARKETPLACE CREATION
DARWIN AND DARWINISMS

Figure 6.1 Portrait of Charles Darwin. © Wikimedia Commons (public domain).

The Great Debate

At the end of June 1860, about seven months after Darwin's *The Origin of Species* was published, an event that has come to be known as the "Huxley-Wilberforce debate" took place in Oxford, England. In the common story of this debate, about Darwin's theory of natural selection, Bishop Samuel Wilberforce (1805–73) is said to have inquired whether Thomas Henry Huxley (1825–95) thought he had been descended from a monkey through his grandmother or his grandfather. Huxley, goes the story, whispered to his companion, "the Lord hath delivered him into mine hands," and replied that he was not ashamed to have a monkey for his ancestor but would be ashamed to be connected with a man who used great gifts to obscure the truth.

It is a fine story. Unfortunately, there is no good evidence that it ever happened that way.

The first account of the debate appeared in 1887 in Francis Darwin's *The Life and Letters of Charles Darwin* and seems to have been inspired solely by stories told by Thomas Huxley himself. But the story was too useful to be ignored by writers near the turn of the twentieth century, who wanted to show the church persecuting science. It quickly attained mythic proportions along with the trial of Galileo as a precautionary tale. However, immediately after the debate itself, public discussion of the debate essentially disappeared for thirty years. Historians have not been able to confirm the popular version of the story from primary sources. So, what did probably happen?

Only a few years before the debate, the paleontologist Huxley had been a scathing and vocal critic of evolution. Charles Darwin had made a point of sharing his theory and evidence with Huxley before Darwin's book was published in order to forestall a negative review. After publication, Huxley was convinced and wrote a favorable review in the *Times*. Meantime, Darwin's primary scientific opponent, Richard Owen, tutored Bishop Wilberforce, F.R.S., an amateur scientist. Wilberforce wrote a long unfavorable review. As the British Association for the Advancement of Science (BAAS) gathered for their annual meeting in Oxford, there was a buzzing discussion concerning the pros and cons of Darwin's ideas. The organizers decided to move a lecture by chemist and photographer John William Draper from Monday to Saturday where it could occur before the participants scattered. Draper presented, "On the Intellectual Development of Europe, considered with reference to the views of Mr. Darwin and others, that the progression of organisms is determined by law." Anticipating a crowd, carpenters worked Friday night to construct additional benches for the Oxford hall. The hall was full and held hundreds.

Draper and family members described the reaction to Draper's paper in personal letters. They don't mention Huxley. In fact, Draper seems to have been pleased by Wilberforce's reaction, a somewhat surprising conclusion, since Draper became the founder of the "conflict thesis" about the relations between religion and science. If Wilberforce had argued vociferously against Draper's points, one would think Draper would have noticed. Why did Draper not mention Huxley? Perhaps the room was so crowded and noisy that Huxley's voice did not carry. Another possibility considered by twenty-first-century historians is that the Wilberforce-Huxley exchange actually occurred in private. Whatever might have happened, Wilberforce and Darwin remained quite friendly. And Darwin's theory spread throughout Europe in a variety of versions applied to a multiplicity of areas.

This small vignette illustrates an important aspect of Darwin studies: virtually everything we know about Darwin and Darwinism has been disputed. Nevertheless, as we shall see in this chapter (and in succeeding ones), Darwinian ideas altered not only biology but also virtually every other intellectual field. As the roots of liberal capitalism grew stronger, they were able to produce new variant forms. The theories of Charles Darwin were based on metaphors derived from political economics. With biology as a support, the justification for a competitive worldview nourished social forms as varied as global imperialism and domestic opposition to welfare programs.

Chapter Map

The ideas of Charles Darwin transformed how Europeans saw themselves and the world around them. But Darwin depended on many other ideas as he developed his own theory of the transformation of species over time. We begin with Darwin's biography and then discuss the books and ideas that influenced his theory of natural selection. We move through theology, geology, philosophy, economics, and biology in order to see where Darwin's ideas about "descent with modification" came from. Darwin anticipated many objections but was somewhat surprised by two telling scientific threats to his theory. We also see a very similar theory proposed by Alfred Russel Wallace who disagreed with Darwin on the human mind.

In Germany, Darwin's ideas were modified to fit a different culture. Ernst Haeckel developed a goal-directed evolution. Fredrich Nietzsche used his version of Darwin's idea to construct an influential philosophy of human freedom that still resounds today. In Russia, the anarchist Peter Kropotkin suggested that evolution was based on cooperation rather than on competition. He pointed to the clear implications for organizing a humane society.

But especially in England and America, other thinkers argued that Darwin had shown that only ruthless competition and survival of the fittest were adequate to build the ideal society. Social Darwinism justified cutthroat capitalism and global imperialism.

Whatever their conclusions, Darwinians of all stripes focused on the individuals of a species as the site of changes that eventually affected the species as a whole.

The Early Charles Darwin

Charles Darwin (1809–82) was born into an upper-middle-class English family in 1809. His maternal grandfather was the very successful ceramicist Josiah Wedgwood (Wedgwood china is still a standard for excellence), and his paternal grandfather was the physician Erasmus Darwin. Erasmus had been an important member of the Birmingham Lunar Society that often met at Soho House, the house of the entrepreneur Matthew Boulton, who had partnered with James Watt to develop and sell steam engines. Both were quite wealthy, as was Charles Darwin's father, Robert Darwin, physician to important members of society. Charles never had to work for money a day in his life. Charles Darwin was an unenthusiastic student who initially was destined to study medicine. However, when he entered the medical college of the University of Edinburgh, he was so sickened by viewing operations that in those days were carried out without anesthetics that he fled the operating theater and ultimately the university. He transferred to Cambridge to study divinity. In his examinations, he actually came in 10th out of 178. In fact, he was quite taken by the logic behind William Paley's use of nature to argue for the existence of God (see the following text). What interested Darwin the most, however, was natural philosophy (science). He spent a great deal of time with botanist John Steven Henslow and enjoyed walking through nature with him. He also studied geology with Adam Sedgwick and traveled to Wales to measure geologic strata with him.

In 1831 Darwin was offered a position as captain's companion to Robert Fitzroy, who at that time as captain of the naval survey ship Beagle was assigned to chart the waters and coast of South America. Ten years before, Spain had withdrawn from its South American colonies, and various European countries saw value in taking their place in one way or another. The UK needed to be prepared for armed struggle (or a colonial enterprise). Given the strict hierarchy of the British navy, captains of ships, who generally came from the aristocracy, had no one to talk to. Many had returned from sea having gone mad from solitude. The navy therefore had developed the custom of sending a socially appropriate companion to dine and converse with the captain. That was Darwin's first job, although he later also became the ship's naturalist. When Darwin later developed his theory, a primary source of data was the material on species that he had collected while sailing on the Beagle. From 1831 to 1836, Darwin collected plant and animal specimens from South America, read voluminously, and corresponded with friends and teachers. By the time he landed back in England, some of his correspondents, notably his friend and teacher John Steven Henslow, had released many of his letters. Naturalists eagerly awaited the Darwin collection. Darwin's father made sure his son was supported financially to live the life of a gentleman scientist. Before continuing with Darwin's story, and the publication of his theories, we shall look at some aspects of the intellectual climate within which he worked.

Darwin's Predecessors

Divine Design

William Paley (1743–1805) was a noted ethicist whose book *The Principles of Moral and Political Philosophy* (1785) was read well into the nineteenth century. Charles Darwin was required to master it for his Cambridge degree. After he sat for his exams, Darwin continued to read Paley, focusing particularly on *Natural Theology: or, Evidences of the Existence and Attributes of the Deity* (1802). In this book, Paley developed an idea that began in the seventeenth century: the argument from design. The main idea is that if we follow the development of science and see more and more of the details of the "machine universe," we will see that the universe is an intricate and interlocking design that could not have appeared by chance.

Suppose we stub our toes on a stone and wonder how the stone got there, begins Paley. It would not be absurd to think that perhaps it had always been there. But if we find a watch in the path, the former answer is absurd. We must assume that at some time someone had made it. Intricate machines cannot arise by pure chance. Some intelligent being designs them. Therefore, since the universe is like a machine, it must have been designed by some intelligence.

In 1766 David Hume (see Chapter 1) had refuted the argument from design in a supposed dialogue among four friends, and Paley set out to refute Hume's arguments. For instance, Hume's character Philo said that the analogy between the universe and a machine is imperfect. We know how watches are made, but we have never seen a universe made. Paley said that even if we had no knowledge of how a watch was made, nevertheless we would know that someone had designed it. Paley even said that if a watch had been designed that could make other watches (like biological organisms, one assumes), and even if the watch we found had been made by one of these watch-making watches, we would still know that there was design behind the watch.

Paley was not particularly concerned to convert atheists, but he did want to bolster the faith of people who were deists. Never once does he try to prove Christianity. He wrote that if one were convinced of the truth of the argument from design, then curiosity might lead some people to investigate the sources of revealed religion. Certainly, Darwin was convinced—until he had developed his own theory. One principle that seemed to recur in many of Paley's books was an evidence-based faith in the goodness of God. He used this principle to state a basic ethical principle. Since we are designed to be close to God, we ourselves should act for the good. For Darwin, Paley provided the best evidence and argument that the universe developed according to an intelligent design.

Evolution as Progress

In this text, we have already discussed several ideas of progressive development. In the Enlightenment, Condorcet argued for progress in human history and for a hope for further progress in the new age of science. Hegel had developed a theory of history that saw the progressive development of freedom and an ultimate union of all people in recognition of the Absolute. As scientists studied embryos, they saw a progressive development from fertilized ovum to an organism ready for birth. In fact, the development of the embryo was often described as the "evolution" of the embryo. The word "evolution" connoted progress in a preconceived pattern.

Geology and Time

In the eighteenth century, the Scotsman James Hutton (1726–97) developed a theory of geology called uniformitarianism. If one looked carefully, one could see evidence of geological change all over. Before Hutton, geologists had developed theories of catastrophic change, like Noachian floods. But Hutton said that the processes of change were daily occurrences: erosion, for instance. Hutton's uniformitarianism demanded immense amounts of time. In fact, Hutton claimed that there was no vestige of a trace of beginnings. The processes had gone on forever and seemed destined to continue.

Hutton's countryman Charles Lyell (1797–1875) continued the uniformitarian approach in new and path-breaking research. His *Principles of Geology* (1830–3) came out in three volumes while Charles Darwin sailed on the Beagle. Darwin got copies of the books, which he read avidly. It was Lyell's book that convinced Darwin that the earth had lasted for at least hundreds of millions of years. Darwin later became a good friend of Lyell. But not until the end of his life did Lyell support a theory of evolution, and when he did, he supported Lamarck (see the following text). He always referred to Darwin's theory as an adaptation of Lamarck's. Lyell studied volcanoes, earthquakes, and strata and leaned heavily on fossil evidence.

One evidence of geologic change was fossils, knowledge of which was expanding yearly from the work of collectors. Fossils seemed to transform from one geologic stratum to another. In fact, one could use similarities in fossils to show that a stratum in, say France, had existed at the same time that a stratum in Scotland did. A strange thing was noticed about fossils. They seemed to be the imprints, in rock, of previously existing organic forms, both plants and animals, but most fossils apparently had died out by the time the next stratum was laid down. They seemed to have become extinct. If one looked at fossils in ancient strata, they seemed to be simpler than fossils in later strata. That is, organisms in later times had more parts than did the earlier fossils. Eventually, very late in geologic time, mammals emerged. Mammals are definitely more complex than, say, shellfish. Paleontologists noted this phenomenon, and some began to construct theories of progress. Perhaps species had evolved overtime.

The existing Aristotelian idea of nature was known as the "scala naturae" or "ladder of nature," also known as "the great chain of being." At the bottom of the ladder lay inorganic materials; moving up a rung one found plants, then lower animals, then higher animals, capped by humans. Theologically, one could posit angels and, at the top, God. Every species had a rung in the ladder. The fossil evidence seemed to indicate that although there was an archetypical ladder, it was only realized materially as time went on. That is, perhaps God had designed a system in which organisms, at a prearranged time, climbed up to the next rung. The universe, perhaps, was progressive.

But if one preferred to believe that the universe was designed in perfection, then perhaps many of the so-called species were actually degenerate forms of earlier more perfect types. Comte de Buffon (1707–88) argued that what we called species were degenerated types, perhaps pulled in a downward direction by environmental factors. It was hard for any eighteenth-century thinker to believe that God had originally created a less-perfect universe.

As scientists studied comparative anatomy, they began to see that certain traits were connected to other traits in the same fossil. For instance, herbivores had teeth that were distinct from carnivores, and their hoofs were different from paws with claws. They began to find pieces of fossils and, with some confidence, make statements about the organism to which that fossil part had belonged.

Evolution by Inheritance of Acquired Characteristics

Jean-Baptiste Lamarck (1744–1829) became known for a theory that any characteristics that an organism acquires as it grows in a specific environment are passed onto its offspring. This theory is often referred to as the inheritance of acquired characteristics. Ironically, Lamarck did not think this idea was his most important. In fact, he thought that the inheritance of acquired characteristics was a process so obvious as to be commonplace.

In 1809, the year of Darwin's birth, Lamarck published *Philosophie zoologique* (*Philosophy of Zoology*), in which he laid out his ideas. Early in his career, Lamarck believed that species were fixed. Later, as he studied the fossil record more carefully, he realized that there must have been transformations over time. Lamarck eventually thought the great chain of being was obvious as one observed nature. The fossil record showed clearly that the chain did not physically exist in the earliest years, but that gradually more and more complex species were added to the world. For Lamarck an inner special force, a force that led to more and more order, drove organisms to attempt to move up the ladder of nature. Since simple organisms were constantly created chemically by spontaneous generation, there would always be simple organisms climbing the ladder of nature from the bottom. But organisms whose hereditary lines stemmed from an earlier spontaneous generation would gradually have worked their ways up the ladder of nature toward more complex forms.

Lamarck's second process was an organic force that led organisms to adapt to their surroundings. His first law of adaptation was a law of "use and disuse" of organs. If an organ were needed in a certain environment, it would be strengthened in the first generation, and in succeeding generations it would grow stronger. On the other hand, if an organ were superfluous in an environmental context, it would begin to grow weaker and, eventually, over several generations of the same environment, wither away. Primary examples used by Lamarck to show new traits stimulated by environmental changes were the mole's blindness, the absence of teeth in birds, and the presence of teeth in mammals.

His second law was that over time these additions or subtractions would be inherited, if they were present in both sexes or in the sex that bore young. Thus, a mole born in the sunlight would still be blind, although if moles began to move into the light, over generations it is possible that their eyes would gradually be strengthened. How many generations? Lamarck was not specific, although he did seem to think time was essentially unlimited. Lamarck used a famous example to describe the formation of a species. Suppose a certain antelope browsed on a bush in an environment favorable to bushes. If a drought arose, then the shallow-rooted bushes would begin to die out. Deeper-rooted trees, however, would be able to drink from underground aquifers, and

Figure 6.2 Comparing the evolution of giraffes according to Lamarck's theory (top) and Darwin's theory (bottom). In Lamarck's theory, the environment calls forth new traits. In Darwin's theory, the environment "selects" from variations. © De Agostoni Picture Library/Getty Images.

would begin to thrive. Over time, the antelopes would have to stretch for higher and higher leaves. Short-necked antelopes would starve, but longer-necked antelopes would be able to survive. As the roots had to reach deeper, the trees would get higher, and the antelopes' necks would strain to lengthen. Finally, the antelopes would have been transformed into giraffes. A new species would have arisen over many generations of stretching antelopes.

Lamarck presented the first fully formed evolutionary theoretical system. But in France, major scientists of the day, like Cuvier, rejected it. Lamarck's book was published during the Napoleonic Wars, and in England it was hardly noticed until a few decades later. The geologist Charles Lyell spent six pages discussing Lamarck's ideas and criticizing them on the basis of a lack of scientific rigor. Later in the century, the German Ernst Haeckel (see the following text) used a version of Lamarck, and Charles Darwin in later editions of his book *Origin of Species* (1859) also used a version of Lamarck's conceptions.

Lamarckism echoed the Enlightenment idea that social problems were related to bad environments. If one wanted to reduce crime, for instance, one could reduce poverty. Lamarckian biology was always interesting to social radicals, and as we shall see, it informed agricultural policy during the Soviet Union in the mid-twentieth century.

Malthusian Catastrophes

While on the Beagle, Darwin had a great deal of time to read some of the major scientific works of the day. He continued this program of reading upon his return. According to Darwin, his ideas gelled in 1838 when he read Malthus's "An Essay on the Principle of Population" (1798).

The question Thomas Malthus (1766–1834) tackled was whether poverty could be eliminated. Despite the general optimism of Malthus's muse Adam Smith, Malthus denied that the growth of wealth achieved through competition, division of labor, and free trade would ever be sufficient to eliminate poverty. For Malthus, the growth of population would always outstrip the supply of food. Human beings were doomed to forever periodically experience famine and starvation.

Malthus assumed that human beings had two basic drives: (1) a need for food and (2) a need for sex and procreation. He argued that the population would always expand geometrically. (Today we would say, "exponentially.") If, say two units of population existed in one generation, the next generation would increase by some multiple, say, for ease of calculation, by a factor of two. So, two units of population would become four, and then eight, and then sixteen, and then thirty-two, and so on.

Food production can never double in that way, said Malthus. To expand food production, one has to clear more land, drain swamps, build terraces in mountains, and so forth. The most that can be achieved in terms of growth in production is to add units. So, if the two units of population had two units of food to eat, the next generation could have four, then six, then eight. If one unit of food feeds one unit of population adequately, we see that the first generation is properly fed (two population; two food) as is the next generation (four population; four food). However, the next generation will experience shortages (eight population; six food), and the generation after that will have some starvation (sixteen population; eight food), and by the next generation all will have collapsed (thirty-two population; ten food).

Some people will always be able to have enough to eat. They will be smart enough, or strong enough, or wily enough to find ample food for themselves and their families. Others will be unable to find food at all. They will be robbed, tricked, or otherwise deprived. Eventually there will be a mass die-off. Population will return to sustainable levels, and the cycles will start off again. As an Anglican clergyman, Malthus saw this process as a way God taught virtuous behavior. Malthus's theory was in this way a kind of theodicy, explaining how a good God could allow suffering in the world he had created.

This message was so bleak that few in the nineteenth century took it seriously. Europe was experiencing unprecedented prosperity, overall, so faith in progress continued unabated. The Malthusian catastrophic message returned in the second half of the twentieth century. But when Charles Darwin read Malthus, he realized that this principle of the eternal press of competition could explain the differences he had seen in the Galapagos years before when he was on the Beagle. He had this insight in 1838. He wrote a short description of how the process of species change might work, and then he continued to collect evidence and examples. Darwin realized that a theory of evolution would be quite controversial, and he was unwilling to experience the unpleasant opprobrium that would be cast his way. He was particularly concerned that his children would suffer.

Darwin's Theory

For the twenty years after he read Malthus, Darwin continued to work as a naturalist, publishing influential books and becoming well known for his sober, careful observations. During the 1840s and 1850s Darwin accumulated scientific awards and recognitions. But he did not publish the theory that he had devised back in 1838. It did serve, however, as a template for his research as he looked for examples of natural selection in his studies. Eventually Darwin wrote over 200 pages outlining his findings and left it with colleagues to be published if he should die.

In 1858, Darwin was shocked to receive a paper by Alfred Russel Wallace that outlined a theory much like Darwin's. Darwin asked his friends what should be done. They decided to offer Wallace's work and Darwin's paper at the same time to the Linnaean Society. In 1859 John Murray published *On the Origin of Species by Means of Natural Selection, or the Preservation of Favoured Races in the Struggle for Life* (known hereafter as Origin or *Origin of* Species).

Darwin built his theory on two metaphors: (1) nature is a breeder and (2) nature is a free-market society. Essentially Darwin took the classical economics of Adam Smith, Thomas Malthus, David Ricardo, and John Stuart Mill, and read it into biology. It seemed to fit beautifully.

Chapter One of the *Origin* focuses on pigeon breeding, all the rage in Victorian England. Darwin noted that breeders are able to make the most fantastic varieties of pigeons by choosing to breed pigeons with the desired traits and not breeding those that had undesired traits. Perhaps a more modern example is dog breeding. A Chihuahua is the same species as a Great Dane. All of these varieties of dogs have been bred by the same process described earlier for pigeons. But the desired traits have to be present in the pigeon (or dog) at birth. The breeder cannot create them; the breeder can only choose them. This selection process is referred to in the title of Darwin's book: natural selection. Nature chooses.

Since the breeder needs to find the desired traits, the key to selection is variation. Every individual of every species looks a little different, or behaves a little differently, from every other individual of the same species. Thus, in Chapter Two Darwin takes great pains to demonstrate that in nature each species contains individuals with very different traits. The point is, there is variation aplenty in nature.

Finally, sixty pages into the first edition, we find Malthus's argument applied to nature. There is competition for survival, and only certain individuals will be able to survive. Early in the chapter, Darwin notes:

I should premise that I use the term Struggle for Existence in a large and metaphorical sense, including dependence of one being on another, and including (which is more important) not only the life of the individual, but success in leaving progeny. Two canine animals in a time of dearth, may be truly said to struggle with each other which shall get food and live. But a plant on the edge of a desert is said to struggle for life against the drought, though more properly it should be said to be dependent on the moisture.[1]

That is, Darwin recognizes that he is arguing from metaphor. The "struggle for existence" is applied to two plants out of sight of one another, "struggling" to get water during a drought. Clearly, this is not a "struggle" as the word is usually understood, but it is necessary to Darwin's argument that all of the actions of organisms that bear on their ability to survive and leave progeny be seen under the general term "struggle." A lion may hunt a gazelle, and the two struggle with another, but this struggle is not the Darwinian kind. Struggle for Darwin is the "struggle" of two gazelles to avoid being lion food, or the struggle of two lions to successfully bring down a gazelle. The action is all within the same species (sometimes same genus). The argument is exactly the same used by Adam Smith to show why competition produces wealth. Darwin needs the metaphor to prove his point.

Darwin's Chapter Four, "Natural Selection," completes his argument. Given all of this natural variation, nature makes her selection. But since variations are generally slight, a species does not change rapidly. The process is very gradual, and one change may take thousands upon thousands of years. If a variation that is favorable to survival and production of progeny is selected, it has to be reselected thousands of times. Only gradually will the unfavorable variations begin to die out. Darwin needs Hutton's and Lyell's presentation of geological time that is essentially unlimited. At the very least, the time needed for the selection of all the species on earth will be hundreds of millions of years. But gradually some traits will become extinct, and others will be chosen, and species change will occur.

We now see the importance of Darwin's Chapter One, in which breeders select organisms for propagation. Selection, of course, is a human trait. But if nature is personified, then nature too can select. In Darwin's argument, sometimes nature is the situation within which organisms compete. Nature is a free-market society. Sometimes nature is the chooser, the breeder. One can see why the wealthy Darwin was well situated to describe natural selection. It is hard to see Marx coming up with this particular argument.

In the rest of the book, Darwin endeavors to be as fair as possible. The very next chapter, Chapter Five, presents the difficulties of the theory, the main one being that the fossil record shows big jumps from one species to another. As Darwin notes, the transitional species are absent. But he also expresses his faith that "*natura non facit salutum.*" (Nature does not make leaps.) How does he explain this difficulty? Darwin tells us that fossils happen only occasionally. Almost all of the time, dead organisms decay without a trace.

Darwin discusses many issues with copious examples. He considers instincts, geographical distribution, the importance of barriers, like large rivers or mountain ranges, to separate individuals of the same species and let them develop in unique environmental conditions. Eventually he sums up his argument in an eloquent presentation of environmental complexity.

> It is interesting to contemplate an entangled bank, clothed with many plants of many kinds, with birds singing on the bushes, with various insects flitting about, and with worms crawling through the damp earth, and to reflect that these elaborately constructed forms, so different from each other, and dependent on each other in so complex a manner, have all been produced by laws acting around us. . . . Thus, from the war of nature, from famine and death, the most exalted object which we are capable of conceiving, namely, the production of the higher animals, directly follows. There is grandeur in this view of life, with its several powers, having been originally breathed into a few forms or into one; and that, whilst this planet has gone cycling on according to the fixed law of gravity, from so simple a beginning endless forms most beautiful and most wonderful have been, and are being, evolved.[2]

In this paragraph, Darwin sets the stage for the science of ecology. All species are interconnected. The tangled bank represents a small subsection of tangled nature. And we humans are part of the grandeur.

Contrary to popular belief, Darwin never claimed to have a theory of evolution. As we have seen, the word "evolution" connoted progressive development, unfolding according to a preset plan. Darwin explicitly said that nature could only act on variations that presented themselves. The variations were random, or at least their unknown cause was not part of Darwin's theory. Darwin referred to his theory as "natural selection" or "descent with modification." The implications were staggering. Life developed randomly. There were no higher or lower organisms. There were only life forms that had somehow made it through the selection process to live today. Bacteria, cockroaches, and human beings were equivalent in their success in making it through the lottery of natural selection. Nature selected not for some kind of preset notion of higher or lower, but rather for the ability of a variation to survive and reproduce in higher numbers than other less successful variations in a particular set of environmental conditions. Of course,

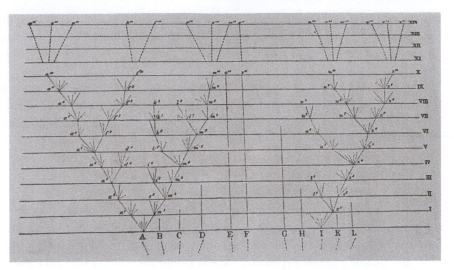

Figure 6.3 Diagram of evolution in Charles Darwin's *The Origin of Species*, 1859. The eleven species at the bottom change as time passes. Each horizontal line represents 1,000 generations. Some species become extinct. By the top of the chart, after 14,000 generations, A has become eight different new species and I has become six new species. Only F of the original species continues unchanged. © Photograph by David Galaty.

as Darwin pointed out, the principle of division of labor led to increasingly complex and specialized organisms.

Darwin's model was a randomly branching tree. Genera were branches that divided into twigs that became new branches or disappeared entirely. There was no way to predict the direction of growth of this tree. There was no central trunk.

> As buds give rise by growth to fresh buds, and these, if vigorous, branch out and overtop on all sides many a feebler branch, so by generation I believe it has been with the great Tree of Life, which fills with its dead and broken branches the crust of the earth, and covers the surface with its ever branching and beautiful ramifications.[3]

Darwin had very little sympathy for the idea that the biological world is designed to give the least possible pain to its creatures. No theodicy could rescue the structure of seeming cruelty observed in nature.

> Finally, it may not be a logical deduction, but to my imagination it is far more satisfactory to look at such instincts as the young cuckoo ejecting its foster-brothers—ants making slaves—the larvæ of ichneumonidæ feeding within the live bodies of caterpillars—not as specially endowed or created instincts, but as small consequences of one general law, leading to the advancement of all organic beings, namely, multiply, vary, let the strongest live and the weakest die.[4]

In this original version of Darwin's book, we see the idea of survival of the fittest. Nature did not display any sympathy for the weak and downtrodden. Instead, nature decreed that they should die. This Darwinian abandonment of theodicy may be a watershed moment in the history of ideas.

Darwin was clear about the impact of his teachers on his thought. He sent copies of the book to scientists like John Herschel and Charles Lyell. They received it badly. Herschel called it "the law of higgledy piggeldy."[5] Herschel's objection was that it seemed evident that the random process was guided by plan, by a designer. Darwin's system was like trying to write Shakespeare by randomly combining words. How could a random process produce human consciousness with the ability, for instance, to build a science that accurately mirrored nature?

But Darwin's book was a commercial hit. It sold out, went into extra printings, and, as the criticism poured in, went into rewritten extra editions. The argument hit the nerve of common sense. If one were a Victorian middle-class person, it would be hard to argue against one's own worldview. Of course, the rest of Europe was not Victorian, and we shall shortly see how the *Origin* was interpreted in other countries.

Two Telling Counterarguments

William Thomson, Lord Kelvin, was one of the founders of thermodynamics, as we have seen. He was a religious man, but not a dogmatist. But he wanted to use the new thermodynamics to calculate the age of the earth. As one descended into mine shafts, the temperature became measurably hotter. If one extrapolated from the difference in temperature at the surface to that at different depths, one could calculate the temperature at the center of the earth. If one further assumed that the earth had once been a whirling ball of hot gases that had gradually cooled down and congealed, then one could use thermodynamics to calculate the age of the earth. In 1862, Kelvin carried out the calculations and found that the earth was probably of the order of 20–400 (most likely no more than 100) million years old. This was not enough for Darwin's theory to work. Kelvin was arguably the most prestigious and one of the most accomplished scientists of his age. Darwin had no recourse but to recalculate his theory.

Fleeming Jenkin (1833–85), a professor of engineering at the University of Edinburgh, provided another objection to Darwin's theory. Jenkin assumed that heredity was produced as a blend of the traits of both parents, the prevailing theory at the time. He showed that if an individual had a favorable trait, the mate of that partner was unlikely to have the same trait. Therefore, the favorable traits would be diluted. In a few generations, the favorable trait would cease to exist. Darwin required many generations for a trait to become dominant in a population. He realized that this was a telling argument.

Luckily, Darwin could lean on Lamarck. Perhaps, he wrote in later editions, there is a mechanism by which nature can evoke a change in traits. Perhaps nature is not a passive chooser, but a more active participant. But even given that adjustment, still, to

Darwin natural selection and descent with modification were the primary mechanisms for species change.

In time, both Kelvin's and Jenkins's arguments would be refuted. Kelvin had known nothing of radioactivity, but when one added radioactive processes to the production of the earth's heat, the age of the earth expanded tremendously. This argument could not be made until the twentieth century. Similarly, when the genetics of Gregor Mendel were rediscovered and applied in the twentieth century, a new mechanism for heredity was discovered.

But part of Darwin's genius was not to try to answer the question of heredity. When Darwin was writing, cell theory was in its infancy and chromosomes had not been discovered. When he did, in a later book, try to deal with the problem of heredity, in a theory known as pangenesis, he was wrong. Darwin, however, tried to stick to his metaphorical argument. His book was a rhetorical success and gradually was absorbed into biology for a decade. At the end of the nineteenth century, few biologists were still interested in Darwin, as scientific interest turned from long-term transformation to short-term stability in theories of inheritance. In the 1930s–50s, his theory was reinterpreted and widely used.

Darwin's Competitor

Alfred Russel Wallace (1823–1913) was the immediate stimulus to Darwin's publication of his long-simmering theory. Wallace was a naturalist who initially collected specimens and investigated the distribution of species in the Amazon basin and the Rio Negro. Unfortunately, on the way back to England his ship caught fire, and Wallace lost almost all of his specimens and notes. Undaunted, Wallace started over in the Malay peninsula. In the 1850s, he began to correspond with Charles Lyell and also with Darwin. Some of Wallace's papers began to lead Lyell to reconsider his belief in the fixity of species. Lyell was thus quite taken with Wallace's developing views on the development of species, but Darwin saw them as reflecting the general progressivism and hierarchical order of nature at the time. His own views, as we have seen, emphasized the random production of variations.

However, around 1858, Wallace reflected on Malthus's essay on population and realized that it might provide a way of explaining the development of species. He wrote a paper to this effect and sent it to Darwin to forward to Lyell if Darwin thought it had any merit. Darwin was shocked to see his own ideas in someone else's handwriting—but he sent the paper to Lyell asking what should be done. Darwin's son was, at that time, seriously ill with scarlet fever, and Darwin had no stomach for engaging in scientific controversy. He left the matter in the hands of his friends, who, as we have seen, sent both Darwin's and Wallace's work to the Linnaean Society, along with older correspondence from Darwin that demonstrated his priority in formulating the theory of natural selection and descent with modification.

Although Wallace and Darwin's views were similar, there were important differences. Wallace opposed Darwin's metaphor that nature is a breeder and said that variations chosen by nature were very different from variations chosen by breeders. In his 1858 paper, Wallace compared the mechanism of selection to a governing regulator on a steam engine. The Malthusian approach was seen as a way of keeping the entire ecosystem in balance. In this way, he was one of the founders of the focus on systems rather than individuals.

The two thinkers differed most, however, in their assessment of mind. Wallace was convinced the human mind came from nonmaterial causes. He was not a Christian, but he did have an interest in spiritualism. Along with several physicists and other scientists of the late nineteenth century, Wallace thought spiritualism was a fit subject for scientific investigation.

Perhaps Wallace differed most from Darwin in his assessment of free-market capitalism. He opposed free trade because it was hard on workers. He collaborated with John Stuart Mill during the time Mill turned his thinking in a socialist direction, and Wallace actively opposed private landownership. Wallace thought the government should own all land and lease it to those who would make it most productive. At the end of the nineteenth century, as Darwin's cousin Francis Galton began to advocate eugenics for the improvement of the human race, Wallace opposed the idea. He did not think that we could have an assessment of the ideal characteristics of human beings without social class bias.

Both Darwin and Wallace made the change of species believable. But neither had the last word in the nineteenth century. Scientists with different bents and different national backgrounds interpreted the theory in their own ways. And Darwin's theory was not only used in science. Fairly quickly after the theory was announced in 1859, it was reintroduced into social theory. The status of human beings was called into question. Were human beings just smart animals? Were humans just another species? Was there a way they could continue to see themselves as close to God, just a little lower than the angels? Could humans still be seen as the possessors of immortal souls? What did Darwin's ideas imply for ethics and morality? These were not questions that Darwin himself had asked, at least not publicly or in print. Darwinism quickly outran Darwin. Thinkers in every country interpreted Darwin in the light of their own national histories and concerns. The ideas associated with Darwin's name often had little to do with what Darwin himself thought. Darwin became a symbol, an icon.

German Darwinism

When Darwin's ideas got to Germany, they provoked analyses that had very little to do with the English basis of Darwin's metaphors. German thought had been dominated by a philosophy springing from Immanuel Kant, and as we saw in the third chapter, German Idealism responded to Kant by denying Kant's distinction between the world of the human mind and a world outside of mind. Idealism was essentially speculative; truth was sought by examining thought itself. Soon science itself became speculative.

But a few years after the death of Hegel, German science returned to experiment, German philosophy returned to Kant, and sometimes the two intermixed. A few biologists and physicists, most notably some of the students of the German physiologist Johannesburg Mueller, thought that someday the phenomena of life would be explained according to physical (mechanical) principles. The foremost German physicist of the later nineteenth century, Herman von Helmholtz, was one of these young physiology students. Helmholtz, the multidisciplinary student of physiology and medicine, based a path-breaking proof of the law of conservation of energy on a Kantian analysis. A few years later, Helmholtz, an expert on the physiology of sensation, discussed how nerves always transmit the same sensation, no matter what the source. A blow on the head will cause the optic nerve to stimulate a sensation of light, as the victim of the blow sees a flash of light. Light waves stimulate sight in optic nerves, but the same rays stimulate heat sensations when they hit the skin. What we experience, then, is determined more by our physiology than it is by stimuli from the world outside of us. When scientists study their observations, they are deluded if they think they are studying mainly a world outside of the phenomenal world. Scientific theories reflect the minds that think them. This is scientific Kantianism. It is philosophy aided by scientific analysis.

But neither Helmholtz nor his friends Emil du-Bois Raymond and Ernst Bruecke nor the younger scientists like Rudolf Virchow that followed their lead, could see exactly how one might simplify the study of life into a problem in mechanics. When Darwin's theory was announced, Helmholtz could see the way. To him, Darwin had provided a method of explaining life in physical terms, and he was willing to call the nineteenth century "Darwin's Century."

Because official Christianity supported the institutions of government, radical Europeans, including radical Germans, often denied religion. Since the eighteenth century, radicals were often materialists who denied the existence of anything other than the material world. Marx and Engels, for instance, saw themselves as "scientific materialists." But neo-Kantianism made a hash of naïve materialism. Naïve realists wanted to discover the hard, real world, beyond thought; what they got was another idea, the idea of the material.

In the economic world, there had also been an increasing emphasis on material comforts and monetary wealth. Classical economics emphasized the study of money relations as a replacement for other human needs or wants. Often representatives of the new "working class" emphasized making sure that workers got their share of monetary wealth. As we have seen, Marx and Engels criticized just this tendency, but that didn't stop other workers' advocates from asking for higher wages as a primary step in increasing worker welfare. And even moralists like the utilitarians emphasized "the greatest good for the greatest number" and tried to quantify "good" in monetary terms.

Around 1860, German thought faced a kind of crisis. Darwin seemed to provide answers to many of the dilemmas. Darwin's system of natural selection seemed to be a description of the material world that was not just a projection of our own sensory and thought processes. Darwin also seemed to provide a natural description of historical progress. Darwin described a world that seemed to be getting "fitter" and more complex, not because God had willed it, but because that was the way the world worked. The world worked that way whether or not human beings were thinking about it, or even whether or not human beings existed.

So, when Germans considered Darwin, they saw a definition of progress, and they saw a confirmation of atheistic materialism. It was impossible for them to replace their own questions with the simple industrial pragmatism that had motivated much recent British thought. This was true even at the scientific and biological levels. We will explore two versions of German Darwinism: the scientific version of the biologist Ernst Haeckel and the philosophical version of the philosopher Friedrich Nietzsche.

Ernst Haeckel

Ernst Haeckel (1834–1919) was known as the German Darwin. He was a foremost zoologist who was recognized and feted for his work of prolific publication. But Haeckel saw Darwin through the lens of his German background. He saw the nation as a whole that subsumed individuals. He was a romantic biologist who believed that biological forms were mental archetypes. As a result, he had no compunctions about transforming the Scala Naturae into a tree, a la Darwin, and seeing the process of descent with modification as a true evolution, a preformed developing process. For Haeckel, the main branches of the tree were the preformed genera, and the limbs that branched off were environmental modifications of the main forms.

A zoologist, Haeckel started as an embryologist who later coined the phrase: ontogeny (the development of an embryo) recapitulates phylogeny (the development of evolution), that is, the developing embryo goes through the stages of evolution that preceded it. Thus, a bird's embryo will look like a fish, and then a frog, before it becomes a bird. The German Karl Ernst von Baer (the discoverer of the mammalian ovum in 1827) had emphasized that embryos follow different patterns, never going through the adult stages of "lower" species. Darwin agreed with Baer that embryos only share initial general forms and diverge from one another during development. But Baer also agreed that there is a general law of evolution that directs where the process is going. The general intellectual ethos in Germany emphasized unities and systems, whereas the British tended to emphasize pragmatism and the importance of individuals. The implications of the ideas of Lamarck were much more appealing in Germany than the more radical ideas of Darwin that seemed to point to a lack of underlying order and random variation. Haeckel's scientific views reflected his social views and vice versa. In 1906 he helped found the German Monistic League and wrote several essays outlining their aims. Monism was based on the idea that all is a unity. There is no separation between a spiritual and a materialistic world, but rather spirit is incorporated in the material. We are all parts of one stupendous whole, as the eighteenth-century poet Alexander Pope had claimed. For Haeckel, social science derived from biology. The whole has a structure, but this structure is seen in processes

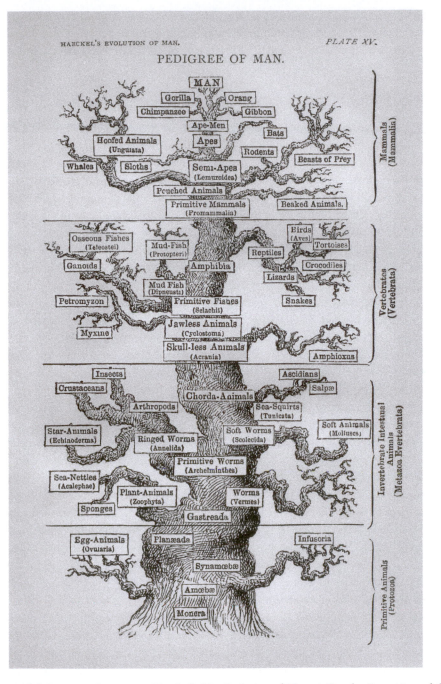

Figure 6.4 Diagram from Ernst Haeckel's *The Evolution of Man. A Popular Exposition of the Principle Points of Human Ontogeny and Phylogeny*, 1883, p. 183. Here there is one huge trunk of animal life leading to Man at the top. Different groups grow separate branches as the tree moves through the phyla over time. This diagram differs significantly from the former diagram drawn by Darwin. Haeckel saw ordered change while Darwin saw random selection. © Wikimedia Commons (public domain).

of development. Just as an embryo develops in one direction, toward an adult being, so the universe is developing according to a plan. This approach reflected Hegel's idea of an evolving humanity that ultimately will be organized as a unity into the absolute state.

Friedrich Nietzsche

It may seem strange to include Friedrich Nietzsche (1844–1900) in a chapter on Darwin, especially since in some of his work he was quite critical of Darwin. But Nietzsche had a tendency to eat his own, as he struggled to emphasize his own uniqueness, and many scholars are convinced that his system was built on a Darwinian base. As we discuss Nietzsche, we can see just how far-ranging Darwinism's influence was. Nietzsche was not a scientist, but rather a philologist, a student of ancient languages, and from his secondary school days he studied Greek, Latin, Hebrew, and French. In his university studies, he was lucky enough to meet and study under Wilhelm Ritschl, who was enchanted by his student. Even though Nietzsche had not completed his residency requirements for the Ph.D., Ritschl wrote a strong recommendation for Nietzsche to become the professor of philology at the Swiss University of Basel. He described Nietzsche as the only student from which he himself had learned, a "phenomenon," the leader of all the young philologists in Leipzig, who could not wait to hear Nietzsche speak. He assured the Swiss that Nietzsche was, like the Swiss, a free spirit who did not at all share the German devotion to obedience and order that was so prevalent in Prussia, and also was not an agitator as many Prussian left-wingers were. Although Ritschl had no hope that his letter would work, surprisingly it did, and at the age of twenty-four Nietzsche became perhaps the youngest full professor in the German-speaking world.

In the course of his studies, Nietzsche read a great deal of philosophy, including Schopenhauer, Ludwig Feuerbach, and Friedrich Albert Lange. He became acquainted with Darwin, as he read Lange's book, *A History of Materialism*, and, in fact, before he was offered the professorship, he was ready to abandon philology to study for a degree in philosophy. Darwin opened up brand-new possibilities for Nietzsche, as for other German thinkers. For Nietzsche, Darwin displayed the possibility of seeing all of human experience as a struggle of the weak against the strong. Nietzsche was especially concerned with the human expression of values and morality. For Nietzsche, all human values could be understood as expressions of the will to power.

But how, then, did European values come to represent the interests of the weak and the meek? What kind of will to power would emphasize "turning the other cheek" or loving one's enemies? To answer his question, Nietzsche turned to philology. The ancient world had been composed of masters and slaves. Morality was defined by the masters, and "good" was defined as "what I want." Bad was defined by "what I don't want." That is, noble humans who lived by power defined morality. Morality was an expression of their will, nothing more, and nothing less.

But, said Nietzsche, the "sly" slaves had somehow turned the tables on their masters. They redefined "bad" by turning it into a new term: "evil." Evil was what God did not want. Good became "what God wants." And it turned out that God wanted what was in the slaves' best interest. For a slave, a good master is one who is kind. From the slaves' point of view, a good master is one who doesn't punish them, who cares for and protects them. Nietzsche shows the development of "slave morality" by showing the derivation of the words "good" and "evil."

Furthermore, the slave morality emphasized a world beyond the vale of tears, pain, and misery within which we find ourselves. Yes, the slaves might find that they were trapped on this earth, but after death they would be freed and would find a world in which they triumph. In God's heaven, the wealthy and the powerful would be thrown down and face eternal punishment, while those who had lived simply and lovingly would be rewarded. The trick was not to be seduced by the rewards of material life, but to eschew material pleasures for the eternal pleasures of heaven.

How could powerful people be convinced to renounce the world and sensual pleasure? How could a rational person be convinced to become ascetic? The trick was to use guilt formation. If someone restrains angry and aggressive impulses and does not express them against another person, the impulses must go somewhere, and the anger is turned inside. The anger turns into guilt. And now the priest can advise the sufferer, "You are the cause of your own pain." Your bodily desires are the cause of your unhappiness. And so, the ascetic can get pleasure out of self-punishment. By punishing himself, the ascetic is atoning for his own sin.

So, for Nietzsche, Western culture was hopelessly lost. Where could we look for a model to emulate? Nietzsche found the world of Homer, the world of the pre-Socratic Greeks. In this world, strength was a good thing. Heroes vied with heroes, pitting their strength against one another. Good was defined as "arête," the Ancient Greek word for "excellence." The person of true excellence was worthy of praise, and no one pitied a person who did not display arête. Nietzsche yearned for a world in which the strong and excellent unapologetically expressed themselves. Slaves were useful in constructing the buildings and monuments made possible by the strong. Nietzsche had no use for democracy, socialism, Christianity, or feminism. The necessity for struggle was something Nietzsche thought was foreign to women in general. He rejected a life of caring for others, especially the weak, and saw women as the primary caregivers of society. As a result, Nietzsche often expressed misogynistic statements when speaking of women in general. Specific women, like the Russian writer and psychoanalyst Lou Andreas-Salomé, were excepted. Since at times in his writing Nietzsche indicates that women are potentially higher than men, his misogynism has been a source of contention for Nietzsche scholars.

If all values are expressions of a will to power, then any search for eternal truths is bound to fail. This insight Nietzsche owes to Darwin. Darwin eliminated the ladder of nature, a preformed plan for the design and organization of species. Instead, species formed when accidental traits proved to be advantageous in the struggle for existence. Nietzsche applied the same approach to values. A philosopher with an idea used every persuasive method available to attract others. The struggle among ideas was like the struggle for existence. Some persuasive attempts were successful, while others fell by the wayside. For Nietzsche, the history of Western thought was the history of a struggle for power among philosophers. Every successful philosophy was nothing more than an expression of the will to power of its author.

Realizing that absolute truth does not exist, truly strong people will recognize that they, and they alone, are responsible for their own actions, evaluations, and ethical decisions. Few such people presently exist, but Nietzsche predicts that they will exist in the future. Such people are the Übermenschen, the "overmen," sometimes unfortunately translated as "supermen." Nietzsche's book *Also sprach Zarathustra* (*Thus Spoke Zarathustra*) shows one such overman, Zarathustra, who descends from the mountain to declare his insight: to live an authentic life, we must realize and accept that we alone are responsible for who we are and what we do. No one can remove this awful burden from us, because there is no one else at a higher plane. We live as if on a tightrope strung over a deep abyss. The fall into unmeaning is terrifying. Of course, there are others struggling for power over us who would have us believe that they know truths and that we should follow them, but these clever persuaders are just part of the will to power.

A good test of our authenticity is to ask whether we would wish this very moment would recur eternally. For we have created this moment out of the constraining material of the physical world and our fellow human beings. If a demon were to tell us that this moment would eternally recur, would we see the demon as blessed or as an evil being?

Nietzsche's message was not delivered in the logical paragraphs of traditional philosophy, but rather in brief anecdotes and aphorisms. He numbered his paragraphs as if each one were a new point. His message was often nonlinear and full of unformed insights. In a sense, the actual medium was part of the message. He wrote as he wanted to live, in spurts of power. Nietzsche's aphoristic style of writing allowed him to display a wide-ranging set of ideas, all of which cannot be described here.

But one important idea, developed early in his career when he was still friends with the innovative, path-breaking anti-Semitic composer Richard Wagner and Wagner's wife Cosima, was that of the Apollonian and Dionysian. Apollo stands for reason and order, Dionysus for passion and chaos. For Nietzsche, both stances are valuable because they reflect human life as it is. The Greek tragedies of Sophocles represent the best of a balance between the two poles. Tragic heroes like Oedipus are overcome by fate and the chaotic. They can come to recognize their state but are powerless to do anything about it. Unfortunately, said Nietzsche, Euripides and his contemporary Socrates replaced Dionysian chaos with Apollonian reason. For Nietzsche, Western civilization had been sliding downhill ever since, with a few valiant exceptions that failed. It was important to restore the Dionysian for humans to be able to lead honest, truthful lives.

Art, especially as seen in drama, was important to Nietzsche as an expression of human aesthetic creativity. Nietzsche saw all values as created by humans, and he preferred that these values reflect beauty and affirmation rather than ugly negations.

Thus, in a sense, humans create their own illusions as they struggle to express their inner force upon the world. But Nietzsche also seemed to somehow demand that authentic Overmen lead a truthful life. The balance between creative illusion and authentic truth in Nietzsche's writing is hard to find. In a sense, Nietzsche seemed to want us truthfully to recognize our precarious existence in a Dionysian chaos before we set off to shape our own aesthetically inspired world and struggle with our peers to impress our own will in human society.

What, then, is Nietzsche's relationship to Darwin? Like Darwin, he used a genealogical approach to studying the emergence of our own world. For Darwin, the units of genealogical analysis were observable traits in organisms, for Nietzsche the units were words and their meanings. Both Darwin and Nietzsche saw a lack of an overarching plan for development. Later interpreters of both saw unplanned development as a key idea, and thus Darwin's theory came to be called "evolution," even though there was no progressive evolution in his pure conception. Nietzsche could have been the Darwin of values.

But Nietzsche later renounced Darwin on several grounds. First, Darwin was a scientist, and Nietzsche saw science as his age's main ascetic project, a project that shunned passion and bodily desires and channeled life force into intellectual work. Scientists, in this regard, were like Christian monks. Second, Darwin saw the action of the environment as the key factor in the modification of species, whereas Nietzsche saw an inner life force as key. As we have seen with the biologist Haeckel, Germans tended to take the side of Lamarck, who, as you will recall, saw an inner force causing organisms to change in response to a changing environment. For Nietzsche, a noble individual is not merely subject to the whims of fate, but uses his inner strength, his inner striving, to impress his world against the whims of other people and other forces that would overcome him. For Nietzsche struggle is life. For Darwin, organisms use whatever variations they have received as they struggle to survive to reproduce. Nietzsche saw a noble using all his inner force to become more than he was given by nature.

Ironically, Nietzsche was himself not a strong man. He was seriously injured when he had a horseback-riding mishap, and muscle injuries followed him throughout his life. He suffered from a variety of ailments and soon found he could not function in his professorial role. Eventually he had a psychotic break upon seeing a horse beaten in the streets, and he lived the end of his life, uncommunicative, under the care of his exploitive sister. His sister, Elisabeth Förster-Nietzsche, became the executor of her brother's manuscripts, and edited them to make Nietzsche's writing seem to reflect her own nationalist, anti-Semitic, and militaristic views. She produced a book of heavily edited writings entitled *Der Wille zur Macht* (*The Will to Power*) that was quite useful to the Nazis as they justified their war of conquest and program of genocide in the Holocaust. Only in the last several decades have scholars had access to all of Nietzsche's unpublished work and been able adequately to rectify his sister's interpretation and to represent what Nietzsche intended.

Figure 6.5 Prince Peter Kropotkin © Getty Images.

Evolution from Cooperation

The Russian Peter Kropotkin (1842–1921) was born a prince, a title he renounced at the age of twelve. His father controlled large tracts of land and almost 1,200 serfs. When he was fourteen, Peter went to St. Petersburg to join the elite corps of pages, a kind of military school with work in the palace. He graduated first in his class and joined the tsarist army, volunteering to serve in Siberia. In Siberia, he first read anarchist ideas as well as the liberalism of thinkers like John Stuart Mill. He was assigned to a geographic survey expedition and soon became more interested in science than the military. Returning to St. Petersburg, he began to work with the Russian Geographic Society and to study mathematics in the university. When he resigned his commission, his father disinherited him.

In Russia, the main intellectual questions usually had to do with the best organization of society. Russia was still a feudal country in the mid-nineteenth century, which meant that large landholders with control over serfs held great power. The serfs were tied to the land and owed at least one-third of their production to the lords. As Western Europe developed from a feudal into a modern industrial society, the technological (and thus military) power of the West increased, leaving Russia and other agriculturally based feudal societies behind. Russian intellectuals throughout the century debated how Russia might develop. Many of them studied in Western Europe; others were exiled in the West for questioning the regime. Most intellectuals realized that Russia needed to find new ways to economic, social, and political development.

After Russia was humiliated in the Crimean War of 1853–6, it was clear to the tsar that something had to be done, and he decided to free the serfs in 1861, in part so that they might become factory workers. He noted that it was better to free them by decision from above than to have them decide to free themselves from below. But freeing the serfs involved having many of them pay for their land on an installment plan as many others were left landless. Some serfs thrived, others didn't. Concern shifted to the peasant question rather than the emancipation question. In the West, it was no secret that the working class was no happier than the Russian serfs, and the most successful governments, like those of the UK and Prussia (Germany by 1871), made significant concessions to workers in the form of votes and social programs. Democracy was coming, and the thought struck terror into aristocratic hearts in both the West and the East.

Kropotkin was part of this intellectual ferment, even as he continued to work as a scientist. By the age of thirty, he had become an anarchist. He spent 1872–6 in jail in Russia where he was allowed to continue his work in his cell. He published an important paper on the dates of the ice age while imprisoned. Just before his trial, his friends helped him escape. In a comic finale, they all went to a posh restaurant to celebrate his release, reasoning correctly that the police would never look for him there. Most of the rest of his life was spent in exile in Western Europe.

As he put together all his notes on species in Siberia and added his notes on peasant societies, he applied this knowledge to the theory of evolution. He noted that every species he had studied had not been involved in competition with one another so much as cooperation. Wolves hunted in packs. Reindeer came together and worked as a herd. He began to think that the emphasis on struggle was misapplied. Not that there was no competition, but competition was a minor note when compared with cooperation. His primary scientific book was published in English from magazine essays. *Mutual Aid. A Factor in Evolution* (1902) eloquently made the case for cooperative evolution. Kropotkin added the point that preindustrial and noncapitalist societies also emphasize competition. The peasants of Russia had a great deal of a governmental autonomy at the local level and formed associations in which they worked together.

As an anarchist, Kropotkin's idea was that people should come together in mutual agreements. The idea of a central state distorted human nature. In industrial societies, workers should control the factories by mutual agreement. As Kropotkin became more and more involved in political organizations, he found himself bumping up against Marxists, who wanted to secure a dictatorship of the proletariat. Kropotkin and his fellow anarchists were opposed. The main issue that separated anarchists was how to achieve the downfall of centralized power so people could begin to build the associations that would produce a new, humane, society. Many anarchists thought that acts of terror would be necessary, and in fact, they succeeded in assassinating the tzar in 1881. Other assassinations preceded and followed, but none had any effect on the existence of centralized government. They only strengthened the resolve of the authorities and convinced ordinary citizens to turn away from reform. Kropotkin seems to have approved of "propaganda by the deed" but he himself did not participate in acts of terror. When Lenin and the Bolsheviks took over the Russian government in 1917, Kropotkin could only approve. At last, there had been a true revolution, even if it was not the anarchist revolution he had hoped for. And at his funeral in 1921, Lenin allowed thousands of anarchists to wave anti-Bolshevik banners in mourning.

Social Darwinism

Social Darwinism is a phrase that is almost always used pejoratively. Few people ever referred to themselves as Social Darwinists, but many made arguments that reflected the phrase. The Social Darwinist argument is that since Darwin showed competition is behind the progress of species, competition and "survival of the fittest" is a law of nature that should be applied to individuals and to societies. Social Darwinists argued that if people were unsuccessful in competing in the industrial world, it showed that they must have inferior traits. Perhaps they were too lazy or too mentally challenged to compete. At any rate, the best thing that could be done was to let them die. Charity only preserved these traits, allowed those that have them to breed, and weakened the human race. Social Darwinism at the social level argued that some peoples had been unsuccessful in constructing societies that could compete successfully against the West. Western nations were justified in taking these societies over and reforming them in a Western mold. Thus, the so-called law of nature of natural selection through competition justified warfare and imperialism. Eugenics, an idea championed by Darwin's cousin Francis Galton, usually had a Social Darwinist edge. Eugenics was a fashionable idea among intellectuals in the early nineteenth century until the Nazis' genocide, argued on eugenic principles (Jews are an inferior race), brought eugenics to a screeching halt.

A famous example of Social Darwinism is seen in Rudyard Kipling's poem "The White Man's Burden":

> Take up the White Man's burden—
> Send forth the best ye breed—
> Go bind your sons to exile
> To serve your captives' need;
> To wait in heavy harness
> On fluttered folk and wild—
> Your new-caught sullen peoples,
> Half devil and half child. (First stanza)[6]

In this poem, written to the United States when that country made the Philippines a colony after the Spanish-American War of 1898, Kipling argues the Philippinos are incapable of developing a humane society on their own. The United States would be doing them a great service ("To seek another's profit/And work another's gain") by administering them as a colony. And the implication is that if, in the process, their culture changed to resemble that of the United States, they would be better off, even if they resented the change.

Herbert Spencer

Herbert Spencer (1820–1903) was the widest read English thinker in the nineteenth century. He was the first philosopher to sell over a million copies of his works. Because he coined the phrase "survival of the fittest" to describe Darwin's ideas, he is often referred to as a Social Darwinist. And occasionally, he (and, as we shall see in succeeding chapters, virtually every other European thinker of the latter nineteenth century that bothered to comment on such matters) did make Social Darwinist-like remarks. But Spencer was against militarism, patriotism, and imperialism. It is ironic that because of his phrase, he is often mentioned as the paradigm example of a Social Darwinist.

Spencer's main project was to show that at every level—the physical, the organic, the human, and the social—nature was organized by one overarching principle, that of progressive evolution. His system was complex and included dissolution and death as well as evolution and progressive change. He was a Lamarckian who believed there is a force within humans that leads them to adapt to circumstances. Under the proper conditions, these adaptations would be passed on to future generations. He thought people would best develop to a higher level if they experienced their circumstances as fully as possible, because such experience would evoke the inner forces that produced change. Spencer was a supporter of private charity; but he was not a supporter of government programs to help the poor. Opposition to government charity is the extent of his Social Darwinism. To Spencer, humankind would eventually become more altruistic and less violent and militaristic, and eventually, governments would not be needed because people would instinctively get along and do the right thing.

Spencer was influenced by a religious upbringing that by his teens had transformed into an implicit deism. That is, he thought that there was a plan behind events, although he did not embrace any sort of anthropomorphic deity. One of the reasons Spencer's books were so compelling to the Victorian reading public was that he provided a way people could believe in the progressive development of humans and human society without believing in God. In fact, Spencer supported belief in science and in the unity of all knowledge. Spencer was a self-conscious stylist who strove to write clear, readable prose. His books, however, were quite long as he supported his points with volumes of examples. He tried very hard to master all branches of knowledge and to present their findings in as clear a way as possible. Reading Spencer, people could think that they, too, were mastering all the knowledge of nineteenth-century Europe.

Conclusion

A major theme in the mid-nineteenth century was transformation in the natural and human worlds. Transformation in the geological and organic worlds could be seen in the mountains, rocks, and fossils. Transformation in the human world was seen everywhere and clearly demonstrated in the Crystal Palace Exhibition of 1851.

As thinkers tried to apply Darwin's insights to the social world, they developed an ethnocentric and class-centric approach. Individuals who were in the middle or upper classes seemed to have inherited the traits that allowed them to successfully negotiate modern society. But those who were poor or criminal were seen to have inferior traits. Similarly, societies that were successful in the world of commerce, war, and imperialism must have a structure and a set of inhabitants that were superior to the structures and inhabitants of less successful societies.

Darwin's theory was based on the competition among individuals of a species. The species itself emerged from the makeup of the individuals who comprised it. In this respect, it fit the needs of a liberal society. But we have seen that although individualists increasingly dominated European elite thought, not everyone agreed with individualism. Some, like the socialists discussed in the previous chapter, thought that the form of society could be changed to create a humane and nurturing space for the individuals. In the next chapter, we will look at the theories, some insidious, that underlay nationalism and other group and social analyses.

CHAPTER 7
NATIONALISM AND OTHER "ISMS"

Figure 7.1 Proclamation of the German Empire at Versailles. Painting by Anton von Werner. Werner was present and was commissioned to make several paintings. The paintings were altered to meet the needs of the commissioners. © DEA/G. DAGLI ORTI/De Agostini/Getty Images.

New Nations

On January 18, 1871, German military bands played enthusiastically as troops marched around the French Palace at Versailles. Inside, in the Hall of Mirrors, King William of Prussia, joined by twenty-five leaders of other German states along with generals and diplomats, worshipped at a field altar at one end of the hall. All present ended the service with a loud rendition of the German hymn "Now Thank we all our God" ("Nun danket Alle Gott") as they prepared to join together to create the new German Empire. Otto von Bismarck, the Prussian minister-president and North German Federation chancellor, proclaimed the Empire, and the Grand Duke of Baden shouted: "His Majesty Emperor (Kaiser) Wilhelm!" Bismarck was now chancellor of the German Empire.

Four months earlier, on September 20, 1870, Italians completed their unification as King Victor Emmanuel of Italy entered Rome and set up his household in the Quirinal Palace. A few weeks later, Pope Pius IX sequestered himself in the Vatican and left Italy to the secular world. The pope's one consolation was having called the first Vatican Council in July 1870, in which the delegates condemned rationalism, naturalism, materialism, and pantheism and also proclaimed the doctrine of Papal infallibility in matters of faith or morals. The years 1870 and 1871 were indeed eventful!

Of course, these official acts of unification were only public show. The real unifications had been accomplished in three ways: (1) by connecting all parts of Germany and Italy technologically, especially by rail and telegraph, (2) by decades of acts of war and diplomacy that either forced or persuaded the leaders of smaller states that were to be sewn together that unification was desirable and inevitable, and (3) by decades of inculcating national ideas into the peoples of the new Germany and Italy. In 1800 most of the people who lived in these areas would not have thought of themselves as German or Italian. They lived locally, spoke local languages, celebrated local traditions, and remained leery of their neighbors. By 1870 their descendants generally accepted that they were German or Italian, even if they still spoke and lived locally.

Chapter Map

The story of this chapter is in part the story of the building of national consciousness and the rise of a theory known as nationalism. A nation was defined roughly as a cultural and linguistic entity. People who shared a language and shared cultural traditions were known as a "nation." The theory of nationalism stated that all members of a nation deserved to have a state so they might govern themselves. Thus, part of the task of nationalists was to build a case for such a non-self-evident proposition. But a more difficult task was to actually construct some sort of cultural entity that could be called a nation. Only after nations had been created could nation-states follow.

Nationalism thus relied on advances in linguistics, national histories, questionable scientific studies of race, and unearthing medieval stories and myths. It also depended on the web of connections provided by technologies such as the railroads and telegraph.

Others also began to define themselves as members of newly understood groups. Urban feminists argued about how best to understand the common experiences of women. Jews found themselves left out of national theories and subject to anti-Semitism. Out of their experience arose the Zionist movement.

Napoleonic Nationalism

Before the French Revolution, the word "nation" tended to refer to the nobility that ruled over peasants in feudal monarchies. Serfs were irrelevant to the aristocrats, who usually

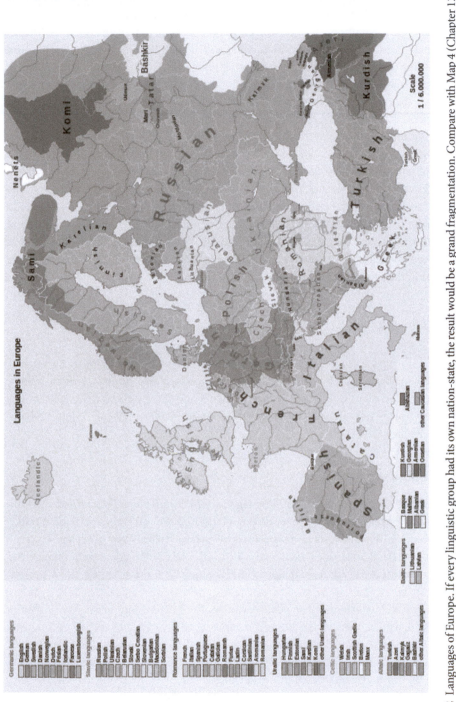

Map 2 Languages of Europe. If every linguistic group had its own nation-state, the result would be a grand fragmentation. Compare with Map 4 (Chapter 13) depicting the unity of Europe. Ironically, focus on national groupings leads to fracturing, while a focus on individual equality leads to unity.

were descendants of the serfs' ancestor conquerors. Something that is very personal to us today, like choice of religion, was determined by the ruling prince.

The French Revolution and the rule of Napoleon changed all that. As the idea of the French Nation formed early in the process of revolution, property rights and constitutional government were available to all citizens. As the revolution radicalized, the state assumed religious authority as it abolished the aristocratically oriented church. A state religion, complete with rites, holidays, and (new) traditions replaced Catholicism. Eventually, France was able to recruit an effective citizen army motivated to fight for a nation to which they themselves belonged. This nation included all of the peoples who lived in France, with their various dialects and traditions, and thus had a cosmopolitan aspect. The arts and the sciences blossomed in France and were symbols of what France thought she had to offer the world. The French nation, then, began to see itself as more civilized than other nations. And many French began to view civilization as an aspect of nationhood. French government bounced from Napoleon to restoration of a Bourbon king and then to a new Napoleon with a new Empire in the third quarter of the nineteenth century, but the French nation-state continued to remain more receptive to inclusion than the German states.

German Nationalism

Napoleon Bonaparte's success in almost conquering Europe galvanized other Europeans. Especially in Germany, thinkers simultaneously condemned godless French culture while urging Germans to emulate France in the creation of a new German nation. The main early voices were the romantics Johan Gottfried Herder (1744–1803) and Johann Gottlieb Fichte (1762–1814).

Johann Gottfried Herder

Herder developed a philosophy of language in which language determined thought. One cannot express thoughts except through language, but all languages are not alike. In fact, for Herder, meaning is determined by the way words are used; there are no preformed eternal meanings to which words of each language attach themselves. Rather, as words are used in particular contexts along with other words, the meanings evolve.

The logical conclusion is that people who speak different languages have different thoughts. A nation, then, was a linguistic entity. And when we think about linguistic nations, we become aware that different peoples have different customs, foods, traditions, religions, and practices. Herder thought it unlikely that people could love all humanity as much as they loved their own families and tribes.

For Herder, the totality of human experience was a dance of nations. Each nation was an important part of the whole. Herder was a dedicated cosmopolitan. He supported human rights and hated absolutism. He was an egalitarian who thought that there was only one class, the people, a class that included monarchs, political leaders, and working people but which did not include "the rabble." It was up to the state to ensure that all people had the opportunity to be educated and have a minimum standard of living. Herder appreciated international travel, exchange, and trade. He strongly condemned war, colonialism, and any other sorts of attempts by some nations to dominate others. Where there was intercultural mixing, Herder opposed homogenization, or the necessity of some nations to lose themselves in the presence of a master nation.

Herder's establishment of linguistic variation as a sign of variation in ways of thinking or worldviews provided nineteenth-century nationalists a way of thinking that brought the primacy of nations to the fore. Not all of these thinkers were as appreciative of other cultures as was Herder. Unfortunately, a belief in essential national differences combined with ethnocentrism provided a way for other nationalists to argue for the need of some nations to conquer others.

Johann Gottlieb Fichte

We first met Fichte in Chapter 3 as one of the founders of German Idealism. In 1807–8, as Napoleon swept through Prussia, Fichte wrote *Addresses to the German Nation*, a book that was later seen as a founding document of German nationalism. For Fichte, a supporter of the French Revolution, Napoleon had betrayed republican ideals and negated the revolution. As a result, Fichte called upon Germans to take up the cause of freedom, become aware of themselves as a nation, and resist Napoleon and his threat to human progress. Fichte borrowed from Herder the concept of nationalism and the essential differences among all nations. When Fichte wrote his book, Napoleon's troops occupied Berlin, to which Fichte had returned after first fleeing the invading troops. Napoleon's ability to foster a sense of national feeling among the French inspired Fichte

Figure 7.2 A picture of Johann Gottlieb Fichte addressing the German Nation 1807–8. © Getty Images.

to try to foster a national feeling in Germans. The difference, Fichte claimed, was that the French nationalism was cosmopolitan and thus cut off from a natural nationalism. Germans alone had the ability to rekindle an organic nationalism.

Fichte proposed a new form of education for Germans in which love of Fatherland and German culture would be prerequisite. Training in national sentiment and allegiance would predate even reading and writing. Fichte advocated that all children be removed from their homes to avoid contamination with nonnational ideas. They would be cared for in the schools and returned to their families when their education was complete.

Fichte saw the divisions of Germans into a multitude of states as a perversion of true German feeling. The rulers of these various political entities acted in their own interests rather than in the interests of Germany. Even if one of these princes were able to prevail over the others, a Germany united under one of the existing states, say Prussia, would become Prussian rather than German. What Fichte proposed was nothing less than the cultivation of a new way of thinking in all the states in which Germans lived. When this program was completed, Germany would arise because of the sentiment of all the people, not because of pacts among princes. The early Germans, claimed Fichte, were a confederation of small groups with a central leader whose powers were carefully delegated. They learned absolute government from other, non-German groups, like the Romans, but absolutism did not fit the German spirit.

This German spirit is carried, said Fichte, by language. The first speakers of a language saw the world a certain way, and even though languages change over time, new words carry the same meaning as the old. There is continuity to thought, because language precedes the thought. Germans who were brought up to speak a non-German language can never recapture the connection with their ancestors that a true German feels. He concluded that Germans link mental life to action, whereas non-German-speaking Teutonic people separate mental activity from life and see mental culture as a kind of game. Germans were destined to take the lead in developing the new culture of Europe. And what better people than the Germans—who had produced artists and thinkers of the caliber of Goethe, Kant, and Beethoven?

For Fichte, there was a supersensuous realm of existence within which Germans lived. True meaning in life resided in individuals' ability to realize that their lives stemmed from the whole. Fichte dismissed people who thought that the individual stands alone and makes a life. In time, all individuals disappear. Only the nation persists. Individuals were, then, specks dispersing in the wind. They did not exist in any long-lasting or eternal way. God has given us the nation and has united individuals with their spiritual form, which is the nation.

Fichte's ideas were not immediately useful. Germans did not suddenly leap to overcome their differences. But the building of industrial organizations in the Western part of Germany, a tariff union that made possible the transportation of goods and peoples across borders, and, of course interstate railroads and telegraph lines, all of these and more led to a situation in which Fichte's lectures were resurrected and became part of the ideology that was embodied in the German Empire under the Prussian king and German emperor.

Italian Nationalism

Some Italian voices had advocated for a unified Italy at least since Niccoló Machiavelli (1469–1527). In the nineteenth century, however, the unification movement (known as the *Risorgimento*) bore fruit with the accession of Victor Emmanuel, king of Piedmont-Sardinia, to the Italian throne in 1861. Arguably, the most effective voice in a welter of nationalist voices was that of Giuseppe Mazzini (1805–72). Mazzini combined journalistic analysis with a talent for organizing and proved an effective leader. It is worth noting that Mazzini was a republican who believed in democracy, and so the accession of a king was a distinct compromise for him.

Mazzini was born in an area of northern Italy that was ruled by the French. His father was a radical revolutionary, a supporter of Robespierre and the Jacobins, while Mazzini's mother was a pious Jansenist who believed that we are predestined to sin and hell, and we can only be saved by divine grace. Mazzini did not grow up in a family that favored compromise and half-measures. Catholics and the pope condemned both of his parents' beliefs, yet Mazzini built his analysis on the importance of the church.

In his early adulthood, Mazzini joined the secret political group called the Carboneria and was arrested and exiled. From France, Mazzini helped found his own secret society, Young Italy, with the motto "God and the People." He hoped that a general popular insurrection would produce the unified democratic republic that he hoped for. For a time, during the revolutions of 1848, Mazzini found himself a member of a triumvirate ruling Rome. The republican troops (led by Giuseppe Garibaldi, the general who later led successful troops in the battle for Italian unification) were no match for the French army that had responded to the pope's frantic pleas for help, so Mazzini returned to exile. As the wars for unification went on, Mazzini found himself in disagreement. He had in mind a populist, republican revolt, and until Rome was finally subdued and the unification of Italy complete, he did not support the monarchical government.

As his thoughts developed and were expressed in articles and books, Mazzini emphasized collaboration among all Italians. He was opposed to Marxism and the idea that the bourgeoisie and the proletarians have opposite interests. To the contrary, he was in favor of one Italian nation under God. In the 1860 "Doveri dell'uomo" ("Duties of Man"), Mazzini argued that all people first and foremost are humans, members of the human race, and they should feel a kinship with all people. But individuals are helpless to right wrongs if they are individuals standing alone overlooking the vastness of humanity. People need the association of others to have any noticeable effect. Therefore, God has given us nations, people who share our language and customs, with whom we can work to achieve a better world.

Unfortunately, evil governments have broken up these natural nations for their own gain. The members of these governments only recognize their own clans, and the rest of humanity is there for them to exploit. God, however, will not allow this situation to persist. With God's help and approval, we will restore our nations, and the states of the world will be formed as governments of nations. Mazzini argues that nations, when armed with state power and governed by the people, democratically, can effectively right wrongs and create a good society. To Mazzini, the highest good was to love and support one's nation. The nations together, then, could promote the universal good from which he started this analysis. His watchwords were education, labor, and the franchise.

Mazzini was a strong supporter of women's rights. He believed that equality between the sexes was necessary to build a truly democratic society. Interestingly, he was convinced in these views by an Englishwoman, Jessie White Mario, who dedicated herself to the unification of Italy after hearing of atrocities committed in Italy by foreign troops. White made her living as a journalist, and her exposés of poverty were influential in helping ameliorate conditions.

Nationalism was a thriving idea in the nineteenth century, and, of course, it continues to be a strong force in contemporary Europe. In the nineteenth century, it offered a religious goal for which people were willing to die. Whether nationalism represented the interests of small nations oppressed by a larger power, like the Greeks or Serbs under the Ottoman Empire, or the interests of large nations split among a number of powers, like the Germans or Italians, that is, whether independence or unification was called for, the call to identify with a nation and offer one's life and fortune to help it gain political power was a compelling call.

Finding the Nation in Languages

Before the nineteenth century, most European language studies focused on Greek, Latin, Hebrew, and other ancient languages. However, colonialism brought Europeans into contact with non-European languages, and scholars began to examine them. The field of Orientalism extended from the languages and ideas of the Near East to studies of Indian thought along with the study of Sanskrit in British India. But the British, led by James Mill and Thomas Macaulay, tended to look down on Indian culture. Only a few scholars were interested in devoting rigorous thought to Indian language and culture. One of these scholars, the Scot Alexander Hamilton (cousin of the American), went to Paris to study Sanskrit manuscripts there. Moored in Paris during the Napoleonic Wars, Hamilton taught Sanskrit to Europeans in France.

Friedrich Schlegel

One of these Europeans was the German Friedrich Schlegel (1772–1829), the German Romantic who had so influenced Schelling in Jena. The study of the connections between Sanskrit and European languages that produced our current concept of the Indo-European languages thus passed from Great Britain to Germany. Realizing the connection between Sanskrit and German, Schlegel theorized that the Germans had come from India. Schlegel's 1808 book, *On the Language and Wisdom of India*, may have been the primary cause of an "oriental Renaissance." In the book, Schlegel mistakenly claimed that German came from Sanskrit, rather than recognizing that both came from an earlier, lost language. He also argued that the history of language cannot be studied by just noting the similarity among words, but rather had to be established by looking at the structure of the various languages and comparing these structures. Schlegel focused on inflection, that is, how a word changes to mark things like tense, number, person, mood, and so forth. Thus, Schlegel popularized the notion of comparative grammar.

Jacob Grimm

Others used Schlegel's book to develop the idea of the superiority of the German or Aryan (from India) race. About the same time, Jacob Grimm (1785–1863) had studied the evolution of the German language by comparing the grammatical structure of various German languages. Grimm studied how a sound in a word changes over time, and he was able to show that if one posited a regular occurrence of sound changes, one could show how related languages diverged from one another. For instance, one could show that if the early language from which all Indo-European languages evolved had a word for "ten" that was "dekm," one could derive Latin "decem," "Greek deka," Sanskrit "dasa," and Gothic "taihun." Since these sound changes occurred throughout a given language, one could compare other similar words using the derived sound changes. The study of sound changes was thus a powerful method for reconstructing the historical evolution of language families.

Grimm was also interested in German legal institutions, and, with his brother Wilhelm, he published studies of German folklore. From the Grimm brothers we have received the materials of several Disney movies. Thus, studies of the history of German language and culture supported German nationalism.

Comparative and historical "linguistics" (the word was coined in the late 1830s) developed a methodology and a set of experts. Franz Bopp (1791–1867) studied verb conjugations rather than Schlegel's inflections. Bopp was able to compile a set of comparative grammars of Sanskrit, Avestan, Greek, Latin, Lithuanian, Old Slavic, Gothic, and German. Bopp had no use for romantic ideas, but rather strove to take part in developing a real science of language. Later in the century, linguists used the model developed in the study of Indo-European languages to study other language groupings.

Wilhelm von Humboldt

Perhaps most notable was Wilhelm von Humboldt (1737–1835), who learned his Sanskrit from Bopp. Humboldt had a rich and varied career as a diplomat, government servant, philosopher, and linguist. He founded the Berlin University that was eventually named after him and developed a theory of education involving engaging students in social situations, like apprenticeships, in order to make them "well-informed human beings and citizens."

As a linguist, Humboldt extended studies to languages outside of the Indo-European grouping. For Humboldt, all languages were rule-governed systems and not just correspondences between things and sounds. Meaning reflects the ideas of the social group that uses it, and therefore the users of different languages will think differently about the world. Humboldt distinguished between a "linguistic worldview (*Weltansicht*)" and a more general worldview (*Weltanschauung*).

The flow of words can be suspended while human beings reflect, and during reflection the flow of sensations is also suspended. Language-based thought creates a consciousness that one set of circumstances is different from another and the knowing subject is different from the objects of contemplation. Through language we impose order on the formless flow of impressions. That is, language allows us to orient ourselves in the world.

Words do not occur apart from other words, but the linguistic sounds of language occur only in a system of sounds. Understanding between solitary minds can occur only because we speak in a similar language system and, even then, understanding only occurs through dialogue. Thinking is not a solitary, but rather a social act. And in order to fully comprehend that act, we should study a language's literature, science, and philosophy. Humboldt's study supported the idea that different nations, defined by different languages, were culturally different from one another.

Fascination with the Medieval

Beginning in the eighteenth century, some writers and scholars became fascinated by the stories and lore of their medieval pasts. The motives were many, but the effect was to recall a golden past age when noble was an adjective as well as a noun, where everyone had a social position, and where, as Robert Browning wrote, "God's in his heaven—/All's right with the world."

In 1760 the Scottish poet James MacPherson published *Fragments of Ancient Poetry*, a translation of works that he said he had collected from oral interviews in Scottish Gaelic. He claimed that a legendary poet named Ossian had produced the tales. By the middle of the nineteenth century, MacPherson's book had been translated into virtually every main European language and had been depicted in art and opera. Although controversy over the authenticity of his materials continues to this day, there seems to be a consensus that he had indeed unearthed valuable folk tales and that he himself had a part in shaping the poetry. However that may be, all over Europe writers began their own quests to bring the "medieval" (a word coined in the nineteenth century) world into modern Europe.

Walter Scott

Walter Scott, himself a Scotsman, wrote the widely popular *Ivanhoe* in 1819. Set in twelfth-century England, *Ivanhoe* involved a love story between a Christian and a Jew set against the enmity between Norman barons and Anglo-Saxon peasants. Through his historical fiction, Scott created dilemmas that reflected the politics of his own day. Scott was one of the first writers of historical novels, and he had no scruples about combining history and fiction in other ways. When King George VI was scheduled to visit Scotland in 1822, Scott was commissioned to orchestrate the pageantry, including the king

Figure 7.3 Walter Scott monument, Edinburgh, Scotland. © Photograph by David Galaty.

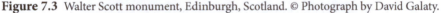

wearing a tartan, and thus the tartan became a major symbol of Scottish identity. When Scott wrote *Kenilworth*, he had his Queen Elizabeth enter her castle in a quite similar ceremony. Eventually the English became fascinated by Scottish culture.

The Gothic revival accompanied this literary fascination with the medieval, beginning in the mid-eighteenth century. By the nineteenth century, Gothic architecture became common. It was associated with high church, or neo-Catholic, Anglicanism, and in this guise, it spread throughout the United States as well. The British Houses of Parliament (built in the 1840s) are other examples. In literature, the Gothic novel emerged, one of which was Mary Shelley's *Frankenstein*, followed by many novels, including Emily Brontë's *Wuthering Heights* (1847). Brontë's novel is a story of love triangles, class snobbery, revenge, thwarted desire, and ultimately of death and unhappiness. It is a complex, intricately plotted book, and is still seen as one of the best novels England has produced.

Medievalism also motivated the decision in 1848 of seven artistic friends to found the Pre-Raphaelite Brotherhood. Essentially the Pre-Raphaelites thought that art had gone astray in the High Renaissance and had become mechanistic and overly mannered. They wanted to return to the art of the thirteenth century to emphasize imitation of nature and society as they are truly seen—in intense color. Dante Gabriel Rossetti in particular wanted to explore the connections between romantic poetry and art, and his sister, Christina, herself became an excellent poet. Essentially, they saw an integrity in medieval culture, as well as a spirituality, that had been lost in the intervening centuries.

As romantics, they wanted to restore such values. Their literary heroes were John Keats and Alfred, Lord Tennyson.

Richard Wagner

In Germany, the medieval orientation was highlighted by the later operas of Richard Wagner (1813–83), a flamboyant composer of what he called a *Gesamtkunstwerk* (a total work of art) that united several of the arts in a way that allowed each of them to play an important role. In his young adulthood, Wagner was a democrat and a socialist who liked to live beyond his means. All of these tendencies forced him to flee—either from creditors or from post-1848 conservative governments. Throughout his life, Wagner engaged in stormy affairs and marriages. In exile, he developed new theories of music that he actualized after his return to Germany in 1862. Soon thereafter, the young king of Bavaria, "mad" King Ludwig II, invited Wagner to Munich, paid off Wagner's debts, and supported his operas. As Wagner's operas increasingly concerned medieval myths, Ludwig, enchanted, built a fairy-tale-like castle at Neuschwanstein beginning in 1868. By 1875, Ludwig had an opera house (*Festspielhaus*) along with a home for Wagner and his family built on a hill in the city of Bayreuth. This became the site of an annual festival, a veritable orgy of Wagnerian operas.

An excellent example of Wagner's fascination with the medieval is his opera *Tristan and Isolde*, sometimes cited as the origin of modern music. Wagner always wrote both the score and the libretto for his operas and made both work together. *Tristan and Isolde* is a story of a knight who falls in love with his king's betrothed. Such a love could never be consummated and had to end in death—a "love death." In the overture, one can hear a series of chords that move from key to key and never resolve into an ending. The listener sits in a state of anxiety, waiting for the music to resolve into a final chord. Thus, the music itself reflects the state of mind of Tristan who can never find peace.

Wagner's operas included his famous "Ring Cycle" that includes *Das Rheingold*, *Die Walküre*, *Siegfried*, and *Götterdämmerung*. The Ring Cycle lasts fifteen hours, and is usually played in four successive nights. The story involves a ring forged by a dwarf that gives the bearer the ability to rule the world. The ring is, of course, stolen—by Wotan, the king of the gods—but it has to be given to the giants in payment. The operas concern the complex attempts to get the ring back. Eventually Siegfried is successful, the ring is given to the Rhine maidens, and the gods and Valhalla are destroyed. As Wagner wrote these operas, he used the musical idea of the *leitmotif* in which a musical phrase stands for a character or an idea. He also used large orchestras to express a wide range of emotion. His last opera, *Parsifal*, was overtly nationalist, anti-Semitic, and tended to offend traditional Christians.

National Histories

The case for nationalism was not merely an intellectual analysis; for a new nation to emerge, the people who supposedly made up that nation had to feel their kinship with each other deep in their bones. One way to build a national consciousness was to construct a national history. The modern profession of history was largely born in the nineteenth century, and one theme that almost all historians shared was progress. Hegel saw history as the unfolding of the world spirit and the realization of the absolute. The Hegelian Karl Marx saw history as a set of class struggles that would result in the humane freedom of a classless society.

Thomas Macaulay

The English historian Thomas Macaulay (1800–59) also saw English history as the unfolding of liberty, but he insisted that the craft of the novelist be combined with that of the archivist so that "two hostile powers," Reason and Imagination, might be brought together. For Macaulay, a historian must be absolutely true to the materials, the facts, of history, yet the narrative that emerges should be "affecting and picturesque." Macaulay, in his 1828 essay "History," surveyed historians from the Greek Herodotus to the writers of his day to show the imbalance of historical narrative on one side or another of the Reason/Imagination conundrum. In his own time, Macaulay thought, "The best historians of later times have been seduced from truth, not by their imagination, but by their reason." They seek general principles that are deduced by a few phenomena, and then they distort the other phenomena to suit the theory. But as they apply reason mistakenly, they also neglect narrative. For Macaulay, it is important to capture the spirit of an age, and, in order to do so, perhaps make editorial decisions about which documents to include or emphasize. Macaulay set out to write a history of England that met his own criteria.

Macaulay's *The History of England from the Accession of James the Second* was published in two parts in 1848 and 1855. Mid-nineteenth-century England was riding high, with the Crystal Palace Exhibition (see Chapter 4) of 1851 demonstrating to the world the power of English technology and political influence. For Macaulay, British history demonstrated a country that had overcome superstition and had built a constitutional government based on freedom of expression and belief. The relatively new UK was a country in search of a nation. That is, the Welsh, Scottish, and Irish were peoples whom England hoped and expected would become a part of a large nation with a common tongue (English) and common laws and aspirations. Macaulay's four-volume book begins with events in 1685 and ends in 1697. Thus, it concerns itself mostly with the Glorious Revolution (1688) and its aftermath, a revolution in which Parliament established political supremacy over the crown. As such, this book supported the primacy and superiority of English, and British, culture.

Macaulay and Lord Acton, the English Catholic historian, were perhaps the foremost exponents of what in the twentieth century was derided as "Whig History," that is, historical works meant to show that the march of events moved ever upward toward liberty and freedom of expression. As Acton described Macaulay, he "had done more than any writer in the literature of the world for the propagation of the liberal faith."

Histories of France and Germany

In France, the emphasis was less on the principles of liberalism and more on the beneficial work of "the people." France's gift to the world had been the revolution and subsequent constitutions supported by the people. The principles of liberty, equality, fraternity were more important than the development of parliamentary rights. But emphasizing these principles also undermined the histories written by monarchists. Jules Michelet (1798–1874) published a nineteen-volume *History of France* in 1867. He began with the medieval period and worked his way forward to the revolution. His emphasis throughout was on the people rather than the leaders. By writing this history, Michelet demonstrated to the French that they had a deep-rooted culture and nation, whatever the political circumstances had brought in each age.

In Germany, the emphasis lay squarely with the state. Most of the German historians served Prussia, and from Hegel onward they saw the development of the state as their theme. Leopold von Ranke (1795–1886) was known for his claim that historians should write history "as it really was." To Ranke, every age was distinct, and he did not approve of Hegel's philosophy of history as a drive toward a goal. But he also said that undoubtedly there was some coherence to the movement from one age to another. Ranke saw the Teutonic peoples and the shape of modern Europe emerging from the great migrations from Asia through a variety of events like the Crusades. Ranke, influenced by Friedrich Schelling, saw God acting in history. What Ranke's readers could also see was the German nation underneath the variety of political processes and divisions. For Ranke, it would be a mistake for Germans to reenact the French Revolution, for it would break the continuity that was so important in the development of a people. The Prussian state was a spiritual being which had developed over centuries; it was a gift from God.

Each country of Europe developed a national history that saw history through the lens of its own culture. Most national historians were proponents of a law of progress. The past was leading us inexorably toward recognition of the rights of their nation. It was not clear to these historians that all nations had the right of self-determination. For instance, once the Hungarians had won the right to teach their children in Magyar, they were not willing to allow the same privilege to the Serbs in their part of the Austro-Hungarian Empire. The various nations of Europe were too intermixed to permit a "one nation-one state" principle. In fact, for one historian, Arthur de Gobineau, intermixing was causing a problem. In Gobineau we see that behind national patriotism often lay a deeper motive: racism.

Racial Theories

When Europeans began a centuries'-long enterprise of conquering other peoples and colonizing the lands on which these non-Europeans lived, they faced a problem: Were these people actually human in the same sense that Europeans could be said to be human, or were they a different, though very similar species? By far the most used textual reference was *The Bible*, and the best evidence seemed to indicate that the date of creation was about 6,000 years ago. In the seventeenth century, the Archbishop Ussher, a noted scholar, calculated the date of creation as 6:00 p.m., October 22, 4004 B.C. Ussher had laboriously acquired and compared manuscripts from many Middle Eastern sources in order to calculate his date. For anyone who wanted to calculate the time necessary for significant biological change to happen; however, the period of 6,000 years was too short. Therefore, the consensus was that God had created the peoples of the world as they appeared today.

There were two alternatives: polygenism (the creation of human times in different places and at different times) and monogenism (one point of origin for the human species). In the early nineteenth century, the favored theory was polygenism. In this version, God created the various races of humans at different times. The most recent creation was the establishment of the white races, and these seemed to Europeans to be the smartest and most able of the races of the earth. White natural superiority provided a rational for both slavery and imperialism, but even to those Europeans who practiced neither, the superiority of the white race often seemed apparent on moral and aesthetic grounds. That is, the argument was frequently made that whites were just more beautiful and acted more ethically than people from other races.

With the geological evidence that the earth had existed for hundreds of millions of years (at least), and Darwin's development of an argument for the gradual transformation of one species into another, monogenism seemed to be more persuasive to many intellectuals. Nevertheless, especially in France, scientists continued to argue for polygenism, even arguing that there was no evidence that aboriginal Australians could interbreed with whites. But especially in Great Britain, monogenism carried the day, with an argument for the impact of the environment on the gradual alteration of visible traits like skin color. Environmental monogenism still allowed for an argument of superiority, on the grounds that environmental influences had caused some races to decline in intelligence while others advanced.

Count Joseph Arthur de Gobineau

Count Joseph Arthur de Gobineau (1816–82) was therefore preaching to a continental-sized choir when he developed his "scientific" racist theory. Gobineau came from an aristocratic and quite politically conservative French family. His mother's family had lived in Saint-Domingue (Haiti) in the eighteenth century, and Gobineau was haunted by the possibility that he might have an ancestry of African origin. His mother left Gobineau's father for the tutor of her children and frequently moved with the children in and out of the eastern border of France. At one point, impoverished, she was imprisoned for fraud, a humiliation Gobineau never forgave. At the age of nineteen, Gobineau moved to Paris to become a writer. He moved in with an uncle and began to publish reactionary essays and serialized fiction. After the "Bourgeois Monarch" (Louis Philippe) took over the throne in 1832, Gobineau despaired of seeing a restoration of a legitimate heir to the Bourbon throne. Everywhere Gobineau looked, he saw the rule of money—something he deplored while desperately desiring more wealth. When he wrote about Germans, he applauded East Prussia and its rule by landed aristocrats (Junkers) but feared for the middle-class rule that seemed more and more likely with the commercial success of the customs union (Zollverein). Gobineau saw French noble aristocrats as a race apart, descended from Germanic Franks who ruled in Gaul in the fifth century. The other French classes descended from inferior Celts and other riffraff.

For Gobineau, who hated the increasingly powerful capitalist class and who saw himself as the product of a superior caste that had been defeated in the French Revolution, there was no alternative but to declare the end of civilization. After the democratically inspired revolutions of 1848, Gobineau decided to write *An Essay on the Inequality of the Human Races*, a 1,400-page tome. This huge book made his reputation. Gobineau argued that there were three human races: black, yellow, and white, and each of these races created a different sort of culture. He argued that blacks were strong physically but weak mentally. The yellow race was materialistic, and therefore able to thrive. The white race, to Gobineau, was the most intelligent and the most beautiful, and uniquely held the artistic ability to create beauty. If anyone discovered an intelligent or creative member of the black or yellow races, that person was probably created through miscegenation. But Gobineau did not press this issue too hard, for he was willing to grant that talented individuals existed in all cultures. He was willing to grant the existence of creative black or yellow people, but nevertheless, the entire race, taken at the average, was distinctly inferior to the average of the white race. One of his telling arguments claimed that anatomy was destiny:

> The dark races are the lowest on the scale. The shape of the pelvis has a character of animalism, which is imprinted on the individuals of that race ere their birth, and seems to portend their destiny. . . . The negro's narrow and receding forehead seems to mark him as inferior in reasoning capacity.[1]

Gobineau argued on the basis of language studies that the Aryans of Hindu legend had spread their genes throughout the area where Indo-European languages were spoken. He extolled the Indian caste system that maintained the superior Aryans at the top, and criticized the Buddhists, who had argued for the possibility of universal enlightenment, as promoting a sexual mixing of castes.

So, Gobineau traced an imaginary set of migrations in which Aryans originated in Siberia and, retreating against Asian hoards, moved toward India and Europe. Yellow races came from the Americas and black races from Africa. The beauty of Persian epic poetry and Persian women proves that they were Aryan. They became inferior when they mixed with Semitics who had themselves mixed with blacks from Africa.

Gobineau was not only a racist but also a classist. It was inconceivable to him that any commoner could be as intelligent or generally as noble as a purebred aristocrat. The downfall of France, Gobineau claimed, was due to the democratic mixing of the classes.

For Gobineau, as for many Europeans, the advent of democratic institutions, however well-guarded against actual control by mid-nineteenth-century working classes, signaled a terrible decline in Western civilization. The anti-Semitic Gobineau saw the Jews as an alien race that could bring down European culture. The German race seemed to have preserved Aryan traits the best. For Gobineau, as for Hegel and Fichte before him, the Germans were the hope of Europe. His book convinced the anti-Semitic composer Richard Wagner, and Wagner's son-in-law Houston Stewart Chamberlain later wrote a racist book, *The Foundations of the Nineteenth Century* (1899), that influenced Nazi anti-Semitism. The consequences of this point of view in the twentieth century were to be catastrophic.

Scientific Racism

While most European scientists harbored the idea that different races have different capacities, there were some, in the biological, medical, and anthropological sciences, who set out professionally to prove this assumption. The flaw in these studies is that however scrupulous the experimental design, the experiments assumed what they set out to prove. And indeed, experimental design was difficult. If scientists wanted to show quantitative differences in capacities, say for intelligence, or physical strength, or persistence, or for nurturing, the question was, what should they measure?

One answer was to focus on intelligence and measure the relative size of brains. Scientists could remove the brain and then fill the skull with little BBs. When the BBs were poured into a graduated cylinder, scientists could see exactly how much room there was in the skull. They assumed that intelligence was directly linked to brain size. One of the most famous scientists carrying out such experimental programs was the French anatomist Paul Broca (1824–80) after whom Broca's area, in the frontal lobe of the brain, is named. Broca engaged in research in a number of areas of medicine. For our purposes, we shall look at his studies in the French Anthropological Institute, which Broca founded in 1859 (the year of the publication of Darwin's *Origin of Species*). Broca measured skulls, weighed brains, even assessed forearms (to see if the length of the forearm could be tied to apelike bodies), and tried to be as scrupulous as he could. As these studies continued, a major test was whether they supported what everyone knew: that whites were superior to other races. Unfortunately, brain size was not correlated with the supposedly more intelligent races. When eminent and successful people donated their brains for study after their deaths, there were several embarrassingly small brains.

When Broca began studying the size of various parts of recently harvested brains of various races, and of the placement of the hole in the skull through which the spinal cord passes (foramen magnum), he hoped to find that blacks were closer to apes than were whites. In fact, as he carefully reflected on his results, he found that according to his experimental design, blacks should be more intelligent than whites. Clearly, a rethinking of the experimental design was needed, and Broca was up to the task.

Figure 7.4 Brain studied by Paul Broca. © Apic/Hulton Archive/Getty Images.

Broca and most of his colleagues realized that brain size is positively correlated with body size, and since no one claimed that larger people are more intelligent than smaller people, scientists had to correct for differences in body size in order to accurately compare two people. The issue of body size clearly affects any comparison between men and women, although some misogynist scientists used uncorrected data to show that women were inherently less intelligent than men. Women scientists showed the flaw in such reasoning.

By the twentieth century, scientists realized that determining intelligence by studying brain size was a hopeless endeavor. Today the nineteenth-century data remains in the records, but nineteenth-century use of that data to reach conclusions is worthless. Nonetheless, the impact of these scientific studies was enormous at a time when science was becoming the standard of objective truth. And the conclusions persisted in the twentieth century among nonscientists. Meanwhile, those scientists who wanted to continue to correlate intelligence with some measurable trait turned to intelligence testing. And although many institutions that wanted to sort human beings by "smartness" used intelligence testing, with its famous factor called IQ, the accuracy of intelligence tests is highly contested, and in general, has been discredited.

Finding Criminals

Cesare Lombroso (1835–1909) was an Italian from Verona who pursued literature, linguistics, and archaeology before settling on medicine. About ten years after he finished his degree and began practicing, he became a professor specializing in forensic medicine. His most famous work, *The Criminal Man*, was published in 1876. Lombroso argued that criminals shared certain anatomical traits. He was trying to identify anatomical disparities between the insane and the criminal, when he was given the chance to observe the skull of a well-known criminal. He reported having a "flash of inspiration" in which he realized that criminals were throwbacks to earlier stages in evolution. He saw similarities between criminals, savages, and apes. All had "enormous jaws, high cheek bones, prominent superciliary (eyebrow) arches, solitary lines in palms." He saw ability to withstand pain and a love of tattooing and orgies, among other propensities. They all wanted not just to kill but to mutilate and cannibalize.

Lombroso's theories quickly attracted opponents. Earlier in the century, the main approach to criminological theory, the classical school of criminality supported by Cesare Beccaria and Jeremy Bentham, emphasized rational people making free choices. They argued that increasingly severe punishment should be used as a deterrent. To Lombroso, crime was hereditary, and he therefore opposed punishment in favor of isolation, exile, or, sometimes, execution. Lombroso discouraged looking at the environment from

Figure 7.5 "Avere Una Bella Cera—Wax Portraits Exhibition." Wax heads made by a Lorenzo Tenchini, a student of Cesare Lombroso, to show criminal types. © Marco Secci/Getty Images Entertainment/Getty Images.

which criminals had come, because criminality was present before the environment could have made a difference. Better to study the actual criminal's biological traits. His daughter reported, however, that later he found that disease and environment played a part and that there was a "graduated scale leading from the born criminal to the normal individual."

Interestingly enough, because criminals were associated with "savages" and apes, Lombroso creatively described animals with human traits, like the adulterous stork that killed her husband or the male ant that raped and killed a female ant with atrophied sexual organs because he lacked access to female ants with reproductive powers.

Lombroso was highly influential around the turn of the century since he was one of the founders of forensic psychology and of institutions for the criminally insane. He may have coined the word "criminology." In several countries, expert witnesses from the Lombroso school testified in trials concerning the criminality of a defendant who had "criminal" features and traits. How many innocents with unfortunate physiognomies spent their lives in prison because of the force of Lombroso? In literature, from Tolstoy to Bram Stocker, characters cited Lombroso as they assessed the criminality behind other characters.

Women's Lives

The questions of women's rights, or how to make the lives of women better, did not initially center on voting rights. In fact, for most of the nineteenth century, most citizens, male or female, did not have the right to vote. Universal male suffrage was enacted for most European countries between 1870 and 1918, and most European women were not enfranchised until the twentieth century. Citizen voting did not make much sense unless there was a parliamentary government. Even then, most people lived on small farms and were not very interested in the issues discussed in Parliament. Generally, voting rights were an issue either for those with property or those residing in cities.

In the eighteenth century, a few women, like Mary Wollstonecraft or Olympe De Gouge, demanded education for women and marriage equality. These continued to be demanded by many middle-class women along with economic rights, like the right to control the money they brought into a marriage or earned while married. As the Industrial Revolution grew stronger, there were more demands that women be allowed to work or to set up businesses without the permission or supervision of their fathers or husbands. Another important issue for many women was protection from prostitution.

As we have seen, early socialists like Saint-Simon or Fourier (see Chapter 5) argued for the complete emancipation of women and the inauguration of ideal societies. Many women theorists incorporated these ideas into their analyses. In 1833 the communitarian-entrepreneur Robert Owen published a manifesto, "Appeal to Women," excerpted from the French feminist newspaper *La Femme Libre*, a newspaper that used only first names of women to avoid retribution. Their appeal included: "Let us refuse as husbands any man who is not sufficiently generous to consent to share his power. . . . We prefer celibacy to slavery." And: "Universal association is beginning; among nations there will no longer be relationships other than industrial, scientific, and moral; the future will be peaceful."[2]

George Sand

The writer George Sand (Aurore Dupin, baroness Dudevant) echoed the sentiment in her 1832 novel *Indiana,* as a wife responds to her husband:

> You resorted to violence and locked me in my room; I went out through the window to show you that there is a difference between exerting an absurd control over a woman's actions and reigning over her will. I passed several hours away from your domination; I breathed the air of liberty in order to show you that you are not morally my master, and that I look to no one on earth but myself for orders.[3]

When the revolutions erupted in 1848, women put their own concerns on the table alongside those of their male colleagues and fellow revolutionaries. They had two kinds of issues: (1) access to various goods like jobs or education and (2) public equality, including the right to own property or to vote. In France, the journalist and former follower of utopian socialist Saint-Simon, Jeanne Deroin (1805–94), argued vociferously for the vote for women. The government should concentrate on ending the struggle between women and men by ending male privilege, she insisted. Deroin emphasized the maternal duties of women by arguing that they could only protect their children by publicly working to construct French society. A founder of feminist newspapers like *Voix des Femmes* and *Politique des Femmes*, Deroin also founded women's clubs and associations.

Louise Otto

The German Louise Otto (1819–95) founded two journals especially for women, *Frauen-Zeitung* and *Neue Bahnen*. She also founded the German Association of Female Citizens (*Allgemeiner Deutscher Frauenverein*) and published several novels and poems that promoted her ideas. In Frauen-Zeitung, she clarified her position: "I do not belong to those so-called 'emancipated' women who have discredited the phrase 'women's emancipation' by devaluing woman to become a caricature of man."[4] She believed that women, because they were different from men, could accomplish more to achieve "world salvation." Otto, a socialist and a Christian, focused on women who suffered from poverty and misery.

Otto sought to distinguish her ideas from "Georgesandism," a German movement to imitate the French writer George Sand. Sand was caricatured for illegally wearing men's clothes, smoking in public, and engaging in multiple affairs. Otto emphasized women as good citizens who showed faith and courage in building a moral country. But Sand's radical individualism, important as it was, was not all France had to offer to women's movements. The playwright Victor Hugo grasped the possibilities as he declared that the nineteenth century would proclaim the right of women.

Deroin and Otto's emphasis on the distinct qualities of women is an important theme in nineteenth-century women's movements, especially in Continental Europe, even after activist women began to focus on the vote. Women deserve to be included in government because they are different than men and therefore have insights and abilities that are presently unrepresented. In a sense this position stakes out an "essentialist" position. Just as many nationalists claimed that their nation had different traits and insights from other nations, women like Otto saw women as a kind of a nation with deeply imprinted traits and points of view. The view that women should have political rights because they are different from men also echoed the rationale of those who would withhold the right of women to have a public voice. The two sides argued the same position but reached quite different conclusions based on that position.

Eliza Burt Gamble

The publication of Charles Darwin's books, especially *The Descent of Man, and Selection in Relation to Sex* (1871), caused several women to react to Darwin's apparent anti-woman bias. Such a woman was the American Eliza Burt Gamble (1841–1920), who wrote a book *The Evolution of Woman* (1894) in which she argued, "scientists, generally, seemed inclined to ignore certain facts connected with this theory which tend to prove the superiority of the female organization"[5] Darwin had written that males have to compete to be selected by a female, and says, Burt, if this is true, then the woman is the "intelligent factor" whose will selects the supposedly superior traits of men. Furthermore, some of these traits, like hairiness, are argued in other scientific works that describe the hierarchies of primates, to be a sign of inferiority. In fact, the female of many species is able to reproduce not only sexually but also through parthenogenesis. More boys are born, but more girls survive. Gamble goes on to show how women were once supreme in society. Warfare allowed her to be subjugated, but that disability is being rectified in modern society. In short, this feminine critique of Darwin emphasizes not that women are just as good as men, but that women are better in almost every way.

Alternative Approaches

The other view was that women are essentially the same as men. As Harriet Taylor (see Chapter 2), the soulmate and wife of John Stuart Mill, wrote in her article "Enfranchisement of Women" (1851): "That civil and political rights acknowledge no sex, and therefore the word 'male' should be struck from every State Constitution."[6] Taylor called for a "partnership" and a "coequal share" in private industry and government. She and other feminists looked up to the leadership of the United States in establishing a true democracy in which women were organizing to demand suffrage. Despite its flaws, the United States seemed to offer a model of a state in which the ideal was equality for all.

In the third quarter of the nineteenth century, radical women focused on many emergent issues. For instance, the Crimean War (1853–6) provoked antiwar movements that sought to cross European boundaries to bring women from different countries together. The Swiss Marie Goegg argued that reeducation of women concerning the evils of war could lead these women to train their young sons not to glorify war and national glory through military conquest. In 1905, a woman, the Austrian writer Bertha von Suttner, won the Nobel Peace Prize for her work in opposing war, beginning with her 1889 novel *Lay Down Your Arms*.

In Scandinavia, *Clara Raphael: Twelve Letters*, a novel published in 1850 by the Dane Mathilde Fibiger, rang true to women. In the novel, Clara refuses to marry in order to achieve her goal of pursuing knowledge. Scandinavian women organized groups to discuss women's literature and their own desires to realize their intellectual potentials. In England, Florence Nightingale, the famous nurse of the Crimean War, also wrote about the suffocation of privileged women in the life of the family. Individually, women in various countries began to apply to universities and professional schools, and some were admitted. One of these, the homeopathic physician and midwife Jenny P. d'Hericourt, was able to use physiological and medical arguments to argue that women and men's brains were equally well equipped. Women can be as rational as men, she argued, while men can also be as emotional as women.

By the time of the Franco-Prussian War in 1870, women were ready to organize at both national and international levels. The argument began slowly to pivot from particular issues that affected women's lives to the vote. If women had the vote, the argument ran, then their representatives in Parliament could enact the legislation to deal with all the other problems. Of course, as long as monarchs and emperors ran the governments of Europe, votes had almost no effect.

An important difference between England and continental European countries was that England had a long-established parliamentary government. The vote was much more important to women in the UK than it was to women in states with strong monarchies and weak parliaments. Early in the nineteenth century, many British liberal voices had expressed concern that the unpropertied or the uneducated might not have the capabilities for participation in public life. But gradually a series of reform acts brought the franchise to increasing numbers of workingmen. It was relatively easy for women to make the case that if the country was headed down the road to universal male suffrage, then there was no reason to exclude women. In the UK, those men who did not already have it got the vote in 1918, along with some women. Suffrage for all adult women followed in 1928.

In Germany, many feminists worked for other causes as well as women's rights, such as socialism and pacifism. A focus of many feminists was women's need for the right to work with decent pay if they were to fulfill their missions as mothers. Creative literature supported their positions. In 1880, Henrik Ibsen's feminist play *A Doll's House* was debated all over Europe. That play was followed by a plethora of others in which female protagonists challenged the expected norms of society.

As the nineteenth century drew to a close, a complex web of new challenges to feminist goals called for creative thinking. The demographic transition (in which families have fewer children when they move from rural to urban areas) began to be apparent in Western European countries. Governments called for women to have more children to support the nation. Unfortunately, there were significantly more women than men, so many women could not marry and have children. Inter-European wars as well as imperialist projects had sopped up male lives. Unmarried women still needed jobs. Throughout the later nineteenth century, reform legislation had created new protections for women in various industries. But this reform legislation also had the effect of limiting the number of jobs available to women. Some of the legislation, for instance limiting the ability of women to work at night, worked in favor of workingmen's unions, and often women saw the restrictions as attempts to keep them from making the higher wages available with night work.

Women reacted to these issues involving the balance of work inside and outside the home, as well as maternal activities, in various ways. Different women had different needs, values, and opinions. Some women who were opposed to limiting night work for women noted that the only work activity that was not prohibited to women at night was prostitution. In many European countries, governments regulated prostitution to protect against venereal diseases. Increasingly it was apparent that there was no one-size-fits-all solution to women's issues, but that women needed to both vote and participate in government so that their voices would become part of the debate.

Zionism

As Napoleon swept through Europe in the first decade of the nineteenth century, he brought the egalitarian and universalist ideals of the French Revolution, as he understood them, along with him. One effect was to emancipate Europe's Jews and to take steps to allow them to assimilate to European societies. As Napoleon fought to replace feudalism, Jews were able to move out of their ghettos. Although after Napoleon's defeat several countries moved to enact restrictions, in Western Europe Jews essentially remained citizens. For several generations, German Jews experienced the ability to be educated and to pursue careers just as other Germans could. Many families began to orient themselves more secularly than religiously, and many families converted to Christianity.

Unfortunately, emancipation left them in many ways more isolated than they had been when they lived in ghettos. In ghettos, they had a tight religious community. Once they left the ghetto to pursue bourgeois careers, however, they identified with the nationalities of the lands in which they lived. The people of those nationalities, however, did not accept Jews as true fellow nationals. And Jews found that they themselves were not sure how to fit in. When dietary laws were inconvenient in the new forms of daily life, when the Sabbath included community activities with non-Jews, and when Jewish customs collided with gentile practices, how should an emancipated Jew act? Especially in Eastern Europe several nationalities tended to live side by side in countries that had changed their boundaries and their rulers throughout the past few centuries. When Poles, Lithuanians, Germans, and Russians all worked for nationalist ends, where should a Jew try to fit in? Which languages should the Jew use?

Jewish emancipation along with racial nationalism exacerbated the continuous anti-Semitism that had simmered throughout the nineteenth century. The idea that Germans (or French, or any other nation) were essentially different from other European nations led many Germans to question the existence of alien races in their newly unified land. After all, "race" in Europe was tied to the idea of "nation." While Americans focused on skin color, Europeans also focused on language and relation to the particular ancestral tribe that might have migrated out of Asia early in the Common Era. In short, a nation-based wrath enveloped Jews at the end of the nineteenth century. The old canards were supplemented by new accusations, like the fraudulent *Protocols of the Elders of Zion* that purported to be the records of Jewish leaders plotting to take over the world by controlling the world economy and taking over the presses of many nations.

Throughout the nineteenth century, a few Jewish voices had begun to explore the possibilities of a migration to the land of Palestine—the belief that Jews should move to what today is Israel is known as Zionism. Moses Hess (1812–71) was a socialist colleague and friend of Karl Marx. As Hess wrestled with the problems raised by capitalism and nationalism, he began to feel that the Jewish nation should have its own state in the land from which they had sprung. But for Hess this new state should be based on socialist principles. In his book *Rome and Jerusalem* (1862), Hess looked at Italian nationalism and realized that Jews needed the same thing. Just as Rome symbolized Italy, so Jerusalem symbolized Jewish state. The book, destined to be an important source of Zionist ideas, was read by few at the time.

In 1881 in Russia there began a series of pogroms that became massacres. Between 1881 and 1884, over 200 pogroms occurred. Leo Pinsker (1821–91), an emancipated Jewish physician from Odessa, began to rethink the entire emancipation project. To Pinsker, Jews had been treated as passive recipients of emancipation. They were not actors but rather acted upon. Pinsker thought that freedom could not be a gift. Freedom had to be taken. In 1882 he wrote a pamphlet entitled, "Autoemancipation." In it he described the difference between emancipation—offering rights to individuals—and national consciousness—creating a group that could act in its members' own interest. Europeans, he said, treated Jews as a nation, but they were not treated as the members of other nations were. The reason was that Jews had no state and therefore could not reciprocate. They were a dependent nation. Not only that, but their religion taught them to wait passively for God to send a Messiah. Instead of waiting for God to send Moses, Jews should develop their own leadership.

In 1873, the long depression that lasted in some countries more than two decades, led many Europeans to cast about for scapegoats to blame for their families' sudden economic miseries. Stock exchanges went under, bank panics ensued, and some people lost their life savings. Jews, caricatured as moneylenders, were often blamed, and the old accusations of the use of gentile blood in Jewish rituals were resurrected.

Theodor Herzl

Theodor Herzl (1860–1904) was an excellent example of an emancipated Jew. He was born in Pest (one part of today's Budapest) in Hungary. His parents were secular Jews, and his father was a successful businessman. When he was eighteen, the family moved to Vienna, where Herzl studied law. Eventually he became a journalist and sometime playwright. He was a great supporter of Germany as the leader in European culture and hoped that his educational formation (*Bildung*) in German civilization could enable him to become a leader in Central Europe. In 1895 the outspoken anti-Semite Karl Luger was elected to be mayor of Vienna, and Herzl was shaken to his core. The emperor of Austria-Hungary, Franz Josef, refused to approve the election, but by 1897, on the fifth try, the emperor finally acceded after he was begged to do so by the pope. Herzl, as a journalistic correspondent in Paris and London, had seen anti-Semitism in other countries as well, and in 1895 he began reluctantly to rethink the possibility of Jewish assimilation. He now thought combating anti-Semitism was fruitless, so he began thinking of a way for European Jews to escape Europe and find their own homeland.

Herzl assimilated and effectively publicized the ideas of Zionist thinkers like Moses Hess. For Herzl, a new Jewish state should be socialist. A noted journalist, Herzl understood the power of symbols. He dressed the part of a statesman, and he insisted on only meeting with heads of state. Without an organization behind him, Herzl became the spokesperson for an idea. He understood the power of public opinion.

As a Jewish nationalist, Herzl became convinced that Jews were essentially different from peoples of other nations and that Jews deserved their own state. He had given up on the idea that Jews might become Germanic, or any other European nationality. He established the Zionist ideas with a book, *Der Judenstaat* (*The State of the Jews*), in 1896.

Herzl considered a few different places where a Jewish state might be inaugurated, including Argentina and East Africa, but he realized that for historical reasons, as well as the importance of Jerusalem in current Jewish practices (like the Passover Seder service), the Ottoman province of Palestine would be a better choice. He proposed paying the Turkish (Ottoman) public debt in return for the right to settle in Palestine, a plan that received support at the highest levels of Ottoman government, but which was ultimately rejected by the sultan. He considered the relationship of Jews with Arabs in the new state and called for giving Arabs rights as individuals. He did not consider the possibility that Arabs might themselves create a national movement.

Herzl's friend Max Nordau (1849–1923), another emancipated, educated journalist, addressed the first Zionist Congress in Basel, Switzerland, in 1897. His argument began: "The Western Jew has bread, but man does not live on bread alone." Jews needed more than material success. The problem, argued Nordau, was that emancipation had come not from the heart, but rather as an intellectual proposition. During the French Revolution, French citizens got rights because they were human beings. Consistency demanded that since Jews were human beings, they too should have rights. There was no recognition by the French of the wrongs that had been done to Jews over the centuries. The French (and later other Europeans) did not embrace the Jews as people. Instead, the Jews were a kind of geometric proposition, like the metric system. "The men of 1792 emancipated us only for the sake of principle." So, after emancipation, there still remained the old sentiments of hatred toward the Jews. Non-Jews were not ready to accept Jews as equal. The Jews has not had a chance to develop a talent for politics. With their own state, they would have the chance to do so.

At the beginning of the twentieth century, Zionism was still only a set of ideas. But the cruelty of the twentieth century produced the Holocaust, and the Holocaust propelled its survivors out of Europe. Many found their way to Israel. Zionism came alive after the Second World War.

Conclusion: The Dreyfus Affair

After the 1871 defeat in the Franco-Prussian War, France was left in a state of shock and outrage: shock at how easily they had been defeated and outrage at the loss of territory and the size of the monetary indemnity. The result was a spirit of *revanchism* (thirst for revenge) that led to heightened nationalist feeling among a vast majority of French citizens. This nationalism partially played out in an increase of anti-Semitism that in 1886 was fanned into flames by a scurrilous book, *Jewish France,* by Éduard Drumont.

In 1894 a housekeeper and clandestine French intelligence agent in the German Embassy in Paris found a discarded note showing the Germans knew about a top-secret new French artillery weapon. Looking for the spy, the French military identified Captain Alfred Dreyfus, a Jew from Alsace (and therefore German speaking). Having decided that Dreyfus was guilty, the top officers in the military took steps to make sure that his guilt could be proven. They found self-proclaimed experts in handwriting to link Dreyfus to the note, and they suppressed testimony by an actual expert in handwriting analysis. Éduard Drument, who after publishing *Jewish France* founded an anti-Semitic newspaper, *La Libre Parole* (Free Speech) revealed the ongoing investigation and condemned Dreyfus. The minister of war gave an interview in which he declared Dreyfus guilty. Only a few citizens reserved judgment. Each day people looked for the next piece of journalism that could illustrate the nefarious actions of the Jewish traitor.

Dreyfus was convicted, but unfortunately for those who had staked their reputations on his guilt, he was innocent. As Dreyfus went to Devil's Island in exile, new documents were forged to make sure he never came back. A new head of Military Intelligence, Georges Picquart, investigated and discovered in the secret files proof of Dreyfus's innocence. He found proof that Major Walsin-Esterhazy was the actual spy. The high command, running scared, tried to cover up Esterhazy's crime. Intellectual leaders increasingly came to the conclusion that the leaders of the military had committed an injustice. They nation split into outraged Dreyfusards and virulent anti-Dreyfusards. But Esterhazy was quickly acquitted, while Picquart was convicted.

In 1898, the lionized author Emile Zola, by that time a committed Dreyfusard, published an emotional article entitled, "Je Accuse . . .! in which he detailed the cover-ups and forgeries committed by the top military and other leaders. A debate opened up, and eventually Zola was tried for libel. The trial was tightly controlled, and Zola lost, fleeing to England to avoid imprisonment. But the courts became involved. Dreyfus's conviction was overturned. Dreyfus was brought back to face a military trial once again.

Once again, he was convicted. But this time the possibility of a pardon was raised. If only Dreyfus admitted his guilt, he could be pardoned. Exhausted, Dreyfus agreed. In 1899, the country wanted to move on. But moving on was impossible. Books and articles continued to appear, on both sides of the question. Finally, in 1906, the Supreme Court, having exhaustively studied the evidence, decided to remove any idea of the guilt of Dreyfus. He was restored to the army with a promotion.

Theodor Herzl was in Paris and observed with a breaking heart the way that anti-Semitism had run amok. Clearly, much of the French citizenry harbored hatred for Jews. He cited the Dreyfus affair as he made his case for Zionism.

At the beginning of the twentieth century, European intellectuals were largely nationalists who saw essential differences among the peoples of different nations. The idea that different groups had essentially different qualities had scientific backing that took a long time to be refuted by later scientists. Indeed, it still lingers with us today.

CHAPTER 8
REDEFINING INDIVIDUALS AND SOCIETY
SOCIOLOGY, ECONOMICS, AND CLINICAL PSYCHOLOGY

Figure 8.1 Photograph of Marianne and Max Weber, 1893. © The History Collection/Alamy Stock Photo.

Marianne Weber: Intellectual and Wife

Marianne Weber (1870–1954) faced a crisis. Her husband Max, six years her senior, adored his mother, a somewhat distant, very moral, socially conscious woman. Marianne too admired her mother-in-law and tried to emulate her. Unfortunately, Max's frustrated father, also named Max Weber, had sufficient libido and joie de vivre to leave him unsatisfied with his more ascetic wife. In June 1897, Max initiated a quarrel with his father in which he accused his father of selfishly making demands on Max's mother. Two months later, his father died. Max was distraught, blamed himself, and began to experience mental disorders that left him unable to work. He had to ask for relief from his teaching duties and eventually resigned from his prestigious post as professor at Germany's Heidelberg University. Marianne continually cared for her stricken husband. She also continued to attend lectures at the university (she and Max had worked to get women the right to study there) and to foster a discussion circle there. She rejoiced as Max began to slowly recover his ability to work. How ironic when she discovered that the cause of his recovery may have been an affair with their friend Else Jaffe, and also with Mina Tobler, a pianist. Max had married a woman like his mother and had suffered the same sorts of frustration as had his father.

Nevertheless, Marianne ignored the affairs and supported Max in his career. She also set out to make a career for herself. She began to use the methods of the new sociology, of which her husband was one of the founders, to understand the experience of women in a patriarchal society. She noted how the rapidly changing industrial world provided new work opportunities for women even as they lived in traditional, male-dominated marriages. She set out to use marriage as a case study for society at large. Eventually, she concluded that marriage was "a complex and ongoing negotiation over power and intimacy, in which money, women's work, and sexuality are key issues." She found that most of human society and social action does not take place within the boundaries of law, but rather there is a "middle ground of immediate daily life." Since women do the child rearing, shopping, and caretaking of families, they control this middle ground. And the middle ground is where the self and identity are created. In some ways, marriage provides a protective framework within which women can shape society and human identities.

Marianne Weber proved a prolific author and became a leader of German feminism in the twentieth century. Eventually she received an honorary doctoral degree from the University of Heidelberg. She spoke to large crowds as a public speaker, until Hitler ended the Federation of Women's Organizations.

Chapter Map

In the previous chapter, a new kind of group emerged. Nationalism grew in romantic soil but incorporated a new idea: the nation as a linguistic and cultural entity. Near the end of the century, scientists grew interested in studying social groupings, and the field of sociology spread its roots. These new shoots, entangled with the rootstock of nineteenth-century individualism, produced unexpected species in the coming century.

In this chapter, we see how the emerging social sciences used both individual and group-oriented analyses to understand human beings in society in very different ways. Max Weber saw cultural structures persisting over time in different guises. Emile Durkheim saw the existence of social facts that did not exist at the individual level. All focused on new methods, often using statistics and mathematical approaches.

Economists began to use newly developed mathematics and focused on relationships that were amenable to mathematical treatment. They began to look at margins, the effects of one more transaction, not big picture questions. They assumed that value and utility could be measured by price, that is, that human values were amenable to quantification. They also sought ways to connect economics to sociology.

Finally, psychologists like Sigmund Freud sought to understand mental structures. Freud developed a theory of mind in which a variety of structures and processes interacted. With Freud, human beings were no longer rational actors but, rather, beings beset by unconscious and overpowering urges.

The ideas of Freud, along with those of Darwin and Nietzsche, challenged the traditional views of what a human being was. Twentieth-century thinkers would have to operate on new terrain.

The Birth of Sociology

Max Weber (1864–1920)

Max Weber, along with Auguste Comte, Karl Marx, and Emile Durkheim, is generally considered one of the founders of modern sociology. In contrast to Marx, who thought the methods of production created the base on which culture was built, Weber saw culture as the underlying factor in social action. Weber came of age in the wake of the unification of Germany as an empire under the aegis of the Prussian king. He was born into a family that was well connected politically and academically.

Perhaps the most striking aspect of Weber's milieu was the rapidly increasing urbanization experienced by Germany. Berlin was the most striking, adding half a million people every thirty years, people from many cultures and countries. As they flooded into Berlin, the city underwent constant development, including the introduction of new water, sewer, and transportation systems. Mark Twain called Berlin the Chicago of Europe, a city of industry and commerce, no longer a backwater of European cities. An unanticipated result of all this development was that Berlin's inhabitants experienced a human-made environment. Unlike the rural settings from which their grandparents came, a setting dominated by nature and natural disasters, Berlin was an entirely human world. When Nietzsche had written that God is dead and we have killed him, he was presciently speaking for the experience of people living in a human-made world. Nietzsche called into question the existence of any natural laws outside of those constructed by humans. When Weber read Nietzsche, the philologist's message made sense.

The gifted Weber had eased his boredom in the lower grades by reading the collected works of Goethe. He was steeped in German culture. As he read philosophy, he was most attracted to neo-Kantianism which emphasized Kant's belief that nature in itself was unavailable to human knowledge; only the phenomenal world of mind could be known. As Weber's career proceeded, he increasingly felt the impossibility of ever discovering natural laws that pertained to the human, social world.

Weber attended law school at the University of Berlin, where he spent his first two years enjoying the student, urban culture. He swung between law and history in his studies, and his first major works involved the history of law and economics. By 1891 he had not only passed the bar examination but had also obtained his doctorate in law and written his habilitationsschrift, a major postdoctoral work that demonstrated a German PhD's fitness for academic employment. He began to find his intellectual home in the historical school of economics, a school that eschewed the theorizing of the British classical economists (like David Ricardo). The historical school saw economics as a cultural product that varied from country to country. They therefore thought that the best way to understand economic issues was to use comparative history, employing statistics, studying development over time in different cultures, and comparing the results.

As a young academic, he lectured but also consulted with the government, most notably concerning the influx of Polish farm laborers to replace the urban-bound German workers. Weber studied the arrival of Polish workers in German cities and eventually wrote the lion's share of the report. As a result, Weber joined a league that opposed allowing Polish workers to enter to compete with German workers. But Weber's critique was not economic but, rather, cultural. He saw the Poles as a threat to German culture, and he blamed the large landowners of the East, the Junkers, for sacrificing Germany's needs for unity to their own desire for low-waged workers.

As we have seen, Weber was haunted by the possibility that he had killed his father, and he fell into a deep depression that led to his resignation from the university. For a few years, he could do no work. Eventually he was able to begin writing again and produced his most influential book, *Die protestantische Ethik und der Geist des Kapitalismus* (*The Protestant Ethic and the Spirit of Capitalism*) in 1905. He became involved in government and politics, and when war broke out in 1914, he was a strong supporter of Germany's involvement. Like many other intellectuals, he became disillusioned by the end of the war. He returned to teaching in 1919 and began to write what he saw as his magnum opus, *Wirtschaft und Gesellschaft. Grundriß der verstehenden Soziologie* (*Economy and Society*). Unfortunately, he died of the flu in 1920. His wife edited the book and prepared it for publication in 1921–2.

Weber contributed several important ideas to the development of sociology as a discipline, although he tended to see himself as a historian of law and an economist. He wanted to understand the rapidly changing society around him, but he believed that human sciences could never be approached totally objectively. Human beings understood their lives as full of meaning and choice, and sociologists could not separate themselves from their humanness. They themselves contributed interpretation and meaning to their search to understand the interpretations and meanings of others. Since Weber rejected the possibility of finding laws of society that were independent of a human context, the only way to proceed was to understand all human activity as cultural in nature and the sociologist as a creature embedded in a society. To study the underlying structure of economy in the German society of his day, Weber used historical, cultural analysis. That is, he sought a similar structure in the past that might have informed the capitalism of his day. He found that, as we shall see, in Calvinist Christianity.

Weber saw in his society a structure dominated by bureaucracy, and he sought to understand its structure and subtext. One of its features was an emphasis on rules that were themselves an outcome of a rational process. In his view, the society was becoming increasingly rationalized. In the process of rationalization, human creativity was suppressed. Bureaucrats were expected to follow the rules laid out in the grand rational structure and thus had very little room for creativity. Weber's studies of bureaucracy and rationalization broke new ground in sociological studies.

Weber's cultural approach can be contrasted with the approaches of other founders of sociology. Auguste Comte (see Chapter 5) called his system positivism and emphasized sociology as the top of a hierarchy of sciences, one that included the laws of the sciences below it and to which sociology added its own objective laws. Karl Marx (see Chapter 5) emphasized the determining factor of economic activity. To Marx, all cultural products, the institutions, laws, and primary ideas, were a superstructure that was supported by an economic base. One could understand culture as a product of economic structure. To Emile Durkheim (see the following section), sociology should be data driven. Durkheim emphasized the collection of statistics that could be analyzed to produce accurate generalizations about society.

Many of Weber's main themes are raised in *The Protestant Ethic and the Spirit of Capitalism*. In this book, Weber sought to understand just what made capitalism work and why someone would consider acting as a capitalist. For Weber, modern capitalism was the pursuit of money to make more money. In earlier forms of capitalism, people invested money to achieve a purpose important to them. But in modern capitalism, profit is pursued for its own sake, and the capitalist is a person whose life is devoted to that goal. In fact, capitalism seems to have become an ethic. Why would such pursuit have become the central good of modern life?

Weber's method was to seek the roots of the essence of capitalism in another historical era. He did not seek to find capitalism itself, but rather an approach to life that had the same structure as capitalism. The issue for the sixteenth-century Calvinist was the doctrine of predestination. Calvin emphasized the qualities of an all-knowing, omniscient God. Such a God must know all that would ever be. God must know whether a person will be saved or damned. Since God is all knowing, nothing people do can change their fate. Helping the poor, going to church, saying one's prayers are all ineffectual. Confessing one's sins is useless, as is the absolution of a priest. God already knows whether you are going to hell of heaven; He has decided. It is preordained. God is remote and His will beyond the understanding of mortals.

What people can know is how they are spending their lives. They can look at their own actions to get a hint of whether or not they are to be saved or damned. Do they work hard and save their money? Are they, as the Gospel parable suggests, adding to their money rather than hoarding it? They can also look at the result of their work. If they seem to be successful, it might be a sign that God has favored them.

Weber pointed out that this approach to religion is very different from many others. In Catholicism, a person can hope for salvation through the church. Helping the poor will be rewarded by God, while hoarding one's money in the face of suffering may be a quick road to damnation. Mysticism of various sorts is another approach. Mystics seek a relationship with God, which they gain by eschewing the things of the world and devoting their lives to prayer and meditation. Weber considered a number of non-Calvinist Protestant sects in order to show that in their own ways they focused attention on the spiritual realm in order to gain salvation. They did not have the same ethic as Calvinism.

The Calvinist way was a lonely way. One died alone and faced an afterlife fate in the absence of family or friends. The emphasis was all on individuals—who scrutinized their lives looking for clues to their predetermined fate. This system of thought encouraged industrious pursuit of the position in life to which God had called one. Acceptance of God's call was a vocation, a calling. It encouraged abstemious saving. It discouraged enjoyment of worldly pleasures. And where there was little spending, saving occurred. The Calvinist became wealthy without really trying. However, the Calvinist cared little for the money, but rather for what the money signified: a life lived according to God's will, a sign of God's approval.

As capitalism arose in Europe, it was practiced in many ways, said Weber. For instance, in the "putting out" approach to textile manufacturing and sale, an entrepreneur, acting locally, would buy wool, put it out to peasant workers to prepare and weave, and then sell the resulting cloth to make a good living and a profit. The profit would be used to buy more wool to start the process over again. But such a capitalist might have other goals, like building a better house, or drinking imported wine, or building monuments in the community, or even helping the poor. When a Calvinist-informed capitalist entered the textile industry, that capitalist had a calling: excelling in the textile trade to fulfill God's will. In a kind of social Darwinian competition for survival, the capitalist with a single-minded calling would win out. As non-Calvinists also competed, they found that only by adopting the Calvinist ethic could they succeed. By the eighteenth century, capitalism had itself adopted an ethic, and to show what the spirit of capitalism had become, Weber cited many of the maxims of Benjamin Franklin ("He that idly spends five shillings worth of time loses five shillings and might as well throw five shillings into the sea" or "For six pounds a year you might have the use of one hundred pounds, provided you are a man of known prudence and honesty"). Honesty, or the appearance of honesty, was important. What had been spiritual had been transformed into something utilitarian.

Modern capitalism, in a Darwinian-like process, overcame other forms of capitalism. Lost in the process was any particular idea of God or God's will. Capitalists needed a calling and they needed to devote their lives to the making of money, but the making of profit had become the whole reason for their devotion. Efficiency in making profit was paramount, and it turned out that the best way to be efficient was to calculate. That is, reason in the pursuit of profit was the most efficient way to make a profit. And rationalization was the province of science, invention, and engineering. Machines began to take over, and machines were nothing if not rationally constructed entities.

Furthermore, human behavior could be rationalized into sets of rules that governed the actions of entire cadres of workers. Bookkeeping, inventory, and plant layout: organization began to dominate the factories of modern capitalists. Bureaucracy expanded. And bureaucracies demanded well-trained expert workers, each a professional actor in a small part of the enterprise. Bureaucrats ideally made very few idiosyncratic, creative decisions. They followed the rules so that the entire bureaucracy could work smoothly. No matter how well educated, no matter how eminent a person's upbringing, that worker should be replaceable by another expert. A rationalized society moved seamlessly while people served as the cogs.

As Weber surveyed this modern society of bureaucracy, rationalization, and modern capitalism, he could see that it produced material comforts, but he was forced to ask: For what? Was there any meaning in this society other than the progress defined by the results of rational action? He was led to state, at the end of his book:

> The Puritan wanted to work in a calling; we are forced to do so. For when asceticism was carried out of monastic cells into everyday life, and began to dominate worldly morality, it did its part in building the tremendous cosmos of the modern economic order . . . the care for external goods should only lie on the shoulders of the "saint like a light cloak, which can be cast aside at any moment." But fate decreed that the cloak should become an iron cage. . . . No one knows who will live in this cage in the future. . . . For of the last stage of this cultural development, it might truly be said: "Specialists without spirit, sensualists without heart; this nullity imagines that it has attained a level of civilization never before achieved."[1]

For Weber, modern capitalism could have occurred only in Western Europe, for only in Western Europe did Calvinism become, for a brief time, a major force. The spirit of capitalism was an ethic born in a unique time and place. Other forms of capitalism could exist, did exist, and had existed in other cultures, but not in this superefficient, rationalized form.

Western Europe had moved from a religiously oriented society, a world of spirits and gods, to one of monotheism, to a world of rationalization. It had become disenchanted. Science had displaced religion. But science could only answer how the world worked. It could not answer why it existed, where it came from, or where it was going. It could not tell human beings who they were or what they should do. Weber studied in the wake of Nietzsche, who, Weber thought, had perfectly captured his times. In the modern age, all individuals had to answer their own questions of value. It was a world of a bureaucratic machine, supported by modern capitalism, but it was also world of multiple human gods whose judgments were informed by individual taste. It was not a world of natural processes, not a world of magic bubbling brooks.

Emile Durkheim (1858–1917)

Emile Durkheim was born into a devout family of French Jews. Durkheim, however, decided not to follow his family and to lead a life apart from religion. He studied at the École Normale Superior and studied classics. He also read Auguste Comte and Herbert Spencer, and after he completed his dissertation, he decided to switch to social

Figure 8.2 Photo of Emile Durkheim 1900. © Bettmann/Getty Images.

sciences. Unfortunately, France did not have any social science curriculum. He passed a rigorous examination to become a teacher in secondary school or above, and from 1882 to 1885 taught philosophy in high schools. Eventually he studied sociology in German universities. In Germany, he reported, he began to abandon the Cartesian-inspired search for clear and distinct ideas in order to embrace the complexities of empirical studies in which the most useful categories were never easily apparent. In 1893, he wrote a doctoral dissertation, *De la division du travail social* (*The Division of Labor in Society*) *and* began to publish articles. While at the University of Bordeaux, he taught the first social science course at a French university, published three books: his dissertation, *Les règles de la méthode sociologique* (*The Rules of Sociological Method*), and *Suicide*, and he also founded *L'Année Sociologique*, the first French journal in the social sciences. In 1912 he came out with *Les formes élémentaires de la vie religieuse* (*The Elementary Forms of Religious Life*). The First World War devastated him. His own son died early in the war, and many of the students he had mentored died in the trenches. Durkheim died of a stroke in 1917, before the war ended.

Durkheim's contributions to intellectual history came in two forms: he was interested in developing a methodology for the social sciences and he explored the existence of social facts that did not exist at the individual level. In this latter enterprise, he was an innovator in the philosophy of knowledge, or epistemology.

Durkheim was motivated in his studies to understand the vast changes that were sweeping French, and European, society. Along with many other scholars studying the social sciences, he saw modern life as producing individual isolation and despair. Social cohesion was crumbling as institutions fell to the pressures of technology, urbanization, and population growth. In his first book on the division of labor, he differentiated between an organic solidarity of more primitive societies and a mechanical solidarity of industrial societies. In the organic solidarity of earlier societies, everyone had a place, and there was a shared collective conscience that included everyone and that defined the norms and behaviors of the entire group. Of course there was crime, but that is a given social fact in virtually every society. In industrial society, this collective consciousness weakened. The only way to maintain order was with repressive laws and penalties. The effect on individuals was to leave them wondering where they fit in. Labor was divided for efficiency, so everyone played a very small role in whatever the society produced or did. This led to efficiency, but also to a variety of social ills.

In *Suicide*, Durkheim demonstrated his method of approach. He began with quantitative, statistical, data. Where statistics had been adequately kept, they showed that the suicide rate varied from society to society. Durkheim carefully considered the possibility that this rate might be caused by individual psychological illnesses or that the statistics might be explained by the differing weather conditions or that some cause other than the society might lead to these results. Eventually he determined that a suicide rate was a social phenomenon. Somehow each society was structured in such a way that different structures led to different rates of suicide.

If he had not had such solid quantitative, thus exact, data, Durkheim would not have been able accurately to determine the point of causation. But in this case, if the cause of suicide rate had been psychological, it would have been studied properly by psychology. If it were economic, it would have been studied by economists, and so forth. Durkheim, however, saw the cause as a social fact, a concept of which other sciences were leery. The role of sociology was to study social facts. These were facts that affected the behaviors of individuals in the society.

These social facts were external to every individual, but they were real constraints upon the actions of these individuals. They could be conceived by individuals, but they were not constrained by the ideas individuals might have about them. However, these social entities could be studied scientifically, using the methods already developed in the social sciences. Durkheim credited Comte for this insight. Sociology stood at the peak of the sciences. However, it needed the input from these other sciences, for societies were composed of people who themselves were mammals with biological processes, and their biology was greatly affected by their chemistry which depended on physics. But sociology could not be deduced from these other sciences, because they did not recognize or study the new kind of real entity that Durkheim called the social fact. Sociology thus had a subject matter and a hand up from its older cousins in the development of methodology.

Since sociologists were themselves both individuals and social beings, they themselves had to be affected by social facts. Sociologists, like other scientists, had to adopt the distant, value-free perspective that allowed good data to be collected and analyzed. Essentially Durkheim recognized that the biases of the observer could affect the scientific results, and the only answer was to recognize this problem and strive to avoid it by practicing a rigid methodology. Later in the twentieth century, sociologists were forced to recognize that they could not get out of their own skins. The observer would always influence the results, and it was best to be up front about that. Similarly, we will see, quantum physicists would be forced to recognize that the very act of physical observation affected the results. But Durkheim prescribed a rigid adherence to objectivity.

In his book on suicide, once Durkheim had determined that suicide rates were social facts, he set about to analyze the essential differences in societies with different rates. He found that a key factor was the amount of social cohesion. Catholic societies had a lower rate of suicide, and they were also more organic. People knew who they were and what was expected. They had a place. But in the more Protestant areas, where industrialism and the extreme division of labor predominated, there was more social fragmentation. People could easily find themselves lost when they no longer had private social supports (like family bonds) that gave their lives purpose and meaning.

Once he recognized the social structures that affected the suicide rate, Durkheim set out to categorize the various types of suicide. He found

1) People that committed suicide out of an inflated sense of themselves (ego).

2) People that committed suicide altruistically because they thought the society needed it.

3) People who did not fit in the society (anomie).

Of course, his typology has been replaced, and today it is mostly of interest methodologically. But his last term, "anomie," deserves discussion because to Durkheim it was a characteristic of the modern, socially fragile, society he wanted to understand. To Durkheim, in modern society there was no general moral guidance to individuals. Division of labor in organic societies was done cooperatively, and all understood where they were needed to play their parts. In mechanical society, division of labor was too general, and the actors were too distant, for anyone to understand the role each played.

In his book *Les formes élémentaires de la vie religieuse* (*The Elementary Forms of Religious Life*—1912) Durkheim concentrated on early religious forms as seen in other cultures and applied his method. At the end of the book, Durkheim began to reflect on the nature of knowledge. He found that religious practices and beliefs reflected the society in which they exist. In this sense, religion could not be untrue, any more than society could be untrue. Society emerged in the interaction of individuals. A solitary individual may have sensory impressions, but these are not generalized into words. But when individuals begin to communicate their impressions, they create language. Words, then, do not correspond to particular instances; they express generalities, the possibility of similar individual sensory impressions to many people in many times. We are born into a language and have no control over it. The language controls us and the ways we organize our thoughts and think about the world. No one knows all the words in the language that person speaks. The language lies outside of any person. It may reside in a comprehensive dictionary (that must be constantly out of date as language evolves), but even before dictionaries, language existed.

Modern science emerged from religion and religious questions. Thus, science is itself a social form. It uses logic, and logic itself is a social form. By this Durkheim means that science and logic, like religion, express the social relations of the societies that have created them. One cannot properly juxtapose an ideal society with the flawed society in which one exists, because the ideal society is one of the forms of the real society. Ultimately, this approach reaches to an analysis of thought itself.

Kant had separated the structures of thought, the categories, from the sensory impressions that the categories organize. He put the categories into our minds, along with the sensory impressions, and then postulated an outer, unknowable world that had stimulated our sensory systems to create sensations that seem to be the actual world outside of the individual mind. Durkheim put the categories into society. People in a society experienced an order of events that moved in time. Their language contained words and concepts that expressed a sense of time. Thus, even the way that people experienced time, space, and causality was created by society. Such experience was a social fact.

For Durkheim, when Socrates discovered that words were universal and general, and he began to explore the meaning and nature of the concepts (forms) that important words expressed, it seemed to him that he was discovering reality. The forms existed beyond human beings in a different plane of existence. But Durkheim thought he had discovered the actual nature of the forms and the plane in which they existed. The plane in which the forms existed was society. Words, and their relationships, are social facts.

Words, language, logic, methods of inquiry, science, all not only exist in society; they express the relationships and experiences of the people that live in that society. As society profoundly changes, so must the fundamental structures of thought change. Such a process of change is neither easy nor nondisruptive. It may be expressed violently. One of the reasons that Durkheim's fundamental reanalysis of thought and knowledge was not as influential as that of others was that most of the students he mentored perished in the First World War. Durkheim died in grief.

Truth at the Margin: A Revolution in Economics

In the 1870s, the field of "political economy" changed its orientation, especially in the UK, and by the 1880s it had become just "economics." As economics separated itself from noneconomic issues in the analysis of society, it became much more mathematical. Why? A number of scholars trained in physics and engineering changed their orientations and began to use the skills they had learned in studying physical and biological sciences to tackle economic questions. Furthermore, as we have seen, physicists made use of new developments in mathematics, particularly the ability to solve partial differential equations, to open new vistas in the fields of thermodynamics and of electricity and magnetism. As they did so, abstractions like "energy" and "field" became refined and were treated as more fundamental than entities that could actually be observed using the human sensory system.

Differential calculus allows a person to analyze tiny changes at a moment in time. For instance, "60 kilometers per hour" describes what happens in one hour's time. But how can it make sense to use that same expression in an instant (as the odometer in an automobile does)? Differential calculus allows us to slowly shrink both distance and time until both approach zero. The answer is expressed in kilometers and hours. As the field of differential calculus developed, equations using differentials (think infinitesimal amounts) could be written. Solving these equations, however, was very difficult, and it took years to develop ways of solving many of these "differential equations."

But what is a "partial differential equation?" Suppose two or three (or more) different quantities are being compared (like kilometers and hours). What happens if you want to examine what happens if only one of them changes? Then you hold the others constant and allow the one you want to examine change. In equation form, such a study is called a partial differential equation. For example, you eat many foods but have an allergy to something. If you hold all foods constant, but gradually reduce your intake of one of them, you are doing a study that mimics a partial differential equation. Partial differential equations are like the expression, "all things being equal, we can say." For example, James Clerk Maxwell used partial differential equations to develop his theory of the electromagnetic field. Pieces of the field were moving in all directions, but if all of them stopped while only one dimension continued, he found that he got a swirl. If a car is moving and the brakes are applied to only one side of the vehicle, it will turn around and around. This operation of a partial differential equation is appropriately named a "curl." Major developments in partial differential equations took place in the 1830s and 1840s and beyond. These mathematical developments allowed physicists to invent the new field of thermodynamics and new conceptions for electromagnetism.

The young economists, people like the Englishmen William Stanley Jevons (1835–82) and Alfred Marshall (1842–1924) studied mathematics as students. They grew up studying thermodynamics and electromagnetism and excelled in mathematics. When they turned to economics, it was natural for them to think in physical and mathematical metaphors. It was natural for them to compare small changes in the relationship between two quantities. For instance, supply and demand are related, but how? As the supply of a good increases, the price for one of these goods decreases. But as demand for the good goes up, the price will rise. How can we compare these two variable quantities? The new mathematical economists could solve the problem, and Alfred Marshall illustrated it in the now iconic supply and demand curve diagram.

Suppose the curves refer to automobiles. We see "price" on the vertical axis and "quantity" on the horizontal axis. If we just pay attention to the demand curve, we see that as the price gets lower, the demand for automobiles gets higher. More people want a cheap car than an expensive car. At a low price, the quantity demanded increases. Now,

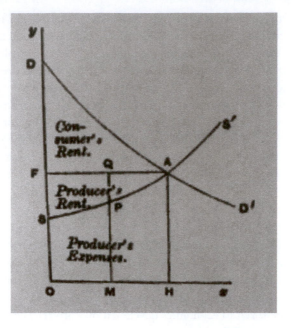

Figure 8.3 The original supply and demand graph made by Alfred Marshall in *Principles of Economics*, 1890. The graph shows losses expected to either producer or buyer when quantity demanded does not equal quantity supplied. © Wikimedia Commons (public domain).

if we just pay attention to the supply curve, we see that at a low price, producers are not willing to produce many cars. Maybe they will produce a car to give to their parents, but no more. However, as the price rises, as they can make more and more money on the car, they are willing to make more and more cars. If they could, they would overcharge for the cars. But notice that at a high price there is partially no demand for the cars. What is the balance point? How many cars should the producers make?

The new economics looked at the problem in small increments, or margins. Since one couldn't make a fraction of a car, the changes had to come in whole cars. What was the profit in making one more car? And then one more? The difference in the price you could charge was not much, but it was something. Each new car increased the supply, and as more and more cars entered the car market, consumers had more and more choices. They wouldn't choose the more expensive car (if all cars are the same). The producer would make a lower profit on each car. The new economists said that the change of one car was a "margin" of one car. They wanted to know what would happen "at the margin." The answer to the automobile manufacturer's dilemma, it turned out, was that one should stop producing new cars at the point where the marginal supply equals the marginal demand.

Marginal thinking is very different from the large-scale thinking of Adam Smith or David Ricardo. Adam Smith had asked where the wealth of a nation comes from. The new economists were asking whether a manufacturer should make one more thing. Adam Smith's analysis was almost entirely a verbal argument, made on the basis of idealized situations. The methods of the new neoclassical economics were rooted in mathematics. It wasn't that these economists were uninterested in large geographic areas and large amounts of time, but rather that their mathematical techniques were more suitable for smaller-scale analyses, important economic questions that had hitherto been unaddressed.

Times had changed. Whereas Adam Smith had observed a new sector of society, industrialists, and had argued on their behalf and against government interference, by 1870 the industrial economy was apparent to everyone. Karl Marx and Friedrich Engels had developed a comprehensive argument on behalf of the other side of the industrial society, the proletariat, or workers, but an economics that spoke to the needs of industrialist decision-makers had not yet been developed. Industrialists, of course, were not waiting for the economists to tell them how to make decisions.

Besides Jevons and Marshall, a few of the other path-breaking neoclassical economists were Léon Walras (1834–1910) and Vilfredo Pareto (1848–1923), both Swiss, the Austrian Carl Menger (1840–1921), and the Irish Francis Ysidro Edgeworth. There also were other schools of economic thought like the German historicists exemplified by Wilhelm Roscher (1817–1924) and later by Max Weber. Despite the differences exemplified by these various nationally oriented schools, their differences paled in comparison with the truly alternative approach to economics developed by Karl Marx and Friedrich Engels (see Chapter 5).

William Stanley Jevons

Born in Liverpool, Jevons (1835–82) grew up in an economically interested household. His favorite university subjects were chemistry and botany, but for financial reasons he stopped studying and went to work in Australia as an assayer. He returned to England and the University of London, where he not only continued to work in the physical sciences but also began to turn his attention to the moral sciences. He was first known as a logician and professor of mental and moral philosophy at Owens College, Manchester. Wearied by the need to prepare so many different subjects, he took a professorship in Political Economy at University College, London. He later drowned in a swimming accident in 1882.

Jevons based his economics on a theory of utility, first developed by Jeremy Bentham (see Chapter 2). Comparing utility to gravity, he noted that utility could not be observed directly, but that it could be known by its effects, just as gravity is not seen directly but is demonstrated in the fall of bodies. Utility was seen in the choices human beings made. One of his goals was to demonstrate how economic statements could be phrased in mathematical equations. He essentially derived basic integral calculus as he discussed economic questions, and he showed how equations could be illustrated in graphs. For instance, he drew a graph to indicate how a pleasure is reduced in intensity according to the time that it is felt. The vertical (y) axis was intensity, and the horizontal (x) axis was time. He began by dividing the time into minutes.

He then slowly reduced each moment until each was a small fraction of a second. The graph of boxes became a smooth curve. Thus, an issue in describing how pleasures acted

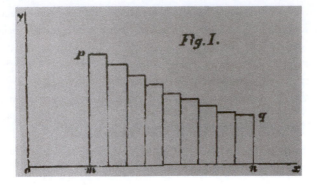

Figure 8.4 Graph of descending increments in W. Stanley Jevons, *The Theory of Political Economy*, 1888, p. 30. Illustration of how one can shrink the width of the rectangles until they lie under a smooth curve as all the rectangles approach straight lines. What is being measured here is the intensity of the feeling of pleasure or pain, as Jevons tried to use utilitarian ethics to make economic decisions. © Out of Copyright (public domain).

in individuals could be mathematized. He continued this process as he developed the basic principles of economics.

Since, as he claimed, "Economics does rest upon the laws of human enjoyment," the whole of economics was based on the individual and individual choice. For instance, the aforementioned graphs could be made to represent the consumption of food. Each fraction of a second (each point on the line) represented a small quantity of food. As more and more food is consumed, the amount of pleasure and utility lessens. The decision to consume or not to consume is always made at one point, that is (using the term developed by Alfred Marshall—Jevons used "degree of utility"), at the margin. Marginal utility is thus a derivative of total utility (the area under the curve). And, as Jevons said, "the final degree of utility is that function upon which the Theory of Economics will be found to turn."

Jevons wrote on several topics related to economics, and his books *The Coal Question* and *A Serious Fall in the Value of Gold* are two excellent examples. In the first, Jevons developed his famous paradox. If the use of coal becomes more and more efficient (i.e., if less coal is used to achieve the same effects), coal will become cheaper and more coal will be used. Jevons's paradox bears directly on modern efforts to reduce fossil fuel use by making fossil fuels more efficient. He also wrote on logic, developing an approach later used by the twentieth-century philosopher Karl Popper, and on the physical sciences.

Alfred Marshall

The London-born Marshall (1842–1924) studied physics at St. John's College Cambridge, where he received the second-highest score in mathematics (second wrangler). He suffered through a period of moral doubts that led him to switch fields to philosophy. Beginning with metaphysics and theology, he worked his way through philosophical fields until he arrived at political economy. He was attracted to economics because it provided suggestions on improving the lives of the working class. He realized that economics needed the help of other fields, like sociology. For Marshall, economics must be allied with social and political forces to make a difference in the lives of workers. But by using the mathematics he had learned at Cambridge, and attacking economic issues with physical analogies, he hoped to show that economics had an important role to play in solving social issues.

Marshall became a leader in the field of economics by writing a path-breaking textbook, first published in 1890. Eventually the eighth edition became the textbook of choice for decades. Marshall emulated Jevons in using illustrative graphs, and he saved most of the rigorous mathematics for footnotes. He wanted to produce a book that people would read. His famous prescription was the following:

> 1) Use mathematics as shorthand language, rather than as an engine of inquiry. 2) Keep to them till you have done. 3) Translate into English. 4) Then illustrate with examples that are important in real life. 5) Burn the mathematics. 6) If you can't succeed in 4, burn 3. This I do often.[2]

Essentially, Marshall compiled the marginal approach to economics and contributed his own analyses to it.

In particular, Marshall developed the use of supply and demand curves to understand prices and the relationship between quantity and price. A supply and demand curve (see aforementioned text) is like scissors, two curves that intersect at the point where ideal price is determined. The earlier classical economists, like Ricardo, had developed a theory that value depended upon labor, and Marx had also used the labor theory of value in his analysis. Jevons had substituted a utility theory of value, although utility could not be directly determined. Marshall pushed the question of value to the side and used price as the key variable. Price could be seen to be determined directly from the relationship between supply and demand. If one wanted to continue to use the concept of value, one could link it directly to the price. Socialist thinkers noted that labor (human beings) had been replaced by money (an abstraction) in this transformation.

But he also continually suggested that the exclusive use of mathematical economics would distort the public welfare. Especially in his appendices, Marshall discussed issues in which economics bordered on other topics. He thought that people had duties as well as rights and that the wealthy had a duty to contribute their wealth to society. He recognized that for the wealthy to pay taxes to public education would seem onerous to them, since they sent their own children to privately funded schools, but they had an obligation to do so. He thought labor unions were essential to achieving a just society, and that labor unions should also work for the common good.

The Lausanne School

Léon Walras (1834–1910) began professional life as an engineer. He tired of working as an engineer, and after working in several fields, he ended in political economy at the University of Lausanne, Switzerland. Eventually he and his colleague Vilfredo

Pareto founded what was to be called the Lausanne school of economics. Independent of other economists, like Jevons, he came up with the idea of marginal economics. His main contribution to economics was a general equilibrium theory in which he used several interlinked equations to determine the point at which prices would be stable. He was concerned not with one market, or one product, but with the entire economy. He began with equations describing the behavior of two people in a bartering relationship, and then developed equations for more and more complex market systems. He was able to ensure that there were at least as many equations as there were variables to be solved for and, thus, that his system of equations was solvable. He was able to show that if other markets are stable, then the last market to be analyzed must also be stable.

Walras's colleague Vilfredo Pareto (1848–1923) was an Italian born in exile in Paris. Eventually his family was able to return to Italy, and Pareto earned a doctorate in engineering at the University of Turin. In the 1880s, he began to turn to political economy, and argued forcefully for a laissez-faire, unregulated, economy. In 1893 he succeeded Walras in the chair of Political Economy at Lausanne, where he continued the practice of doing mathematical economics. He developed the Pareto Principle, otherwise known as the 80-20 rule, in which in any society 80 percent of the property will be owned by 20 percent of the population. This has been generalized to other situations in which 20 percent of a group monopolizes 80 percent of a quantity that is intrinsic to the group. He also introduced "Pareto optimality," the idea that a system has achieved maximum economic satisfaction when no one can be made better off without someone being made worse off. This idea became, in the hands of others, the idea that a perfect competitive market produces a wealth distribution that is "Pareto optimal."

As Pareto continued his mathematical research, he found that the ideal systems that were the prerequisite for a mathematical treatment seemed not to produce results that were replicated in society. He began to turn to sociology to understand the complexities of society better than he could with mathematics. In his book *Tratto di sociologia generale* (1916) (*The Mind and Society*), he introduced the concept of the circulation of elites in which he claimed that in any revolutionary change one set of aristocrats is replaced with another. Pareto assembled reams of data from many societies in many centuries as he tried to understand how people get wealth and power. He found that wealth and power are always distributed so that very few have most of it. It seemed that there must be a social law, "something in the nature of man." Meanwhile at the bottom people always starve. That is, for Pareto, there is no real progress in history.

If we compare the approach of the marginalists of whatever nationality with the approach of Max Weber to questions about the nature of capitalism, we can see the difference between the German historical school and the new approach of marginal economics. Weber and other German economic thinkers thought that economics was a human science that could not ignore the motives and ideas of individual humans. Economics existed differently in different cultures, because different cultures represented different worldviews. Historical inquiry involved the compilation of a great deal of data from different eras and different countries and then cross-comparing it to see how the problems of making a human life were solved differently. Weber's study of the origins of capitalism, discussed earlier, was paradigmatic.

The economists who developed the marginal approach thought that they had discovered economic laws that persisted across cultures and across times. Especially with the work of Marshall to minimize individually varying human wants as an economic question, replacing "utility" with price, the marginalists saw themselves as founding a rigorous, mathematically based science.

Of course, there was an alternative approach that saw itself as scientific, and that was Marxist economics. Marx and Engels used a variation of Hegel's theory to develop what they saw as laws of historical development. To the Marxists, human desires and goals tended to be the same in the same culture, and any culture was defined by the ownership of the means of production. There were thus three different approaches, with variations in different schools—and these schools tended to be organized on national lines. Of course, economists in different countries were free to adopt the approaches of economists from another country. Perhaps the most striking example of this trend was the movement of the Austrian school to the United States in the twentieth century.

Clinical Psychoanalysis: Sigmund Freud

Sigmund Freud was a confirmed pessimist. He constructed a new form of psychiatry, psychoanalysis, and, in so doing, developed a map of the human mind, eventually influencing virtually every field in the humanities and social sciences. Nevertheless, as he reflected on his work, he noted that the best he could do was turn neurotic misery into common unhappiness.

Sigismund Schlomo Freud was born in 1856 in the village of Freiberg, Moravia (Příbor in today's Czechoslovakia), at that time part of the Austrian Empire. Freud later recalled a golden age of belonging in a small town that was shattered when, at the age of three, his father's failed business dealings put the family on a road that soon led to Vienna. Freud's father was an avid student of the Torah, and Freud himself was an academic standout. Freud began studies at the University of Vienna at the age of seventeen and soon joined the medical school. He studied neuroanatomy with the noted anatomist Ernst Brücke and graduated with an M.D. degree in 1881. He started work at the Vienna General Hospital as a researcher, but time spent in the psychiatric clinic led to a growing interest in clinical medicine. By 1885 he was appointed lecturer (docent) at the hospital, but quickly left on a fellowship to study in Paris under the famous neurologist Jean-Martin Charcot who was using hypnosis in his clinical research. Study under Charcot soon led Freud to specialize as a clinician in medical psychopathology, the study of sicknesses of the mind. Although Freud's dream was to connect mental phenomena to activity in the brain, leading him eventually to write an unpublished *Project for a Scientific Psychology* (1895). In his clinical work, he was unable to find a direct use for neuroanatomical studies.

Figure 8.5 Photo of Sigmund Freud and his daughter Anna Freud, who also became a psychoanalyst and theoretician 1913. © API/Gammo-Rapho/Getty Images.

In 1886 Freud began work as a private practitioner in Vienna using hypnosis to treat hysteria. Eventually he gave up hypnosis and developed a "talking cure" in which patients were required to report anything that popped into their heads as they described their symptoms. As Freud developed his "free association," he found that when patients described their dreams, they produced thoughts that allowed Freud to analyze what eventually seemed to be unconscious material that had been repressed. When Freud's father died in 1896, producing in Freud depression and disturbing dreams, Freud analyzed his own dreams and was dismayed to find that he harbored a deep hatred of his father that centered around Freud's own attraction to his mother and subsequent rivalry with his father.

Eventually this shattering insight led Freud to formulate a theory of the Oedipus complex, a theory that claimed that all children went through a stage of attraction to the opposite-sex parent and rivalry with the same-sex parent, a situation that was eventually resolved by the child's identity with the same-sex parent. Unresolved Oedipal issues could lead to neuroses, including pedophilia and homosexuality. During the Oedipal period, thought Freud, boys develop castration anxiety and girls develop penis envy.

In 1899 Freud published his dream studies in *The Interpretation of Dreams*, a book that was based upon Freud's overarching insight that a dream is the fulfillment of an unconscious wish. The idea of the unconscious was quite controversial. Until Freud, the mind was seen as the same thing as consciousness. Sensory impressions, ideas, fantasies, daydreams, emotions, analyses, and so forth are all carried out in consciousness. The idea that any of this mental activity might be unavailable to a conscious mind seemed to challenge common sense itself. How could I wish for something unconsciously? How could I not be aware of how I feel? How could I perceive things yet not be aware of them?

Freud not only postulated an unconscious, but he also claimed that as much as 90 percent of human mental activity was unconscious, hidden to the conscious mind much as most of an iceberg lies below the sea, invisible to people on the surface of the ocean. At the surface of the unconscious lay the preconscious, wherein lay material that was not presently in consciousness but that was available to it. Between the unconscious and the preconscious was a censorship function that forbade the entry into consciousness of repressed, forbidden material. Such material might be forbidden emotions (like hatred of one's father), violent impulses, forbidden desires (like incest), traumatic memories, and the like. In dreams, postulated Freud, forbidden ideational content disguises itself in seemingly fantastic stories that are suggested by association. Many of these stories are roughly based on recent occurrences—but there is no demand that the stories be logically coherent. The censor in the preconscious examines the ideas that are wafting toward the surface and judges that these fantastical ideas are unthreatening and thus may enter consciousness. We awake, then, vaguely remembering dreams that make no sense: no sense, that is, until the psychoanalyst hears them and is able suggest an interpretation.

In the next five years, Freud published *The Psychopathology of Everyday Life* (1901), *Jokes and their Relation to the Unconscious* (1905), and *Three Essays on the Theory of Sexuality* (1905). In these Freud elaborated his theory. An important addition was a theory of drives. For Freud, an "it," usually translated as "id," occupied much of the unconscious. In this id was the pleasure principle. All children are born with a pleasure principle that centers in attaining pleasure and avoiding pain, and most of the pleasure involves food, which the baby gets by sucking. This pleasure principle includes libido, a drive that engages generalized sexual impulses. The libido centers on sucking and orality in early months, but then moves on to anal gratification, genitalia, and eventually to genital sex.

A few years after birth, however, the child has realized that it is not the only being in the universe and that the rest of the universe is not centered on giving the child pleasure or reducing the child's pain. The child then has to develop a reality principle. It realizes that it has to delay gratification and learn to do certain things in order to get things that give pleasure or reduce pain. This reality principle largely occupies the ego.

After the reconciliation of the Oedipal issues and the identification with the parent of the same sex, the child begins to develop an "ego ideal." That is, it internalizes important elements of the parent's personality. This ego ideal becomes the over-ego or superego. The superego is largely unconscious, but it leads the children, and then adults, to feel guilty when they violate the superego's strictures.

As Freud refined his theory of sexuality, he began to feel constrained to define a normal progression of development. The baby is in the oral stage and gets libidinal pleasure from sucking. Later, as children become aware of their feces, they get pleasure in having produced something with smells and textures. They may feel like they want to play with their new production. Parents react with toilet training that is designed to control their children's output. Later, children find their genitals and enter what Freud calls a Phallic phase. They enjoy playing with their genitals and feel the pleasure of infantile masturbation. After the Oedipal stage, children enter a latent period. But as puberty approaches, they enter a genital phase that ultimately centers libidinal energy in the penis or clitoris/vagina.

If progress through any of these stages is blocked, for instance by parents forcing toilet training or punishing children for masturbating, the child develops unconscious resentments and fears. Since the child's feelings are unconscious, they cannot be resolved directly and usually continue into adulthood. One of the defense mechanisms ("defense" because they defend the person from experiencing the pain of forbidden feelings) is projection. A person may project feelings onto other people. For instance, if a person feels forbidden anger, that person may see other people as angry, on the attack. Another defense mechanism is introjection, in which people do to themselves instead of to others. Instead of expressing anger outwardly, introjecting people may experience bodily pains, stomach cramps, headaches, and so forth. The most severe form of introjection is suicide in which a person avoids killing another by killing the self.

Unresolved development can also lead to personality disorders that can be seen as a complex. For instance, unresolved anality might result in messiness issues: by becoming either obsessively neat or completely messy.

Freud began to see the personality as responding to large drives that encompassed many of the mechanisms described earlier. The main drive was eros, the life force. Next to that was libido, the drive for sexual fulfillment (in which "sexual" is generalized and may involve something as gentle as stroking or as violent as sadistic bondage or torture). After the First World War and the killing of millions, Freud felt that he had to posit a third drive, thanatos, or the death wish. Every organism runs down and gradually feels more need for rest than activity. In its extreme form, thanatos projected involves killing, often on a mass scale, as in the war.

Beginning in the 1920s, Freud began to try to apply his theory to explain social phenomena. He used a variety of ways of applying what was essentially an individual method to derive social truths. In the essays comprising *Totem and Taboo* (1913), he seemed to imply that a primal act, like an early group of sons killing and eating their father, was somehow impressed into memory so that the Oedipal complex and other psychopathologies were universal. He took a similar approach as he argued in *Moses and Monotheism* (1937) that Moses was precisely this figure for the Jews. In this argument, Moses was an Egyptian who led a select group of followers out of Egypt, but that these followers subsequently killed their savior. Appalled by what they had done, they founded a monotheistic religion in which Moses was not only a human figure but also, in the deep recesses of the unconscious, worshiped as a god.

In *Civilization and its Discontents* (1930), Freud discussed how civilization maintained itself by prescribing what individuals could and could not do. By regulating the sex drive, civilization was able to use the repressed libidinal energies to encourage hard, socially useful work. Since individuals could not get what they really wanted, they lived desperate lives as they compensated by doing art, science, or any other socially approved work. In this approach, Freud did not use his theory of universal unconscious primal memories, but rather developed an analysis of an individual response to the overarching structures of civilized society.

Conclusion

As people moved into cities from the farms, the urban world provided a vastly altered experience from the rural landscape. In the countryside, one's surroundings seemed to be created by a divine being. Now people lived in a world that human beings had clearly created. And while "acts of God" still occurred in fires and floods, such acts were fewer and farther between. The acts of humans were more likely to create the catastrophes of collapsing buildings or the terrifying events of protesting explosions. It seemed as if a new human being was emerging. The new sociology, economics, and psychology, together with the Nietzschean critiques of thought, the Marxist ideas about class and history, the Darwinian notions of species change, and the Social Darwinist ideas of the superiority of Western culture and middle-class ideas, provided an intellectual framework that could not have been understood in the beginning of the nineteenth century.

Of course, the changes in technology and thought had their own impact on the arts and sciences. And it is to the modernist revolutions that we now turn in the next chapter.

CHAPTER 9
THE EARLY MODERN WORLD

Figure 9.1 Marie Curie in her laboratory 1898. Note how very basic this laboratory is. © Culture Club/Hulton Archive/Getty Images.

Marie Curie

In 1910 Nobel Prize-winning Marie Curie (1867–1943) had a problem. Four years after her husband and co-prize winner Pierre Curie had been killed by a horse-drawn vehicle, she had an affair with physicist Paul Langevin, who was estranged from his wife. Right-wing agitators hounded her in the press and reviled her as a usurping foreigner who did not understand that in France a woman had a place in the home. Her reputation needed serious repair.

Fortunately, at this low point in her life she was awarded the 1911 Nobel Prize in Chemistry, leaving her to this date as the only person to win the two prizes in two different scientific fields (Linus Pauling's second prize was the Peace Prize). When the First World War came to France, Curie decided to help wounded soldiers. She developed radiological centers at the front to enable X-rays to be taken as soon as possible—and also to use radium as a sterilizing agent, since penicillin had not yet been imagined. This selfless work burnished her reputation. After all, in tending for others, she was doing women's work. Who could not approve?

An American journalist, Missy Meloney, convinced Curie to write an autobiography in which Curie would tell the personal side of her studies of radium. When Curie died of cancer from her constant exposure to radiation, her daughter Eve wrote a second, quite personal, biography, unlike many biographies of male scientists that concentrate on work alone. Children's books about Marie Curie continue to be published. She inspires young people to this day.

As you read this chapter, keep in mind that something similar could be written about the lives of virtually every figure discussed here. The early modern period was a period in which individual biography was part of success. Einstein, Picasso, Stein, and all the rest not only presented themselves but also had the help of many people in the forming of their legends. These legends also often obscured the community nature of artistic and scientific masterworks.

Chapter Map

This chapter is about the intellectual and artistic responses to the rapidly changing technological and social world at the turn of the twentieth century. The chapter begins with what is often known as "the Second Industrial Revolution." Electricity, automobiles, telephones, radio, film, and so forth transformed the life experience of Europeans.

Intellectuals thus lived and thought in a new ecosystem. They realized that traditional assumptions were insufficient to support their endeavors and so began to look deep beneath the obvious to find structures and relationships from which one could reconstruct meaningful thought. As they did so, they began to look at the form their assumptions took. Not only did these radical challenges change our ideas about the world, but they also changed our ideas about how to portray, create, and think about the world.

In the first decade of the twentieth century, geometric ideas began to dominate, as cubist artists tried to depict movement in time and space on a canvas. Meanwhile in physics the fourth dimension, time, turned out to be best understood as another dimension of space. A large part of this chapter explores and explains the scientific ideas behind the theory of relativity. Relativity theory broke with long-established assumptions as scientists convincingly demonstrated that space seemed to contract and time to dilate as velocities approached the speed of light. There was no absolute space and time—only spacetime.

Artists and scientists also challenged ideas about the basic units of their fields. Biologists studying heredity saw that many problems resolved if they assumed that somehow there were units of heredity, genes. In music, composers challenged the structure of tonality within which individual notes had been defined and developed a music in which one note had no tonal relationship to other notes. Without key (tonal) structure, music sounded dissonant and even ugly to the untrained ear, but to musicians the new atonal system freed them to compose new materials.

In physics, scientists were willing to consider that the basic units of matter, atoms, might be composed of other, more basic units, like electrons and protons. They also found that seemingly continuous substances like energy or light could best be understood if they had, sometimes, a particle-like structure. Thus, it seemed that the submicroscopic world could be understood best in terms of units: or quanta. Quantum theory described a spacetime that made no sense in terms of the human world.

The Second Industrial Revolution and the New World

The last few decades of the nineteenth century saw changes in the technological, institutional, and social structure of society that are often summed up in the phrase "second industrial revolution." We have already discussed some aspects. A spate of inventions transformed society so quickly that anyone who had lived just a few decades could not help but notice the difference. These inventions stemmed from several extensions of transportation and communications infrastructure as well as from the new energy sources of petroleum and electricity.

The Bessemer process enabled steelmakers to produce vastly increased quantities of high-grade metal. Since steel is more durable than iron, railroads were able to extend their range with new long-lasting steel rails. As railroad building accelerated, new telegraph lines hummed alongside the right of way to enable the coordination necessary to juggle trains whizzing past each other. Longer-range railways meant that materials (like steel) could be shipped quickly over long distances, thus facilitating more rail building. But more than steel was shipped, and businesses were able to grow larger by opening outlets and factories throughout a country.

As businesses grew larger, they needed new laws to enable them to operate effectively. For instance, the older laws required owners of businesses to bear the liability if their businesses created harm or owed debts. Investors could lose their houses and bank accounts if businesses failed badly. Such liability exposure deterred investors from buying ownership shares in growing companies. To enable investment, the "limited liability" corporation was invented. Stockholders were liable for the value of their stock, but liability did not extend beyond that. Their personal lives were protected. Publicly owned "corporations" became in many respects "human bodies" under financial laws and were able to raise the capital they needed to grow rapidly when conditions were favorable.

Although the early industrial revolution was concentrated in England, Belgium, and France, a newly unified Germany jumped eagerly into the industrial race. More than any other government, Germany invested in technological and scientific research. They also encouraged corporations to merge into cartels (the *Konzern*) so that the economies associated with size could be realized. Business competition was much less important in Germany than in England.

As businesses expanded, they sought improved and new products to manufacture and sell. The need for products stimulated inventors. As Alfred North Whitehead noted in

1925, "The greatest invention of the nineteenth century was the invention of the method of invention." In every industrialized country, talented people scrambled to be the first to patent a new product. What were these products?

We have already discussed the radio, invented and developed by the Italian Guglielmo Marconi. But before Marconi presented his wireless telegraph, the Americans Alexander Graham Bell and Elisha Gray had invented the telephone, a speaking telegraph, in 1876. In 1877 both Germany and the UK had established short telephone systems. By the end of the decade, Europe had begun the process of wiring itself for conversation.

Perhaps the most important set of inventions were those concerned with electricity. Electricity provided light, as Joseph Swan in Great Britain, followed closely by Thomas Edison in the United States, invented the incandescent light bulb in 1878. In order to light cities and factories, central power stations had to be built, and the first one was probably in Surrey in 1881. Soon neighborhood after neighborhood exchanged gaslight for electric lighting. Developing these electrical systems involved many technical problems, both in developing appropriate equipment and in discovering how to link equipment together into a system. But once the electrical generating equipment was built and available, other uses for this new power source were found. Electric motors began to replace steam engines in factories. Motors were much quieter and more efficient than steam engines for many purposes. Electric trams in cities began to replace horse-drawn trams.

In transportation, the extension of railroads continued apace, but two competitors began slowly to arise. The modern improved bicycle entered the stage in 1876. Ten years later, the German Karl Benz patented the first automobile. Both of these inventions relied on two other developments. The first was vulcanized rubber and the pneumatic tire. The second was modern methods of paving roads. Tarmac was patented in 1901.

But automobiles also needed a third: petroleum refining, first developed in Scotland in 1848. Although petroleum products were used mostly for lubrication and kerosene lighting, by the twentieth century the unwanted byproduct, gasoline, came into its own. The automobile transformed European society in the twentieth century. The oil industry became a global giant.

In order to manufacture automobiles, a great deal of precision is required. Moving parts, pounding and rotating thousands of times every minute, have to precisely mesh with each other. The tolerance for error is miniscule. We have already seen how machine tools for boring accurate holes in iron blocks as well as and screw making machines, enabled high pressure and efficient steam engines to be developed. But these early precision tools were crude in comparison to those needed at the end of the nineteenth century. Industry standards needed to be defined, and precise measuring instruments to ensure accuracy had to be developed. In America, Henry Ford used 32,000 electrical machine tools to make his Model T Ford. Interestingly enough, European methods of automobile manufacturing relied on individual expert workmen shaping and filing and fitting parts together. The Americans relied on interchangeable parts that were manufactured to precisely fit together. Thus, the assembly line, with its conveyor belt speed, was early used in America but was quite late coming to Europe.

Perhaps the most striking invention in transportation was the airplane in 1903. Several inventors had tried to create a heavier-than-air craft, but the American bicycle manufacturers Orville and Wilbur Wright found the answer as they concentrated on control systems rather than engine power. Just a little more than a decade after the Wright brothers flew 200 feet at an altitude of 10 feet with a 6.8 miles per hour speed, at Kill Devil Hills (near Kitty Hawk), North Carolina, airplanes in the First World War flew for hours at hundreds of miles an hour at 15,000 feet. By the 1920s, airplanes were transforming mail delivery, travel, freight delivery, and entertainment.

Amid the upheaval caused by these changes in energy sources, materials, communications technology, and transportation methods, a host of other inventions continued to transform society. Phonographs allowed people to preserve sounds. Without ever going to a concert or an opera Europeans could hear the voices of the most famous singers and orchestras. The movie camera started an entire industry, led initially by the Lumière brothers in Paris in 1898. Elevators allowed buildings to be built higher, and the vertical shape of cities changed in decades. Refrigerated railcars and ships allowed the transportation of meat and other perishable foods thousands of miles from region to region and country to country. Nitrogen-based fertilizers greatly increased farm productivity. Urban growth continued unabated, and cities slowly became healthier with effective treated water and sewage systems, along with legislated quality standards. All of these innovations interacted with one another to create millions of possibilities. European cities were exciting places to be at the turn of the twentieth century.

Imagine Marie Curie, born in 1867. When she was still young, she grew up in a house lit by candles or gas, drank water carried from a neighborhood tap into the house, used a latrine in the back yard, created entertainment by visiting with her friends or reading, and traveled around the city in a horse-drawn coach or on foot. She lost her sister and her mother to diseases that today would have been just an inconvenience. But when she was a teenager, telephone systems began to be built in Western Europe. At the age of forty-three, in 1910, Marie Curie would have experienced almost all of the changes we have just discussed. She could have owned an automobile if she had not sunk every cent into research, and could have had a telephone in her house. She certainly drank purified water from a tap, flushed her waste into a toilet emptying into a sewer system, bought food in Paris that had been shipped from America, went to see the latest silent film at the cinema, went home to listen to a concert on her phonograph, stayed up late reading in a room lit by electricity, and traveled across the ocean in a steel liner powered by high-efficiency steam engines. In 1912 she would have heard how the sinking Titanic used radio to summon ships to rescue survivors who had been able to fit into the insufficient lifeboats. By the 1920s, she listened to radio for entertainment.

In short, the big news of the turn of the twentieth century was that the modern world was different. No one had ever experienced a world like this one. Embracing the modern felt exhilarating to many young scientists, artists, and thinkers, even while the newness of the modern world was a horror to others. The Italian Filippo Tommaso Marinetti wrote, "We are going to be present at the birth of the centaur and we shall soon see the first angels fly." The modern centaur was the automobile, combining not humans and animals, but rather humans and machines. And the automobile led Marinetti to write further, "We declare that the splendor of the world has been enriched by a new beauty: the beauty of speed. . . . We want to sing the man at the wheel, the ideal axis of which crosses the earth, itself hurled along its orbit."

Form

As thinkers tackled the implications of this new, modern world, many of them realized that they would have to reimagine the very forms of thought. The most basic expression of "form" is spatial shape. Euclidean geometry studies the laws and relationships among various spatial forms. But more generally, "form" is expressed in patterns. A limerick has a form, because it must be expressed in a pattern. The rhyme scheme is aabba, the meter mostly anapestic. If a rhyme does not have this exact form, then it is not a limerick. Each field of art or science uses a variety of forms to express ideas.

Usually, form underlies an idea, but the idea is about something else. It is useful to distinguish among "form," "content," and "subject matter." For instance, if an artist paints two trees next to each other, their branches intertwining, and entitles the painting "Love," we might say that the subject matter is trees, the content is love, and the form is a set of relationships among colors and brush strokes. During the turn-of-the-century period, artists often began to let the subject matter, as perceived by the eye, become less distinct until it sometimes disappeared altogether. Eventually both the content and the subject matter folded into an examination of form. Paintings began to be about painting and literature about words. Form became content. Forms folded back on themselves as form studied itself.

An example can be found in the works produced by the Spanish Pablo Picasso working in France and the German Albert Einstein. Neither knew the other but both realized that they would have to reconceive the basics of their respective fields in order to deal adequately with new modern questions. Both decided to investigate space and time.

Space, Time, and Geometry

Cubism

With Pablo Picasso's (1881–1973) "Les Demoiselles d'Avignon" ("The Young Ladies of Avignon") modern art was firmly established. The Andalusian Spaniard Picasso was born into an artistic family. His father was an artist and art teacher who was responsible for Picasso's early training. Picasso began staying for periods in Paris after 1900. He was desperately poor and politically leaned toward anarchism. In his early years, Picasso painted representational art with unusual colors to represent emotion. He went through a blue period and a rose period on the way to his modernist break. Picasso's legend grew with the support of Gertrude Stein, an expatriate American author who decided, with her brother Leo, to collect avant-garde art. Picasso became one of her favorites, and she exhibited her purchases at salons in her home.

In 1907 Picasso began to respond to a variety of influences, including Gauguin and Cézanne. He visited an exhibit of African art in Paris and related that to ancient Iberian sculpture. He saw these pieces through the lens of Gauguin's primitivism. But he was also influenced by mathematics and philosophy. The mathematician/philosopher Henri Poincaré had written about the idea of a fourth dimension as time. Maurice Princet, the author of mathematics books on the geometry of four dimensions, was a frequent visitor to Picasso's studio, The Bateau-Lavoir (his friends claimed his studio looked like a laundry boat on the Seine), where young artists tended to gather. Princet included sketches of four-dimensional figures in his book.

Picasso was taken by the idea of representing the fourth dimension. Representational painting, after all, is an optical illusion in which a two-dimensional surface appears to have three dimensions. Why not add a fourth? But the fourth is tricky, because the eye and brain cannot see time, the fourth dimension. We can easily see the three spatial dimensions of the world in which we live, but we can only see one moment in time. If we could see time in the same way we see space, we would see someone enter a room, walk around it, and leave the room, all in overlapping figures. (In fact, Marcel Duchamp later portrayed that with his "Nude Descending a Staircase" in 1911.) For Picasso and his colleagues, reality was full of motion.

So, the new painting was a mélange of influences as Picasso took a drawing of women in a brothel and added elements from Iberian and African art. But then he added motion. A side-view nose is painted onto a front-view face. We see different brief moments in a moving scene all pasted together. Many of Picasso's supporters scoffed, including, it is said, Leo Stein.

Figure 9.2 Marcel Duchamp and his painting *Nude Descending a Staircase*. This is a painting of a process: four dimensions (three spatial and one time dimension) depicted on a two-dimensional canvas. © Bettmann/Getty Images.

Figure 9.3 Artist Marcel Duchamp. © Getty Images.

Picasso kept the painting in his studio for the next seven years. But his friends all saw it, and it changed the character of modern painting. In 1907 Daniel Kahnweiler began to hang Picassos in his gallery and wrote analytical works explaining the new art to his customers.

The French painter Georges Braque began to work with Picasso in developing the new style known as cubism in which everything was depicted through a geometric scheme. The point of cubism was to depict the visual world through intersecting planes. A forehead might be defined by one plane, the cheeks by others. These planes were ideal constructs that often moved beyond the figure. But as these planes intersected, one could see a dim figure emerging. Soon more and more artists were painting cubism. Eventually some painters abandoned the world of the senses altogether. Art had become abstract geometrical shapes made of colors. Emotion faded as form took over. At this point, subject matter, form, and content merged to become one.

Picasso's cubism approached art from several different assumptions. One is that there is no privileged perspective. From the time of the Renaissance, artists had used a one-point perspective to achieve the three-dimensional illusion. Cubism gave this up. Second, the reality that was being painted included motion, that is it depicted both time and space. Third, it implied that there is a hidden aspect to reality that is not immediately available to the senses or to common sense. This point implied that art did not have to correspond to perceptual, visual experience. Thus, fourth, paintings can be abstracted from experience. What is left is pure geometry, but there is an assumption that both space and time are amenable to geometric treatment.

All of these assumptions can be found in Einstein's relativity theory, although there is no evidence that young Einstein and young Picasso knew of one another's existence.

Scientific Conundrums

When scientists became convinced that light was a wave, all were agreed that something must be waving. That something was called "aether." No one knew what it was, but clearly it filled all space, because light reaches us from the stars. Since planets move through space without slowing down from friction, scientists realized that the aether must be exceedingly thin. But since light consists of transverse waves that cannot be maintained in something as thin as the atmosphere but only in something as thick as tar or jello, scientists realized that they could not even imagine what aether might be. In fact, perhaps the most pressing physical problem in the nineteenth century was to solve the structure of aether. Using increasingly ingeniously designed equipment, scientists were able to measure the speed of light in various materials (air, water, vacuum) with impressive accuracy. But what supported the light waves was a mystery.

In 1887 the American physicists Albert A. Michelson and Edward W. Morley developed an extremely sensitive apparatus called an interferometer that was able to split a light beam and bring the two parts back together again after they had traveled different paths. They hoped that they could show the effects of the earth's path through the aether. Since the earth was moving though the aether as it circled the sun, at some time in the year it should be creating a current, or wind, in the aether. For instance, if in December it was moving at the same speed as the aether, in June, when the earth was moving in the opposite direction from what it was moving in December, it should be going against the aether wind current. The two halves of the split light beam should be moving at different speeds and should interfere with one another when they were brought back together.

No effect was found.

Some physicists thought that the aether must be carried along with the earth. There were reasons based on other experiments, however, to think that the aether was stationary in space. Perhaps there was a partial drag of aether around moving objects.

The Irish physicist George Fitzgerald and the Dutch physicist Hendrik Lorentz hypothesized that physical objects contract slightly in the direction in which they are moving. They were able to calculate equations that showed that if the Michelson-Morley apparatus contracted in the way that the equations demanded, then the light waves moving through the ether would come back together exactly as if they had not been affected by their motion through the aether. They had no explanation for such a contraction, but if such a contraction occurred, then the Michelson-Morley results could be explained.

The French mathematician, physicist, engineer, and philosopher of science Henri Poincaré (1854–1912) also worked on the mathematics of the Lorentz contraction and helped show that they could be seen as mathematical transformations. He corresponded with Hendrik Lorentz and suggested new and better ways to formulate the mathematics and to interpret the meaning of these new ideas in physics. Poincaré had worked for the

French government to establish time zones, and as part of this work he had considered how to synchronize clocks. He realized that light should be considered to move at the same speed, independent of the speed of the source of light in order to simplify the mathematics as much as possible. He wrote about considering time as a fourth dimension. But he didn't quite find the theory of relativity.

Albert Einstein and the Special Theory of Relativity

The young physicist Albert Einstein (1879–1955) ultimately solved the problem by analyzing the process of measuring moving bodies. He apparently was not particularly trying to explain the failure of Michelson and Morley to find evidence of the ether, but rather was trying to find a way to reconcile the contradictions between Newton's mechanics and Maxwell's electrodynamics.

Although he was born in Ulm, his father Hermann Einstein and his Uncle Jakob soon founded an electrical company in Munich, and brought their families there, where they lived until Albert was fifteen, when business failures led to the Einstein family's move to Italy. Albert excelled in mathematics, and his father hoped he would become an electrical engineer. Soon Einstein moved to Switzerland to study for the entrance examinations to the Swiss Federal Polytechnic University, where he enrolled in the mathematics and physics program in 1896. The same year he renounced his German citizenship to avoid being drafted.

The Serbian Mileva Marić joined Einstein's class as the only woman studying physics and mathematics. Einstein and she became good friends, then lovers, then spouses in 1903. Before they were married, they had a daughter, Lieserl, as Einstein referred to her in his letters, who was born in Serbia and never returned to Switzerland. Historians have concluded that she either died of scarlet fever or was adopted and lived under a different name. In 1904 their son Hans Albert was born and in 1910 Eduard. Einstein's mother strongly disapproved of the marriage, and it soon began to feel the stress. The two separated in 1914 and divorced in 1919, when Einstein married his cousin Elsa.

After graduation, Einstein was unable to land a teaching position, and he eventually got a job in the Bern, Switzerland, patent office with the help of a friend's father. Einstein had grown up surrounded by electrical apparatus in his father's business, and he found that at the patent office he had to deal with questions about electrical equipment. Among the questions he had to deal with were the transmission of electrical signals and the synchronization of clocks. The theoretically inclined Einstein thought deeply about these issues. In fact, a key to his method was a "thought experiment" in which he assumed perfect apparatuses in order to test the logical possibility of a hypothesis.

Eventually he decided that he needed to concentrate on what he saw as the fundamental act of physics: measuring. Only when something is measured can it be treated mathematically. But he also wanted to reconcile the gulf between Newton's corpuscular theory and Maxwell's field theory. So, he based his theory on two fundamental assumptions, one from each approach: From Newton he took the first law, the law of inertia, but he turned this into a principle: (1) all inertial reference systems, that is, systems moving in a straight line at a constant speed, are equivalent. In short, there is no way to determine whether such a system is at rest or in motion. From Maxwell, he took the invariance of the speed of light in a vacuum. (2) Light in a vacuum will be measured at the same speed (symbolized by "c") no matter how fast its source or the observer of the light is moving.

And that is it: the special theory of relativity. The rest is following out the consequences of these two postulates.

In order to measure something that is moving past an observer, the observer has to have a ruler and make two observations at exactly the same time. The observer has to see first one end and then the other end of that thing being measured. Thus, these two observations have to be simultaneous. But what does simultaneous mean?

Einstein supposed a train with an observing person inside it was moving very rapidly (close to the speed of light), but very smoothly (an inertial reference system), past an observer on the ground. He further supposed that there were two lightning strikes, and the person on the ground saw them simultaneously. The person on the train would not see them simultaneously, because the train would move away from the lightning flash behind it and toward the one in front of it. The observer on the train would see the forward flash first, followed later by the rearward flash.

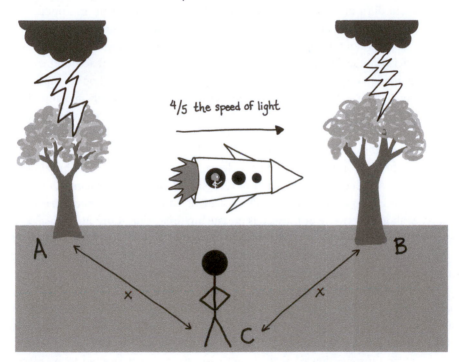

Figure 9.4 Relativity of simultaneity. Both the person in the rocket and the person on the ground are entitled to think they are at rest. The person on the ground sees simultaneous lightening strikes. The person in the rocket sees first one, and then the other. Each thinks the other's observation is caused by the motion of the observer. It is impossible, then, to define simultaneity for all observers. © Drawing by Kassel Galaty.

But the person in the train was in an inertial system, and according to Einstein's first postulate, an inertial system cannot be distinguished from a system at rest. The person on the train, then, would think that the train is at rest and the person on the ground was moving very fast toward the back of the train.

But you protest, come on! The person on the ground is the one who is really at rest. Einstein would respond, "Really?" The earth is rotating about a thousand miles an hour. It is moving around the sun. The sun is whirling through the Milky Way Galaxy. The Milky Way Galaxy is whirling through space. Who is really at rest?

So, the theory of special relativity said that it is impossible to be sure that an observer is actually making simultaneous observations when that observer measures something that is moving. In fact, if an observer is moving just as fast as the thing being measured, that observer will measure the length of that thing as longer than the first observer who sees the thing moving. What will the difference in the measurement be? Exactly the difference that was predicted by Lorentz and Fitzgerald.

If one follows Einstein, the explanation of the failure of the Michelson-Morley experiment to find any motion through the aether is that the apparatus and the light beams appear to shrink. There is no material shrinkage, but the structure of the act of measuring moving things creates different measurements, and each measurement is as valid as the next. Einstein did not refer to the Michelson-Morley experiment in his famous paper of 1905 "Zur Elektrodynamik bewegter Körper" ("On the Electrodynamics of Moving Bodies"). The point of the paper was to reconsider the basic assumptions of physics. But other physicists noticed that Einstein had provided an elegant way of accounting for the Michelson-Morley results while all the other explanations were ad hoc attempts to use the traditional theories to explain anomalous results. They seemed ugly in comparison.

There were further results from Einstein's unpacking of his two basic postulates. A measurement of time involves a measurement of distance (how far did a clock's hands move?). Observers in two different inertial reference systems will measure time differently. The faster a clock is moving, the slower time will seem to pass. Einstein points out that this result occurs with all kinds of clocks. A plant that is dormant in the winter and blossoms in the spring is essentially measuring time. A human body that reaches puberty at about age twelve or thirteen is measuring time. Thus, Einstein later said, if an identical twin leaves her sister on the earth and travels very fast into space, turns around and comes home, the two twins will be different ages. The twin on earth may have aged forty years, while the space-bound twin may have aged two years.

From 1911 on, this phenomenon, called the "twin paradox," has captivated scientists and non-scientists alike. Essentially, it provides a theoretical way to travel one-way in time. Unfortunately, such a time traveler into the future can never return to the past to tell the story to friends and family.

Essentially, Einstein showed that certain assumptions that seemed to be essential to a physical understanding of the universe were disposable. For Einstein, aspects of nature that could not be observed were not needed in physics. Newton had assumed that in order for his mechanics to work one needed to assume that there was an absolute time and an absolute space, even if only God knew what that was. Einstein said that unobservable absolutes should not be part of physics. Neither time nor space existed in an absolute form, apart from being measurable. Energy and mass were similarly measured differently in different inertial systems. Aether was not observable and thus was not appropriately part of physics.

Perhaps the most famous of Einstein's equations is $E = mc^2$, the amount of energy inherent in matter is equal to the mass times the square of the speed of light. Since the speed of light is a huge number (186,000 miles per second), and a huge number squared is a gigantic number, only a little bit of mass could produce a large amount of energy. This equation in a few decades was used to calculate the amount of energy released in an atomic bomb.

The General Theory of Relativity

Einstein and others realized that his theory did not deal with accelerated motion, but only with inertial motion. He was not sure how to generalize his theory. But he did have a brilliant insight sometime before 1907. In one of his famous thought experiments, he asked what experiment could distinguish between the experience of accelerating and the experience of being in a gravitational field. Suppose a person were in a windowless room that was being towed faster and faster (accelerating) by a rocket ship. The floor of the room would push against that person's shoes. Suppose that same room were on the surface of a planet. The floor of the room would push against that person's shoes. The experience, said Einstein, would be the same. That is, acceleration and gravitation were indistinguishable. He raised this observation to a principle, the equivalence of gravitational mass and inertial mass.

Applying his equivalence principle to special relativity, Einstein was able to show that clocks would run slower in a stronger gravitational field than they would in a weaker gravitational field (or no gravitational field). He was also able to show that light would seem to bend in a gravitational field. To show this, we might imagine the same windowless room. In the accelerating case, if a person shoots a bullet in one side of the room, the room will continue to accelerate upward while the bullet passes through the room. The bullet will therefore exit the room at a lower point than it entered it. In a gravitational field, of course, the bullet will fall as it moves horizontally. The same thing will happen to a light beam generated on one side of the room. As the room continues to accelerate, the light beam will hit the wall on the other side at a lower point than the point of generation. Therefore, in a gravitational system, light must deviate from a straight line.

In geometry, the shortest distance between two points defines a straight line. The best way to generate a straight line is with a beam of light. Strings and chains sag in a gravitational field, but a beam of light is seen to move in a straight line. That is why surveyors use telescopes to determine a straight path through the air. But if light actually bends in a gravitational field, how would one practically find a straight line? Space would appear to curve.

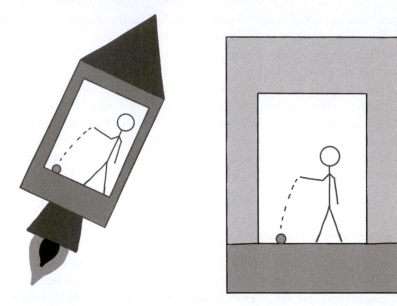

Figure 9.5 Equivalence of acceleration and gravity. A person in a windowless accelerating rocket will experience the same effects as a person in a windowless room in a gravitational field. No experiment can determine who is accelerating and who is in a gravitational field. © Drawing by Kassel Galaty.

Figure 9.6 General relativity, deflection of light due to sun's gravitational field. © Getty Images.

Einstein's mathematician friend Marcel Grossman suggested that he look at non-Euclidean geometry, the geometry of curved space. The surface of the earth is a good example of a non-Euclidean geometry. On the surface of the earth, the shortest distance between two points is the arc of a great circle, which is why airplanes often fly across the poles instead of following the straight line of a flat map. Since the shortest distance between two points is still the definition of a straight line, lines in the geometry of spherical surfaces are curved. One might say that the space itself is curved, just as we say that the surface of the earth is curved.

But of course, the shape of the universe is more complex than the surface of the earth. In 1908 the mathematician Hermann Minkowski (1864–1909), a former mathematics teacher of Einstein who later regretted his mediocre assessment of Einstein's mathematics abilities, published a theory of four-dimensional spacetime. He showed that space and time could no longer be considered to have an independent existence, but that both space and time were parts of a larger whole: spacetime. He was also able to show that although space and time contracted and dilated, there was an interval in spacetime that did not change with motion.

Einstein was able to use this conception as he figured out how to add gravity and acceleration to the relativity theory. The problem was to show how spacetime was affected by the presence of matter. If a straight line was practically defined as the path of light, and if light was "bent" in the presence of a massive body, then four-dimensional spacetime itself could be described as "curved." The question was how much it is curved. After years of intellectual struggle, by 1915 Einstein had the answer, and he published his field equations.

In the traditional, Newtonian view, pieces of matter sent out gravitational forces that attracted other pieces of matter. These gravitational forces acted across empty space to pull pieces of matter together. Orbits of planets (like the earth) were maintained by balancing inertia with gravitational forces.

In the Einstein view, there were no forces acting at a distance through empty space. Spacetime assumed a shape that defined what lines matter would follow as it moved through spacetime. Every point of spacetime could be said to have a number that showed just how matter would behave as it moved through that point. Of course, the number associated with a point changed as matter moved closer or farther from the point. So as matter moved around, the shape of spacetime constantly shifted. Only if there were no matter in the vicinity would spacetime have a flat shape like Newton had thought empty space had.

When the shape of all space is expressed as an interconnected whole, we have what is called a field theory. Einstein had developed a gravitational field theory to complement Maxwell's electromagnetic field theory. And as we have seen, field theories have a different structure than particle/force theories. A field theory is a theory of a unified collectivity, unlike a particle theory that concentrates on units. Still, the two field theories did not merge into one. Gravitation had a different form than electromagnetism.

After the First World War, the British physicist and astronomer Arthur Eddington organized expeditions to the southern hemisphere to view a total solar eclipse to test

Einstein's prediction that light would be bent in a gravitational field. The sun was massive enough that measurable bending should take place. In normal conditions, the light from the sun obscures the stars in the sun's vicinity. But if an eclipse darkened the sun, the stars should be visible. If a star did not appear exactly where it was predicted to appear without bending, then it would be possible to measure just how much the position deviated from the expected one. Einstein's equations were precise enough to make an exact prediction, and in fact, Einstein's theory was borne out. When Eddington announced the results, Einstein's theory made headline news. From 1919 on, Einstein was the first modern scientific superstar. He was an icon, and his name became associated with genius, as in, "He's no Einstein, but he's pretty smart."

In the 1920s, and beyond popularizers of science made the primary results of the special and general theories available to the general educated public. Philosophers and scientists began to debate what it might mean if time were variable, if we lived in a four-dimensional world, and so forth. The British author Virginia Woolf was stimulated by her understanding of Einstein's theory to explore the various meanings of time in her 1927 novel *To the Lighthouse*. In that book, the longest chapter only covers one day, while the shortest chapter covers ten years. Woolf played with perception and point of view as she considered what reality might actually be. The lighthouse is many things, depending on who is observing it and from where.

Science Fiction

In the second part of the nineteenth century, a number of authors began to think about scientific and technological discoveries and ask what would happen if some discovery were made. Science fiction novels used imaginary technology as a way of exploring the ills of present society and building utopias or dystopias. But science fiction also served to spark the imaginations of people in every rank of society and to stimulate them to imagine possibilities out of the ordinary. The Frenchman Jules Verne (1828–1905) became one of the most translated authors in the world.

One of the possibilities treated by science fiction writers was time travel. For instance, the French astronomer and writer Camille Flammarion (1842–1925) wrote *Lumen* in 1887 in which an alien being zooms through space faster than light. The being catches up with light that has left the earth and is able to see time move backward. He sees armies lying dead on a field rise and march backward to the beginning of the battle as their bullets fly back into their rifles. In 1895 H. G. Wells wrote *The Time Machine* in which the protagonist is able to fly into the future and back again. He goes to a distance future to find that humans have evolved into two separate races, descendants of the former useless leisure class, who have lost all initiative, and descendants of the former worker class, who live in the dark and keep the indolent leisure class alive as food. He then travels thirty million years into the future to see a dying earth lit by a dimming red sun. When he returns to his own time, he finds that only three hours have elapsed.

In 1884 Edwin A. Abbott published *Flatland: A Romance of Many Dimensions* in which the world is populated by geometric figures who live in two dimensions. The protagonist, A. Square, dreams about a one-dimensional world occupied by points. He tries to convince the monarch of Lineland that there could be a second dimension and so enrages the monarch by his heresy that he tries to kill A. Square. Later, a sphere from a three-dimensional universe visits A. Square. The sphere appears to be a circle because in two dimensions all that can be seen is a cross section of the sphere. But as the sphere moves up and down through the third dimension, the circle gets bigger and smaller and eventually becomes a point and disappears for a time. The sphere picks up A. Square and shows him Flatland from above. A. Square is able to see that his world is but a small part of reality, and that Spaceland encompasses much more. Once he realizes the possibility of more dimensions, he suggests to the Sphere that there might be a fourth dimension. The Sphere rejects that possibility, but A. Square realizes the truth. In the discussion of the lives of people in Flatland Abbott satirizes his own society. But the enduring power of the book is that it presents the possibilities of multiple dimensions. *Flatland* became a success after Einstein published his general theory of relativity and the idea that space and time are wedded together into a four-dimensional continuum.

New Units

One part of the modernist revolutions concerning form was to explore the basic units that had hitherto served as the basis for analysis and/or creation. Between 1870 and 1910, artists began to experiment with brush strokes and color in new and unexpected ways. Musicians began to examine the use of notes, cut away from tonal context, as the basis for composition. In biology, heredity was analyzed using the idea of units, or genes. In physics, continuous substances like light and energy were seen to have a discontinuous character; everything seemed expressible in terms of a new word for unit pieces, a quantum. In literature, some authors began to explore and analyze words as the basis for fiction. And in social thought, adults were given the vote independent of class, race, or gender. In this section, we will explore each of these ideas in turn.

Genetics

Although reproduction and heredity had been studied throughout the scientific period, genetics starts with the Austrian monk Gregor Mendel (1822–84). Between 1856 and 1863, Mendel studied the effect of crossbreeding on the traits of pea plants. He concentrated on seven characteristics, like seed color, pod shape, and plant height. First, he isolated plants that always bred the same characteristics that it had itself. For instance, a green seed would always produce a green seed. Next, he cross-pollinated true-breeding green-seeded plants with true-breeding yellow-seeded plants. In this case, all of the offspring had yellow seeds. But when he bred these second-generation plants with one another, one-fourth of the seeds were green. The same results held for the other seven traits. Mendel coined the terms "recessive" and "dominant" to describe the traits he was observing. In this example, yellow is dominant, and green is recessive.

Mendel deduced that each parent plant passed these traits randomly to their offspring. Each set of traits was independent of the others. One could calculate the ratios in which traits were passed on by doing simple statistical calculations. Thus, each of the traits existed in a unitary form: either yellow or green, tall or short. The idea that traits might exist as units ran counter to general ideas about heredity. The predominant idea was that offspring blend the traits of their parents. A green seed and a yellow seed would produce a greenish-yellow seed. A tall plant and a short plant would produce a medium-sized plant. Furthermore, in succeeding generations, the plants would tend to return to type. This blending idea of inheritance contained no room for discrete hereditary units.

Mendel communicated his results to the Natural Science Society of Brno, and his papers were published in their journal. And there the matter stood. Mendel was called into administrative service, and practically no one read the journal articles. Mendel died unknown as a scientist in 1887.

But meantime, research continued.

Francis Galton

The child prodigy Francis Galton (1822–1911), cousin of Charles Darwin, ranged widely across intellectual fields. As a young man, Galton was an explorer in Africa, but in his thirties he married and wrote scientific papers based on measurement in meteorology, psychology, criminology, and statistics. After his cousin, Charles Darwin, published *The Origin of Species*, Galton became fascinated by human variation and heredity. Like most of the rest of Europe at the time, Galton was a racist and was fascinated by the question of why Europeans were so much richer and powerful than the inhabitants of other regions. In 1873 in a letter to *The Times*, he actually recommended that the Chinese send their excess population to Africa to improve the breed. But most of Galton's work was done using British subjects. He painstakingly studied the biographies of eminent men and their relatives so he could apply statistics to show that the traits necessary to eminence were inherited.

He then turned to studies of twins who were raised in different families so he could study the differential effects of "Nature" and "Nurture" (he coined the terms). He thought that the data lay on the side of nature. He therefore developed recommendations for what he called "eugenics," deliberate policies to improve the British population. He thought all children should have a chance at a first-rate education and that financial inheritance should be minimized. People who did not have high abilities should be put in celibate situations, and "the better sort" of immigrants and refugees should be welcomed and offered citizenship. Galton also defined "dysgenics," practices like the late marriage of eminent people that worked against improving the British "race."

Galton was befuddled by the tendency of offspring of various species to revert to the mean. It seemed that in the long run it might be impossible to actually improve the breed without serious culling of unwanted offspring. By his development of statistical studies in biology and his recognition that gradual changes could not produce permanent changes, he helped define a set of research problems that would lead to a rediscovery of Mendel's work. Galton himself did not rediscover the idea of unitary factors in inheritance because he concentrated on traits that seemed to be distributed continuously because they were supported by multiple sets of genes.

Mutations

The Dutch botanist Hugo De Vries (1848–1935) and the German botanist Carl Correns (1864–1933) both began to do experiments that were closely allied to those that Mendel had made. In 1900 Correns cited both Mendel and Darwin and put pressure on de Vries to do the same. de Vries had studied new, previously unobserved, traits in primroses and had named these new traits "mutations." He suggested that large jumps in traits, saltations, would enable evolution to occur whereas gradual changes could not be supported. The Englishman William Bateson (1861–1926) translated Mendel's papers into English and argued that Mendel's theory should form the basis of a new science of heredity. In 1905 Bateson coined the word "genetics."

But for Bateson, a gene was not a material substance located in one part of the organism. It was rather a kind of stable energy state in the whole organism. Bateson, the Danish botanist Wilhelm Johannsen and others were unwilling to see genes as anything other than a state of the whole organism. There was not enough evidence, nor indeed was there even a whisper of a theory, to show that some specific part of an organism could change the organism as a whole.

This lack of theory and evidence changed as the American T. H. Morgan began to see parallels between the pairing of chromosomes and the Mendelian theory of dominant and recessive traits. If, in hybrids, there were two factors for a trait, then the pairing of chromosomes could perhaps explain how the two factors were brought together. Morgan worked out an ingenious method for mapping traits on the chromosomes of fruit flies, and by the 1920s most Anglo-American biologists were convinced that somewhere on a chromosome the factors for heredity lay. But the opposite view dominated in France. One problem was that no one could see how a gene might affect the development of an embryo. The chromosomal gene did not support further research or theorizing in embryology or in most areas of biology. That connection would wait for the 1950s.

Music: Tonality and Atonality

The nature of music in the nineteenth century was in part shaped by the social upheavals of the Industrial Revolution. As a strong middle class emerged, there was a demand for musical entertainment. Performances moved into large halls, and orchestras became larger, with stronger instruments. But music also was performed in middle-class parlors. Many middle-class young women were trained at the piano so they could perform for family and friends. Sheet music sold widely.

Stylistically, the music was tonal, that is it was played in a key, like the key of C or the key of G. A characteristic of tonal music is that each note has a particular role, depending on the key. So, for instance, in the key of C Major, the note C is the home, or tonic, note. A triadic chord built on C (C, E, G) is a basic tonic chord, and in most pieces the ending drives toward the tonic. However, in the key of G Major, the G note and chord are the tonics. C is the fourth tone from G, and the C chord is called the subdominant. In the key of G Major, a musical piece drives toward resolution in the tonic G. Try humming a song, like, say "Twinkle, Twinkle Little Star," and see how difficult it is to stop singing one note from the end. The song drives toward resolution.

In the traditional tonal system of the nineteenth century, each key had associated with it a scale made of eight notes. Since there were thirteen possible notes between any octave that began and ended a scale, five tones were outside the scale. These notes were used in a variety of ways, but they usually provided a feeling of dissonance—or changed the tonality, for instance from Major to Minor. However, when the key changed, such as from C Major to G Major, some of the dissonant notes became part of the scale, and scale notes became part of the dissonant group. For instance, in C Major, the note F# is dissonant, but in G Major it is the seventh note of the scale. Try playing a C Minor chord (C, E flat, G) and then a C flat Major chord (C flat, E flat, and G flat). The E flat is common to both chords, but in the first it has a minor sound and in the second it has lost the minor sound and is part of a Major sound. Can that E flat be said to be the same note in both contexts? The artist Marcel Duchamp provided us with a similar question. He hung a urinal in an art exhibit and titled it "The Fountain." Can a urinal become a work of art if it is moved from a restroom to an art gallery?

By the second half of the nineteenth century, many composers were working to stretch the tonal structure by, for instance, frequently changing the key and thus the tonal structure of the piece. One of the most striking examples is Richard Wagner's (see Chapter 7) opera *Tristan und Isolde* (first performance 1865). The opera concerns itself with forbidden love that cannot be consummated and that ends in the death of the two lovers. Wagner used dissonant chords that resolved to other dissonant chords that never resolved back to the tonic chord. The listener was dragged from irresolution to irresolution, never finding the release of a return to the home. The reader is encouraged to listen to the "Overture" to hear this effect. The opera continues in this suspended state until, in the "Liebestod" (Love-Death), Isolde dies and the music resolves.

But all the experiments of the later nineteenth century remained tonal. Individual notes had a part in a greater whole and were defined in terms of that whole. As tonal structures changed, the role of the individual notes changed, but they still were defined by the key structure. A human analogy might be a person who plays different roles in different social situations and acts differently depending whether she is at home, at work, in the gym, or serving as a school volunteer. Context matters.

In the beginning of the twentieth century, a logical but still jarring innovation was made by the Austrian composer Arnold Schönberg (1874–1951). Early in his musical career, Schönberg worked tonally as he continued the innovations begun by Wagner and Liszt and tried to balance them with the more conservative approaches of composers like Brahms, who worked in the aura of Beethoven. By 1908 Schönberg, who was in a personal crisis because of his wife's infidelity and in a musical crisis because the logic of his composing was pushing him against the boundaries of tonality, produced pieces that in parts gave up tonality altogether. By 1909 and his *Drei Klavierstücke* (Three Piano Pieces), he had left tonality completely. Although Schönberg did not like the word, he

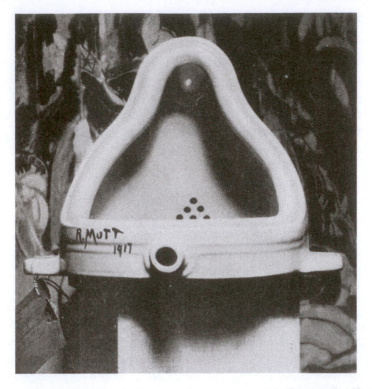

Figure 9.7 Satiric art: "The Fountain" by Marcel Duchamp, 1917. Photograph Alfred Steiglitz. Original Print and negative destroyed. This cropped photo was in the 1917 magazine "The Blind Man." Duchamp's work asks whether art is created by context. © Wikimedia Commons (public domain).

had established the principle of atonality. In atonality, there is no particular key, and the individual notes have no relationship to one another except the "distance" or interval between them. Schönberg used all twelve notes, and since there was no scale, there was no thirteenth note to end a sequence.

Notes in an atonal system were thus free of context. Musically, they were radical individuals. The entire piece took shape only because the individual notes moved in a planned relationship with one another. Schoenberg avoided repetition and often sought dissonance, not only because of the jarring emotional quality but because he had a musical idea he was working out. Sometimes a sequence of notes was used also as a chord, so that which was chronological became simultaneous. Later, in his twelve-tone technique Schönberg established rules for choosing the notes, such as a rule that said that all twelve tones had to be used with the same frequency so that no one note would be emphasized. Audiences were frequently confused and angry, especially at the beginning of the atonal approach. At times, their vocal reactions drowned out the performers.

Thinkers battled during the modernist period over the primacy of the individual and the primacy of the society, or the state. In a musical form, in a non-verbal language, similar battles took place as well.

Atomic Structure

The British J. J. Thomson (1856–1940), working with cathode-ray tubes, discovered a new particle, the electron, that was much smaller than an atom. The word "atom" comes from the Greek for "not able to be cut." Clearly, with Thomson's results, atoms were not the basic units of matter. Perhaps the basic units were electrons? But since very few pieces of matter in the world are electrically charged, there must be a positive something to balance the electrons. And since electrons are so tiny, most of the mass of an atom must be made of the positive part. Putting all this together, Thomson suggested that atoms were composed of a positively charged "stuff" with electrons embedded in it. This was dubbed the "plum pudding atom."

In 1898 Henri Becquerel had shown that photographic-plate-effecting rays emitted by uranium were composed of "alpha" particles that turned out to be positively charged helium ions. Thomson's student Ernst Rutherford (1871–1937) suggested that scientists shoot the positively charged alpha particles at a thin sheet of gold foil and measure the deflection. These experiments showed that the atom actually had a dense but very small positively charged nucleus and that the electrons orbited far away from the center. Thus, Rutherford suggested that the atom had a planetary structure. Just like planets orbiting the sun, electrons orbited the nucleus.

But, electrons, unlike planets, have an electric charge. An orbiting electric charge (or any accelerating electric charge) radiates energy. The orbiting electrons thus should radiate energy, slow down, and spiral into the nucleus, creating a plum pudding atom. Rutherford's planetary model was unstable. There was no reason it should exist. But the gold foil scattering experiments showed that it did exist. Physicists were not sure how to explain the problem. The answer, it turned out, lay hidden in another area of physics.

Early Quantum Theory

The German physicist Max Planck (1858–1947) decided in 1894 to develop a theory that would explain the distribution of heat by a "black-body" that could radiate heat along with light at all frequencies. The theories used at that time did not coincide with experimental results. Planck found that if he assumed that heat energy was given off in little packets (quanta), the mathematical theory would accurately predict what was observed. But no one could imagine how the light associated with heat (think "white hot" or "red hot") could come in particle form. Light, physicists thought, was a wave that spread out over space. Thus, Planck's quanta made no intuitive sense.

In 1905 Einstein used the same idea to explain the photoelectric effect. In this effect, when light is shone on a metal, it causes an electric current by bouncing electrons out of the metal. But if a lower-frequency light is turned up in intensity, no electrons are emitted. There is more light, but still no electrons. Only when the frequency of the light is increased are more electrons discharged. Einstein showed that if he assumed that light comes in little packets, he could explain the photoelectric effect. Each packet can impart energy to an electron. But if there is not enough energy in a packet to bounce an electron out of the metal, it does not matter how many packets hit the electron; the electron will not budge. However, when the frequency is increased, there is more energy in a packet, and now only one packet will be enough to dislodge an electron. These packets of light energy are called "photons." Einstein presented his theory as a "heuristic." It worked, but he could not really see why light should come in packets, that is, he could not see any reason why the theory should work.

So as scientists wrestled with the problems of the planetary theory of the atom and tried to explain why the electrons did not spiral into the nucleus, there was a precedent. In 1913 the Dane Niels Bohr (1885–1962) suggested that electron orbits were fixed in the space of an atom. An electron could be in one orbit or another but could not exist in other, nonorbital, areas of the atom. If an electron emitted exactly the right amount of energy, it could drop down into a lower orbit. If an electron absorbed exactly the right amount of energy, then it could jump up to a higher orbit. But it could not emit or absorb an amount of energy that would send it into any of the forbidden places in the atom.

No one could explain why there should be fixed orbits or forbidden spaces, but the theory worked to explain several problems. Perhaps the most important problem was to explain the existence of spectral lines. A spectrum line occurs when light is emitted by an element or is absorbed by an element. Thus if, say, hydrogen emits light, that light comes in certain frequencies and not others. If the light from hydrogen is put through a prism and then photographed, one sees the lines. Each element has unique spectral lines. So, if Bohr's theory were accurate, the lines would come as electrons radiated energy. They could only radiate the amount of energy that would allow them to move to one of the lower orbits: no more, no less.

But why would an atom have fixed orbits?

In 1924 the French physics student Louis de Broglie (1892–1987) asked himself why waves like light could be seen as particles, whereas particles like electrons could not be seen as waves. He decided to develop a theory that rectified this imbalance. De Broglie supposed that electrons did have waves. In his vision, an orbit was like a tuned guitar string. A guitar string can support one main note and also overtones of one half, quarter, eighth, etc. of the main note. It cannot support other notes unless its length is changed. For de Broglie, if electrons were like notes, then they could only exist in an orbit of the proper length. De Broglie submitted this idea as his doctoral dissertation. It won him the Nobel Prize.

In 1926 the German physicist Erwin Schrödinger (1887–1961) developed a wave mechanics in which the electron was a wave. In his seminal paper, he was able to derive the spectral lines of hydrogen and show the Bohr model of atomic structure could be explained. The German Max Born (1882–1970) suggested that the wave was not the electron itself, but rather represented the probability that an electron could be found at any place in the atom.

At about the same time, the German Werner Heisenberg (1901–76) spent an academic year on a Rockefeller fellowship to do research under Niels Bohr in Copenhagen. There he engaged the problems concerning the structure of the Bohr model of the atom. Later, back in Germany, Heisenberg suffered from severe allergies, and he fled pollen-rich

Göttingen to stay for a time on Helgoland. When his hay fever disappeared, he decided to list all observations concerning spectral lines. Essentially, he began to create a matrix. As he mused, he decided he needed a mathematics in which when terms are multiplied together, the answer varies depending on the order in which one multiplies them. He was struck by the idea that the intensity of spectral lines varies with the probability that an electron will make the orbital transition that produces that line. If the probability is high, more electrons jump that way, and the radiation becomes more intense. When he got back to Göttingen, he teamed with a graduate student, Pascual Jordan, who understood the mathematics of matrices. The two created matrix mechanics, a theory that was mathematically equivalent to Schrödinger's wave mechanics.

It was clear from Heisenberg's initial approach, postulating quantities in which changing the order of multiplication changed the answer, that two quantities multiplied together would be uncertain. Out of this characteristic of the theory came the Heisenberg Uncertainty Principle. One cannot know exactly the position and momentum of a particle at the same time. Position multiplied by Momentum minus Momentum multiplied by Position is not equal to zero. If Heisenberg's theory was accurate, then the Heisenberg Uncertainty Principle was inescapable. We cannot simultaneously be sure what both the position and the momentum are.

Although Heisenberg's theory was mathematically equivalent to Schrödinger's, the two physicists disagreed about the meaning of the theory. For Schrödinger (joined by Einstein), the atom had a structure, and the laws of nature were deterministic. Uncertainty lay in our human inability to measure precisely. For Heisenberg (joined by Bohr), the uncertainty of the theory was intrinsic to nature. There was no deterministic structure to the atom. Nature at its core is only probabilistic.

Later philosophers asked if this fundamental uncertainty existed in the everyday world. Perhaps, for example, random electrons in the brain could be the source of free will. Let us consider an example. A grain of salt contains about 1.2×10^{18} atoms. That's over a sextillion. An electron or two could be anywhere in the room, according to probability calculations. But that would do nothing to change the location of the salt grain. In short, the Heisenberg Uncertainty Principle is very important at the atomic level, but rarely does it make a difference in the everyday world.

Except!

Schrödinger, in order to show the absurdity of the Heisenberg/Bohr interpretation of quantum theory (known as the Copenhagen interpretation), concocted a thought experiment. Suppose a cat is in a box with a vial of poison, and the vial can be broken by a switch triggered when an atom emits some radiation (a quantum phenomenon affected by uncertainty). Outside the box, we cannot know whether the atom had emitted the radiation or not. Is the cat alive or dead? According to the Copenhagen interpretation, a quantum state cannot be known until it has been observed. Observation forces nature to make a decision. But until an observation has been made, the quantum state does not exist in any of the possibilities. It exists in all of them. The cat then exists in a state of being both dead and alive. Schrödinger and Einstein thought this was absurd. To them the Heisenberg Uncertainty Principle existed because we were unable to observe some aspect of nature. But nature still had a definite form. It was unknown to us, but it still existed.

Einstein and Bohr spent several conferences debating this issue. Einstein would construct a thought experiment in which the exact position and momentum (or time and energy) could be measured. Bohr would retire to think about it and would then emerge to refute Einstein's example. In one famous case, Bohr showed that Einstein had neglected the theory of relativity! Einstein never succeeded in showing Bohr he was wrong. In fact, in 1935 Einstein, Boris Podolsky, and Nathan Rosen wrote a paper, "Can Quantum Mechanical Description of Physical Reality Be Considered Complete," in which they argued that since the theory predicted the "absurd" conclusion that the wave functions of two or more particles would become entangled and stay entangled as the particles moved far apart—until a measurement was made—the theory must be incomplete. In fact, today quantum entanglement is one of the foundations of the emerging field of quantum computing.

Other Explorations of Units

With the widespread use of photography in the second half of the nineteenth century came a desire to reproduce photographs in printed materials. By the 1880s, methods called halftone were patented. In halftone, an image is broken up into dots of various sizes and distances from one another. If the dots are large and dense, the image looks black. But as the dots get smaller and move away from each other, the image lightens until it is very light gray, or, with no dots, white. By the 1890s, most newspapers and journals included photographic reproductions using this technique.

In 1884, Georges Seurat (1859–91) began to work on a large painting called "A Sunday Afternoon on the Island of Grande Jatte." He painted small dots of color that blended just like halftones. Instead of blending the colors on the palette or on the canvas, Seurat depended on the viewer's visual apparatus to do the blending. Essentially, he was showing that blended colors were actually composed of small units. Only a few artists used the technique, called pointillism, but in the twentieth century it was quite interesting to cubists who were working mathematically. Physicists and psychologists found the study of color to be good source of theoretical ideas, and in the twentieth century artists resurrected their mathematical approaches. Using dots provided something that could be counted and measured.

The expatriate American author Gertrude Stein (1874–1946), the patron of Picasso, experimented with words as the ultimate units of a book. In *Tender Buttons* (1908), Stein played with the relationships of words with objects and words with words as she explored her own internal reactions. In doing this, she often implicitly raised the issue of how words force us to see the world in certain ways. Stein saw herself doing in literature what Picasso was doing in art, especially with cubism. Perhaps her most famous exploration of words is "a rose is a rose is a rose."

Conclusion: The First World War and the End of a World

In the beginning of this chapter, we quoted from soon-to-be fascist Filippo Marinetti's (1876–1944) *The Founding and Manifesto of Futurism* (1909). Marinetti wanted the world to change, and he wanted to use force. The first point in his Manifesto was, "We want to sing the love of danger." And he developed this idea until he declared, " We want to glorify war—the only hygiene of the world—militarism, patriotism, the destructive gesture of libertarians, beautiful ideas worth dying for and contempt for women." In fact, he spoke for his times. Young Europeans from all over the continent hankered for their time in the field of battle. Young men from every country thought that their country would win easily.

Why not? In the past decades, Western Europeans had used the technologies of machine guns, barbed wire, steam, and iron to destroy African forces armed with obsolete weapons. It turned out that equally armed Europeans could only fight to a standstill: four bloody years in trenches and millions of lives lost. Eventually the strangling blockade of the British navy and the entrance of the United States were enough to force the Germans to sue for peace.

But Europe had been transformed. The tzar, the kaiser, and the emperor were gone. Absolute rule based on heredity disappeared. Many of the old elites were sent packing. The brightest minds of its Europe's youth were decimated in battle. And as we have seen, the old certainties, the old methods, the old worldviews were mortally damaged. New modern ideas stood ready in the wings. But no one escaped the war with optimism. The ideas behind European rebuilding will be discussed in the next chapter.

Figure 9.8 Study for *The City Rises*, painting by Umberto Boccioni, 1910. Boccioni illustrates the futurists' obsession with speed and power as the definers of the modern world. Compare Marinetti's "The Futurist Manifesto." © Leemage/Hulton Archive/Getty Images.

CHAPTER 10
SEARCHING FOR A NEW WORLD ORDER

Figure 10.1 Millicent Fawcett addressing a meeting, 1913. © Topical Press Agency/Hulton Archive/Getty Images.

Two Reformers

Social reformer and suffragist Emily Hobhouse (1860–1926) grew increasingly angry as she heard of the internment of Boer women and children in British concentration camps during the second Anglo-Boer War in 1899. By 1900 she had organized a relief fund and set off for South Africa to deliver it and to investigate. Her outrage alternated with despair as she realized how dire conditions for the interned Boers were. She wrote letters back to Britain and took advantage of every chance to expose British atrocities in the press. At least 28,000 Boers, mostly children, died of exposure, starvation, and disease. The camps scandalized Europe. By the time she returned in 1901, she was persona non grata for the wartime government, who nevertheless felt obliged to send an investigatory commission.

Forbidding Hobhouse to reenter South Africa, they chose Millicent Fawcett (1847–1929), a moderate reformer and suffragist to lead the study. Hobhouse's supporters called it the "Whitewash Commission." Fawcett's motives were to show that women could be useful in wartime work, and therefore worthy of the vote. She was pro-British and supportive of her government in wartime. Nevertheless, the commission verified Hobhouse's findings and made recommendations for reform of the camps just as the war was ending. In fact, the Ladies' Commission was a historic first for women during wartime and was recognized as such. Fawcett returned to her leadership position in the suffragist movement.

When the First World War broke out, the pacifist Hobhouse opposed it with all of her strength. Fawcett and other suffragist leaders like Emmeline Pankhurst suspended protest activities to support he government during the war. When the war ended, all men and many women got the right to vote. By 1928, universal adult suffrage existed in the UK.

Chapter Map

Europe's Great War cleared the ground of the vestigial remnants of early collectivism. Hereditary emperors and monarchs disappeared, leaving only constitutionally constrained shadows. The ideological roots of these defunct systems remained and struggled to regrow in new forms. Capitalism and liberal democracy survived the conflagration but were forced to mutate by including political egalitarianism; country after country offered all adults the right to vote. The roots of absolutism, grafting themselves onto the tubers of Marxism and Nationalism, gave rise to communist, fascist, and Nazi governments—a new forest of political ideas—that confronted democratic capitalism.

In the arts, creators pushed open new vistas in the modernism movement. They explored meaninglessness, absurdity, the unconscious, and the general angst facing people adrift in a changing world. Some philosophers developed new forms of logic and redefined the limits of philosophy. Other philosophers started with consciousness as they explored what it is that human beings really know and what the human condition must or can be.

The Ideas Behind the Great War

The Great War (the First World War—renamed after the Second World War) was arguably the single greatest catastrophe in Europe since the Black Death of the fourteenth century. Even the winners emerged more relieved than triumphant. Before the war, large numbers of the populations of the countries of Western Europe felt excited and optimistic; after the war, they mourned their devastation. Paradoxically, before the war each country was sure of victory in a few months. What was the source of this optimism? Why were so many countries unable to sense the disaster that awaited them? What ideas lay behind the decisions to fight?

Clearly, the politics of Europe were complex and clandestine as the century turned. Secret societies and secret treaties created a shifting and fascinating landscape of intrigue. But that compelling story does not reveal what led masses of people to act and react. What ideas shaped the European world picture in such a way that war seemed to be not just the only answer, but also an attractive one?

Imperialism

In 1884 the chancellor of Germany, Otto von Bismarck, sponsored a meeting in Berlin to divide the continent of Africa among the industrial countries of Europe. All recognized that what we now call "the scramble for Africa" might lead to war. The scramble had been triggered by Belgian king Leopold's decision to create his own personally owned colony in what is today the area comprising the Democratic Republic of the Congo. But countries did not just want colonies. They wanted to rule an empire. They wanted prestige. Germany especially developed a *Weltpolitik* (World Policy) that emphasized Germany becoming a worldwide power.

They also wanted wealth. Both Conservative and Marxist thinkers were convinced that new markets and increased trade were necessary to maintain social order. In 1916, in the middle of the Great War, the Russian exile Vladimir Ilyich Ulyanov, better known as Lenin (1870–1924) wrote *Imperialism, the Highest Stage of Capitalism* in which he argued that the free-market capitalism based on competition had changed into a capitalism based on monopolies. Cartels and trusts had replaced industries organized around many competing small businesses. Most production, most employment, most profits, were generated by a very small number of large businesses. Slightly less than 1 percent of businesses controlled most of the economy.

These monopolies were echoed in the banking industry, and a new kind of capitalism, finance capitalism, had been born. To Lenin, the first imperialistic urge was this drive to swallow up competitors, as well as suppliers and other businesses. The imperialism of possessing other lands, then, was a natural extension of the attempts to build financial empires. Financial imperialism, branching into geopolitical imperialism, was the inevitable consequence of the capitalist system. Fish had to swim, birds had to fly, and capitalists had to build empires.

Lenin based his analysis in large part on the work of John A. Hobson's *Imperialism: A Study* (1902) in which Hobson presented a similar analysis of imperialism but then suggested that it didn't have to be that way. Hobson suggested that taxpayers paid dearly, with no real gain, to help investors make money in colonies. If countries instead enacted laws to protect incomes, reduce child labor, protect unions, and so forth, the people of the country would be much better off. Lenin disagreed, and wrote that until capitalism ended, imperialism would continue to exist.

Other writers emphasized the good that Europeans could bring to colonized people. By bringing the Christian religion, by educating, by curing, and by investing in railroads and other infrastructure, Europeans could create enormous benefits. Some Europeans were convinced that it was their moral duty to civilize others. So, another rationale for imperialism was exemplified in Rudyard Kipling's "The White Man's Burden" (see Chapter 7).

Imperialism tinged with misplaced altruism was an underlying theme in rationales that ultimately led to war.

Militarism

Since Napoleon had forced Prussia to vastly reduce its army, Prussia, and then Germany had adopted policies to ensure that the nation would always be ready for war. Year after year citizens were trained as soldiers and then returned to civilian life. Officers came from the landed gentry, and they too were required to undergo training. These officers also provided the citizens who ran the civilian governmental bureaucracy. In effect, the citizenry was trained to obey the government, and this tendency ran across political party lines. The British Empire also had a large cadre of people across the world who were trained to serve and obey and who were proud to be part of the armed forces.

Militarism does not necessarily answer an obvious national need. Various economists have argued over the years that money spent on the military actually weakens a country economically. Pacifists have made a variety of arguments in favor of reducing armaments and avoiding war. But the upper classes of Western Europe were convinced that the use of arms was necessary to advance the national interest, and this was especially true of Germany.

Militarism was exacerbated by Social Darwinism, which viewed all social life as a struggle. As the English statistician Karl Pearson (1857–1936) put it in *National Life from the Standpoint of Science* (1902):

> The scientific view of a nation is that of an organized whole, kept up to a high pitch of internal efficiency by insuring that its numbers are substantially recruited from the better stocks, and kept up to a high pitch of external efficiency by contest, chiefly by way of war with inferior races, and with equal races by the struggle for trade-routes and for the sources of raw material and food supply.

From this point of view, the most important part of national policy was military policy.

Between 1898 and 1912, Germany and Britain engaged in a naval arms race. Although Germany gained, by the time the two countries agreed to a halt, the British still had more than a two to one edge in ships. In addition, France, Austria, Italy, and Russia all introduced conscription systems that increased the number of trained personnel who could be called on in case of emergency. They had been stockpiling arms and preparing for war, at least since 1880.

The countries had also all prepared strategic plans that assumed they might be going to war with any of a number of other European countries. They all aimed to mobilize using well-timed railroads and to strike quickly. The German approach included a two-front plan in which they would quickly overcome the French and then wheel around to fight the Russians who would be forced by their antiquated infrastructure to mobilize more slowly. All countries, then, had been on high alert for years.

These two sets of ideas, imperialism and militarism, were not sufficient to explain the war. But they were necessary. Given the interlocking alliances, the cat-and-mouse games in the Balkans, and an unanticipated a Serbian assassin in Sarajevo, war fever flared into war.

A War of Invention

Not only soldiers went to war, but also scientists and inventors. The pacifist Albert Einstein, who had recently been recruited to direct the Kaiser Wilhelm Institute for Physics in Berlin, was appalled at the readiness of his colleagues to discover new and improved means of killing other human beings. Like other nationalistically oriented Europeans, scientists were eager to show how they too could help their countries. Einstein's colleague Fritz Haber, who had invented ways to produce artificial fertilizers that greatly increased farm productivity and helped feed millions, successfully invented poison chlorine gas.

Most of the inventions of the war were based on older ideas that were linked to new technologies. For instance, when barbed wire backed by stationary belt-fed machine guns turned every assault into carnage, inventors combined internal combustion engines used by automobiles, thick steel plating, and armored treads to create the tank. The tank could roll over barbed wire and small ditches with ease. Flamethrowers, invented just before the war, were fearsome weapons that when fired through a trench burned alive anyone who was there.

The possibilities of the newly invented airplane were clear. Airplanes were used to scout behind enemy lines and to help aim long-range artillery. But clearly, they could also serve as an offensive weapon if they could be mounted with machine guns. Unfortunately, machine guns firing through a propeller could shatter it. A Dutch inventor, Anthony Fokker developed a "synchronizer" that allowed the machine gun to fire between the spinning blades of a propeller. Both sides soon had the technology, and air battles could commence. By the end of the war, radio transmission between pilot and ground became possible. And along with airplanes came guns specifically designed as antiaircraft weapons.

The list of inventions was extensive and included submarines, depth charges, ultrasound submarine detection, aircraft carriers, improved radio transmission, steel helmets, tracer bullets, flare pistols, stainless steel, more accurate artillery, and much more. Interestingly, some of the inventions for war had other uses. For instance, the zipper was invented to fasten soldiers' pockets more securely. "Cellucotton" made from wood pulp was used to replace scarce cotton. It not only served as a new kind of bandage but also stimulated the invention of both the sanitary pad and facial tissues.

Medical advances allowed more seriously wounded soldiers to return home than had survived any previous war. Using the nineteenth-century innovations of antisepsis and anesthesia, doctors were often able to avoid amputation. Planners devised a system of transporting the wounded by ambulance to a field hospital, where wounds could be cleaned, debrided, and disinfected before surgery was performed on the soldier, who could then be shipped home if necessary. The British biochemist Henry Dakin developed a sodium hypochlorite solution that could kill bacteria without burning the flesh. Blood typing had been discovered shortly before the war, so anticlotting solutions to keep the blood flowing allowed transfusions for the first time to save soldiers who would otherwise have bled to death.

And medical inventors worked hard to perfect prosthetic limbs and other body parts. A result of such aids was that as the war progressed and after it ended, many more veterans were alive than would otherwise have been the case. But many of those who survived had disfiguring treatments, as infected tissues were liberally removed. In fact, plastic surgery soon developed to deal with faces that had been mutilated. Others suffered from "shell shock," what we now call posttraumatic stress disorder (PTSD). The returning soldiers were all too often broken in body or spirit, or both, and the populations at home saw the horrors of war firsthand.

Ideas Emerging from the Great War

Ideas Behind the Peace

The armistice that ended the Great War took place on the eleventh minute of the eleventh hour of the eleventh day of the eleventh month, November 11, 1918. Soon thereafter, allied forces occupied Germany's Rhineland, the strangling British blockade was ended, and food and supplies entered Germany. Talks to hammer out the peace began in January 1919. The primary French motives were revenge, reparations, and future safety. The British were divided between those who thought Germany should pay and those who looked forward to a peace of reconciliation. The Americans brought fourteen points to the table that emphasized reconciliation and avoiding war in the future. The Italians wanted more territory. The Germans had vainly hoped for negotiations that would respect their equal place as a great European nation.

The end result included a triumph for the French, a humiliation for Germany, and a complete redesign of Eastern Europe. Germany was forced to admit guilt for the war, pay an enormous sum in reparations, accept troops on their western lands, disarm and remain disarmed, and give up territory. The Austro-Hungarian Empire was broken up, and Austria and Hungary became new, truncated, democratic countries. Czechoslovakia was created, and Poland's independence guaranteed by the Germans. A corridor cutting through Germany gave Poland access to the sea and isolated the eastern portion of Prussia. The Balkan countries were united to form the new kingdom of Yugoslavia, and Romania gained territory. The Ottoman Empire was dissolved, and modern Turkey was born.

An underlying enigma was the issue of nationalism. As the Austrian Empire was broken up, it was impossible to juggle new state boundaries to include mostly members of a single nation, understood as a linguistic and cultural entity. The Austro-Hungarian Empire had never been composed mostly of German-speaking Austrians or Magyar-speaking Hungarians. Also included were Ukrainians, Romanians, Poles, Jews, Serbs, Czechs, and many more national groups. The Versailles Treaty tried to ensure national rights and the protection of minorities, but in fact, that was impossible.

John Maynard Keynes (1883–1946), the representative of the British treasury to the Versailles conference, wrote *The Economic Consequences of the Peace* (1919) in which he argued that the treaty was a disaster for the economic future of Europe. A large portion of the population of Great Britain thought that the treaty was unfair to Germany, and this perception played a role in the later passive response to the rise of Adolf Hitler. Keynes argued that a prosperous Europe needed an integrated and fair economic system, which the treaty made impossible. He also argued that the allies had reneged on the agreements they made at the time of the armistice. Essentially Keynes supported Woodrow Wilson's fourteen points—which was more than the US Senate did when they refused to join the newly formed United Nations—modeled on Wilson's suggestions. But Keynes also pointed out that Wilson was completely ineffective. To Keynes, Wilson had ideals without strategy.

For Keynes, the treaty did nothing to help the Central Powers become integrated into the new Europe. "It is an extraordinary fact that the fundamental economic problems of a Europe starving and disintegrating before their eyes, was the one question in which it was impossible to arouse the interest of the Four [The leaders of the allied countries]."[1]

Figure 10.2 Photograph of John Maynard Keynes, 1929. © Bettmann/Getty Images.

Keynes called the peace "Carthaginian," referring to Rome's determination to completely destroy their enemy Carthage. He predicted inflation and economic stagnation. Keynes's prescience was born out in the next decades. His reputation soared.

The Economic Aftermath of War

The first inklings of what was to come were found in demonstrations and riots in several countries as workers and others demanded significant change. In Germany, Communist uprisings were put down, and its leaders Karl Liebknecht and Rosa Luxemburg were assassinated. The Social Democrats (SPD) took over the government under the new Weimar Constitution, and President Friedrich Ebert set about dealing with the demands of the Versailles Treaty as well as the domestic situation. In 1923 Germany underwent an enormous hyperinflation that had been building since 1921, largely because of Germany's response to the insistence of the allies that they keep up with reparations payments. In 1922, a loaf of bread cost about 160 marks. By the end of 1923, it cost over 200 billion marks. People went to work to get paid for the day and then rushed to the store to buy groceries before their pay dwindled to nothing by the end of the

Figure 10.3 German hyperinflation: Worthless banknotes, 1923. © Universal Images Group/ Getty Images.

day. Eventually issuing a new German currency controlled the inflation. Loans from US banks helped the Germans keep up their payments in the 1920s. But the economic instability was a harbinger of coming events.

Even the economies of the victors were shaken by the aftermath of the war. The prewar European economy had been predicated on free trade (punctuated by some tariffs) and the strength of a British pound that was pegged to a gold standard. But during the war Britain lost not only men but also money from exports. By the end of the war, many of England's buyers in other countries had looked elsewhere for manufactured items. During the war, Britain used up its financial reserves. Eventually the UK had had to borrow billions from America to fund the war. Great Britain had been trying to get the last bit of use from antiquated machinery in the turn-of-the-century era, while countries like Germany and the United States, with new and improved machinery, pushed hard as they challenged Britain's industrial leadership. Throughout the 1920s, growth was sluggish. When the British government reestablished the gold standard pegged at prewar rates, the effect was deflationary. There was not enough money in circulation to fuel greater economic activity. Nevertheless, the middle class was able to enjoy new consumer items like automobiles. European countries on the continent faced similar problems but in general had an even worse time than Great Britain.

New Political Structures

Universal Liberal Democracy

Most of non-Soviet Europe turned to liberal democracy after the war. The liberal democracies, Great Britain and France, had won, and the new countries from Poland to Austria wrote constitutions enshrining democracy. The main argument in favor of universal democracy was that excluded groups, like women and nonproperty owners, had continually demonstrated, and sometimes revolted, as they demanded the franchise. It was clear to members of these nonvoting groups that upper- and middle-class males had rarely legislated in the interests of nonproperty-owning males. Instead, parliaments had adopted policies of paternalism in which fathers and husbands, or business owners and managers, were trusted to look after those under their care.

In the nineteenth century, unified Germany had adopted universal male suffrage, but they had organized the government so that the Reichstag, the lower house of parliament, could be over-ruled by the Bundesrat, the Imperial Council of Rulers of German States, as well as by the Kaiser. Thus, no country had yet attempted actual democratic rule based on universal adult suffrage. Instead, elites controlled the little democracy that there was.

This changed after the First World War, in some countries quickly, in others slowly (France did not institute female suffrage until after the Second World War). The prewar society that the poet Ezra Pound called "a botched civilization" had died. There were still remnants of hereditary monarchs with power, but in most countries that retained a monarch the power shifted to the parliament. Hereditary nobles still had prestige, but little power.

What was the argument for universal adult democracy besides the convenience of avoiding political demonstrations demanding the suffrage? One could argue that all human beings had been created equal, but that clearly was not literally the case. Different people clearly had different talents, intelligences, and interests. Most people had little interest in following politics. In fact, throughout the nineteenth century the inability of most noneducated people to contribute intelligently to voting presented a major problem for people like John Stuart Mill, who otherwise felt keenly the need to provide for the working classes. The best that could be said then was that universal democracy was a terrible system, but it was better than the alternatives.

But reformers in Western Europe had instituted public schools in the nineteenth century, and illiteracy had been almost abolished. Newspapers for the working classes allowed non-elites to follow the issues of the day. In 1911 the German/Italian Robert Michels argued in his book *Political Parties* that democracy would always produce oligarchies (the iron law of oligarchies). Democracy would produce parties, and parties would turn into bureaucratic oligarchies. James Bryce, an erstwhile British ambassador to the United States, wrote in 1920 that politicians would always be responsive to economic interests, and those interests would provide politicians the wherewithal to convince constituents to support them. In short, universal adult suffrage would not be a threat to a country but would provide a political placebo allowing people to think that their opinions and actions mattered. And so it turned out. European democratic institutions focused on political parties, and individual voters by and large voted a party line.

There was another form of equality that was more defensible than the argument that people had essentially the same abilities to understand politics and vote intelligently. The ideal was that all people should be equal before the law, irrespective of their abilities, ethnicities, genders, ages, or other characteristics. In the nineteenth century, women, serfs, and workers were actually governed by different laws than were upper-class males. Slowly, with the emancipation of serfs and a variety of labor protection laws, that situation was changing.

Not everyone agreed that all should be equal before the law, especially with regard to women. Most men and many women thought that women had a special place in the family that a man could not provide. But more and more people began to believe that even if that were true, women should have the same rights as men. And those who were not propertied males realized that if they were to become equal before the law, they must have the vote.

Outside of politics, the postwar world increasingly respected experts. Technology was demonstrably making life better for most people. Water systems needed engineering expertise. Pilots needed to be trained. The hope of many was that a government elected by the people would in turn entrust decision making to experts. Heredity had proved a terrible way to insure expertise. The largely aristocratic Officers Corps had proved disastrously incompetent in the management of the war. But perhaps training the brightest people, irrespective of class, would produce experts who could be called upon by democratic governments. Thus, the best argument for universal democracy lay, almost paradoxically, in the possibility of a true meritocracy.

The Great Depression and the Challenge to Democracy

By the end of the 1920s, the collapse of the American economy and a reduction in world trade hit Great Britain hard. Unemployment went from 10 percent in 1929 to 20 percent (three million workers) by 1933. The Great Depression of the 1930s affected countries differently and at slightly different times, but most found it hard to know what to do. Both France and Britain elected socialist parties during the 1930s as they sought to deal not only with the economy but also with its effects on working people. In Central Europe, the Great Depression was devastating. Germany fell hard, and the Austrian bank Creditanstalt collapsed and was taken over by the government. The repercussions echoed in Poland and Central Europe. The rise of Adolf Hitler was directly related to the pains of the depression.

But all of these countries got no effective help from economists. In general economists were still neoclassical, so they focused on the actions of corporations and individuals rather than nations. There was as yet no good theory about economic action at the national level. Economists thought that governments should maintain a strong currency, regulate economic abuses by rogue firms, and otherwise get out of the way.

For example, the generally accepted "Say's Law" claimed that whatever was produced would find a buyer. If a product did not sell, then its price was too high. If goods were stockpiling, the only reasonable response from the government was to wait for the market to catch up. There was no generally accepted theory of insufficient demand. Similarly, the cause of unemployment was seen as the refusal of workers to accept the wages offered or to travel where jobs were. There was no generally accepted theory of systemic unemployment, and all unemployment was seen as voluntary.

In 1936 John Maynard Keynes published his famous *The General Theory of Employment, Interest and Money*, and about the same time a group of Swedish economists led by Gunnar Myrdal (1898–1987), known as the Stockholm School, came to very similar conclusions. According to the traditional view, people saved money in banks that was then used for investment. An economic recession happened when investors did not borrow the money to invest. In short, the problem was that the public saved more than entrepreneurs were willing or able to invest. According to the economics of the time, this situation should right itself, because with more money in savings and fewer buyers for those savings (investors), the cost of those savings should go down, that is, the interest rate should fall. In this view, saved money was like any other commodity. If there was a glut of shoes, the price of shoes should fall.

But Keynes saw that in fact investment was not picking up during the depression years. Keynes was preparing and writing his book in 1935, when the Great Depression had been running for six years with little sign of recovery. What was wrong? Keynes realized that sometimes, like during the Great Depression, much unemployment is involuntary. He saw that the problem was that people without any money couldn't save. Lack of investment did not reflect a glut of money, but too little of it. The old economics was wrong.

Without enough money, Keynes maintained, demand for goods would sink. Lack of demand meant that businesses could not sell their product and so had to let workers go. The jobless workers were unable to buy, so demand further declined, driving the economy into a vicious cycle. But if there were an increase in money in the economy, then interest rates would drop, and entrepreneurs should be willing to invest. As they did so, jobs would increase.

One way to put money into the system was to have the government invest in public works projects. If the government hired workers and paid them a stipend, the workers would spend their money on consumer goods. In fact, the effect of paying previously unemployed people a stipend was that by spending it they would stimulate further economic activity. Workers would buy food, which would lead to employment among storekeepers and farmers. They would pay rent that would stimulate construction. Thus, by injecting money into the economy by giving it to workers, the amount of money in circulation would multiply. Keynes noted that the decision to consume or save was affected by social and psychological factors.

Additionally, if the government invested in public works, then the infrastructure of the country would be improved. Although Keynes was quite interested in public works, the issue was controversial enough that he did not discuss it much in his book. Keynes, tongue in cheek, noted that if the government were to bury bank notes deep in mines, private companies would hire workers to dig up the bank notes, and the effect on the money supply and the economy would be the same as if the government funded a public works project.

Governments had already been taking some of the steps recommended by Keynes. Many of them had been investing in public works projects to put people back to work. They did this in spite of the recommendations of economists to do nothing. Out-of-work people are likely to revolt. A society with mass unemployment has become a sick society. Democratic governments needed to be responsive to public groundswells. In Great Britain, the pound was unlinked from the gold supply, and the government could take steps to expand the money supply. It cut interest rates and devalued the pound, for instance. In the south of England, housing construction provided jobs. However, in Wales and northern industrial areas, unemployment continued at crippling levels. Keynes's *General Theory* described what was happening and provided an explanation of what was working.

Although Keynes's opponents called him a socialist, he was anything but. He did not advocate that the government take over industries, but rather that the government should act to boost the money supply and get the economy moving so that private industry could function effectively.

Communism

The first great political break occurred before the war was over. Russia had suffered greatly during the war, mostly due to its continuing feudal-autocratic structure and its inability to compete with developed industrial states. Overwhelming battle deaths, food shortages, and general privation led to mutiny and revolt. In February (using the Julian calendar then in use), the tsar was forced to abdicate, and members of the Duma (Parliament) formed the Russian Provisional Government dominated by representatives of the landed aristocracy and wealthy capitalists. The Provisional Government decided to continue the war. Meanwhile, a national network of workers' councils, soviets, also developed. Among the leaders of the soviets were Bolsheviks, led by Lenin. Lenin advocated an immediate end to Russia's participation in the war, restoring land to peasants, and feeding workers in the cities. Eventually in October the Bolsheviks took over the government by force. They indeed negotiated an end to the war, ceding territory to Germany in the Treaty of Brest-Litovsk, and began to establish a communist state. As they struggled to figure out just how to put their ideas into practice, they also had to fight a civil war against noncommunist Russians. This war continued until 1922. Lenin was seriously ill between 1922 and 1924, when he died and was replaced by Stalin. The government of the new Soviet Union was therefore based on the ideas first of Lenin and second of Stalin.

Lenin's Program

In 1887, when Lenin was seventeen, the tsarist government executed his brother Alexander for plotting to assassinate the tsar. Lenin, who had also recently lost his father, then became a committed revolutionary. He became a Marxist, translated *The Communist Manifesto* into Russian, and began to wrestle with the problem that Russia was a peasant country with only a very small industrial working class. Marx had predicted that capitalism would be overthrown by factory workers, and for Marx, capitalism should already have turned peasants into workers before a true communist revolution could occur. The problem for Lenin was that peasants were tied to the land and were serfs in a feudal system—although some peasants, kulaks, had become more like small businessmen than workers. Lenin began to theorize that industrialization would draw peasants into the cities where they would become part of the proletariat. In 1897 Lenin's activities caught up with him and he was exiled to Siberia for three years. In 1900 Lenin moved to Switzerland where he began to write in earnest. Left-wing thinkers were divided among a variety of positions, and as Lenin became surer of his own views, he began to enter into the polemical fray. Although he moved all over Europe, when the First World War broke out he located again in Switzerland, until, after the February Revolution, he was granted passage through Germany back to Russia. The Germans hoped that Lenin, and other dissidents that they put on the same sealed train, would cause problems for the tsar and his army.

In 1902 Lenin had written a pamphlet entitled *What Is to Be Done?* in which he differentiated between organizations of workers and a true revolutionary party. One part of the European left wing, the anarcho-syndicalists, focused on organizing workers into trade unions so that united they could influence government policies in favor of workers. Lenin wrote that individual workers had been brought up in capitalist countries and did not have the intellectual tools to know what was truly in their interests: the abolition of capitalism itself. He recognized that both he and Marx had grown up in middle-class households and had been well educated. They could see through the capitalist ideological facade and understand how the bourgeoisie actually ran their governments. He considered himself to be a professional revolutionary who spent all his time studying and preparing to lead the revolution. Only a small group of similarly committed professional revolutionaries could counter the subtle persuasions of capitalist representatives and act decisively to bring about a real revolution in which capitalist oppression would end once and for all.

Lenin also saw himself as a democrat, however. He wrote that free discussion among party members should precede any vote. However, once the vote was taken and a decision made, it was incumbent upon all party members to get behind the decision and cease debate. Effective, united action was crucial. His slogan was, "freedom of discussion, unity of action." Lenin supported free elections in all groups from the bottom to the top of the party. In that way, even communists at the bottom had a say about who would represent their group.

But voting had little to do with Lenin's conception of democracy. True democracy was based on Marx's adage: "From each according to his ability; to each according to his need." Only generations after the end of capitalism, with its well-taught competitive mindset, could such a slogan exist in action and not just in concept. Only people who had become used to working together to meet society's needs, that is, people who had not been raised in a competitive capitalist environment, could instinctively act in the best interests of the whole.

Lenin, echoing Robespierre and the Jacobins, thus argued that the revolutionary vanguard, the Communist Party, should lead in the overthrow of capitalism. They would take over the administration of the state in the interests of workers and peasants. Before the revolution the state had represented the interests of the oppressive bourgeois class. Since the bourgeois state represented property and money, it co-opted intellectuals who constructed falsely persuasive arguments to convince the oppressed that the state was acting in their interests. But after the revolution, in the absence of an oppressive class, the state really would work in the interests of the proletariat. At this point, the state apparatus would be used, in the domestic sphere, primarily to organize work activity. For instance, water mains would need to be built and maintained. Expert workers would know how to do that. Ultimately, they would not really need state supervision to do their jobs. In foreign affairs, the state would be needed to organize defense, diplomacy, and trade—until all countries had become communist. At some point, the state would become superfluous and would "wither away."

Lenin argued against a "one-size-fits-all" definition of a communist state. He recognized that each nation (defined as a cultural and linguistic entity) had a different culture. He argued for the right of nations to self-determination. Russia included many different nations, and Lenin argued that each nation should decide how best to proceed after the revolution, given its own priorities, as long as it did not restore oppression. He realized that national identity was important to people, and that they would fight to maintain it; at least in the short run, the best answer would be a federation among the proletariat of all nations.

In the face of an immediate civil war, Lenin had to put some of these ideals aside. The red army as well as urban workers needed food, and Lenin instituted the New Economic Policy (NEP) in which peasants were allowed limited local capitalism: the possibility of a profit from raising their crops. The government would not requisition food from farmers (which had led to hoarding and refusal to produce) but rather would levy a tax administered by banks. He also nationalized all industries and worked to coordinate them, keeping them from competing with each other. Only the state would supervise foreign trade.

Stalinism

The Georgian Joseph Stalin (1878–1953) was the secretary general of the Communist Party, a post that was supposed to disinterestedly administer the will of the party's Central Committee. But Stalin was in charge of appointing local party leaders, and soon he had a cadre of his supporters in key positions. Lenin recognized the power Stalin had accumulated and near the end of his life warned Stalin's main opponent, Leon Trotsky,

Figure 10.4 Vladimir Ilyich Lenin and Joseph Stalin. Photo was altered to add Stalin to convince the country that he was close to Lenin. © Hulton Deutsch/Corbis Historical/Getty Images.

to remove Stalin from his post. After Lenin's death, a power struggle ensued that by 1929 left Stalin in complete control of the party and the Soviet Union.

Trotsky and other leaders thought that continued revolution in other countries was essential for the Soviet Union's ultimate success. Stalin recognized that after the war communist revolutions in industrialized European countries had failed. He therefore advocated building socialism in one country and required foreign communist groups to work to support the success of the Soviet Union. His main opponent was Trotsky, but he succeeded in exiling Trotsky from the Soviet Union. Trotsky continued working for continued revolution until Stalin had him assassinated in Mexico City in 1940.

Stalin parted with Lenin on the treatment of the peasants and, starting in 1929, abolished the NEP and began the collectivization of agriculture—that is, replacing small farms with much more productive large-scale agriculture. The idea was that peasants were to become agricultural workers who would be gradually integrated into the proletariat. In order to accomplish agricultural collectivization, Stalin ordered the arrest and deportation of the kulaks, the richest peasants who would likely lead the resistance to collectivization. Peasants revolted in various areas of the Union of Soviet Socialist Republics (USSR), but these uprisings were summarily stamped out. By 1936, over 90 percent of peasants had been collectivized.

The speed with which collectivization of agriculture was carried out illustrates a major motif in Stalinism—a sense of urgency and a concomitant willingness to sacrifice millions of individual lives to accomplish what Stalin thought were the needs of the Soviet Union. Stalin could feel the hot breath of the capitalist countries closing in on the Soviet Union. In the 1930s, Stalin was convinced that another war with industrialized Germany was inevitable, and he realized that the largely rural Soviet Union would be unable to cope. Stalin's goal, then, was to accomplish in a decade what had taken capitalists a century and a half. He wanted to turn the Soviet Union into an industrial powerhouse. Lenin had been able to hope that at least a few other European countries already would have had successful communist or socialist revolutions. Stalin had no such illusions.

In 1928 the planning arm of the Communist Party (Gosplan) announced the first five-year plan: the establishment of basic heavy industry. Gosplan recognized that certain forms of production, like steel, were necessary to the development of all other production. All economic activity in the country was to be bent to that end. Laborers and managers alike worked overtime to dig mines for iron ore, to build new industrial cities (like Magnitogorsk), and to create new factories. By the end of 1932, Stalin could announce that the plan had achieved its goals. The Soviet Union was second in the world (behind the United States) in heavy industry.

Stalin's second five-year plan was announced for 1933. It focused on continuing to improve heavy industry but also transportation and communications. Childcare was to be set up to allow mothers to join the workforce. The third five-year plan, beginning in 1938, was to focus on tanks and other weapons. It was interrupted by the invasion of the Soviet Union by Germany in 1941.

Stalin also brought cultural production under state control. By doing this, he also tried to eliminate national feeling among minority ethnicities, something Lenin had warned against. He demanded a culture for the masses, which resulted in a demand for socialist realism in art. This style promoted communist themes like the dictatorship of the proletariat. Stylized realism was used to clearly depict heroes and villains. Modernist art was seen as decadent, and abstraction was opposed. Stalin also promoted school building and the abolition of religion and religious institutions.

Soviet communism, building on Marx, had no use for individualist values. The proletariat, that is, the class of all workers, was considered much more important than any individual worker. Communism was dedicated to abolishing all classes other than the proletariat, so in its ideal form, everyone who was able would work, and all would understand that the meaning of their lives was defined by their relationship to the group. For many, communism became a religion. Communism's historical dialectic claimed that at the end of history, class warfare would come to an end in a realization of the true purpose of human life. Fighting for communism was a crusade for humanity that should lend meaning to a person's life. Communism was thus made attractive to many thinkers in capitalist countries, especially in the context of the meaninglessness of the First World War, the suffering of the Great Depression, and the angst and despair that many felt.

Fascism

The constitutional, democratic monarchy of Italy did not last long after the end of the war. Italy had had a disastrous war and a disastrous peace. Although Italy had been promised territory by the allies in return for military alliance and support, when the Versailles Treaty was finished, Italy received a fraction of what they had hoped for. Immediately there were protests against a government that had not negotiated effectively. In addition, workers, inspired by the Russian Revolution, began to occupy factories and other workplaces. There was rioting in several cities. Many Italians wanted law and order more than anything. After a swirl of events, fascists marched into Rome in October 1922, and former socialist Benito Mussolini (1883–1945) became the prime minister. The fascists were a nationalist party with a ruthless streak. Mussolini used assassination and secret police to consolidate power. His Blackshirts carried out thuggery in the streets, and although there was opposition, it was weak. Mussolini had support among the military and also among business elites. By 1925 Mussolini had arranged not to be responsible to parliament. He was Il Duce, the head of the government. He remained in that position until near the end of the Second World War when he was overthrown and executed.

Strikingly, many leaders in democratic countries approved of Mussolini. After all, Mussolini opposed socialism and communism. He had put an end to the partisan fighting in which a significant participant was the Italian Communist Party. Winston Churchill in 1933 declared that Mussolini had shown the way to overcome socialism through his courage and effectiveness. It is worth noting that to Western European conservatives by far the greatest threat was communism. Moneyed elites had a great deal of influence in a capitalist democracy, and communists were very clear that they wanted to remove the money from elites and turn them into workers. By 1933 there were no rich people left in the Soviet Union. But while employment boomed in the Soviet Union, the West had entered into a deep economic depression. Not Italy, however. Mussolini had used both subsidies and public works to ensure that reasonable living standards for Italians continued.

What then were the basic principles of fascism? In 1932 the Hegelian philosopher Giovanni Gentile (1875–1944) helped Mussolini write "The Doctrine of Fascism." Gentile was a right-wing Hegelian, which meant he broke with Marx over the importance of thought. To Gentile, the dialectic existed in thought, not in Marx's material economic relationships. So, Mussolini's piece began with the idea that in action, ideas were always present. Fascism was spiritual and opposed to materialism, and spiritual individuals could only exist as part of the nation. Fascism called upon individuals to renounce self-interest and to find true human value as a part of something larger. Thus, fascism saw itself as an ethical movement that called for human beings to develop themselves physically and morally so they could act effectively for the nation. A sense of history and tradition would show human beings where they have come from and where they must go.

Fascism rejected Marxism because it pitted class against class. All classes were equally valuable, so workers and capitalists should come together to act in the interests of the nation. The state was more than the sum of its individual members. One could not use the vote to find out what the state needed, because voting emphasized a summing-up process rather than the transcendence of meaning. Thus, fascism was a corporate theory. Just as a body is more than the sum of the cells, so the state was more than the sum of individuals.

Fascism involved rejection of a number of things. It rejected individualism. It rejected Marxism. It rejected liberalism. Fascism rejected pacifism, since only in struggle could

Figure 10.5 Photograph of Giovanni Gentile, framer of fascist ideology. © Mondadori Portfolio/ Getty Images.

the nation understand itself. It rejected parliamentary democracy as a sham. Fascism saw itself in the light of the theory of evolution. Nature acted only for the good of the species, not for the good of individual organisms that perish in the struggle of natural selection. One can see Hegel, Darwin, and Nietzsche all at work in Mussolini and Gentile's discussion of the aims of fascism. In their minds, fascism was a totalitarian idea, and the nation should be governed in its totality. In fact, they claimed that although the nineteenth century was a liberal, and thus an individualist, century, the twentieth century would be a fascist, and thus a corporative, century. Economics would be based not on competition but on cooperation among enterprises, all coordinated by, and in service of, the state. Just as soldiers multiply their strength by acting together as an army, so the citizens of a nation would become stronger by working together under a central leadership.

In the 1930s, Fascism seemed, to those in liberal democracies, as a possible future. Fascism valued the contributions of capitalists. It didn't want to expropriate anything. But it seemed to want to solve problems, of which there were many.

In Spain, the struggles between monarchists and Republicans led to a civil war beginning in 1936. It pitted the right-wing Nationalists against the left-wing Republicans. The Nationalists, led by the leader of the Falange, General Francisco Franco, were supported by Nazi Germany. The Republicans received a modicum of support from the Soviet Union. Since Stalin's Soviet Union was pushing hard to develop modern armaments, Stalin curtailed support for communists in other countries. Thus, Germany's military aid lopsidedly outpaced the Soviet Union's. The Nationalists won, and Spain would be fascist for almost the next half century.

Nazism

During the unrest following the First World War, German right-wing nationalist groups were among those agitating against liberal democratic government. Among these groups, a myth claimed that Germany had been about to win the war when Jews and socialists stabbed the nation in the back. In fact, Germany's food and supplies had been exhausted, the army was revolting, and the supreme commander, Paul von Hindenburg, told the Kaiser at the end of September that Germany had lost the war and must have an immediate armistice. One of the right-wing groups was the National Socialist German Workers' Party (NSDAP, known informally as the Nazi Party—actually a derogatory term used by opponents of the party) led by Adolf Hitler. A twenty-five-point program was drafted in 1920 by Anton Drexler and served as the theoretical basis for the rise of the Nazis.

The twenty-five points began with the goal of uniting all Germans into a "Greater Germany" that would include Austria and other border areas that included Germans. The definition of "German" occurred in the fourth point. The basis was not language, but rather blood. Thus, Jews, who were viewed as having different blood, could not be citizens of Germany. Only German citizens could vote or hold office, and all noncitizens would be subject to different laws, designed specifically for foreigners. Immigration of non-Germans would be prohibited, and all recent immigrants would be forced to leave. Laws would be changed to reflect a German rather than a Roman tradition (meaning that all law would be based on the superiority of the Aryan race).

According to the twenty-five points, the state and its citizens would have mutual obligations. The state would be obliged to create a livelihood for every citizen, and every citizen would be obliged to work. The work, both mental and physical, could not clash with the interests of the whole nation, and should promote the general good. There could be no unearned income, no rent seeking. All companies that were held by trusts or cartels would be nationalized. The slogan was: the good of the community before the good of the individual.

The state would ensure the welfare of all through old-age pensions, health care for mothers and children, education accessible for all up to the highest levels, including physical fitness activities, and financial support for gifted poor children. All would be taught the "concept of the state," and all information media, including newspapers, would be staffed and run only by German citizens. No foreign investment would be allowed.

Thus, from its origins the Nazi Party was an extreme racist and nationalist party that wanted to expel non-Germans. It promised work and financial support for all complying citizens, and also declared its intention to take over and supervise all economic and informational activities. Like the Italian fascists, it declared its intention to be totalitarian—that is, to coordinate all activities within the totality of the state and nation. But unlike the Italian fascists, the Nazis were avowedly racist. Both the Italian fascists and the German Nazis had well-developed paramilitary wings that provided them a measure of independence from the state police and military.

In the chaos of the 1920s, including hyperinflation, economic difficulties, and heightened political tensions, the Nazis gained adherents. In 1925 and 1926, Hitler published a two-volume story of his life entitled *Mein Kampf* (*My Struggle*) that declared his aspirations—a book that was promoted vigorously by the party. In the elections of 1932, the Nazis won a plurality of the votes, which, in the absence of willingness by any other party to form a coalition government, led President von Hindenburg to offer the chancellorship to Hitler.

The Nazis disdained communists and socialists, but they also disdained right-wing parties that promoted the interests of the rich instead of the interests of the nation. In fact, in his speeches Hitler criticized capitalism as having Jewish origins. He was clearly antidemocratic and anti-individualistic. The only European countries that he could envision working with were the UK (a German derivative, he thought) and Italy (because it was fascist).

When he had consolidated power, Hitler set about building up the military might of Germany. He supported the armaments industry and set about building the autobahns, the world's first superhighways, to transport troops and material quickly. As a result, Germany barely felt the Great Depression before it had ended. Without knowing it, Hitler had applied Keynesian prescriptions by using massive government expenditures to jump-start the economy.

Artistic and Philosophical Movements

Literary and Artistic Responses in the West

Somewhat ironically, both the winners and the losers of the Great War felt a sense of loss and unease. Both visual and literary artists created worlds of anxiety and despair. In 1920 the Irish poet William Butler Yeats wrote "Things fall apart; the center cannot hold;/Mere anarchy is loosed upon the world, / . . . The best lack all conviction, while the worst/Are full of passionate intensity." And as Yeats looked into the future, all he could ask was, "And what rough beast, its hour come round at last, / Slouches towards Bethlehem to be born?"

Thomas Stearns (T.S.) Eliot (1888–1965) began his poetic exploration of indecisive anguish with the well-received "The Love Song of J. Alfred Prufrock" (1915) in which the protagonist is almost unable to descend a staircase because people may see that he is thin and going bald. He has "measured out my life with coffee spoons." A signature Eliot approach was to assume that his readers had been widely educated in several languages and to insert quotations without translation or explanation as he alluded to other works. He continued this theme after the war in "The Wasteland" (1922), one of the most influential of all modernist works. It is a poem of sterility in which he begins with the sentiment that April is cruel because it has ceased to bring life.

In France, writers were stimulated by the movements in the visual arts known as dada, a nonsense word used to express the meaninglessness and random character of art in a time of capitalist war. Capitalism used reason in making decisions, but in 1916 it seemed that reason was in the service of unreason as the frightful war carried away everything in its path. Some artists described dada art as anti-art. It was meant to shock and provoke. Soon dada spread throughout the continent. An example is the already-mentioned "Fountain" by Marcel Duchamp, a urinal hung on a gallery wall. In 1919 Hannah Hoch in Germany constructed a collage entitled "Cut with the Dada Kitchen Knife through the Last Weimar Beer-belly Cultural Epoch in Germany."

Dada soon provoked a movement known as surrealism, based on Freudian concepts. The 1917 ballet "Parade," composed by Erik Satie with a scenario by Jean Cocteau, and set design by Pablo Picasso performed in 1917, was described by Guillaume Apollinaire as surrealistic, who thus gave the movement its name. Art, drama, and literature provided outlets for surrealist expression. An example is the Spanish playwright Federico Garcia Lorca, who wrote *The Public* and *Play Without a Title* in the early 1930s. Surrealism, then, influenced all the arts. Politically it tended toward anarchism or communism.

Surrealism in art consisted of reproducing dreamlike, often nightmare-like, paintings in which images from ordinary life were juxtaposed in impossible ways. They frequently melted and morphed into strange shapes. Surrealistic art used symbolism in the same way that dream life was symbolic. Nothing meant what it seemed to signify on the surface. But only through surrealism could one begin to access the true reality of the human mind and the actuality of the nature of the human world. The poet and playwright André Breton (1896–1960) wrote a *Surrealist Manifesto* (1924) that emphasized most of these

«Nous réduirons l'art à sa plus simple expression qui est l'amour.»

André Breton, *Poisson soluble*, 1924

Figure 10.6 A recent art exhibit at the Centre Pompidou-Metz, "Couples Modernes. 1900-1950" posed the question of the various relationships between love and creation. Here a viewer looks at works involving the surrealist artist André Breton and his loves with the fictional Nadja, Valentine Hugo, and Jacqueline Lamba. © JEAN-CHRISTOPHE VERHAEGEN/AFP via Getty Images.

themes. Breton had worked in a neurological ward during the First World War where he found that Freud's clinical approach was helpful. As a poet, he advocated the use of free association through "automatic writing" in which the writer writes whatever comes to mind without censorship. Surrealist poetry had this stream of consciousness quality.

In the UK, stream of consciousness was used to explore everyday life, most notably by Virginia Woolf (1882–1941) and James Joyce (also 1882–1941). Woolf, fascinated by both Freud's and Einstein's theories, wrote inside the minds of her characters. Thought, to Woolf, was disjunctive and jumped from topic to topic. As she changed point of view, the connections among topics changed. Characters worked out their wishes as they thought and acted. Two excellent examples are *Mrs. Dalloway* (1925) and *To the Lighthouse* (1927). Woolf was hounded by bipolar disorder that sometimes verged on psychosis (perhaps exacerbated by rape and sexual abuse by her half-brother), and in the end committed suicide by drowning herself.

James Joyce was an Irishman born in Dublin. His first two books, *Dubliners* (1914) and *Portrait of the Artist as a Young Man* (1916), had only hints of stream of consciousness, but in 1922 he published *Ulysses* in which Leopold Bloom moves about Dublin on June 16, 1904, for eighteen hours, represented in eighteen chapters. The travels of Bloom are based loosely on the travels of Odysseus in Homer's *Odyssey*, and each chapter has its own special character with its own science, color, body organ, and so forth. The stream of consciousness is often quite hard to follow, and notes are needed to guide the novice reader. The next book, *Finnegan's Wake* (1939), dropped any pretense of plot or character development as it explored thought through stream of consciousness and multilayered, multilingual puns. The first and last lines of the book are the same, giving the work a circular character.

Throughout the interwar period, the arts in Western Europe tended to be remote from the experience of average people. But to the extent that they reflected the bewilderment and angst of people who felt buffeted by war and economic depression, they maintained a connection to the predominant Western European mood.

Philosophical Approaches

Analytic Philosophy

In Great Britain and in Vienna, philosophers pursued approaches that were very different from those of philosophers in Germany and France. Analytic philosophy sought rigorous conceptual clarity in statements. They adopted the approach of Gottlob Frege, who had developed a symbolic logic that was capable of translating many seemingly ambiguous statements into a logical form. A disadvantage of this approach was that one had to master symbolic language before one could understand the analysis. The analytic philosophers presumed that any statement could be broken down into "logical atoms." The idea of logical atomism then implied that the world is exclusively made up of independent facts. There was no place for a holistic analysis in which the individual facts changed their meaning depending on a larger context. At the turn of the century, British idealist philosophers had taken a monistic approach, arguing that the world itself was a whole and that parts of it could only be understood in relation to that whole. In reaction, the Englishman Bertrand Russell (1872–1970) embraced logical atomism as he, along with others like Alfred North Whitehead, founded analytic philosophy.

If the analytical philosophers were right that mathematics was independent of human thought, and that mathematics had a logical structure, then by developing logic in its symbolic form, it may be possible to derive arithmetic and mathematics from logic. No need to worry about the way human beings perceived phenomena. In fact, many perceptions and ideas about them were just illogical and therefore untrue, or even nonsensical. The point was to discover the logical structure behind reality. Unfortunately, Russell discovered that any logic that was powerful enough to describe arithmetic would produce contradictions—paradoxical statements. In 1903, Russell wrote to Frege that Russell had discovered that Frege's logic would lead to a paradox. The paradox is similar to the statement "This sentence is false." If the sentence is false, then it is true. But if the sentence is true, then it must be false.

In his introduction to Wittgenstein's *Tractatus Logico-Philosophicus*, Russell wrote, "nothing correct can be said in philosophy," because "philosophy is an activity and not a theory."[2] Philosophy clarifies statements, but it makes no claims.

Wittgensteinian Critique

While the pacifist Russell spent part of the First World War in prison, his student Wittgenstein fought in the Austrian army. During the war and while he was in a prisoner of war camp, Wittgenstein began drafting his seminal *Tractatus Logico-Philosophicus* that was published in 1921. For Wittgenstein, logic can be used to clarify statements of fact and to show their relationships to one another. If one steps outside of logical necessity, however, one cannot find any other form of necessary relations. Following Hume, he noted that we could not be sure that the sun will rise tomorrow. In fact, "A necessity for one thing to happen because another thing has happened does not exist. There is only *logical* necessity" (6.37). For Wittgenstein, logical facts (both about what is the case and what is not the case) constituted the world. But what this logical world meant was outside the world. He stated that there is no value in the world, "and if there were, it would be of no value" (6.41). Thus, ethics and aesthetics could not be expressed and were therefore transcendental.

Philosophers disagree about what the *Tractatus* meant. Some have seen Wittgenstein as claiming that everything that cannot be expressed logically was nonsense and therefore nonexistent. But it seems that Wittgenstein reserved a place in human life for experiences that are not logical, and therefore inexpressible—but not unable to be experienced. "Not how the world is, is the mystical, but *that* it is. . . . The feeling of the world as a limited whole is the mystical feeling" (6.44, 6.45). He went on, "We feel that even if all possible scientific questions be answered, the problems of life have still not been touched at all." Some things cannot be expressed, but only shown. But the only way to learn, he thought, was to study all of the *Tractatus*'s propositions until the student saw them as senseless. "He must surmount these propositions; then he sees the world rightly. Whereof one cannot speak, thereof one must be silent" (6.54, 7). That is the last line of the *Tractatus*. Russell wrote an introduction to the book, but Wittgenstein thought Russell had not understood him.

Then Wittgenstein temporarily left philosophy, feeling that he had nothing more to discover. He became a primary school teacher. As a teacher he was generous with the gifted students and a tyrant capable of physical abuse with the less able learners.

In 1929 Wittgenstein returned to Cambridge and with Russell's encouragement submitted the *Tractatus* as a PhD thesis. Once he was awarded the doctorate, Wittgenstein became a fellow of Trinity College, Cambridge. In 1939 he was elected to the chair of philosophy. Thereafter, he began to change his mind about both mathematics and language. He denied that there were any discoverable mathematical facts.

His developing ideas about language were published posthumously in *Philosophical Investigations* (1953). He began to see that the definition of a word could be found in its use, rather than in its utility in pointing to something outside of language. He devised the idea of language games in which words dance next to each other according to some sort of rules that cannot be rigorously defined. We can only see how the rules work in particular situations. While there may be private languages, said Wittgenstein, rule-based language is public. Even though no one can define the words precisely, all speakers know how words should be applied. Thus, in ordinary language, grammar is not a rigid set of rules created or deduced by authorities but is rather an understanding of which utterances make sense and which are nonsense. Philosophy that explores this kind of grammar is a kind of therapy—not defining truths, but rather helping thinkers discover how they have made an error in thinking they have found a truth. Philosophy, Wittgenstein said, neither explains nor deduces but rather shows the fly how to get out of the bottle.

Logical Positivism

During the 1920s and 1930s, a philosophical discussion group known as the Vienna Circle met regularly to discuss analytic philosophy. Part of their debates concerned the ideas in the *Tractatus*. Wittgenstein often attended, although the circle was composed of more traditional analytic philosophers. Out of this circle, and one in Berlin, came the approach known as logical positivism. Logical positivism sought to find a way to connect the logical propositions examined in analytical philosophy to the world. Logical positivism demanded that all propositions had to deal with observable events. They agreed with Ernst Mach (see Chapter 9) that the mind knows only sensory experience. Only that which can be verified is scientific. Thus, they moved beyond logic to science.

Logical positivism and its various offshoots ruled philosophy in the English-speaking world for several decades. But the hope of analytical philosophers, and logical positivists, that science could be summed up in logic, was doomed to failure. Kurt Gödel's famous 1931 proof that any logical form that was powerful enough to include arithmetic must be either contradictory or incomplete drove the final nail into the coffin of the hopes for a completely logical universe. The zombie corpse emerged from the coffin but eventually succumbed. Philosophers had many pressing issues they thought worthy of discussion and exploration. They were not willing to accept that these issues were meaningless just because they did not deal with observable events in a logical fashion.

Continental Philosophy

"Continental Philosophy" was named by the British to differentiate some of the ways of thinking in Germany and France from the logical, analytical approach in Great Britain. John Stuart Mill had used the term to distinguish the utilitarianism of Bentham from the post-Kantian approaches adopted by German scholars. Bertrand Russell echoed the same theme in the twentieth century. Twentieth-century Continental Philosophy comprised phenomenology and later existentialism. In distinction to the British approach, the Continental approach started not with logic but with consciousness. The world that Wittgenstein had said was inexpressible was the one these philosophers wanted to talk about.

Edmund Husserl's (1858–1938) *Logische Untersuchungen* (*Logical Researches*, 1900–1) introduced the problems and methods that would occupy phenomenologists for the next several decades. Born a Jew, Husserl converted to Lutheranism in his twenties. He studied mathematics, physics, and astronomy before he eventually entered philosophy. He taught at Halle, Göttingen, and Freiburg. When the Nazis took power, he was banned from the library because of his Jewish background. He died of pleurisy just before the Second World War.

Husserl set out to bridge the gap between the objective and the subjective. The British analytic philosophers focused on language (including symbolic languages) and the meaning (or lack of meaning) attached to words and symbols. Husserl began with the units of consciousness that lie behind utterances. We choose, consciously or unconsciously, to focus on something. Thus, whatever is in consciousness is an intentional act, although some conscious experiences are not intentional, like pain. The task of phenomenology is to analyze the structure of consciousness. To do this, we must reflect on our own conscious experience. That is, we must think in the first person. We cannot directly study the consciousness of someone else. So, the meaning of "evidence" is different in phenomenology than it is in other disciplines. We *experience* consciousness; we only *observe* other things in the world, and perhaps engage with them.

An important point, then, is that as we experience, we should bracket off all ideas we have about what is really there. For instance, if we touch a tree, we feel rough bark; we inhale a musky smell; we see brown and green. The actual word "tree" gets in our way as we focus on the phenomena themselves. Kant had used the phrase "thing-in-itself" to refer to that which is outside of consciousness. Husserl calls the "things themselves" what are actually in consciousness. The question of something "out there," beyond consciousness, is bracketed off (a concept borrowed from the ancient Greek skeptics called epoché). The importance of this bracketing is that it allows us to talk about our experiences without being drawn into the question of "how do you know it is real?"

One of the most important insights of phenomenology, then, was that we should trust our experience. Even if we are hallucinating, the hallucination is real and can be described. This idea was translated in the 1960s by the phrase "be here now." And in fact, phenomenologists suggested that their philosophical stance was useful for nonphilosophers. Living in the present is therapeutically valuable. Physicians listening as patients describe their felt experience is also therapeutically valuable. Setting our ideologies and presuppositions aside for a time is personally rewarding. Just experience and describe is the phenomenological attitude.

But phenomenology as a philosophical approach necessitates thinking about conscious experience. In order to think about experiences, it is often necessary to abandon the phenomenological attitude—just experience one's own consciousness—as we attempt to connect different sets of individual experiences. The phenomenologists developed a complex vocabulary to distinguish different sorts of experiences and disparate sorts of bracketing, and this vocabulary often sounded jargon laden to the novice reader. Often the content of philosophical examination was a memory of a conscious experience rather than the conscious experience itself.

For the phenomenologists, even though each conscious experience is individual, there is a kind of similarity among human minds. Phenomenological description happens in the first person (the "I"), but we also have the ability to empathize and to understand that others also have experiences similar to our own. In particular, "I" can assume that another person is intending acts of consciousness just as I do. That is, the tree experience of another may have a different content than my tree experience, but we are both experiencing an intended act of conscious experience—we are both choosing, consciously or unconsciously, to focus on certain experiences. We both live in what Husserl called a lifeworld, a set of beliefs and cultural context that connects our conscious experiences with those of others. Some of the aspects of two lifeworlds are quite different, but others, such as existing in space and time, are common to all. Interestingly, our lifeworlds are constructed intersubjectively, in interaction with others.

Since our worlds are intersubjective, there must be something that we share, that is, something that does not belong to just one individual. The fact that we communicate effectively means that our worlds must be similar in form, at least to some extent. Considerations of this sort indicate that there is something that transcends any one person, but that is shared and sharable by others. This then points to a transcendent consciousness and a transcendent experience. There is a pure, transcendental consciousness that all humans share.

In his last great (unfinished) 1936 book, *Die Krisis der europäischen Wissenschaften und die transzendentale Phänomenologie: Eine Einleitung in die phänomenologische Philosophie* (*The Crisis of European Sciences and Transcendental Phenomenology. An Introduction to Phenomenological Philosophy*), Husserl highlighted his concerns about the directions of modern science since Galileo. For Husserl, modern science had become abstracted from the world it was meant to describe. By not paying attention to the world of consciousness but rather postulating an objective world that could be described mathematically, science had lost its way. Since increasingly modern Europe relied upon science, the crisis in science was a crisis for European thought and life.

Martin Heidegger (1889–1976) was Husserl's research assistant who later succeeded him to the professorship in Freiburg. Born a Roman Catholic, he studied for a time at a Jesuit seminary and later took up theology at the University of Freiburg. In 1933 he was elected rector of Freiburg University.

Heidegger was not willing merely to accept Husserl's idea of intentionality, but rather used it to dig deeper. He noted that we often ask whether things exist, but we do not ever ask what it might mean to exist. The key to Heidegger, then, is the question of what it means to exist. He notes that for us humans, things exist only in their relationship to us. A scientist might study atoms, but our knowledge of those atoms is related to measurements that human beings make, using their machines. The key existent, then, is human existence. Humans are the beings for which Being is a question. He invented a new word for such beings: Dasein, composed of "Da"—there—and "sein"—existence. So Dasein is the being that is there in the world.

According to Heidegger, for human beings the existence of things is related to their utility. "I" do not just contemplate a hammer and think of its "hammerness," but rather I pick up the hammer to pound a nail into something. Of course, I can passively think about the hammer, but in that case it is only passively present. Heidegger thought that philosophers up until his time had been concerned with that which is only passively present. But most of the time we think about useful things. Usually, I think of a hammer as a tool that I am able to use. We are oriented toward the future. If I am not presently using the hammer, I know that I can use it at a future time. Heidegger's major work, published in 1927, was titled *Sein und Zeit* (*Being and Time*). For Heidegger, being must exist alongside time. Unfortunately, he never wrote the book's second volume intended to explicate the nature of time.

We also exist in the world along with others, which makes our world a world with others (a "Mitwelt"). We never have a time when we exist only for ourselves without others, and so there is no way to conceive of an actual Dasein who exists only for itself. The human world (and for Heidegger there is no other kind of world) is made up of interconnected things. Pens go with papers, go with desks or writing surfaces, go with intending to write something, and so forth. Dasein is in a Mitwelt even if that Dasein becomes a hermit. A hermit has defined life in terms of others from which the hermit wishes to escape. In Heidegger's example, if "I" go for a walk and find a boat, I think of the boat as belonging to someone else for which that boat is useful. In Heidegger, we start with an individual consciousness, but we end with a human being enmeshed in a community. Phenomenology leads us in a transcendental direction.

Today it has become difficult to separate Heidegger from his decision to embrace Nazism shortly after being named rector of his university. Scholars have found anti-Semitism in his early letters, and there is ample evidence in later private writings to make the case that he was at heart a Nazi. On the other hand, he himself claimed that from 1934 on, after the night of the long knives (a time of executions of Hitler's political opponents), he was opposed to the Nazi Party. He claimed that he remained a Nazi to protect the university. By the end of the war, Heidegger had been assigned by the Nazis to dig anti-tank ditches.

Conclusion: Love in Scheler and Buber

Max Scheler (1874–1928) was a periodically lapsing Catholic who found his footing after the First World War when he was able to work with the Göttingen phenomenological circle led by Edmund Husserl. Scheler sought to rescue human beings from their definition as merely technological beings whose meaning was utilitarian. For him, the essence of human beings was the ability to love and through love participate in the inner meaning of all things. Knowledge was for Scheler a relationship between beings. Knowledge is not constructed but rather takes place during acts of mutual discovery. The source of the ability to partake in this discovery process is love, a love that directs itself to the infinite. Thus, knowing is an act of participating in the divine.

Scheler found in phenomenology and the idea of intention a way of connecting his insights to an established school of thought. Humans can intend higher or lower values, and for Scheler love was an expression of the best in value. As knowers engage in loving relationship, they form bonds. Thus, a loving human being lives in a community. The highest form of community is the loving community. In such a community the

Figure 10.7 Theologian Martin Buber. © Keystone/Stringer/Hulton Archive/Getty Images.

members are so connected that they feel a responsibility toward the others and for the others. There is a kind of solidarity in which all individuals feel responsible for fulfilling their roles but also feel responsible if others do not fulfill their roles. The community should support each other. The most impoverished society is one made up of solitary, autonomous individuals.

Martin Buber (1878–1965) was a Jew who was born in Austria and raised in Ukraine. He based his philosophy on a development of Kant's distinction between the knowable phenomena of mind and the unknowable noumena of a world outside of mind. This distinction seems to make it impossible for human beings to bridge the gap between different minds. Human connection cannot take place within theoretical reason. But Kant also described a practical reason in which we should never treat another human being as a means rather than as an end. Thus, we can recognize the other in ourselves. Phenomena can be a road to the noumenal world.

Buber was best known for the book *I and Thou* (1923). If people are seen as objects in the noumenal world, they are experienced as an "it." The I-It relationship does not fulfill human possibilities. An I-Thou relationship brings two equal human beings into dialogue. Through this I-Thou relationship with each other, humans are also brought into and I-Thou relationship with God, and, ultimately, for Buber, toward redemption.

Both of these figures were some of the most widely read of the philosophers after the First World War. There was a hunger for love and meaning in the middle of the chaos that was Europe.

CHAPTER 11
TECHNOLOGY AND SCIENCE AT MID-CENTURY

Figure 11.1 Lisa Meitner, 1946. The discoverer of nuclear fission. © Bettmann/Getty Images.

Nuclear Fission and Lise Meitner

Nineteen Thirty-eight was an epochal year for the Austrian physicist Lise Meitner (1878–1968). The first woman full professor in Germany and the head of the department of physics at the Kaiser Wilhelm Institute in Berlin, the Lutheran Meitner was forced to flee Nazi Germany because she had been born into a Jewish family. She slipped into the Netherlands with only ten marks to her name. Her scientific collaborator Otto Hahn gave her his mother's diamond ring in case she needed it as a bribe. Meitner ended up in Stockholm, Sweden, where she was given laboratory space. Her nephew Otto Robert Frisch, a physicist, was also in Stockholm.

But 1938 was not only a trying year for Lise Meitner. It was also a year of professional triumph. After James Chadwick's 1932 discovery of the electrically neutral particle named, appropriately, the "neutron," and the realization that much of the weight of an atomic nucleus was due to neutrons, several scientists in different countries thought that they could perhaps create elements heavier than uranium, the heaviest naturally occurring element, by bombarding uranium with neutrons. Just before she left Berlin, Meitner had been performing such experiments with the chemist Otto Hahn and his assistant Fritz Strassmann. Hahn wrote to Meitner's nephew Frisch telling him that the two had bombarded uranium nuclei with neutrons and found barium among the resulting products. Hahn was not sure where the barium had come from. Up until then, only smaller chunks, like alpha particles (helium nuclei) or protons, had been emitted when a nucleus was bombarded with particles.

Meitner had been collaborating with Niels Bohr, who often traveled to Stockholm from his lab in Copenhagen. Bohr, and others, had suggested that perhaps an atomic nucleus was shaped like a water drop. While the chemist Hahn did not know anything about nuclear science, the physicist Meitner was at the cutting edge. She realized that a water drop could become two drops and that when that happened, the water drop got longer and then pinched in the middle as it overcame surface tension and became two drops. Meitner imagined the same thing happening in a uranium nucleus. She also realized that uranium had more protons than any other element (92). These protons were all positively charged and therefore repelled each other. A uranium nucleus, Meitner realized, was on the verge of instability. If neutrons entered the uranium and destabilized it, the uranium could divide into smaller nuclei that were actually the nuclei of other elements. These two new nuclei would both be positively charged, and each would repel the other. The two would fly apart with a high velocity. Accelerating to a high velocity takes a lot of energy, as anyone knows who has driven a car and calculated the amount of gas needed to so. Where would so much energy come from?

Meitner, working with Frisch, calculated the weight of the two resulting nuclei. They realized that the two new nuclei would be lighter than the original uranium nucleus. Einstein had shown that energy and mass were equivalent ($E=mc^2$). Since the square of the speed of light ("c") was so large, a little mass would produce a lot of energy. In fact, the amount of energy needed to accelerate the new nuclei was equal to the difference in the weight of the uranium nucleus minus the combined weight of the new nuclei. Meitner and Frisch had explained the physics behind what would, in 1945, become the atomic bomb.

Meitner and Frisch published their work about a month after Hahn and Strassman published their paper. In 1945 the Royal Swedish Academy of Sciences awarded the Nobel Prize to Otto Hahn, and Otto Hahn alone, for discovering nuclear fission. Many scientists were surprised at the exclusion of Meitner and Frisch. Meitner had been an eminent scientist in Berlin before the Nazis forced her out. Her work with Hahn before she left Berlin had been crucial to Hahn's discovery. In the 1990s, the records of the Nobel Prize committee were released. Meitner's biographer, Ruth Lewin Sime, had a chance to figure out why Meitner had been excluded. Sime's assessment was that the Prize committee did not understand interdisciplinary work and during the war years did not consult with scientists in other countries. They made a mistake. But Meitner did not lack for later awards and was recognized for her brilliance in the succeeding decades.

After the war, Meitner reexamined her decision to stay in Berlin after the Nazis had started expelling and arresting Jews. She regarded her delay in leaving for Stockholm as a moral failure. As a Lutheran and an Austrian, she had thought she was immune from

Hitler's persecution and so did not emigrate in protest. Afterward she blamed herself, and she also blamed her friend and collaborator Otto Hahn and other scientists who did not leave. As she engaged in this bitter recollection, she took part in the soul-searching self-examination that all Germans had to undergo in the decades after the war.

Chapter Map

In this chapter, we examine developments in technology and science beginning with the Second World War and continuing until roughly the end of the twentieth century. Since the final chapter concerns itself with computers and cyber-ideas, discussion of these topics will wait until then.

The Second World War brought new technology to the world, most notably radar and atomic energy. The atomic bomb and the Holocaust contributed to define boundaries of intellectual history: that which either must not be thought or which is too dangerous to consider. Radar joined other new technologies like jet aircraft and transatlantic phone lines to widen the boundaries of European intellectual life.

After the war, genetic research took a giant leap with the discovery of the structure of DNA. Identifying DNA with the gene raised numbers of methodological and analytical issues. In a few decades, genetic engineering raised the possibility that human beings might design and engineer the shape of life on the earth, raising urgent issues in ethics.

The second half of the twentieth century saw great changes in the ability of physicians to understand, diagnose, and cure diseases. Antibiotics and vaccines allowed the control of diseases like polio, tuberculosis, and measles. Imaging machines allowed pain-free exploration of processes deep in the body. Surgery became precise and focused. Life for Europeans became longer and more pleasant. The human world of 2000 was incomparably better than the world of 1900.

As particle colliders enabled scientists to examine the makeup of nuclei, they found many more particles, some of them with unexpected characteristics. Eventually they were able to construct a theory of particles known as the standard model. Scientists found that they could understand the processes they observed if they posited four basic forces that were mediated by an exchange of particles by other particles.

At the beginning of the twentieth century, scientists thought that the Milky Way Galaxy was the extent of the universe. By the end of the century, scientists thought that there were at least hundreds of billions of galaxies, each containing at least hundreds of billions of stars. The journey of discovery passed through improved and extended telescopes, past ingenious theoretical formulations, to reconceptions of the very stuff of which our world and we are made.

Atomic Bomb

Throughout the war, the United States and Great Britain carried out research on an atomic bomb. They discovered that if a large-enough mass of U_{235}, the isotope of uranium that was fissile (capable of fission), was pushed together, the neutrons that were released in fission would find another nucleus to destabilize before they could exit the uranium mass. If the mass of uranium were not large enough, the neutrons would tend to fly out of the mass before they found their way into an atomic nucleus. The key to the bomb, then, was first to have sufficient amounts of U_{235}. Since mined uranium is composed of 99.3 percent U_{238} and only 0.7 percent U_{235}, and the critical mass for a fission reaction is 123 pounds (56 kilograms) of 85 percent or more of U_{235}, about 15,000 pounds of uranium (7.5 tons) was necessary to produce the fuel for one bomb. Furthermore, the U_{235} had to be extracted from the rest of the uranium.

Since a molecule of U_{235} is slightly less heavy than a molecule of U_{238}, using a process that took advantage of the different weights of the two main isotopes could separate the two forms of uranium. In gaseous diffusion, a lighter atom will tend to move through a membrane with tiny pores more readily than a heavier atom. In a centrifuge, the lighter isotope will fly away more readily than the heavier isotope. In the Manhattan Project, gaseous diffusion proved less problematic than centrifuging, but today, with improved design, centrifuging is the method of choice. In any case, separating time after time after time in a cascading sequence allowed the U_{235} to be gradually purified until the 85 percent purity level was reached. This took a great deal of electrical power and time. There were other techniques of purifying uranium, and other fissile elements, like plutonium (Pu_{239}), but all took large amounts of power and time to assemble a critical mass of fissile material.

Besides figuring out how to produce the fuel for a bomb, scientists had to figure out how to bring two noncritical masses of uranium together quickly enough to create a critical mass so it could explode. Two methods were used: one involved arranging high explosives around the two separated masses so they would be shoved together; the other involved shooting one of the noncritical masses into the other. Most of the research was carried out in the United States at several different sites. Although both the British and American governments offered as many scientists as the project (code-named Manhattan Project) needed, and all the necessary funding, it still took from 1939, when Albert Einstein delivered a letter recommending nuclear bomb research to President Franklin Roosevelt, until 1945 for a few bombs to be readied. On August 6 and August 9, 1945, US bombs exploded over the Japanese cities of Hiroshima and Nagasaki, wreaking vast destruction with tens of thousands of civilian casualties.

The Soviet Union had spies inside the Manhattan Project, so they were able to reproduce the US effort. Additionally, after the European part of the war ended, German scientists were taken to the Soviet Union to help in the Soviet bomb project. In 1949, US president Harry Truman announced that the Soviet Union had exploded an atomic bomb. The "Atomic Age" had begun, along with the Cold War.

In July 1945, Vannevar Bush, the director of the US Office of Scientific Research and Development, wrote a white paper entitled *Science - The Endless Frontier*. Bush argued that science provided opportunities for advancement in every area of life. Basic science offered the knowledge upon which applied science could draw in order to produce new and important inventions. Basic science was like capital, and applied science like the

Figure 11.2 Atomic bomb blast over Nagasaki, Japan, August 8, 1945. The destruction of Hiroshima and Nagasaki changed the world and defined the parameters of the Cold War. © National Archives/Hulton Archive/Getty Images.

interest produced by wisely invested capital. Bush argued that with the wartime emphasis on applied science the world had used up its reserves of knowledge capital. Investment in education and basic scientific research had to be undertaken. The United States and the Soviet Union both supported large-scale research programs. The Western European democracies were financially exhausted by the war, but they too slowly began to support their own programs.

Technological Determinism

But not everyone saw technology as a benefit. Besides continuing protests about the atomic, and later, hydrogen bomb, some analysts began to develop critical theories about the general impact of technology on society. The French scholar Jacques Ellul (1912–94), a professor of History and Sociology of Institutions at the University of Bordeaux, wrote voluminously on religion and technology. At the age of twenty, Ellul had a frightening experience that he interpreted later as being in the presence of God. He gradually underwent an unusual religious conversion process that was informed by reading Karl Marx, Søren Kierkegaard, and Karl Barth. Like Barth, Ellul was a resistance leader in the

Second World War, was given the award of "Righteous Among the Nations" by the Israeli government, and was memorialized at Yad Vashem. He described himself as a Christian anarchist. He thought violence stemmed mostly from nation-states and that it was the duty of a Christian to question and challenge the state. From that stance, he questioned the effect of technology on society.

In 1964 Ellul published *La Technique: L'enjeu du siècle* (translated as *The Technological Society*). He saw technology as any method that involved rationality for the sake of efficiency. Thus, not only machines but also methods of thinking and acting were part of technology. His problem was that technology subordinated the natural world to efficiency. Technology, for Ellul, dehumanized human society. In fact, he claimed, technology had displaced the sacred and had become sacred in its turn. Humans no longer gave up their lives to God but were quite willing to give up their lives to efficiency and rationality. But Ellul also thought the progress of technology was unstoppable. Our lives were constrained; we had sold meaning for pleasure.

We have seen similar themes in the work of Marx, Nietzsche, Weber, and others. We will later see such ideas developed in postmodern thought. Americans and Canadians also developed ideas concerning technological determinism.

Molecular Genetics

We saw in Chapter 9 that biologists had theorized that there was some kind of unit, called a gene, that was somehow connected to observable traits in living organisms (such observable traits are known as phenotypes). Although genes were not observable in microscopes, chromosomes were. Working with fruit flies, American geneticists had shown that changes in phenotypes could be related to reorganization of chromosomal material. It seemed that whatever genes were, they were located on chromosomes. Somehow the chromosomal gene determined the phenotype of the organism. Not every scientist was convinced of this location of the gene. It seemed incredible to some that a molecule or two in a chromosome could carry all the information necessary to the construction of complex characteristics, like eyes or brains. It seemed more likely that the chromosomes were one small part of the action of the parts of the whole organism. Some scientists also saw evidence that the environment affected genetics. The action of the environment was ignored in chromosomal genetics.

Furthermore, although scientists in the English-speaking world developed a research program based on Mendelian and chromosomal genetics, in other countries scientists were not convinced that it was worth leaving productive programs of investigation to pursue the chromosomal line. In France, after the First World War, for example, biologists were more interested in physiology than in the ephemeral gene, and genetics was much more tied to embryological development than it was to cellular studies. In Germany, the education of scientists involved *Bildung*, a comprehensive development of personal values and an exposure to the nation's culture. Thus, German geneticists were much more likely to take a comprehensive look at whole organisms. In fact, at times comparisons were made between the organization of a cell and the organization of the state. The chromosomal approach was much more linked to applied research in agriculture, and indeed in Germany there was a split between the applied and pure geneticists. Of course, after 1933, with the advent of Hitler and the Nazis, genetic research was linked to eugenics and ultimately to the Holocaust.

In England, Darwinian theory made a comeback precisely because of the focus on Mendelian/chromosomal genetics and the theory of mutations as the cause of phenotypic changes. Mutations were spontaneous changes in genetic makeup and were not subject to the reversion to the mean that usually occurred in successive generations of reproduction. If a gene were a small part of a chromosome, then one could imagine how a mutation could occur if chromosomes reorganized themselves, without needing a change in the whole organism. If the mutations occurred in dominant genes, then all organisms that had that gene would express it phenotypically. If the mutation were on a recessive gene, then one quarter of the organisms that had the gene would express it. If the mutation were favorable to survival and successful reproduction, then gradually organisms with that gene would increase as a percentage of the organism's population. Statistical studies done in the 1930s showed that Darwin's analysis would work. Not every country's scientists supported Darwin, including those of the Soviet Union. Communist scientists felt that the action of the environment should act not just by selecting favorable traits (the Darwinian position) but also by evoking favorable traits (the Lamarckian position). A disastrous agricultural research program was pursued along Lamarckian lines under the leadership of Trofim Lysenko.

Chromosomes were known to consist of nucleic acids and proteins. At first, researchers thought that the more complex protein molecules were more likely to be genes than the relatively simpler nucleic acid molecules. However, for a number of reasons a few researchers in England and the United States became convinced that deoxyribonucleic acid (DNA) was the active genetic material in the chromosome. DNA was known to consist of a sugar and phosphate chain accompanied by four bases: adenine, thymine, cytosine, and guanine. A key to elucidating the chemical structure of DNA came from a relatively new technology, the electron microscope. When DNA was crystalized, X-ray photographs taken by Rosalind Franklin working at King's College London showed that the DNA molecule had a helical (spiral) structure. James Watson and Francis Crick working at Cambridge tried to build a three-dimensional model of a helical DNA using pieces of metal crafted to the appropriate shape of the relevant molecules. The task was not easy. How many spiraling strands did DNA have? How were the bases arranged next to the sugar-phosphate chain? Eventually they discovered that research by Erwin Chargaff had shown that the amount of adenine always equaled the amount of thymine and the amounts of cytosine always equaled the amount of guanine. They hit upon a model in which these pairs, A-T and C-G, were arranged on the inside of two spiraling sugar-phosphate chains. All of the angles corresponded to the photographs taken by Franklin, who agreed that they had found the correct model.

The fact that there were two helical strands, rather than one or three, made perfect biological sense. When cells divided, the chromosomes split in two, and one could

Figure 11.3 Working model of DNA. Constructed by James Watson and Francis Crick, 1953. © Science & Society Picture Library/Getty Images.

imagine the two spiral chains "unzipping" themselves. Each chain would have an order of bases that were mirror images of one another, so one could also imagine how each half of the divided cell could construct the other side of the double helix.

But finding the structure of DNA did not explain how DNA might work as a gene. The physicist George Gamow applied the developing theory of information theory to suggest that three bases, or a triplet, were needed to specify one amino acid. Since amino acids were the material of which proteins were made, a string of base triplets could code for a protein. Eventually researchers developed a model in which DNA actually coded for messenger RNA, which carried the information to a part of the cell known as a ribosome where ribosomal RNA actually constructed the protein. Enzymes that govern the activity of a cell are proteins, so essentially DNA was producing enzymes that made the cells in an organism work in certain ways. By the end of the 1960s, researchers were able to specify which triplets coded for which amino acids.

Researchers flocked to molecular biology, convinced that the secret to life lay there. They hoped to be able to explain the multitude of observable organic traits by showing that the cellular processes controlled by DNA could be shown to produce them. Other biologists expressed skepticism. They noted that many layers lay between DNA and actual traits. Cells are complex organisms, and they react to their internal environment. This environment may be simply what food is ingested, what pathogens are causing illness, or the state of anxiety of an organism. The activation of traits may lie in the conditions within the womb as an embryo develops, and thus the expression of traits may be affected by the actions of a separate organism, the mother.

Philosophically, the issue is "reductionism" versus "holism," a subject that this text has presented in a variety of contexts. In reductionism, all the aspects of a higher-level theory can be "reduced" to the parts of a simpler, lower-level theory. In a perfect reductionist world, as envisioned in the positivism of Comte (Chapter 5), physics can explain chemistry that can explain life, that can explain human psychology, that can explain human groups. A well-respected sociobiologist wrote in the 1970s that poetry would be the last biological trait to be explained.

An important reductionist question is: What are the basic units? In *The Selfish Gene* (1976), Richard Dawkins suggested that all of life is an outcome of competition among DNA molecules. The argument is, of course, made through the scientifically questionable rhetorical device of personification. For Dawkins, a cell is just a gene's way of making another gene. However, if we focus on the cell, a good case might be made that the cell is the important unit. Darwin had focused on competition among organisms of the same species. But Darwin also claimed that somehow the competition among individual organisms was for the benefit of the species. One could also make a case that the basic unit was the species.

On the other side, holism maintains that there are very different levels of explanation that do not overlap. In the case of genetics, the classical genetics of the Mendelians has to be rewritten to omit important features in order to fit into the "DNA as gene" definition. The holistic analysis does not claim that DNA is uninteresting but rather that DNA is not sufficient to do all the work of producing phenotypes. In fact, DNA has not been observed replicating itself outside of a cell. Most phenotypic traits are related to multiple genes as well as a variety of environmental factors. The old suggestion that the gene may not a physical entity but rather the state of the whole organism bears looking at if one wants to jump from the intracellular level to the level of the complete organism.

In many ways, the reductionist approach minimizes not only theory but also analysis. The old question of Nature versus Nurture becomes a nonquestion in DNA reductionism. If there is a gene for intelligence, does the presence of that gene suggest that environment does not matter in the development of intelligence? Looking into the cell nucleus may keep us from looking at the organism—or beyond it.

However, focusing on nucleic acids (DNA and forms of RNA) has been extraordinarily useful in a variety of practical ways. Genetic engineering has existed in some form since the early 1970s. The idea was to use technology to directly manipulate an organism's genes. Viruses consist almost entirely of genetic material. A modified virus, then, could be used to insert foreign genetic material into an organism. In the twenty-first century, genetic engineering was used to replace defective human genes with effective ones.

Genetic engineering allowed a variety of medicines to be synthesized. The first of these, insulin, was produced in 1978, and genetically engineered bacteria that produce insulin were used in the synthesis. This process brought cheap and sure treatment to millions of diabetics. The technique has been used in modified form to produce many important medicines. Furthermore, mice were genetically modified to model human diseases like cancer, obesity, and arthritis to name only a few.

In agriculture, genetic engineering has been used to alter crops to stay ripe longer, to resist certain diseases, or to repel pests. Some crops have been modified to taste better, to carry more calories, or to be more nutritious. Some processes have engineered useful drugs or other proteins. The term "genetically modified organism" (GMO), however, has raised a number of ethical as well as practical questions.

What if a harmful genetic variant is inadvertently, or even deliberately, introduced into the world? How do we know what the long-term effects of eating GMO foods are? Companies patent the genes they have produced. Should it actually be possible to own a particular life form? How can we contain GMOs when the wind may blow pollen across fences and fields? In the face of these and other questions, many governments have begun to regulate, or even ban, GMOs. Yet the question remains how effective restrictions can be if a scientist or company wants to violate them. The field of medical ethics is hard at work finding ways to answer such questions.

Science fiction scenarios have suggested that it may be possible to produce a completely engineered human being. What if certain human beings are engineered to be better soldiers, nonfearful killers? Would it be ethical to produce human beings without genetic weaknesses, thus achieving the old eugenicist dreams? What if it didn't work? Might we produce dysgenic creatures? Could human beings be the only species so far to choose their own next step in evolution?

The danger of pursuing reductionist-based genetic engineering is that the holists may have a point. What if it would be necessary to create an environment that is conducive to human betterment? If we developed GMO-humans before understanding what we were doing, we could risk huge, unexpected consequences.

Medicine

One of the most spectacular stories of the twentieth century is the story of improving life expectancy and life quality through improved and more accessible medical treatment. At the beginning of the twentieth century, life expectancy at birth in the UK was 48 years for males and 51.6 years for females. By 2000, the life expectancy was 75.3 years for males and 80.1 years for females. The rest of industrialized Europe had a similar experience. Not all of this increase was due to medicine. Housing and nutrition improved as well.

Twentieth-century medicine began just as the theory that microorganisms cause many diseases began to be accepted by physicians. Stethoscopes were among the more sophisticated devices available. Physicians could diagnose but rarely cure. By the end of the century, the stethoscope had been transcended. Ultrasound was used in echocardiograms to watch the interior of the heart without breaking the skin. CAT scans, MRIs, and low-power X-rays were some of the astounding applications of discoveries in the physical sciences. Medicine borrowed from materials sciences to develop lightweight prosthetic devices, ultrathin threads for stitching tiny blood vessels, and much more. Antibiotics meant that fatal infections were controllable. Synthetic insulin meant that diabetics had hope. Effective surgeries were performed routinely on brains, hearts, spines, and other organs. A physician in 1900 transported to 2000 would hardly have been able to comprehend the changes.

This text will not spend much time on the imaginative research and reconceptions of previous knowledge that made possible the medical advances that changed life in Europe. We will rather look at a few case studies to understand the nature of intellectual work in medicine, drawing parallels to thought in other areas.

The most important medical advances, in terms of the well-being of populations, came in the field of public health. Sewer lines, sewage treatment plants, water mains, and water treatment spread into every part of the industrialized world, including small villages. Water was piped into houses, and human waste was expelled in toilets. Clinics and hospitals were built, and educational campaigns concerning health extended from the medical centers. The 1918 Spanish flu epidemic provided an epidemiological laboratory for public health workers to develop techniques of containment and control as well as healing. One important step was giving sick people blood or plasma transfusions from the blood of recovered patients. This seemed to transfer immunity, and mortality in treated patients dropped 50 percent.

Many public health procedures eliminate disease without understanding what diseases might be addressed. Safe water goes a long way toward ensuring against cholera (see Chapter 4), but water treatment eliminates most waterborne pathogens, many of which were yet to be discovered. The primary danger from unsafe water comes from human beings who, out of economic concern, antiscientific bias, or other reasons, oppose water treatment. Medicine's need to embrace effective treatments without completely understanding the underlying causes highlights a general aspect of the history of ideas. The world has so far proven to be more complex than the most sophisticated thinkers have been able to imagine, and yet these thinkers have been able to conceive of ideas that work in a restricted realm. Physicians and others in the medical fields have to devise plans of action in the absence of complete information.

An important step in medicine was to change the mindset of physicians to appreciate science-based medicine. For example, at the beginning of the twentieth century many physicians resisted the use of the sphygmomanometer (blood pressure cuff and apparatus) on the grounds that one could get more useful knowledge from taking a pulse in a skilled manner. Mere numbers, like blood pressure, they claimed, would reduce the art of medicine to a cold heartless activity. Of course, the blood pressure cuff proved so useful that it soon replaced the sensitive pulse-sensing hands of the physician.

The scientific method in medicine was developed both to avoid experimenter bias and to clearly define the parameters of the phenomena being studied. In the nineteenth century, for instance, German microbiologist and physician Robert Koch (1843–1910) had developed methods of growing bacterial cultures, particularly with the use of agar. At the time, germ theory was not generally accepted. Koch was able to isolate the bacterium that he thought was associated with anthrax. In order to demonstrate that the bacterium caused the disease, he developed four criteria:

The pathogenic organism had to be present every time the disease occurred.

The suspected pathogenic organism had to be isolated from a diseased host and grown in a pure culture.

Samples from the pure culture must cause the disease when inoculated into a healthy animal.

Pathogenic organisms from the inoculated host must be shown to be the same as the pathogenic organisms obtained from the originally diseased animal.

Koch's criteria were designed to guard against a researcher jumping to conclusions upon a new discovery. It was not enough to show that a bacterium was found in a diseased animal. The argument that it actually caused the disease had to be made using experimental evidence.

As part of the scientific approach to medicine, a process of blinding developed. In the nineteenth century, it seemed that an informed expert was better than a noninformed observer. And yet when blinded experiments were carried out, it appeared that experts reached different conclusions than they did when they were unblinded. In 1907 blinded researchers carried out a study of the effects of caffeine, and the practice grew. Patients are notoriously susceptible to a placebo effect in which they report amelioration of symptoms even when they have been given a placebo in place of medicine. A double-blind experiment is one in which both the patients and the administering physicians are unaware of whether a placebo or a medicine is being administered.

Another issue in applying science to medicine is the issue of cause versus correlation. Koch's criteria were designed to avoid reaching a conclusion just because a bacterium was found in a sick animal. Many things can be correlated without having any causal connection. For instance, a rise of population may be correlated with the number of people born with astigmatism. But rise in population does not cause astigmatism.

A similar issue is found in cases where the causal connection depends on the specific makeup of individuals. Smoking is correlated with lung cancer, but some people who smoke do not get lung cancer, and some people who get lung cancer do not smoke. To study such phenomena, a large sample size is needed to produce accurate statistical correlations. Determining the causal connection between smoking and lung cancer involved 22,000 researchers who followed 188,000 men, some of whom smoked and some of whom did not. Within 20 months, it was obvious that smokers died from lung cancer at a much higher rate than nonsmokers. In 1990 a study in the UK compared samples from both 1950 and 1990 involving smokers, nonsmokers, and ex-smokers. Again, the results were born out.

The point is twofold. First, only studies involving large populations observed over many years can determine many medically significant causal relationships. But second, conducting such studies is hard for most physicians who deal with individual patients. The literature in medical journals is still filled with case studies of individuals or small groups. Such studies may be suggestive, but often they are misleading in making overarching generalizations. Before a causal connection can be established, large studies, as well as meta-studies of existing studies, need to be undertaken. The cost and inconvenience of such studies inhibits much medical research.

Perhaps the most important medical innovation besides public health and scientific medicine was the discovery and production of antibiotics. In 1928 the Scottish biologist Alexander Fleming returned to his laboratory from holiday to find that a fungus had contaminated one of his staphylococci bacterial cultures. Fleming guessed that the mold must have flown in through a window. Around the fungus the staphylococci were destroyed, but the bacteria farther away from the fungus were intact. Fleming decided to pay attention to the mold, a species of the genus Penicillium, and found that it released the active agent that he named penicillin. Penicillin killed numbers of different pathogenic bacteria. He also noted that it was hard to cultivate and decided that it would not be practical to use it to fight bacterial infections.

As the Second World War was about to break out, Oxford scientists began to study penicillin. By 1940 they understood its structure and had worked out a way to produce enough penicillin to begin testing. They could stop an infection in its tracks by administering doses orally. It seemed not to be lethal to human beings. However, there was no way that Great Britain could produce enough to make a difference in the war. After America entered the war in December 1941, the Oxford scientists were able to convince American agricultural businesses with large laboratories to get involved. The government persuaded them to waive their previously existing patents. Continued research accompanied manufacturing, and by 1944 there was enough penicillin to treat all allied soldiers who needed it. After the war, penicillin became available to civilians.

Before penicillin, an infected scratch could be lethal. After penicillin, the scratch was an inconvenience. Scientists began the hunt for other antibacterial strains, and a wide variety of antibiotics was developed, some of them effective against a narrow band of bacteria and some wider acting. Although antibiotics were quite effective against bacterial infection, another approach had to be taken against viruses. Researchers developed methods of creating vaccines against certain viral and bacterial diseases, and by the 1950s diseases such as polio were effectively controlled.

In the case of antibiotics, we see a number of different institutional actors involved in the development of the key theories and practices. Academic researchers were important during these early stages. Governments aided them in finding ways to turn discovery into cure. And the governments interceded with businesses to utilize industrially scaled laboratories in which proprietary processes were used to shape the original discovery into a usable and salable product. Physicians and hospitals then had to decide to use the new products as they treated patients. None of these institutions could have accomplished this life-saving production by themselves. In general, making theoretical ideas useful is a complex process, the extent of which is hard to visualize.

Usually in medicine there are two great difficulties: defining the nature of a disease and determining the best treatment. An example will allow us to see the complexities involved in the question of diagnosis and treatment. In the eighteenth-century, physicians described a condition called angina pectoris (literally "choking of the chest"), in which the sufferers experienced a severe generalized pain in the chest that was exacerbated by even minor exertion. Often, they had trouble breathing. The condition would disappear after a time of inactivity, but after a year or so it would occur even during rest. Eventually the sufferers suddenly dropped dead. By the early nineteenth century, autopsies had shown a hardening of the arteries of the heart in some angina-related deaths—but not in others. However, in other autopsies extensive ossification was seen in people who had reported no angina symptoms. In 1867 the Scottish physician Thomas Lauder Brunton discovered that inhaling amyl nitrite, a substance that caused blood vessels to dilate, halted an angina attack within a minute. However, it still was not clear what the cause of an angina attack was. And even with amyl nitrite, the final result was usually a sudden death. There seemed to be no alternative. In 1896 the widely read textbook author Stephen Paget wrote, "Surgery of the heart has probably reached the limits set by nature to all surgery: no new method, and no new discovery, can overcome the natural difficulties that attend a wound of the heart."[1]

In 1912 an American, James Herrick, who was researching coronary thrombosis (clots that formed in coronary arteries) theorized that many people whose coronary arteries were obstructed did not die, because new blood vessels had grown to provide blood by other routes.

Coronary arteries are those that bring blood directly to the heart muscles to supply it with oxygen. Blood travels directly from the aorta to the coronary arteries and into capillaries from which the heart extracts more than three times as much oxygen than does any other organ. Hearts need more oxygen than other organs, and the absence of oxygen in the heart causes the death of heart muscle quite quickly. Herrick's paper provided an explanation for angina pectoris symptoms as well as an explanation for the absence of angina attacks in people who one would have expected to have such symptoms. Herrick suggested that finding a blood supply for the heart from sources other than blocked coronary arteries would keep the heart tissue from dying. No one in his audience seemed interested.

About the same time, a French physiologist suggested that cutting certain nerve fibers might cure the disease. The Romanian Thoma Ionescu first carried out the procedure in 1916, and his patient became free of angina pectoris symptoms. The procedure spread, but researchers soon realized that cutting the nerve treated symptoms but not the disease. In the 1930s, physicians tried removing the thyroid, the gland responsible for regulating metabolism. With metabolism slowed down, the heart needed less oxygen. However, the heart's blood supply was still restricted, so the treatment did not deal with the underlying condition.

In 1935 the American heart surgeon Claude Beck noticed that the patient he was operating on had survived a heart attack and so had some dead heart tissue. The scar from that dead tissue had become attached to the pericardium, the sack that encloses the heart. When he cut the scar away from the pericardium, it bled profusely; new blood vessels had somehow formed. When Beck injected the new vessels with some soot, he found that the soot spread all over the heart. The new vessels had spread throughout the heart muscle. After carrying out much more research on animals, Beck decided to offer an operation to a very sick patient. It is worth noting that in 1935 there were no heart-lung machines, no defibrillators, and no way to stop the heart. All heart surgery was carried out on a beating heart. Beck attached part of the pectoral muscle, and its artery, to the heart wall in order to stimulate the growth of new blood vessels. His patient lived for over fifteen years. A few surgeons used similar procedures, but most did not. It just seemed too risky.

By the 1950s, surgeons were experimenting with using heart-lung machines, hypothermia, and temporary heart-stopping drugs. By the end of the 1950s, it became possible to inject dyes into the cardiac vessels and then use X-rays to determine where the blood was flowing and where it was blocked. A variety of techniques of taking veins from other parts of the body to create bypasses around blockages proved effective. By the 1970s, open-heart bypass surgery was carried out in many European countries.

But were these bypasses effective? How could one determine whether a patient survived because of or in spite of a surgery? Studies had to be designed to compare large groups of patients treated by different methods. By the 1980s, the statistics showed that bypass surgery was effective. At the end of the century, however, a new method was available. Cardiologists threaded catheters through veins and into the heart blood vessels to open vessels and inserted stents to keep the vessels open. Surgeons were often not needed.

In this brief discussion of the struggle to think through diagnostic quandaries and find effective therapeutic procedures for one disease, angina pectoris, we can see the long development of medical thought. The same issues occurred as physicians struggled to understand and treat other sorts of diseases. We also see the incomplete nature of medical thought. New discoveries in in nonmedical fields made possible the invention of new therapeutic measures. The interconnected nature of the body might show that, say, coronary-artery (or other) disease is connected to other bodily processes. We know that coronary-artery disease can be avoided or slowed through exercise and proper diet. Thus, an emphasis on staying well rather than treating sickness has entered the medical field.

In the field of the History of Ideas, a distinction has traditionally been made between pure and applied knowledge. Medicine sits astride that bifurcation, if indeed there is any utility in drawing such a sharp distinction. Often the investigator of "pure" ideas responds to problems created in the applied arts. The two sides feed each other so frequently that it is hard to usefully separate them.

Nuclear and Particle Physics

In Chapter 9, we saw modern physicists develop two theories, relativity theory and quantum theory, which changed the way we view the universe. These two approaches challenged old assumptions about the structure of the universe and of human knowledge, and as such they reverberated far beyond the field of physics. Not only philosophers, artists, authors, social scientists, and other intellectuals and artists found fruit for innovative thought, but also the implications of relativity and quantum theory percolated into the common fund of knowledge. A little industry producing books explaining modern physics for the layperson sprang up. Albert Einstein even tried his hand at explaining relativity theory for beginners in *Relativity. The Special and the General Theory* (1916)

But such books were of necessity far from the ideas held by physicists. Particle physics was based on two very different things: first, observable data like tracks in bubble chambers; second, mathematical theories (or models) that connect observable measurements to one another. The observable data were far removed from whatever was being studied, because the particles were so small that they could not be directly seen. The mathematical models were abstract, but one could try to concoct a visual picture of whatever it is that they referred to. Since both the quantum-level and the nuclear-level worlds were described mathematically in multidimensional spaces that may or may not exist in the physical world, a three-dimensional picture was inadequate at best. Physicists learned to think in terms of the mathematics. The science-for-the-layperson translators thought up analogies and asked if the physicists could accept them.

In the late 1920s, an important problem for physicists was reconciling relativity and quantum theory—a daunting task. As Englishman Paul Dirac (1902–84) developed a relativistic quantum theory, he found a strange result. It seemed that a particle could have either a positive or a negative energy. Dirac imagined that the vacuum was made up of an infinite sea of negatively charged electrons. If one of these negative energy electrons absorbed energy, thus becoming a normal positive energy electron, a hole would be left in the sea. This hole would appear to have a positive charge (because it replaced the negative charge of the electron that had bounced out of the hole). That is, it would appear to be a positively charged particle with the size of an electron. For a time, an observer would see the positive charge near a negatively charged electron, but if the electron fell back into the hole, discharging energy, both the electron and the hole would disappear.

What Dirac had called a hole, turned out to be an actual particle—of antimatter. In 1932 the antimatter particle, the positron, was discovered by Carl Anderson. The Dirac sea was given up in favor of the idea of a set of antiparticles corresponding to a particle of regular matter. When a particle met its antiparticle, the two would annihilate each other in a puff of energy. The idea of antimatter provided a way of thinking about the original big bang. If a particle represented plus one, and an antiparticle represented minus one, then the sum of a particle and an antiparticle would be zero. If there were as many antiparticles as particles in the universe, then the universe would add up to zero. That would explain how something was created from nothing. Matter would only seem to exist, but in sum, it would be nothing. The problem with this approach was that antiparticles seemed to be quite rare. Some physicists suggested that half the galaxies in the universe were made up of antimatter. Others shrugged.

Before the 1930s, the known fundamental particles were the electron, the proton, and the photon (light). But 1932 brought the discovery of yet another particle: the neutron. A neutron was very close to the size of a proton, but it had no charge; it was electrically neutral. It was known that the atomic elements had different forms that had different atomic weights; the different forms of the same element are called isotopes. The existence of the neutron allowed scientists to explain how atoms of the same element, with the same charge (and therefore the same number of protons) could weigh a different amount. The answer was that they had different numbers of neutrons.

Quantum theory was an excellent theoretical instrument for understanding the structure of atoms and small numbers of particles, but it did not work well when applied to large numbers of particles. A new set of theories, known as quantum field theory, was created to study the larger picture. A particular quantum field theory known as Quantum Electrodynamics (QED) was extremely successful in understanding light (and electrodynamics in general) interacting with matter. Charged particles attracted and repelled each other by exchanging photons. One way of thinking about QED was suggested by one of its founders, Richard Feynman. Using the famous Feynman diagrams, he was able to illustrate clearly what the mathematics suggested. He could essentially assume that the photons and other particles began at one place, ended at another, and took every possible route to get there. Each of the infinite paths had a certain probability of occurring, and when he calculated the probabilities, he found that most of them canceled one another, leaving the observed result.

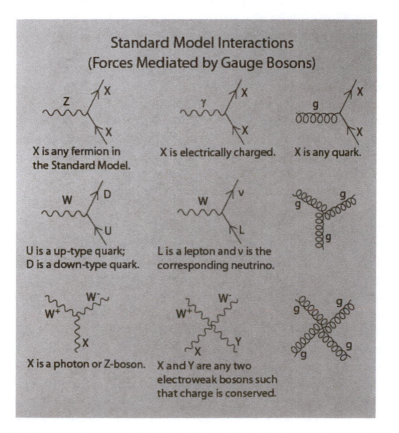

Figure 11.4 Feynman diagrams. Nobel Prize Winner Richard P. Feynman invented a simple way to describe particle interactions. © Wikimedia Commons (public domain).

A consequence of QED was that photons and electrons have the strange property of being discrete—but not individual. All electrons are the same and can be interchanged without changing the situation. This property is not true of stones, planets, or people, although it is possible that our feelings of our own uniqueness and our empathetic projection of uniqueness to nonhuman things produce error in our thinking about an essentially quantum universe.

By the 1940s, there were eight fundamental particles: the electron and positron, the proton and antiproton, the neutron and antineutron, the photon (which it turned out, was its own antiparticle), and another seemingly massless particle called a neutrino.

There were also four basic forces, or interactions. When Rutherford and others discovered that the nucleus was positively charged, it seemed that the positively charged particles in the nucleus should repel one another. Since the nucleus was stable, another force, much stronger than the electromagnetic force, had to be acting at a very short range. There was therefore a gravitational force, an electromagnetic force, and a strong nuclear force. Scientists added the weak force that caused particles to decay into other particles during a radioactive emission.

Researchers ultimately determined that the electromagnetic, weak, and strong forces were caused by two particles sharing and exchanging another sort of particle. For instance, electrically repelling protons bind together by exchanging a massive particle called a pion.

An analogy used by some physicists today to explain how particle exchange seems to exert a force describes two people in boats with their backs turned to each other. One throws a boomerang away from the boat. By Newton's third law (for every action, there is an equal and opposite reaction), the motion of the boomerang away from the boats will send the first boat closer. But then the boomerang circles around and is caught by the person in the second boat. The boomerang hitting the person's hand pushes the second boat closer. Thus, exchange of the boomerang pushes the boats closer. Of course, physicists also remind their audiences that particles do not have the same properties as boomerangs.

The fourth force, gravity, described in Einstein's general theory of relativity, changed the shape of space and time. It seemed to have none of the properties of the forces that acted on particles. For the past century, physicists have been unable to reconcile gravity with the other forces. We will discuss gravity in the following text.

Observing nuclear particles at first involved phosphorescent screens that would light up when hit by a particle and, after 1912, the Geiger counter that clicked when a particle entered it. But the instrument that turned out to be most useful was the cloud chamber. The Scottish physicist Charles Wilson (1869–1959) discovered that he could create a cloud of condensed water. When a charged particle passed through the supersaturated cloud, water droplets would condense along its path. A physicist could actually see the path of a particle.

Beginning in the late 1920s, particle accelerators enabled scientists to create high-energy beams of particles. The particles were sent through powerful synchronized electric and magnetic fields that caused the particles to move faster and faster. As new

Figure 11.5 Photo of particle tracks emerging from neutron-proton collision. Brookhaven billion volt cosmotron 1957. © Smith Collection/Gado/Getty Images.

accelerators were developed, they became larger, and they had to be housed in special buildings. Desktop-sized instruments were no longer sufficient. High-energy beams were used in nuclear medicine and other processes, and they could also be used to bombard other particles. After 1970, the most useful tools were composed of two accelerators that caused particles moving in opposite directions to smash into one another. The results of these collisions could be run through the descendants of the cloud chamber and the resulting particle tracks photographed and analyzed.

As accelerators, and later colliders, became larger and larger, scientists entered a phase that has been called "big physics." They discovered more and more bubble-chamber tracks that looked like new particles with different masses, spins, and other particle-like properties. No one could quite see why these particles, and not others, should exist. Some particles that had seemed like fundamental particles began to fall apart under higher and higher energies. In the mid-1960s, the American Murray Gell-Mann working with the Russian George Zweig, then conducting research in Switzerland, developed a theory of quarks. Quarks came in three versions (up, down, and strange) and did not exist outside of the particles that they combined with one another to create. The quark theory worked well to organize that proliferating stable of particles into a comprehensible system. Many particles could be understood if they were made up of three different quarks. But since quarks could not be observed as individual entities, the question arose: Did they really exist? Perhaps they were only a convenient way of organizing the data. But what became known as "the standard model" worked. Physicists could make predictions that were born out in observations at the large colliders.

Standard Model of Elementary Particles

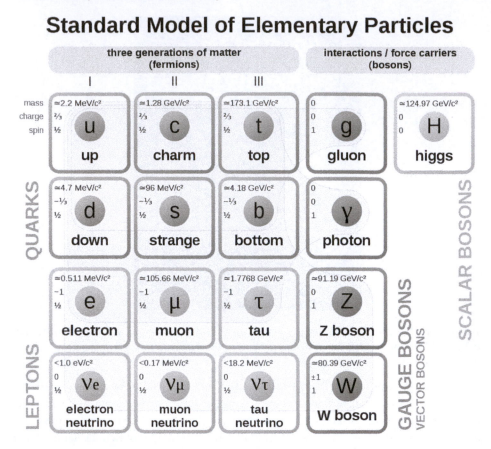

Figure 11.6 Diagram of the standard model. The fermions are particles, like protons, made up of quarks. The leptons are particles like electrons. The bosons are force carriers. © Wikimedia Commons (public domain).

Studying the physics of quarks required huge expenditures and even larger colliders. By the end of the twentieth and beginning of the twenty-first centuries, colliders were many kilometers in diameter. The European Organization for Nuclear Research (CERN), founded in 1954, organized particle physics research throughout Europe. Between 1998 and 2008, CERN built the Large Hadron Collider, the largest in the world, in Switzerland. It is 27 miles in circumference and 175 meters deep.

The Vastness of an Expanding Universe

As Albert Einstein completed the field equations of his general theory of relativity, he noticed that his theory demanded that pieces of matter in the universe would move away from each other. Einstein, like other astronomers and cosmologists of the time, was convinced that universe of spacetime was overall static. He therefore added a factor to his equations called "the cosmological constant." This factor insured that the equations would not predict an expansion of the universe.

Solutions to his equations also showed a universe that had no boundary but was also finite in size. If you imagine the surface of a sphere, you will see that it is finite but that it has no boundary. A person can travel forever over the surface of the sphere without bumping up against an end to the surface. Such a finite yet unbounded surface suggests that the two-dimensional world of the surface of the sphere also exists in three dimensions; the sphere has a volume that in our example is invisible. In the case of three-dimensional space, because there is a fourth dimension, time, three-dimensional space can also be finite yet unbounded. Perhaps there are more dimensions that we cannot imagine because our sensory systems and mental organization are built for four (three space and one time) dimensions. At the end of the twentieth century, an approach called "string theory" suggested that there were ten or more dimensions.

A few years after Einstein's theory was published, the Dutch astronomer Willem de Sitter (1872–1934) used the equations to propose a different geometry for the universe, one known as hyperbolic space. De Sitter's model was infinite, yet static. Simplifying, he began with a mathematical universe of spacetime alone, with no matter in it. He then added atoms slowly. It turned out that any light emitted by the atoms would shift in frequency toward the lower-frequency red part of the spectrum. They would also begin to move away from each other, because of the cosmological constant.

In 1921 the Swedish astronomer Knut Lundmark identified individual stars in the spiral nebula known cryptically as M33. The Estonian Ernst Öpik presented an argument that the Andromeda spiral nebula was 1.5 million light years away from the earth. This is a staggeringly large distance. Light moves at 180,000 miles per second. It goes 5.88 trillion miles in a year, so the distance of one light year is 5.88 trillion miles (note: a light year is a measurement of distance, not time). Multiply 5.88 trillion by 1.5 million and you have Öpik's estimate of the distance to the Andromeda spiral in miles. He actually underestimated. We now think the distance is 2.537 million light years. At the time, most astronomers thought the spiral nebulae were a strange feature of our own galaxy, the Milky Way, and that the Milky Way was the entire universe.

As the twentieth century dawned, astronomers had no way of measuring the mid distances to the stars. The parallax method of measuring distances (in which nearer objects appear to move faster than distant objects: think of the trees beside the road compared with the mountains in the distance as you drive by) worked for nearby stellar objects. But most stars and all nebulae were much too far away to use parallax. If astronomers only knew how bright the stars were, then they could estimate distance by seeing just how much the brightness had faded. But they had no way of measuring how bright the stars were.

The American astronomer Henrietta Swan Leavitt showed in 1908 that Cepheid variable stars (a kind of star whose brightness changed regularly) had a period that varied with its brightness. She could determine this because some Cepheid variables were close enough to use the parallax method. Now astronomers had a way of measuring distance by using brightness. Just find a Cepheid, see how fast it moved from one bright moment to the next, and you could know how bright it was. Then compare its brightness with its apparent brightness, and you would know how far away it was.

In the United States, Edwin Hubble directed the Mount Wilson Observatory with the largest telescope then in use. To get to the telescope, Hubble had to ascend to 6,000 feet above sea level on a nine-mile path. But the climbing was worth it, because he was finally able to see stars and then Cepheids in the Andromeda galaxy. He was therefore able to measure the distance and, at the end of 1924, announce that the Andromeda nebula was actually a galaxy like the Milky Way.

Yet another astounding revelation was to come. If you stand next to the road as a noisy truck approaches, you will notice that the noise seems to rise in pitch. As the truck passes you, however, it makes a kind of zooming sound as the pitch suddenly goes lower. This is known as the Doppler shift, and it applies to all waves, even light waves. If a light source is nearing you, the light will shift toward the blue. If it is receding, the light will shift to the red. Hubble and his colleagues Vesper Slipher and Milton Humason found that the light from distant galaxies had shifted toward the red. The galaxies were almost all rushing away from the earth. The further the galaxy, the more the red shift, and therefore the faster it was going. The universe seemed to be rapidly expanding.

In the 1930s, most scientists were convinced that the universe had always existed. The alternative had theological implications that few wanted to address on scientific grounds. But if the universe was expanding, then perhaps one could, in imagination, run the expansion backward, like a film. At some point, all the matter in the universe would be squeezed into a tiny space. Once the matter was squeezed into a point, one could start the movie running in the right way. The matter would explode in what was known as "the Big Bang." What existed before the big bang? Here, some scientists observed Wittgenstein's dictum: whereof one cannot speak; thereof one should remain silent. Others, like the Belgian astronomer and mathematician Georges Lemaitre (1894–1966), a Catholic priest, happily developed a consistent theory of a big bang. Others also made the case for an unknown being behind the big bang.

But Hermann Bondi, Thomas Gold, and Fred Hoyle offered another alternative in 1948 called the "steady-state theory." They claimed that the universe had always existed. New matter popped into existence at just the rate needed to maintain the density of the universe. As the new matter appeared, it fueled the expansion of the universe. Thus, the universe is not only the same everywhere in space; it is also the same everywhere in time. This idea, that the universe is homogeneous and isotropic in space and time, is called the perfect cosmological principle. In contrast, in the big bang model the universe can be homogeneous and isotropic in space, but not in time. Thus, a cosmological principle that is not perfect is all that is possible.

New telescopes continued to be invented and built. Electromagnetic radiation does not only come in the form of light. Radio telescopes strung radio receivers over a large territory. They were thus able to measure radiation with a long wavelength of several feet. Other telescopes detected X-rays, gamma rays, microwaves, infrared rays, and so forth. Other detectors picked up particles in the form of cosmic rays. Our picture of the universe expanded with each new invention, and new questions confounded the theorists.

Unfortunately for the steady-state theory, new evidence began to emerge in the 1960s that supported the big bang theory. At Cambridge, England, radio astronomer Martin Ryle showed that the energy ranges of extragalactic radio emissions were consistent with a big bang, but not a steady state. The discovery of quasars (extremely bright and highly energetic astronomical phenomena) that seemed to be far away (and thus farther back in time) suggested that the universe had been different in its earlier stages. Discovery of cosmic background radiation at just the frequencies predicted by the big bang theory clinched the deal, at least for big bang supporters. The steady-state theorists continued to try to interpret the data in their favor. The number of steady-state supporters continues to diminish.

The big bang theory also offered the possibility of understanding how the heavier elements formed. Just after the big bang, the universe would have been a sea of energy. How the energy transformed into matter was an interesting theoretical question that has largely been answered satisfactorily. Many elements seem to have been created by the pressures inside stars, but the heavy elements probably needed the pressures involved in the big bang itself.

Stars consist of immense amounts of matter and energy. The gravitational forces are huge, so stars should collapse in on themselves. However, the pressure of radiation being created as hydrogen atoms fuse to become helium atoms, and other sorts of fusions, creates an outward force that balances gravity. As the stars begin to reach the point where fewer fusions are possible, they start to implode under the force of gravity. If there is not enough matter to go further, the stars will turn into dwarf stars. However, if there is enough matter, the stars will collapse so far that the electrons will be forced into the nuclei of atoms, and the negatively charged electrons will combine with the positively charged protons to form neutrons that have no net charge. These neutron stars may give off energy in a pulsing fashion, thus creating the observational entities known as pulsars.

In 1916 the German mathematician Karl Schwarzschild had shown that Einstein's equations, published only the year before, could be solved to predict a singularity, a point where the curvature of spacetime becomes infinite. This seemed to be a mathematical curiosity that had no application to the actual universe, but in 1968 the American John Wheeler showed that at the point where a massive star had collapsed beyond the neutron star stage, it might continue to collapse until nothing could emerge. He called this a "black hole." Light could come in, but no light could get back out again. In 1973 Stephen Hawking showed that at the edge of a black hole X-rays would be produced and fly away from the black hole. Since the 1970s, scientists began to observe black holes everywhere. They lay at the center of galaxies as vast whirlpools of energy that continually sucked more energy in. What their galactic function was, no one knew.

As theoreticians worked on the equations of the universe, a number of issues cropped up. One fundamental issue had to do with the cause and nature of the expansion of the universe. It seemed that it was not just that stars and galaxies were flying away from us, but that spacetime itself was expanding. In 1979 the Russians Alexei Starobinsky and

Andrei Kinde and the American Alan Guth developed a theory in which there was an exponentially rapid expansion of spacetime (a billion times the speed of light) in the first seconds of the universe. This expansion solved a number of technical problems—so cosmologists were convinced that expansion had happened, even though they were not quite sure how.

But the universe held more surprises in store. Besides the initial inflation, the universe had been slowly expanding because of the force of the big bang. This explosive force should be gradually slowed by the force of gravity acting among all the stars and matter in the universe. Scientists had debated for some decades about whether the explosive force would dominate as the universe continued expanding forever, or whether gravity would slow the expansion until the universe started contracting again. Many scientists tended to prefer the expansion contraction model, because it would provide a way to avoid a sudden beginning. If the universe expanded, then contracted to a point and then exploded outward again, this cycle could go on forever.

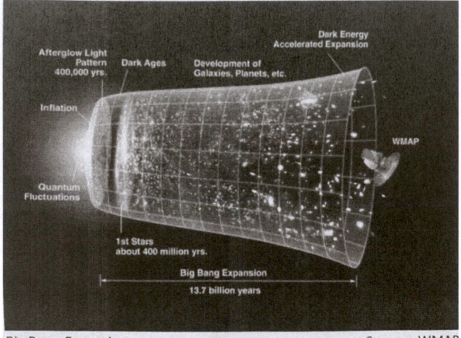

Big Bang Expansion   Source - WMAP

Figure 11.7 Expanding universe. Timeline. A representation of the evolution of the universe over 13.77 billion years. The far left depicts the earliest moment we can now probe, when a period of "inflation" produced a burst of exponential growth in the universe. (Size is depicted by the vertical extent of the grid in this graphic.) For the next several billion years, the expansion of the universe gradually slowed down as the matter in the universe pulled on itself via gravity. More recently, the expansion has begun to speed up again as the repulsive effects of dark energy have come to dominate the expansion of the universe. © Courtesy of NASA (public domain).

In the 1990s, cosmologists got a shock as they analyzed data from the largest telescopes in the world. It seemed that the universe was speeding up. No one had any idea what force might be producing this. Einstein's old cosmological constant was brought out, dusted off, and reinserted in the equations. An arbitrary constant, however, is not an explanation. Scientists introduced the term "dark energy" for whatever might be pushing the universe apart at a faster and faster rate. Dark energy might account for as much as 73 percent of the energy in the universe.

Furthermore, as astronomers observed the spinning of galaxies, they began to realize that the galaxies, and galactic clusters, were spinning so fast that they should fly apart. Just as with stars, a balance of forces maintains galaxies; the gravity of matter pulls them inward, and the energy of the motion of their spin keeps them stable in size. But there was not enough observable matter to produce the necessary gravitational forces to keep the spinning from sending their parts out into space. Imagine whirling a bucket around your head with a rope. If the rope breaks, the bucket will fly off. The rope is analogous to gravity, and in the case of galaxies scientists could not observe enough matter to overcome the centrifugal (inertial) force.

We know that matter exists because it emits, reflects, or absorbs light and other electromagnetic radiation, like radio waves and X-rays. Apparently, there was a kind of matter that did not interact with light. Scientists named it dark matter. So, by the beginning of the twenty-first century, cosmologists were embarrassed to admit that they had no idea what most of the universe consisted of. As far as they could calculate, the universe was composed of approximately 73 percent dark energy, 23 percent dark matter, and 4 percent regular matter. All of our theories are based on observational measurements that support elegant mathematical models. If we can only observe 4 percent of the universe, we must be somewhat humble about the comprehensiveness of our models. Of course, this state of affairs produces abundant work for the next generation of cosmologists.

The Stochastic Universe and the Multiverse

In quantum mechanics, every particle is represented by a wave function that is interpreted as a probability. In the generally accepted approach to understanding the wave function (some version of the Copenhagen interpretation), a particle does not exist as a particle until a measurement "forces" the particle to be some place and not in other places. That is, the particle exists only as a probability until interaction with the macroscopic world of a scientific observer constrains the particle to exist. Even then, if we know where the particle is, we do not know how fast it is going.

No physicist claims to understand what the magic of observation has to do with actually shaping reality. All we can say is that when particles are not being observed, they seem to have an existence as a probability but not as a determinable thing. The Heisenberg Uncertainty Principle implies that at its base, the physical world is probabilistic. The mathematics of probability works quite well, but every attempt to discover a nonprobabilistic model of particle interaction has so far failed.

Several physicists have suggested that if there are an infinite number of outcomes of a measurement, possibly all of the outcomes actually exist. That is, in a larger reality than our own restricted experience, every possible thing that could happen has happened. The idea that every possible path is taken by some version of a particle suggests that at every moment in time there is a grand forking process. Only one particle path leads to the universe we live in, but on some other level, all the other possible universes go on existing and go on branching. This idea is known as the Multiverse.

Strangely, at about the same time the physicist Richard Feynman was developing a forking theory of QED, the Argentine writer Jose Luis Borges wrote "El jardin de senderos que se bifurcan" ("The Garden of Forking Paths"—1941) that presents the same idea at the human level. Every decision that a human being can take was taken in some alternate universe. Time, then, is an ever-forking stream.

A related idea sees the universe as a completely stochastic (random) process. This view does not claim that every possibility exists, but rather that the movement of a particle from one state to another state over some amount of time is unpredictable. We began this text with a discussion of a clockwork universe in which everything was determined. In the stochastic universe, nothing can be predicted. Besides quantum mechanics, this idea is informed by chaos theory. The classic chaos process is known as the "butterfly effect." If a butterfly flaps its wings, weeks later the global weather system will be affected. The idea is that an immeasurably small event can have large consequences—or none. We can never know, so the possibility of prediction is impossible.

If the universe is indeed stochastic, then how is it possible that we discover laws that work. Gravity does not turn on and off. The answer to those that see stochastic processes at work is that the law of large numbers leads us to predictable answers. We may not be able to predict that path of a single particle, but we can predict the path of trillions. One electron in a baseball could be anywhere in the universe. But the baseball, consisting of uncountable numbers of particles, goes where it was thrown.

Conclusion: Science the Authority

The human world was increasingly technological. In the late twentieth century, most people lived in cities, and cities were highly artificial constructs. People traveled, communicated, received and prepared food, stayed healthy, and in general lived their lives supported by, and often controlled by, technology. Intellectual life became more interconnected and more interactive than it had been before. Technology brought new sources into the lives of academic researchers. It also changed the face of medicine, and with it the quality of life experienced by humans.

The relationship between science and technology changed. Whereas the steam engine was invented without a scientific understanding of heat or energy, by the last part of the twentieth century almost all technology arose after basic scientific research. The relationship was also mutual. New technology, like telescopes, produced previously unexpected observations that needed to be accounted for in scientific theories. Thus, new theories and ways of understanding the universe were stimulated by, and in turn stimulated, technology.

Science was the gold standard of human understanding of the physical world. While scientists *qua* scientists did not discuss aesthetic or ethical theory, philosophers and other thinkers were required to stay within the boundaries of scientific understanding as they developed their own theories about the beautiful or the moral. Philosophers often started their work by interpreting the human meaning of various scientific ideas.

Thus, the world described by science had an authority that resembled the authority of the Bible in the early modern world. The molecular structure of genes was not only intellectually satisfying, providing knowledgeable people a way to think about their nature; the molecular theory also was useful in providing new ways of engineering as experts tried to improve the human-experienced world. Similarly, the new cosmology forced humans to think of themselves as very small participants in a vast, strange, wonderful, and frightening universe. Humans began to see just how insufficient unaided intuitive understanding was. Nuclear physics, followed by particle physics, led the human imagination into worlds too tiny to comprehend without greatly expanding the imagination. Nuclear science opened the door to immense amounts of energy that could be used to provide as much electricity as humans could need. It also provided ways of destroying the world that makes human life possible. In nuclear science, as well as in the churning voraciousness of large black holes, humans could glimpse just how closely bound creation and destruction were.

CHAPTER 12
NEW ANOMALIES AND CHALLENGES

Figure 12.1 Leo Szilard and Albert Einstein. Szilard convinced Einstein to inform President Roosevelt of the scientific possibility of an atomic bomb. Since Werner Heisenberg worked for the Nazis, it was possible that Germany would build the bomb first. © Getty Images.

Building and Opposing the Bomb

Hungarian nuclear physicist and inventor Leo Szilard (1898–1964) played two diametrically opposed political roles in the decision making concerning the atomic bomb. Szilard studied and taught at the Friedrich Wilhelm University in Berlin and became a German citizen in 1930. But after the advent of the Nazis in 1933, the Jewish Szilard moved to London where he developed the idea of a nuclear chain reaction, an important step in developing the atomic bomb. Frightened that the Germans might develop the bomb, Szilard, who had moved to New York, wrote a letter to President Roosevelt encouraging him to begin a research project of his own. He and others recruited the prestigious Albert Einstein to sign the letter, and after Roosevelt received it in August 1939, the Manhattan Project was born.

But paradoxically, Szilard opposed using the bomb in war. As the first bomb was readied for testing in New Mexico, Szilard wrote another letter, this time to the overseer of the Manhattan Project, James Byrnes. In this letter, he laid out his arguments against using the bomb. First, He argued that until Japan knew of the bomb and refused to surrender, it would be immoral to destroy cities just as a warning. He was also quite concerned about the worldwide reputation of the United States if it were the first to use the bomb without trying its utmost to avoid having to drop it. When Szilard met resistance, he circulated petitions among scientists, but these also went nowhere. No one in authority would allow the petitions to reach President Truman. And some of the top scientists in the Manhattan Project refused to sign them.

Szilard was not alone in his opposition. Out of the seven five-star officers in the US military, six, including future president Dwight Eisenhower, opposed use of the bomb. Admiral William Leahy wrote that there was no military reason for using a "barbarous" weapon. One concern was that if the Germans had dropped it, the perpetrators would have been hung as war criminals. American officers did not like thinking of themselves as war criminals.

Truman and his advisers decided that the bomb was necessary to save American lives. For decades after the war, the decision about using the bomb was debated in a variety of forums. By the late 1950s, large anti-bomb movements were scattered throughout Europe. As atmospheric testing of the hydrogen bomb spread radioactive fallout throughout the world, opposition grew more intense.

But at the same time, scientists found that nuclear energy could also be harnessed to provide vast sources of electrical energy that could be used to improve the quality of European life. The paradox between nuclear bombs as the destroyers of worlds and nuclear power plants as the servants of humankind echoed inconclusively as Europe strove to build a better future.

Chapter Map

Following the Second World War, the allies (the Soviet Union, the United Kingdom, France, and the United States) faced the question of how to reconstruct Europe in the wake of unforeseen and almost unfathomable destruction. In the end, Europe split into two nuclear-armed camps in a cold war that divided a communist East and a democratic, capitalist West.

The Western allies realized that the Great Depression had exposed the flaws in lightly regulated free enterprise. After the war, Western European economies took off, and the prosperity gave them an opportunity to invent social insurance programs to protect their citizens from the vagaries of the market. Western Europe was built on a capitalist economic base that produced the funding for insurance of an adequate life for all citizens. The communist East adopted the five-year plan system initiated by Stalin. Ultimately, they had to build a wall to keep their most talented citizens from seeking their fortune in the West.

Apart from the theoretical and practical work in the public sphere, other thinkers continued to philosophize. Existentialism emerged from phenomenology (Chapter 10). Existentialists believed that there was no meaning to life until human individuals created it. It was a philosophy of both freedom and responsibility. But a new movement known as structuralism focused on the hidden structures that reflected human minds and human society. Beginning with observations, structuralists built models of abstract networks of relationships explaining human thought and action. These structures were intended to accurately apply to human beings in general, and thus they should have been transferable from culture to culture.

The chapter continues with a discussion of post-suffrage feminism. The Englishwoman Virginia Woolf and the Frenchwoman Simone de Beauvoir wrote seminal books analyzing the condition of women in Europe. European women sought to understand and challenge the underlying patriarchal structures that constrained their thoughts and actions.

In Germany (and for a time in the United States), a school of thinkers known as the Frankfurt School used Marxist ideas in conjunction with other ideas (like those of Freud) to render Marxism relevant to the twentieth century.

Part I: Ideas Worked Out in Practice

Cold War

At the end of the war, Soviet troops controlled most of Eastern Europe. The other allies, Great Britain, France, and the United States, controlled Western Europe. The line demarcating the two zones ran right through Germany. It soon became clear that no one in power wanted to begin a second war among the allies to contest this reality.

In Eastern Europe, the Soviets were greatly respected for their ability to defeat the Germans. From a mostly peasant country after the First World War, the Soviet Union had become an industrial power capable of producing arms and organization sufficient to overcome Germany, the militarily most capable country before the Second World War. For a time, right after the war, it appeared that the Soviet Union was willing to work with noncommunist groups who had the interests of workers and peasants at heart. Few in the East wanted to return to the seemingly failed system of liberal democracy, and the Soviets seemed to be willing to act slowly in implementing land reforms, expropriation of the property of the wealthy, and economic controls to move people slowly toward communist rule. In fact, most Eastern Europeans yearned for social justice more than they wished for a parliamentary democracy controlled by elites. As the Soviets redrew borders, they restored land that had been taken over by Germany. Most Easterners were nationalists, and they were willing to embrace coalition governments that included communists.

In 1946 the American diplomat George Kennan sent a telegram from Moscow describing the Soviet Union as implacably opposed to the United States and set on expanding communist rule throughout the world. Kennan recommended a policy of containment. A few months later, Winston Churchill gave a speech in America in which he accused the Soviet Union of building an "iron curtain" from the north to the south of Europe. The Soviets responded by accusing the British of imitating Hitler by pursuing a racist nationalism that was intent on world domination by expanding the British Empire. The Soviets then accused the Americans of being controlled by monopoly capitalists

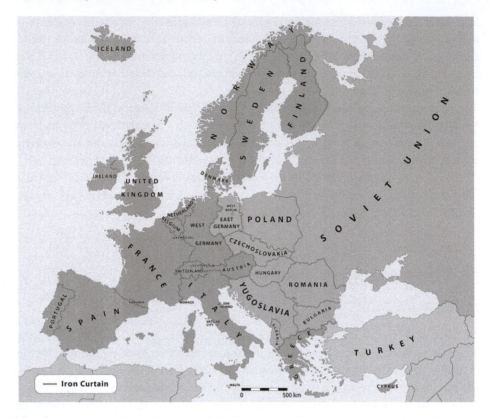

Map 3 Cold War Europe. The result of the Second World War was a Europe divided into two grand experiments: Communism in the East and Social Democracy in the West.

who wanted to wage a war to attain world domination. Stalin defended his attempts to make sure that neighboring countries were supportive and loyal to the USSR. The writer George Orwell coined the phrase "cold war" to describe the situation of enmity without waging war. At that point, Stalin abandoned any idea of building coalition governments in the East European countries controlled by the Soviet Union. Henceforth, all governments would be communist and loyal to the Soviets.

Western Europe was financially supported by the United States. The United States, through the Truman Doctrine, described the conflict as one between freedom and totalitarianism. The United States sent arms to Greece during its civil war and also offered Marshall Plan funds to all European countries including the Soviet Union. The Soviet Union refused the funds on behalf of itself and its satellites. But the countries of Western Europe ultimately received $13 billion ($800 billion in today's dollars). The 1950s were a time of great economic growth and productivity increases in the West.

The sticking point was Germany. After a great deal of negotiating and posturing, Germany was administratively divided among the four wartime allies: The Soviet Union, the United States, the United Kingdom, and France. The latter three combined their sections to produce a united Western sector that in 1949 became the BRD,

Bundesrepublik Deutschland (the Federal Republic of Germany). In the same year, the Soviet sector became the DDR, Deutsche Demokratische Republik (the German Democratic Republic). Both countries housed foreign troops.

The beginnings of the North Atlantic Treaty Organization (NATO) involved a mutual defense treaty signed by France and Britain in 1947. Gradually that alliance grew to include other Western European countries, and in 1949 the United States and Canada were included to form NATO. In 1950 NATO proved its worth in the Korean War. When the BRD was included in NATO in 1955, the Soviet Union and the Eastern Bloc countries created the Warsaw Pact in response.

The tangled roots of European ideas now supported two great political/economic systems, Democratic Socialism and Communism, warily eying one another across a nuclear barrier. Two military alliances faced each other across Europe. These two military alliances never confronted each other directly, although they fought proxy wars in countries like Korea, Vietnam, and Afghanistan. Thus, the Cold War never quite became hot.

One reason that the Cold War never became hot was the presence of thermonuclear weapons. After the atomic bomb, a much powerful bomb based on the fusion of nuclei instead of the fission of nuclei was created. This hydrogen bomb (so called because hydrogen fused into helium, releasing much more energy than was produced in the fission of uranium) was capable of destroying whole cities. At their peaks, the United States had over 30,000 warheads and the Soviet Union almost 40,000. Clearly, they could destroy each other several times over. They were kept from doing so by a doctrine called mutually assured destruction (MAD). Each knew that if they attacked the other, the other could in turn destroy the attacker.

Several dystopian novels explored the world after an incomplete nuclear war. For instance, in 1957 the British author Neville Shute wrote *On the Beach* in which no human life is left in the northern hemisphere, but survivors in Australia await the coming of the cloud of fallout radiation that will kill them all. The populations of both NATO and the Warsaw pact lived in intermittent terror, and scientists pictured a "doomsday" clock on the cover of *The Bulletin of Atomic Scientists* that showed the number of minutes until midnight: doomsday. In 1953, as the Soviet Union tested more and more bombs, it reached two minutes to midnight.

Eastern Europe

Stalin's prewar approach in the USSR, periodic purges and five-year economic plans were the order of the day in Poland, Czechoslovakia, Hungary, Bulgaria, Romania, and Albania. The non-Soviet countries of the East would industrialize. (Marshall Tito in Yugoslavia decided that there were many roads to socialism and refused to subordinate his country to the Soviet Union.) The Soviet Union was determined to extract resources from Germany to pay for the destruction the Germans had wrought during the war. They also made sure that the other countries of Eastern Europe supported them. Where did the investment capital for the industrialization process come from? The answer is from the agricultural sector and the consumers. All resources were turned toward fulfilling five-year plans to build heavy industry. The 1950s and early 1960s saw high employment and increased manufacturing output.

The master plan for each country in the Soviet bloc was to increase productivity in agriculture—meaning that the output per agricultural worker would increase manyfold. The only way to greatly increase productivity was to mechanize agriculture with large equipment, and such mechanization required vast unfenced fields. Thus, small peasant farmers had to be forced to become workers on large collectives or to leave their farms for jobs in the cities. Collectivization of agriculture provided the food for the growing factory-worker population in cities.

Ideally, every citizen would be eligible for social benefits. Education would be universal and free. Older and disabled workers would be provided equal pensions. Childcare would be available for working parents, and a stipend would be paid to families with young children. Health care would be available to all on an equal basis. The reality was necessarily different, especially in the early years. Eastern Europe had been devastated. There were not enough medical personnel to staff the hospitals and clinics. Distribution of food was uneven. A "gray market" developed—goods were held out of circulation to be exchanged in an informal barter system. In short, the reality never lived up to the ideal. For older adults, who remembered the harsh vicissitudes of peasant life, things often seemed to be improving. To their children, however, who had grown up in cities and who were able to access a variety of forms of information from the West, life seemed drab and restricted in comparison with the images and ideas that made their way past the iron curtain. In East Germany in 1953, in Hungary in 1956, and in Czechoslovakia in 1968, revolts instigated by students broke out. In all cases, Soviet tanks and troops eventually entered the country to quell the rebellions. In 1961 the East German government felt compelled to build a wall across Berlin and the country in order to keep their most talented citizens from seeking lives in the West.

Western Europe

The primary problem facing Western European countries was rebuilding their economies. The United States was the natural leader because: (1) the United States was by far the greatest military power and had troops within Western Europe; (2) the United States' industrial infrastructure emerged from the war unscathed; (3) the United States had a larger economy than any European country; and (4) the dollar was the most reliable world currency.

During the war, John Maynard Keynes worked with the American Harry Dexter White to brainstorm ideas about the postwar international economic order. These discussions resulted in conferences where economic policies could be debated, the most important of which was the Bretton Woods conference in July 1944 that included forty-four allied nations. Looming over the conference were the economic failures experienced after the First World War. All wanted to avoid the pitfalls set by the disastrous Versailles Treaty. It was clear that cooperative trade was a surer path to prosperity than trade restrictions.

The most important underlying assumption was the need for open markets. In order to accomplish this goal, all of the members pledged to peg their currencies to the dollar, which in turn was pegged to gold ($35 an ounce), thus establishing a reliable system of monetary exchange. The US dollar became the noncommunist world's reserve currency.

The other side of the agreements was to establish international agencies to regulate trade and monetary flows. Britain, represented by Keynes, proposed that nations running a trade surplus should be required to help trade-deficit countries by loaning them money, building factories in them, or importing from them. The United States, the main surplus nation, vetoed that proposal. Essentially, the United Kingdom was interested in full employment and economic growth, while the United States wanted price stability and free trade. The compromise was the International Monetary Fund (IMF), set up to offer loans to debtor countries based on funds donated by all of its members. The idea was to ensure against large devaluations of stressed currencies. Another new institution, the World Bank (then the International Bank for Reconstruction and Development), focused on loans to countries that needed help in reconstruction. Essentially, the Bretton Woods agreement attempted a regulated world economic system without setting up a world government.

The United States was running a huge trade surplus, which meant that dollars found their way back to the United States, thus creating a world dollar shortage. One answer to this problem was the Marshall Plan, which provided aid to European countries in their rebuilding efforts. Essentially the United States engineered a balance of payments deficit for itself in order to keep the new world economy afloat.

The result of this thoughtful approach to constructing an interlocked world economy was a period of growth in the 1950s and 1960s that astounded prophets of doom who had based their predictions on the post–First World War example. Europe's economy grew at unprecedented rates. Within each country's economy, various processes led to the new prosperity. As in the East, peasants and small farmers, especially in Germany, moved to the cities. Agriculture became more productive and food more plentiful while at the same time factories had sufficient workers. Germany, the land of the *Wirtschaftswunder* (economic miracle), began to import "guest workers" from countries like Turkey.

Developing Nontotalitarian Social Welfare Systems

This prosperity encouraged governments to take unprecedented steps to care for their citizens. Before the war, many Europeans outside of Italy and Germany had been attracted to fascism because all citizens had a place and, at least in theory, those citizens who played their parts were supported. In England and France, the conservative response to the Great Depression was to let the markets work—an option that devastated the many people who were unemployed. In Germany, after the ascent of Hitler, everyone was employed. In Italy, unemployment was relatively low. Of course, unemployment had been nonexistent in the Soviet Union as it rushed to industrialize.

After the war, however, fascism had been thoroughly discredited. Western governments needed a response that combined the social welfare of fascism with an absence of totalitarianism. They found the model in policies they had themselves adopted earlier in the twentieth century. In the late 1940s and early 1950s, Western Europeans developed the modern democratic and capitalist welfare state. They did so out of compassion and conviction, but fortunately the postwar prosperity supported their plans. In fact, it has turned out that the social welfare policies that were adopted tended to increase rather than decrease national prosperity as measured in GDP.

Traditionally the church, especially in Catholic countries, delivered social welfare. In non-Catholic countries, conservative individualists often viewed poverty as failure on the part of the poor. In general, elites thought the free market would ultimately take care of social problems. But by the end of the nineteenth century, it was becoming clearer that mass production could lead to mass unemployment. And whatever the cause of an individual's particular circumstances, mass unemployment was a social problem.

In the middle of the nineteenth century, trade unions initiated unemployment insurance. Private insurance was well-enough established that people understood the idea of sharing risk. The industrial world was a world of uncertainty, and it made sense to establish large pools of people who might pay a premium in order to be protected against misfortune. If everyone paid in, perhaps aided by employers or the government, then everyone would have a claim in case of injury or job loss. Others thought that the government should pay all or most of the premium. Behind this idea is an assumption that occasional need is a normal state of affairs in this new industrial society. Opposed to the idea was the distinction that many made between the "deserving" and the "undeserving" poor.

The first modern national welfare system grew up in recently unified Germany in the 1880s under Chancellor Otto von Bismarck. As the socialists pushed for more protection from the state, Bismarck could see that they posed a threat to him. He tried outlawing socialist meetings, but the socialists still occupied many of the seats in the Reichstag. Bismarck, hoping to head them off, decided to out-socialist the socialists. In 1883, he proposed legislation to provide health insurance for the workers. He mandated that employers pay one-third and workers the rest of the premiums for "sickness care" that workers could draw on for up to thirteen weeks. By 1891 Germany had laws to control workers' hours, restricting children from working more than ten hours, and only in the daytime. They also regulated workplace safety. The Bismarck approach informed efforts in Western Europe during the twentieth century. Both France and the UK instituted insurance-based welfare systems that covered health, old age, unemployment, child welfare, and so forth. No one adopted a system supported by general taxes. Giving money to the poor was too controversial.

Two sets of ideas affected the Western European approach after the Second World War. In 1924, in Sweden, Alva Myrdal (1902–86) and her husband Gunnar Myrdal (1898–1987) coauthored the book *Kris i befolkningsfrågan* (*Crisis in the Population Question*), which focused on how to maintain individual rights for women while still promoting childbirth since Sweden needed population growth. They argued that the society needed to support women, not just for the good of women but also for the good of society. In later books, Alva Myrdal showed how poverty inhibited good childcare and effective education. Meanwhile, Gunnar Myrdal and others developed a Keynesian economic approach that advocated government deficits and spending on public works in hard economic times. When the work of the two Myrdals was combined, the ideas behind the Swedish welfare state emerged. After the Second World War, Sweden led the way as all of the countries in Western Europe developed welfare states of one sort or another.

In Great Britain, a committee headed by Baron William Henry Beveridge (1879–1963) recommended a complete overhaul of the British social welfare system to eliminate the five "Giant Evils" in society: squalor, ignorance, want, idleness, and disease. The postwar legislation emphasized taxation-based programs rather than insurance systems. The jewel in the British welfare crown was the National Health System.

The Western European Idea

Thus, the ideas that generally triumphed in Western Europe were a strong capitalist economy with relatively open trade, international institutions that fostered cooperation and the easy movement of money and goods, a welfare system in which all citizens had health care, family leave, free education, and free health care. In some countries, general tax revenues supported the programs; in others, focused mandatory insurance payments formed the base of a kind of tax. It turned out that most people wanted to work, and societies prospered in the 1950s and 1960s.

Part II: Ideas Worked Out Theoretically

Modernist intellectuals continued to burrow deeper and deeper to find the abstract structures at the center of human knowledge. As structuralists dug, they confronted individualist existentialists who refuted the very idea of core ideas and values as they claimed that each person was free to create value and meaning. The existence of the bomb reminded all that human striving could cease forever.

Existentialism

Directly emerging from phenomenology (see Chapter 10), existentialism was largely the creation of Jean-Paul Sartre (1905–80), who was born in Paris where he studied philosophy and psychology. He taught in various high schools until after the Second World War. During the war, he served France as a meteorologist and spent nine months in a prisoner of war camp, where he read Heidegger's *Being and Time*. After the war, he helped found *Les Temps modernes* (*Modern Times*) a periodical that was a major outlet for intellectuals. After the war, he became perhaps the best-known French author and philosopher. Much of his work was literary, and he was awarded the Nobel Prize for Literature in 1964. He chose to decline the prize, because, as he said, he did not want to be transformed by the award and did not want to take sides in the Cold War.

Figure 12.2 Simone de Beauvoir and Jean-Paul Sartre, 1948. The two great philosophers worked together constantly. © Ullstein Bild Dtl./Getty Images.

The word "existentialism" comes from Sartre's claim that "existence precedes essence." That is, human beings do not have a prefigured meaning, but create their own meaning as they live their lives. Thus, human beings have nothing to live up to. The existentialist stance can be contrasted with a religious stance in which people attain their own meaning by following God's plan for their existence. In this case, their essence (meaning) precedes their existence. Sartre, like many European intellectuals, was an atheist.

Since there is no overarching plan for human beings, they are "condemned to be free." No matter how much they yearn for someone to tell them what to do, there is no one who can do that. If they choose to follow another person's commands or suggestions, then they have made the choice to obey. Sartre told the story of a student of his who during the German occupation came to ask Sartre's opinion about whether he should leave his mother, who was still mourning the death of the student's brother, to go to England to fight with the Free French Forces. The student was torn because if he were to die, it would destroy his mother. The student thought that perhaps he should stay to tend for his mother. Sartre, of course, answered that the choice was up to the student. There was no answer that anyone else could give. And, Sartre remarked, by coming to ask Sartre the existentialist, the student must have known what Sartre's advice would be. He chose to consult someone who would cast the choice back on him. Freedom is always constrained by circumstances, but within those circumstances, we are free to choose.

Sartre noted that there was one value implied in existentialism, and that value was freedom. A writer must always choose "the side of freedom." The choice of freedom, and the recognition that at every moment we are free to choose, is the route to living an authentic life. For instance, if we go to church, we can do that authentically if we do not do it because we "ought" to do it, but rather because we choose to do it. Perhaps most of the people in the church are there for inauthentic reasons: to please God, please their parents, appear pious in the community, and so forth. The correct answer to most requests is not, "I can't," but rather "I choose not to."

We make choices, but we are not alone. Other people who are also making choices surround us, and sometimes the choices of others will affect our own ability to achieve success in our projects. We are historically situated in a world of other free-choosers. Our choices, then, must be made in the context of the present situation. During the war, the German occupation changed the meaning of being French, or being Jewish. Before the war, these may not have been important identity markers for someone. Yet during the war, these aspects of identity changed what one could do. The war affected everyone's actions.

Sartre's first literary success was the 1938 novel *La nausée* (*Nausea*) in which the protagonist finds himself confronted by the meaninglessness of pure being. A depressed Antoine Roquentin undertakes historical research, but he finds himself confronted by a meaningless existence that is like featureless dough. Everything seems contingent, as if it could have been otherwise. Nothing seems firm and fixed. In a key scene, Roquentin sees a chestnut tree and feels a fresh wave of nausea. He sees that the tree has no point; it just sits there randomly, a symbol of all of being that just is—pointless. Eventually Roquentin decides that he can create meaning in art, in writing.

In his 1943, philosophical book *L'être et le néant* (*Being and Nothingness*), Sartre distinguished two kinds of being: being in-itself (lacking consciousness, like rocks), and being for-itself (human consciousness). But being for-itself has no existence until it creates itself; it is like a hole, a nothing. In fact, human consciousness is the action of intention. Intention is not a thing; it is an action; it points to things. Even though we seem to ourselves to have an identity, in fact that identity is all free choice. So, Sartre concludes, because we are nothing, we are free.

Bad faith is an important Sartrean concept. Bad faith is lying to oneself about one's condition. We can lie to ourselves about our identity, for instance thinking that we are the roles we play at our jobs. We can also display bad faith by denying our freedom. Sartre writes of the waiter who plays the role of a waiter but does not express *himself*. We can escape bad faith by realizing that we are free and choosing to play a role. If we are authentic, we realize that we could choose otherwise.

But what about others? The presence of another person leads us to think of ourselves as objects. We see ourselves as if through the other's eyes, and we have a tendency to judge ourselves by what we think are the standards of the other. We feel shame in the gaze of the other. But if that other turns out, on second glance, to be a lifelike mannequin, we can then return to being for ourselves alone. So, introducing the figures of others creates another way of being: being for another person.

Many of these ideas are illustrated in Sartre's fiction. For instance, in "The Childhood of a Leader" (1938) Sartre portrays a character that calls himself an anti-Semite so that he can have an identity. He is afraid of freedom, and so demonizes others to preserve his identity. In his 1944 play *Huis clos* (*No Exit*), Sartre portrays people caught in a room after death. As they gaze at each other, they judge. No one can escape. The meaning, Sartre later explained, was that after death others remember us, and there is nothing we can do to change their memories.

After the Second World War, Sartre declared himself a communist, although communism seemed to violate every principle of existentialism. He explained this by saying that philosophy was not timeless, but rather existentialism was situated in a social world. This was a time, for Sartre, that one should confront capitalism and its effects. But as one might expect, Sartre tried to change Marxism by writing a book, *Critique de la raison dialectique* (*Critique of Dialectical Reason*) (1960) in which he tried to replace the Marxist idea of "praxis" with the existentialist notion of "project," a freely chosen activity in which a person could become entirely absorbed. Sartre became disillusioned with Marxism after the Soviet invasion of Hungary.

Interestingly, most of the existentialist philosophers denied they were existentialist. Since Existentialism is an offshoot of phenomenology, many identified with Husserl and Heidegger more than they did with Sartre and his "existence precedes essence." Other routes to existentialism went through the Danish Søren Kierkegaard or the German Friedrich Nietzsche. Kierkegaard taught that Christianity is subjective, and his philosophy focused on the individual nature of human freedom. Nietzsche taught that human beings are free and as humans express a will to power. Both turned away from the rationalism found in traditional philosophy.

Maurice Merleau-Ponty (1908–61) studied the phenomenologists and combined them with psychology. He maintained that the body and mind were inextricably intertwined. We know, through proprioception, where our limbs are without looking. We do not naturally adopt a "phenomenological attitude" when we interact with the world; we just act. When we think, our consciousness does not just see streaks or smells, but we directly experience things like trees. So, for Merleau-Ponty, philosophy starts with the way people experience the world: with their bodies in action, with their minds seeing wholes rather than parts, and in interaction with other people. He followed the Gestalt psychologists who focused on the whole, the Gestalt, rather than the parts of perception. To them, all parts are parts of a greater whole, the field of perception.

The French-Algerian Albert Camus (1913–60) began his adulthood with a one-year stint as a communist who had not read Marx. He joined the Communist Party because it seemed to offer a way to resolve the growing tensions between native Algerians and French Algerians. He soon moved to journalism where he could investigate the problems raised by both colonialism and fascism. By 1940 he had moved to Paris and become the editor-in-chief of the newspaper *Paris-Soir*. He published the novel *L'Étranger* (*The Stranger*) in 1942 along with the philosophical essay *Le Mythe de Sisyphe* (*The Myth of Sisyphus*), which were complimented by the play *Caligula*. All three emphasized the nature of life as absurd. For Camus, there was no meaning in life, and, therefore, all was random and absurd. In *The Stranger*, a man kills another man for no reason. When he is arrested, tried, and condemned to death, he refuses to find excuses for his act, but accepts the fact that he chose what he did and is responsible for it. In the *Myth of Sisyphus*, Camus starts with the question of whether the absurdity of existence implies that we should commit suicide. His symbol for absurdity is Sisyphus, condemned to roll a rock up a mountain only to see it roll back down when he seems to have completed the task. He wonders what Sisyphus must think as he trudges down the mountain to roll the rock up again. Camus concludes with the idea when Sisyphus recognizes the truth of his fate, he can accept his absurd existence and become happy.

After the Second World War, in which he played a part in the resistance against the Germans, Camus wrote another set of books, a novel, *La Peste* (*The Plague*), a philosophical essay, *L'Homme révolté* (*The Rebel*), and a play, *Les Justes* (*The Just Assassins*). In *The Plague*, Oran is quarantined to contain a fatal disease. Dr. Bernard Rieux stays in the city to treat the victims. He does so because it is his job to treat the sick. He is neither religious nor altruistic, and he knows he cannot win the battle with death. Finally, the battle is over, and the Plague dies down. But Rieux recognizes that the Plague bacillus is still present and that someday it will resume its death-work. The plague is a metaphor—perhaps for the Nazis and totalitarianism. The associated book, *The Rebel*, examines the difference between revolution and rebellion. Revolution attempts to overturn society and government for the better. But the former leaders are replaced by the revolutionaries, who then become tyrants in their own way. The rebel is a person who fights injustice—but has no illusions about perfecting the human condition. Evil must be fought, but our existence continues to be absurd. No perfection is possible.

In 1957 Camus won the Nobel Prize for Literature. He died as a passenger in a car crash in 1960.

Existentialism is essentially a philosophy for the individual. Within a meaningless and absurd world, only the human individual matters. The world is not prefigured, but rather awaits the decisions of individuals who in their freedom make choices. Out of their choices, the world takes shape. But at about the same time that existentialism arose, an analytic approach called structuralism grew up that emphasized the similarity among all individuals and the primacy of culture for the existence of all human beings.

Structuralism

As we saw in a previous chapter, modernist thought often expressed itself as a search for underlying truths that were themselves not apparent in sensory observations or in common sense, that is, on the surface. This search for deep levels of meaning occurred in the human sciences. In linguistics, psychology, anthropology, and sociology, researchers sought to identify structures that underlay human thought, action, emotion, and perception. The structuralist approach was much more interested in studying present-day systems of relations than in examining their historical development. Thus, a distinction between the diachronic (historical: unfolding over time) and synchronic (same time: co-present) studies arose. Although there are important precursors early in the twentieth century, structuralism was mostly developed in the decades just before and after the Second World War.

Structures are sets of relationships. For example, the human brain consists of hundreds of trillions of synapses, connections between brain cells. The relationship of the brain to human thought is defined by the relationships among these synapses. Human thought, then, is determined by a structure, independent of what particular thoughts exist at any one time. A person might be thinking about Marxist or Capitalist theories—it doesn't matter for the study of thought itself. As the quasi-structuralist Canadian critic Marshall McLuhan wrote: "The medium is the message." Our experience of the world changes when we watch TV instead of listening to the radio. It doesn't matter what we see or hear: the fact of engaging in the structure of one medium instead of another makes all the difference.

Unfortunately, we cannot easily observe synapses at work. We experience thought, but we don't experience our brains at work. Structuralists, then, usually do not study brains, but rather the products of human thought and behavior and then seek the underlying structures that generate these human phenomena. It turns out that in principle we are capable of more thoughts than there are synapses (especially since most synapses are not involved with thought). Importantly, then, if the human brain is the generator, it generates only templates that can be filled in with multitudes of ideas.

One way of trying to understand thought was to develop tools to observe the brain at work so we could map synapses. (Today we are attempting this with sensitive electrodes, MRI studies, and the like.) Another way was to examine thoughts, behaviors, and institutions and try to develop models of the underlying patterns beneath these thoughts. A distant hope was that such structures could later be shown to in some way or another to mirror synaptic structures. This latter is the approach taken by most structuralists in the human sciences.

Importantly, the structural models developed by structuralist linguists, anthropologists, sociologists, psychologists, and so forth are abstract. They are abstract because they do not concern themselves with observable entities, but rather with the relationships among a relatively finite set of hypothetical underlying capacities that underlie observable entities. This approach can be contrasted with the approach of phenomenologists who concentrate on direct experience.

Are such structural relationships real in any concrete sense, or are they heuristic tools that allow predictions to be made? Is the only reality in the molecules of the brain cell—or in the utterances or performances of human individuals? Or is there a kind of whole that is expressed in logical or mathematical models? Such questions have lain at the heart of human inquiry for the past several centuries. Is Galileo's claim that God wrote the book of nature in the language of mathematics a useful metaphor even today? That is, do mathematics lie behind our physical and human universes? If not, how can we explain the dependable regularity that we experience in our interactions with a world outside of our own minds?

Linguistic Structuralism

Most structural thinkers find their way back to the Swiss scholar Ferdinand de Saussure (1857–1913). Saussure used the metaphor of the game of chess: the game does not depend on the physical pieces but rather on the relationships among the pieces. For Saussure, the parole (the speech of everyday life) expressed an invisible layer of abstraction called the langue. He saw the relationship between parole and langue as arbitrary. Saussure published little, and much of what we know of his system comes from student notes. But he was the starting point for structuralist investigations, and scholars supported, disputed, and developed his ideas after his death.

For Saussure, language was a human phenomenon. The actual sounds or symbols were merely signifiers of something else, the signified. The signified could be a perception, but it could also be an idea, a feeling, a law, a fictional character, an action, a grammatical form, or many other kinds of mental acts. Signifier and signified together were a sign, and, in Saussure's view, signs were the building blocks of language. A language utterance put signifiers in some sort of relationship that reflected a set of relationships among the signified. Thus, the structure of language utterances reflected an underlying structure among objects that existed outside of language, but not necessarily outside of the human mind.

Different languages use different sounds (words) to signify the same thing. The signifier differs, but the signified remains the same. For structuralists, the same thing holds in culture. Actual cultural forms vary, but they reflect an underlying constant. So, structuralists strive to deduce underlying forms by comparing different languages or cultures. The key is the comparative method.

The importance of the structuralist approach lies not so much in the details of analysis, fascinating as they are, but rather in the assumptions and claims the structuralist approach has made about the nature of being human. To structuralists, human beings were, at base, very similar to one another. By examining language not as just a set of perishable utterances, but as a finite set of semantic and grammatical structures that could generate an infinite number of possible utterances, structuralists hoped to discover something about the structure of the human mind.

Different languages sound and act quite differently. Different languages, for example, have different verb tenses. Some languages include a great deal of information in one word, while others use a string of words to express the same idea. One example that became quite important in the scholarly discussion was the organization of color. Some languages distinguished fine differences in color, while others blurred over such distinctions. The structuralist approach tends to look below such differences to search for commonalities. For structuralists, languages can be translated accurately from one to the other, even if the translation is made with some difficulty. There thus must be an underlying linguistic structure that is expressed differently in different languages.

An alternate approach is exemplified in the Sapir—Whorf hypothesis of linguistic relativity—a claim that different cultures experience the world differently because their language determines their thought. So, for example, if a language lacks a future tense, perhaps that culture does not experience time as having a future orientation. The structuralist answer would be that the language without a clear future tense can get across the same idea by using additional words. In one case, culture determines basic mental possibilities. In the other, we all have the same capabilities, whether or not our languages differ.

We have seen earlier versions of linguistic relativity in the German romantics, many of whom thought that a nonnative speaker of German could not possibly attain the insights available to Germans. In the 1920s, the German linguist Johann Leo Weisgerber (1899–1985) developed a linguistically relative theory of "content-related grammar." As he studied the historical development of German, he found that while early German had many color words, modern German had mastered the same material with only eight words for color. The basic color words, like red and blue, are abstractions, although modern speakers may think of them as concrete. Weisgerber was actually more extreme in his linguistic relativity and his ideas about how language determines experience and perception than either Whorf or Sapir.

George Orwell's *1984* is built in part on the idea of linguistic relativity. In this book, published in 1949, the totalitarian government systematically removed words from the language to limit the thoughts of the citizens. Newspeak made it impossible for citizens to criticize the government. They did not have the linguistic tools to imagine that they might be oppressed.

The main sets of ideas that seemed to make linguistic relativity obsolete were related to the idea of "universal grammar." The German Eric Heinz Lenneberg (1921–75) was forced to flee Nazi Germany when still young. He ended up in the United States, where he became a professor of psychology and neurobiology. In 1954, he and the psychologist Roger Brown published a paper in which they critiqued Whorf's ideas from a biological standpoint. They were committed to the idea that objective reality was the same for all human beings. They decided to study how the different coding systems of different languages in describing color affected perception. They indeed found that Zuñi speakers, who had one word for both blue and green, had a hard time remembering the nuances that were obvious to an English speaker. They understood the differences but didn't react instinctively to the other language. However, they were able to comprehend the language differences.

The American Noam Chomsky most famously developed the idea of a universal grammar. To Chomsky, the brain contains a language center that is the same for all human beings. Language capacity, then, is genetically inherited. Chomsky made a point of refuting behaviorism as the source of language. According to the behaviorists, like B.F. Skinner, we learn language because we are rewarded for saying a word and using it correctly. Over the years, a person learns a language through positive reinforcement. But Chomsky pointed out that language could generate an almost infinite number of ideas. In fact, new ideas could never have been taught through positive feedback. The language center must be capable of generating new forms that are instantly comprehensible to someone else. In a sense, this debate echoes the old nature/nurture debate.

The Universal Grammar approach focused on structure rather than meaning. The idea is to show how a deep structure common to all languages can transform into a surface structure that is unique to each language. Transformational grammar is an exercise in set theory and Symbolic logic. Essentially, this approach in linguistics, by trying to understand how languages can be both comprehensible and infinitely diverse, was searching for the structure of the human mind.

Anthropological Structuralism

Anthropology is the study of human culture in all of its historical and geographic diversity and thus studies both non-Western and Western cultures. Anthropology emerged from the colonial desire to understand the nature of the people they interacted with and brought under colonial administration. As we have seen, in the nineteenth century such studies implicitly defined a higher/lower dichotomy—interestingly, such an evolutionarily based system assumes the psychic unity of all humans. Anthropology remains fascinated with understanding social diversity from the perspective of cultural relativism.

A significant change in anthropological approaches came when during the First World War, the Polish anthropology student Bronislaw Malinowski (1884–1942) was stranded in the British colony New Guinea. Malinowski had the opportunity to do more extensive fieldwork than others had before and so developed the approach of participant observation. He tried to see things from the native point of view rather than judging native practices by Western standards. He emphasized understanding how the institutions of the Trobriand Islanders functioned to satisfy individual needs. This approach was known as functionalism. Other anthropologists later developed ways of seeing non-Western societies through the lenses of Marxism, classical economics, Freudian psychology, sociology, and so forth. All provided fresh insights into the workings of societies.

But out of the work of Malinowski and the many anthropologists who came after him, arose a perspective known as "cultural relativity." Anthropologists were to work to see things from the viewpoint of the other culture without intruding their own values. Cultures are always relative to the contexts in which they function. From this concern, an idea of moral relativism was spawned: the idea that all cultures are equivalent and there is no "best" way of organizing human society. Even when other cultures have seemingly repulsive customs, like cannibalism, anthropologists should see the importance of such practices in the functioning of the society under study. The stance of cultural relativity, including both epistemological and moral relativism, found its way out of anthropology into many other fields and even into public understanding.

Anthropological structuralism, which developed as an offshoot of linguistic structuralism, owes a debt to the French scholar Claude Lévi-Strauss (1908–2009). Lévi-Strauss studied law and philosophy at the Sorbonne. Later he joined the cultural mission to Brazil and taught sociology at the University of Sao Paulo. He and his wife Dina periodically pursued ethnographic work in the Amazon rainforest between 1935 and 1939. They studied several tribes but seem not to have stayed with any of them for more than a few weeks. When Lévi-Strauss returned to France, he had become an anthropologist. Unfortunately, he was quickly stripped of citizenship in Vichy France because he was a Jew. He was able to leave, and he spent most of the war in New York at the

Figure 12.3 Claude Lévi-Strauss in the Amazon, 1936. The great structuralist early in his career. © Apic/Hulton Archive/Getty Images.

New School for Social Research. In New York, he befriended a Russian emigrant linguist, Roman Jakobson (1896–1982). The gregarious Jakobson served as an intermediary bridge for several thinkers who used linguistic insights to develop structural programs in their own disciplines.

The Saussurean Jakobson developed techniques for analyzing and organizing the use of sound in language, focusing on binary distinctions in his analysis of phonemes, the basic irreducible sounds of a language. For instance, a binary opposition might be (1) voiced versus (2) unvoiced consonants. After his relationship with Jakobson, Lévi-Strauss moved to base his system of anthropological structuralism on binary oppositions. He also referred to Hegel and Marx, who both had used the concept of thesis/antithesis in understanding society.

In his linguistic studies, Saussure had distinguished between the signified and the signifier and called the relationship between these a sign. Lévi-Strauss made the same distinction in the study of cultures: what seems to be happening on the surface obscures the real significance of the underlying structural relationship. So, for example, in studying kinship, some anthropologists had focused on marriage and children. Lévi-Strauss, however, saw the atom of kinship in the exchange of women by men, a necessary outcome of the incest taboo. Out of such exchange, families arose. Exchange could be a simple exchange: Group A exchanges with Group B; or the exchange could be more generalized, with Group A sending a woman to Group B, while B sends to C, C sends to D, and D sends to A, completing the circle. The participants did not think of themselves as basically engaging in exchange, but the anthropologist could see that exchange was essential. Exchange, the basis of family building, was what was most important in building kinship and larger social systems. Lévi-Strauss also saw exchange as a universal human structure, using examples from within French culture to make his point.

In order to have an exchange, an inside and an outside group was needed. But Lévi-Strauss saw that if there were only the two (or four) groups, ultimately they would form a well-structured exchange-based group themselves. Thus, there would be only one group. There had to be a third possibility, even if that third possibility were only an idea. Lévi-Strauss proposed that culturally there were concepts that were empty of content until they were filled in, just as there were in language. English uses "thing" to mean just about anything, and so "thing" itself is an empty signifier until a different word is used. "Mana" (spiritual power or force) was to Lévi-Strauss a necessary empty signifier. If there were no empty signifiers, if every word had an exact referent, then the creative power of language (or culture) would cease. Empty signifiers (linguistic or cultural) drive language and culture forward. Thus, although Lévi-Strauss emphasized the synchronic, nonhistorical, nature of culture, his theory implicitly contained a diachronic, historical dimension to it.

As he studied binary relationships, Lévi-Strauss also used a system of analogies. Relationships can mirror or contradict other relationships. So, for instance, in his study of kinship, Lévi-Strauss found that the maternal uncle, who was outside of the nuclear family, was in fact inside the structural unit that generated kin relations. He found that the tie between the maternal uncle and his nephew was a key relationship. He saw that across cultures there was an analogical relationship:

1) The relationship between maternal uncle and nephew is to the relationship between brother and sister

As

2) The relationship between father and son is to the relationship between husband and wife.

This analogy represents the opposing structures of matrilineal and patrilineal descent. And this analogy, Lévi-Strauss thought, existed independent of any particular family. People are born into this analogical structure; they do not construct it. One cannot find it empirically, since it is based on comparison between cultures; one has to use structural analysis.

Similar to kinship, myths have to be understood as structures rather than as stories that refer to some historical event. For Lévi-Strauss, each myth, like the complete Oedipus myth, was composed of little units that he called "mythemes," in analogy with the linguistic concept, "phonemes." Myths have an eternal, nonhistorical, structure. If a myth is retold and the story is changed, the relationships among the mythemes persists.

The anthropologist could see the mythic structure by considering all versions of the myth. Generally, myths contain contradictions and are expressions of the contradictory nature of human thought and experience. If we think of, for instance, the debate between free will and determinism, we can see such a contradiction. Both are part of human experience.

Saussure's distinction between parole (language as it is spoken) and langue (the deeper meaning that is referred to by parole) suggests something that changed with time, as words and grammar rules changed, as well as something that did not change, the deeper layer of human experience itself. Language itself then, contained a contradiction. The third element, the empty signifier, was myth. Myth unwound, thought Lévi-Strauss, in a spiral as humans grappled with the essential paradox of their own lives.

Structuralists often expressed structures in mathematical or logical terms. The observed cultural practices were not as important as the abstract relationships. That which was most real (the structures) was abstract—although the abstract was designed to account for the observable practices. Lévi-Strauss was a Platonist and a Hegelian. He thought human concepts could be expressed by thesis/antithesis/synthesis. These examples only touch the complexity of Lévi-Strauss's structural approach. One can, perhaps, imagine Lévi-Strauss as a kind of Freud figure sitting behind a couch on which a culture reclined. That culture portrayed or spoke whatever came to mind, but Lévi-Strauss knew that the surface content was not what was actually important. Using the theoretical tools that he had laboriously put together, Lévi-Strauss, like Freud, could interpret the actual content of the culture under analysis. Whether the culture was better off after the analysis was debated.

Thus, it is not surprising that psychoanalysis also supported a structuralist approach. For instance, in psychology the French psychiatrist Jacques Lacan (1901–81) developed an approach that he named "the return to Freud." After the Second World War, in the late 1940s and early 1950s he discovered linguistic structuralism in the works of Saussure and Jakobson and also anthropological structuralism in Lévi-Strauss's studies of kinship. By 1959–60, Lacan began to understand psychoanalysis and its approach to the human mind in structural terms. He claimed that the unconscious was structured like a language and began to emphasize Freud's use of words in his analysis of jokes and of dreams. By 1963 he was banned from working as a training analyst and developed his own institution. Soon it was clear that he had founded a new school in competition with that of Freud.

Lacan saw the mind as composed of three registers. The Imaginary register contained images and imaginings. He emphasized that we imagine what we think other people are; we do not know what their essence is. With his new commitment to structuralism, Lacan added the Symbolic register. Lacan saw that people are born into a world of customs and laws—a world of meaning. Meaning, of course, is maintained and mediated by language. The Symbolic register is largely unconscious, and thus the unconscious is structured like a language. Finally, the register of the Real provided a counterpart to the Imaginary and the Symbolic. As we have seen, in Western thought the "real" is a slippery concept—and so it is with Lacan. Sometimes he means by real something akin to Kant's thing-in-itself, something that is behind the phenomena we perceive. For Lacan, the idea of something "missing" like, say, the arms of the Venus de Milo, exists only in the Symbolic. In the Real, nothing can be missing, because the world is what it is, not as it should be. The Real, however, frustrates the Imaginary and the Symbolic as they attempt to construct the world according to their own principles.

Lacan linked these three registers in a topological symbol, the Borromean knot, in which three intertwined circles are constructed in such a way that if one is cut and removed, the other two fall apart. In fact, as Lacan developed ways of creating visual models of the mind, he moved into the complexities of the mathematical theory of topography. Like other structuralists, he wanted to show the mathematical structures underlying his subject matter.

Lacan had no theory of a "self" but rather saw humans developing an idea of a self as they looked in a mirror and heard important others saying, "That's you!" For Lacan, humans learned to play the role of a self. They played this role within the confines of a structure that was given to them. The idea that people can be free individuals was refuted by structuralism. In fact, structuralists tended to oppose the ideas of existentialism and human freedom that were current at the same time.

Structuralism was a system that could be applied in many different fields. Louis Althusser was a Marxist philosopher who emphasized the impersonal structures in Marxist thought. He argued against the Marxist humanism of the Frankfurt School (below), based on the recently released early writings of Marx. Instead, he argued that Marx had an "epistemological break" after Marx began his humanistic writing career and that Marx began to emphasize the structure of society as opposed to individuals. In the field of literary criticism, Roland Barthe approached literature and society by

Figure 12.4 Borromean Rings. The coat of arms of the aristocratic Italian Borromeo family became an inspiration of psychoanalyst Jacques Lacan. The idea is that if one ring is removed, the other two cannot hold together. But together they are a unity. © Drawing by Kassel Galaty.

analyzing symbols and signs. For instance, the romantic idea of drinking wine was important to the French, but the picture of a bottle of wine cementing friendships obscured the pernicious role wine had on health. Like Lacan, Barthe opposed the existential approach.

Second-wave Feminism

In 1929 Virginia Woolf adapted lectures she had given to the women's colleges of Cambridge University, Newnham, and Girton, and published them as the influential book *A Room of One's Own*. Woolf was asked to write on "women in literature," and so decided that as a novelist she would write a fictional essay. The narrator visits Oxbridge and is thwarted at every turn as she is admonished for daring as a woman to use the library or sit on the grass. At each interruption, she loses her concentration. As she reflects on the difference in the quality of food at a male college and a female college, she understands that the male college is much better endowed than the female. And she notes that only in the previous century had women been allowed to control their own money.

She finds that male authors seem to write about women using an angry tone, and as she pursues the seeming anomaly of powerless women being resented by powerful men, she realizes that men depend on women for their own psychological well-being. Without women's fawning support, they could never have built the British Empire. And she suggests that every man has a metaphorical spot the size of a shilling on the back of his head, that only a woman can tell him about. In short, men need women, perhaps more than women need men.

As she analyzes the styles and subject matter of books written by women over the past few centuries, she finds that women write differently than men. There is a women's voice,

Figure 12.5 Statue of Virginia Woolf in Tavistock Park, London. © Photograph by David Galaty.

and women need to encourage one another to foster that voice. But almost paradoxically, she admires women and men who can write androgynously, for every person is a combination of both woman and man. She also seems to advocate incandescent writing, writing that is true, without an axe to grind.

As she assesses what women need in order to write fiction, her answer is that they need independence. They need enough money to support themselves and a place that is theirs alone. With 500 pounds and a room of one's own, a woman has what she needs to let her creative muse soar.

Woolf was writing immediately after the suffragist cause had triumphed. It seemed that women would soon have the wherewithal to build their own places next to men in British society. But even after women had taken the places of men in domestic industry during the Second World War, women faced life as second-class voting citizens. Perhaps the vote was not enough.

In 1949 French philosopher Simone de Beauvoir (1908–86), best friend, companion, and sometime lover of Jean-Paul Sartre, wrote *Le Deuxième sexe* (*The Second Sex*), a book that was badly translated and has only recently been adequately available in English. De Beauvoir was an outstanding student who studied for the postgraduate examination (the agrégation) in philosophy with her new friend Jean-Paul Sartre. He came in first and she second. Though de Beauvoir had no interest in marriage, Sartre described them as "together as one." They each had other lovers, and sometimes shared them. It was a remarkable relationship, cemented by intellectual affinity. But later in her life, de Beauvoir described the essential asymmetry of their lives together. He was the self, and she was the other. She also recognized that Blacks, Jews, and indigenous people were also "others" to those that stereotyped them.

As a phenomenologist, de Beauvoir naturally began her book with her own experience and reported that while men may first be aware of themselves in an activity or career, she finds it necessary to first describe herself as a woman. She quickly moves to Hegel's story of the master and slave to understand her position as a woman. In Hegel's story, the master experiences himself as a subject and the slave as an object, but the slave, always aware of his status as an object, can never be a pure subject. Only through struggle can the slave achieve freedom and selfhood.

But de Beauvoir noted that a woman does not have that option, because she inhabits a body that differs from a man's (a biological given) and because women are dispersed from one another, each living with a man. To revolt against men would be to revolt against her life. Thus, when men see women as the other, the men have an accomplice. Having established women's "otherness," she then turns to science, history, mythology, and philosophy to discover how this situation occurred. The survey is long and captivating.

One of the de Beauvoir's recurring themes is the impact of sex and childbirth on women's freedom. Abortion was outlawed in France until the mid-1960s. Both women and men viewed motherhood as an important role for women, in a way that fatherhood was never conceived. A woman is caught in caring for her child, to which housework was attached, while a man is free to pursue a life outside of the home. De Beauvoir maintains that marriage usually destroys a woman. She also thinks that marriage destroys erotic satisfaction. The only way out, she seems to think, is socialism in which both men and women maintain their brotherhood.

The Second Sex lay fallow during the 1950s, a decade of economic prosperity and putting Europe back together after the war. In the 1960s, however, in both Western Europe and North America, a social movement known as second-wave feminism arose; De Beauvoir's book was a primary source of ideas. There were essentially two separate yet intertwined arms of the movement. One arm was practical: it aimed at legislation and other actions that increased the ability of women to participate in society on an equal footing with men. The other arm was theoretical: it aimed at digging deeply beneath the intellectual assumptions upon which Western culture was based in order to discover the source of women's continual second-class existence. Feminists in each European country took a slightly different tack. The English-speaking world tended to focus on practical concerns, while the French and German feminists tended to emphasize theory more. But both approaches existed in all countries.

An important concept was "patriarchy," taken from the biblical dominance of male leaders of tribes. In feminist usage, the term indicated the general dominance of men at all levels of society. Men were seen as heads of families, leaders of companies, rulers of countries, and even pilots of a romance. Although "The Queen" might seem an exception, the queen in fact was a sovereign, without sex. Patriarchy so defined the social structure of societies that many feminists thought changing this concept was the first step in achieving parity for women.

The Austrian historian Gerda Hedwig Lerner (1920–2013) fled to America after the Anschluss of 1938. As a history professor at the University of Wisconsin and cofounder of the National Organization for Women (NOW), she became an intellectual leader of international feminism. Two books in particular developed important ideas: *The Creation of Patriarchy* (1986) and *The Creation of Feminist Consciousness: From the Middle Ages to 1870* (1993). In her view, patriarchy was a religious concept that kept women away from the divine. Extant written sources almost always expressed a male viewpoint, but as women began to write, they challenged or revised male orientation. By writing, women had been able to begin to think themselves out of patriarchy. For Lerner, patriarchy was socially constructed, so it could be unconstructed and replaced.

The concept of patriarchy enabled the development of combined theories, such as Marxist feminism. In such an analysis, capitalism could be recognized as the underlying source of the shape of patriarchy in industrialized societies—or, given Lenin's assessment of imperialism as a capitalist stage, capitalism could be seen as the source of global patriarchy. Feminist historians found ancient societies that they claimed were ruled by women, or other societies in which men and women held equal decision-making roles.

The socialist British activist Lindsey German (b. 1951) presented a radically different view in which she argued that patriarchy theory did not take account of class. In fact, patriarchy works differently in different classes and at the level of the proletariat is harmful equally to men and women. The issue is capitalism and so the start to female liberation should begin with understanding the position of women in capitalist society.

The British sociologist Sylvia Theresa Walby (b. 1953) suggested that patriarchy took different forms at different times in different cultures. We can see patriarchal forms within the state and the household. We also see it expressed in violence against females, sexuality (in which women's sexuality is controlled) and prostitution, media and popular culture.

Second-wave feminism was expressed through street demonstrations, voting campaigns, legislative lobbying, and self-consciously creating new cultural images. It was a dominant form in the 1960s and 1970s. As we shall see, it gave way to a third wave as the twentieth century drew to a close.

The Frankfurt School

The Institute for Social Research, or the Frankfurt School, was founded just after the First World War in 1923 at the Goethe University Frankfurt. The goal of the School was to investigate how to carry out social research aimed at making society better. Although first intended to concentrate on Marxist ideas, the Communist Party so heavy-handedly tried to interfere with the free expression of ideas by party members that the School decided to break with any intellectual dependence on the Communist Party. While Marxism remained an important source of ideas, the members of the School turned to Kant, Hegel, Freud, and Weber as well. They also freely responded one another's ideas. Thus, the Frankfurt School became an important source of neo-Marxist ideas. As fascism and Nazism gained power and influence, the Frankfurt School tried to develop ways of understanding the phenomenon of such reactionary politics—and since Marx had never seen the phenomenon of fascist socioeconomic systems, new approaches had to be developed.

Although the School worked for ten years in Frankfurt, after 1933 they decided to leave Nazi Germany. Many of them were Jewish. Eventually the School found its way to Columbia University in New York where they stayed until they returned to Frankfurt in 1953. A word for the kind of work the Frankfurt School carried out was critical theory, the study of how a dominant ideology distorts human relationships and how misrepresentations serve to convince people that being dominated is in their own interests. In the Frankfurt School, the dialectical method was used, but it was also used on itself to expose its own errors—as a kind of self-corrective.

The intellectual who was most responsible for developing the Frankfurt program of critical theory was Max Horkheimer (1895–1973), who focused on understanding the relationship between emotion and concepts. He hoped to find ways of showing Italian and German workers how they could resist the enticements of fascism. He showed how positivistic and "instrumental" thinking encouraged a focus on aims rather than on processes. It was easy for human beings to end up being means to an end rather than ends in themselves. Logical, instrumental thinking gained more and more power as technology became more and more important in modern society.

Along with Theodor Adorno, Horkheimer analyzed popular culture as a form of totalitarianism. In their 1947 book *Dialektik der Aufklärung* (*Dialectic of the Enlightenment*), they expressed pessimism over the possibility of establishing human emancipation, much less freedom. It seemed to them that Stalinism, Nazism, and fascism had all found ways of resolving the contradiction between workers and capitalists that Marx had hoped would lead to an emancipatory revolution. A problem, they thought, was that during the Enlightenment philosophy had come to rely too heavily on reason and had then become the servant of technocracy. In the modern world, workers were bought off with goods, films, entertainment that all promised fulfillment. The films seemed all to have the message that only capitalism could bring happiness. Adorno in particular, a trained classical pianist, embraced the atonality of Schoenberg and his students because, unlike popular music like jazz, it expressed human suffering.

Herbert Marcuse (1898–1979) attempted to bring Marx and Freud together into a comprehensive theory in the postwar era. Marx had concentrated on understanding the structure of capitalist society as a structure that determines the ideas and lives of the workers. Freud had focused on individuals and found the structure of their minds. Both Marx and Freud studied pathology and pain, but from opposite ends of the individual-society spectrum. With the rediscovery in 1934 of Marx's 1844 manuscripts, there was a new way to approach Marx. In these early manuscripts, Marx had emphasized the role of alienation, a process in which workers experience themselves as objects. That is, Marx moved into the heads of workers early in his career. Freud was there all the time. With Marx, the constraints of freedom occurred at the social/structural level. With Freud, the constraints on freedom stemmed from human neurobiology.

In *Eros and Civilization. A Philosophical Inquiry into Freud* (1955), Marcuse developed the idea of "surplus repression." He accepted that a certain amount of repression of deep desires (the Freudian pleasure principle) was necessary to allow people to live together. This was the biological base. But he also noted that people in industrialized societies had to repress their basic desires in order to work in a routinized system that dominated them. They did not control their own actions. Thus, the source of Marx's alienation is Freud's repression—except that extra, surplus, repression is needed in capitalist society. People have to work to eat, and the only kind of work available is alienating. Marcuse did not blame capitalists per se, but rather "the technocratic apparatus." Marcuse saw all of Western philosophy celebrating reason, while reason increasingly became a tool of domination rather than of freedom or happiness. Reason became embodied in machines and processes that enmeshed human beings in a rational net. This theme was developed in *One-Dimensional Man: Studies in the Ideology of Advanced Industrial Society* (1964). While Logos was once complemented by Eros, today Logos has won; reason has overcome desire. Marcuse did not advocate replacing reason with desire, but rather allowing both to coexist in the service of human fulfillment.

The psychoanalyst and social thinker Eric Fromm echoed many of these same themes in several books. Like Marcuse, he was born and studied in Germany, leaving only when the Nazis made it impossible to stay. *Escape from Freedom* (1941) described two different sorts of freedom: freedom from and freedom to. The first step for a person caught in social conventions and rote processes was to understand that living in this way was unnecessary. Freedom from was akin to accepting responsibility for one's life, a la Sartre. This was not a pleasant process, and many people found ways of dealing with the pressure to conform. But once people have escaped from dominating structures, the question is how to exercise their authentic selves without falling into a different authoritarian system, like Nazism. Fromm suggested that the way forward was love. He developed this theme in his 1956 book, *The Art of Loving*. He discussed how the ability to love could be learned. Although he advocated loving oneself in an honest way, he opposed taking refuge in extreme individualism.

In the late 1950s and early 1960s, Fromm explored the connections between his neo-Freudianism and early Marxism, especially in *The Sane Society* (1955) and *Marx's Concept of Man* (1961). Rejecting both Western Capitalism and Soviet Marxism, Fromm advocated Socialist Humanism, a society that includes the welfare of everyone in its actions.

These analyses of Marx and Freud emphasized unleashing human desire in the search for authentic existence—and they struck a chord among young adults in the 1960s. Young adults in several European countries used these theoretical approaches as they marched toward the explosions of 1968.

Hannah Arendt

Hannah Arendt (1906–75) studied phenomenology under Martin Heidegger, Edmund Husserl, and Karl Jaspers. An outspoken Jewish intellectual, she became a refugee after Hitler came to power in 1933. After a stay in Paris, she was forced to move once again when the Nazis took France in 1941. She made her new home in New York where she became a noted philosopher of political theory. Her inquiry was dominated by issues raised by the devastating events of the German (Nazi) Holocaust and the Soviet Gulag. In *The Origins of Totalitarianism* (1951), Arendt described a new kind of society built on mass terror, not just the persecution of a regime's opponents but a domination of the entire populace. A totalitarian system seeks uniformity and control in every aspect of life—and thus opposes intellectual, artistic, and spiritual freedom.

But freedom was what Arendt valued most. In *The Human Condition* (1958), she distinguished various kinds of human activities (like work and labor) but reserved her deepest analysis for a *Vita Activa* (active life) in the public sphere. Through this *Vita Activa*, humans create something new in communion with others. Speech is essential to the process as we reveal and discover ourselves by making sense. We find that each of us is unique, that is, we see each other not just as fellow humans, but as individuals. As we give birth to the new along with others, unexpected things happen. The future is unpredictable and the past unchangeable. The only resources we humans possess to resolve these problems are promises (reducing the unpredictability of the future) and forgiveness (reducing the pain of the irrevocable past).

For Arendt (expanding on inter alia Max Weber—Chapter 8 and Edmund Husserl—Chapter 10), modern life increasingly left humans alienated from the earth (shrunk by exploration), our local place (as wealth increasingly became social in global markets), and the universe (as scientific findings replaced our direct experiences). We therefore focused deep within ourselves, the one place that was ours alone. But in the shrunken public sphere, science replaced philosophy—experiment (doing) replaced analysis (contemplating). We worked mainly to stay alive, and clinging to life replaced meaning. The *Vita Activa* was threatened. The break from tradition accomplished by the horrific events of the twentieth century has left us needing to create new ideas (or unearth fragments of old ones) that can support a continuation of a truly human life, apart from bureaucracy and the meaningless search for abundance.

An important question about identity construction in the public sphere is, who gets to participate and where? The locus for public action had been the nation-state. But what about people who are outside of a nation-state? What is the place of refugees? Of persecuted minorities? For Arendt, this question is crucial, because only by living an active life in the public sphere could people realize their identity and humanness. Arendt thought the idea of universal "human rights" was unworkable because there is no common institution that allowed all people to participate. In fact, as recent scholarship has shown, human rights became a concept only in the 1970s after other universalist projects (described in Chapter 10 passim) had failed.

Conclusion

After the celebrations at the end of the Second World War had died away, it was clear to thinking Europeans that Europe would have to be reconceived if the lessons of the Versailles Treaty's failures were not to come back once more to haunt them. But the continent was divided into two mutually irreconcilable camps. No theory could bridge the ideological gap. The postwar years were to represent a kind of social experiment, as communism and capitalism, totalitarianism and democracy, each buckled down to showcase their strengths. The competition took place under the threat of nuclear annihilation. It lasted until 1989 and the fall of the Berlin Wall.

The contradictions inherent in a divided Europe riven by opposing worldviews were unsustainable. Every European institution came under scrutiny including the assumptions underlying thought itself. In the next chapter, we will explore the critique as some Europeans worked to tear things down and others worked to build new structures in society and in thought.

CHAPTER 13
INTELLECT AGAINST REASON
REASON FIGHTS BACK

Figure 13.1 Prague, Czechoslovakia, the Velvet Revolution, 1989. © Peter Turnley/Corbis Historical/Getty Images.

The English Voice of the Velvet Revolution

The Czech Rita Klímová (1931–93) landed in New York City at the age of eight, and all her friends were still in Prague. When the Nazi invasion of Czechoslovakia threatened her Jewish family, they all packed up and fled. By the time the family went home after the war, Rita had gone through junior high school in New York reading *Seventeen* magazine, reciting the pledge of allegiance, and becoming a girl scout. She spoke English with an American, New York, accent. Her musical favorites were Frank Sinatra and Billie Holiday. Once again Klímová had to leave friends and commitments. She went to high school in Prague, and by 1948 she was ready to become a Communist Party member. She sought factory work as a lathe turner making jet engines to become closer to the proletariat and felt that Stalinism was the answer Czechoslovakia needed. She maintained this belief even during the purges in 1952. She received a PhD in economics with a dissertation on the Great Depression and the failings of capitalism, and soon she joined the faculty at Charles University in Prague.

But in the 1960s, as the Czechoslovakian economy faltered, she began to harbor doubts about Marxist economic analysis. She began to apply the Western ideas she had learned and found that they explained what was going on better than Marxism did. Along with the rest of her generation, she welcomed the fresh ideas of Alexander Dubček, the new communist leader who took power in January 1968. When Warsaw pact troops invaded and removed Dubček, she lost her teaching position. She worked as an accountant at the university and began to pick up translation jobs on the side. She moved more and more toward the dissidents who continued to object to the communist regime. She interacted with both Vaclav Havel and Vaclav Klaus, two future presidents of the country. In November 1989, she got a message from Vaclav Havel, who wanted her to translate his announcements, and for the next two weeks she sat side by side with Havel as the communist regime came down around them and Havel became president. As she groped for words, she coined the phrase "the velvet revolution," still used today to describe the nonviolent movements that overthrew one side in the Cold War. In 1990 she became ambassador to the United States, where she remained until 1992 when she wearied from the leukemia that would kill her a year later.

Chapter Map

Around the year 1968, protest movements in both Eastern and Western Europe provoked questioning about the postwar consensus. Throughout Western Europe, young people questioned the loss of ideals the older generations had suffered in the interests of materialism. In Eastern Europe, the soon-suppressed reforms of the Dubček government allowed freedom of speech and expression, while in the Soviet Union dissidents exposed the evils of the Soviet Union's secret prisons, the gulags.

The far-flung fringes of Europe, the colonies, saw the opportunity to become independent after the war had drained European fiscal and moral reserves. Educated European colonials began to celebrate their own non-European cultures and to analyze the nature of discrimination. Their works called into question the myth of European superiority and the inevitability of progress through reason.

As environmental degradation became more and more apparent, Europeans in all countries began to organize to stop the practices that produced such deterioration. The Club of Rome, a new society organized around computer modeling, issued a report that predicted collapse of Western civilization without drastic changes. As if in rebuttal, the green revolution contributed to a slowing of population growth as well as producing more food. Technology kept producing more resources. Climatologists began to recognize and define global warming, a threat that would become apparent in the next century.

All this questioning was accompanied by intellectual and artistic movements known as postmodernism. Postmodernism tended to support a culturally relativistic approach. Postmodernists emphasized the social construction of ideas, as opposed to the existence of ideas that humans could discover through reason or science. They also analyzed language as a self-contained activity that bore no necessary relationship to objects of perception or of a world outside of human beings. Science itself, along with nature, was viewed as a cultural production. Many postmodernists were French, and they analyzed everything from images to texts through a skeptical lens.

During the last two decades of the twentieth century, leaders in both East and West began to move rightward. The Cold War ended as the Soviet Union collapsed. West and East Germany united, and Germany joined the central group of European countries that accomplished European unification in the EU.

Opposing the Postwar Consensus

By the end of the 1960s, in both the East and the West a variety of actors questioned the structure of their societies and governments. Since communist Eastern Europe strove for equality, dissidents there tended to cry out for more liberty and less central control. Conversely, since democratic and capitalist Western Europe emphasized liberty, dissidents there tended to demand more equality and less materialism. Young people everywhere lived in a world connected by television, so they could see, in a way that had never before been possible, how others lived. Increasingly, young people from both sides of Europe had access to education. The growing economies of postwar Europe meant that young Europeans were materially better off, on average, than Europeans in their respective countries had ever been. Europeans also shared the anxieties of the nuclear-armed world. Everyone, on a global scale, shared the experience of mutually assured destruction (MAD).

The United States had taken over the war in Vietnam from the French, and in 1965 had greatly expanded the conflict. They were supported in this struggle by NATO and by most West European governments. The rationale for the war was the strategy of containing, not defeating, communism. But the war was also a colonial war informed by European values; it provided an important general backdrop to West European dissident movements.

On both sides of the iron curtain, 1968 proved to be a seminal year.

Eastern European Movements

Czechoslovakia

In January 1968, Alexander Dubček, a reform-minded leader, became first secretary of the Communist Party of Czechoslovakia with the support of the Soviet secretary, Leonid Brezhnev. Gradually, Dubček began to loosen controls on speech and press and to allow people to move about the country more freely. Relaxing the power of the secret police, he spoke of "socialism with a human face" and began to talk of a transition toward democratic elections. He even talked about mixing the planned economy with a market economy. The result of these steps was that writers and artists felt a new freedom to express themselves without trying to toe an official line. Newspapers, magazines, and television programs began to investigate the country's communist past. New publications sprang up. It briefly seemed that perhaps a communist revolution without totalitarianism was possible.

The Czech experience was echoed in the revolts and demonstrations in Western Europe. Hardline leaders in the Eastern bloc were worried. The Soviets at first negotiated with Dubček and then finally, fed up, invaded the country in late August 1968. The Czechs at first played games with the invaders by, for example, changing street and direction signs. The Soviets were not amused. Eventually, a new first secretary halted the Prague spring experiment. Arrests changed the public mood of exuberance to melancholy. In the West, even supporters of communism began to doubt the possibility that communist totalitarianism could ever "wither away."

The impact of the Soviet invasion on the rest of the communist world was profound. China protested vigorously against the notion that the Soviet Union could tell other countries what proper communist behavior was. Albania withdrew from the Warsaw pact and aligned itself with China. In 1984, Czech author Milan Kundera wrote a novel about the beginning and end of the Prague spring entitled *Nesnesitelná lehkost bytí*, published in French as *L'Insoutenable légèreté de l'être* (*The Unbearable Lightness of Being*). This philosophical inquiry reflected on Nietzsche's theory of eternal recurrence, among other things. The book seemed to conclude that even though every moment is unique, and therefore unimportant, commitment can give a human-scale meaning to a life. The Prague spring was one of those historical episodes that provoked creative artistic exploration.

The Soviet Union

In the Soviet Union, dissidents became more outspoken during the 1970s. For instance, the brilliant nuclear physicist Andrei Sakharov, the major force behind the design of the Soviet hydrogen bomb, became concerned about the dangers of a nuclear world he had done so much to create. He strongly supported negotiating with Americans about a nonproliferation treaty, and his adamant position led to his removal from classified military research. Slowly he went public with his concerns and joined the Committee on Human Rights in the Soviet Union. He began to think of the Soviet Union as akin to a cancer cell that could spread centrally controlled, technocratic society throughout the world. He was awarded the Nobel Peace Prize in 1975 but was sentenced to internal exile and kept under surveillance. Eventually, Premier Mikhail Gorbachev released him in 1986.

One of Sakharov's main supporters in the early 1970s was the author Aleksandr Solzhenitsyn (1918–2008). Solzhenitsyn saw his family farm turned into a collective in the 1930s. He fought in the Second World War, but as the war ended, he was sent to a labor camp in 1945 for criticizing Stalin. During the war, he had witnessed the brutal retaliation of Soviet soldiers toward anyone who resembled a German and was disillusioned about claims to moral superiority by the Soviets. In 1956 Solzhenitsyn was released. He was able to publish an edited version of *One Day in the Life of Ivan Denisovich* in 1962 in which he exposed the Soviet prison system. Since Khrushchev had himself lifted the lid on discussion of the evils of Stalinism, he allowed the book to be studied in Soviet schools. But after Khrushchev was removed from power in 1964, the lid went back on. Nevertheless, Solzhenitsyn was able to work in secret on *The Gulag Archipelago*, a three-volume work that was published outside of the Soviet Union in 1973. It was a detailed exposé of the Soviet Gulag system with detailed discussion of prisoner revolts, brutal tortures, and suffocating oppression. Solzhenitsyn compared the Gulag to the Inquisition and other systems of torture in which the immoral actions of the perpetrators are justified by ideology.

Solzhenitsyn survived a KGB attempt to poison him in 1971, right after he had won the Nobel Prize for literature in 1970. Eventually, he was expelled from the Soviet Union and stripped of his citizenship. He was sent to West Germany but ended up in the United States. He was also critical of the weakening of morality in the United States and feared that Americans would be unable to resist Soviet aggression. He was appalled by American popular culture, but he admired American political liberty, especially the local town hall-style government he saw in New England. A staunch religious moralist, he found little to admire in the modern world.

Western European Movements

Most spectacularly, in May 1968, French students began to demonstrate against capitalism, consumerism, American imperialism, and in general against a variety of seemingly obsolete traditional institutions. Soon demonstrations became street battles, and workers joined students. For a time, the French economy shut down. In several cities, strikers and demonstrators threw up street barricades. The police were accused of brutality and undercover provocation. As unions negotiated with employers and the government, their members refused to accede to the agreements their representatives agreed to. There was no central coordinating body behind the demonstrations, and different groups had different demands. Many students wanted better university housing, more funding for higher education, or less class discrimination in admissions. Workers often wanted better pay, improved working conditions, and job security. Some wanted worker control of factories and the ouster of the de Gaulle government. Many workers mistrusted their own unions, seeing them as too close to the government. Eventually, the brutal tactics of the government evoked support for the demonstrators throughout France. For a few days, President Charles de Gaulle actually left the country. Eventually, he called an election and brought 800,000 supporters to march through Paris in a counter demonstration. The revolutionary sentiments slowly died down.

In West Germany, similar protests took place with a different slant. Young people wanted their parents' generation to take more responsibility for Nazi atrocities and to remove former Nazis, like Chancellor Kurt Kiesinger, from the government. They demanded more direct democratic institutions, especially in universities where they wanted a direct say on policies, including modernization of facilities and expulsion of ex-Nazis from faculties.

Other Western European countries protested along similar lines but with different local emphases. In Sweden, students protested against a proposed tennis match that included players from apartheid nations from Southern Africa. In the UK, protests in Ireland laid the seeds for the later terrorist actions known as "the troubles." In Italy, university students from the lower classes began to agitate against bourgeois, elite leadership. They criticized both communists and capitalists. Eventually, violent radicals from the left and the right sent Italy into a long period of chaotic political uncertainty.

Postcolonial Voices

We have previously examined the assumptions underlying European imperialism: belief in the superiority of Europeans and European culture, as well as a belief that a strong national economy had to be built on conquest and colonies. The idea of progress, elaborated during the Enlightenment, served as a measuring post for European technological culture. As long as technology made human life richer and easier, and as long as science continued to uncover unexpected truths about nature, it was hard to doubt that Europeans were on the right path.

Colonial independence movements called all of these assumptions into question. According to European theory, colonized peoples should have tried to reshape their societies and cultures on a European model in order to experience the fruits of progress for themselves. In fact, many European mother-countries—but not all—had educated large numbers of their subjects to train them in the tasks of administration and governing. Both European ideas and European training proved to be unable to convince colonized peoples to forget their own cultures.

After the Second World War, previously simmering independence movements erupted in almost every European colony. Many of the leaders of these movements were members of the European-educated elite and could write eloquently in European tongues. As a result, their approaches to understanding the pernicious nature of colonialism and its impact on both the colonized and the colonizers became part of the intellectual swirl that made up European discourse. Their perspectives often reversed the prewar ideas of influential Europeans. All over the globe, colonized peoples challenged European ideas as they worked for independence. As an example, we will consider African responses.

One of the most highly regarded English novels was *Heart of Darkness* (1899), written by Polish-British author Joseph Conrad in his third language. The short book exposed the hypocrisy behind European colonialism and showed how rather than being a force for Enlightenment, colonialism was a greedy, brutal activity that ran roughshod over any pretensions of humane conduct. The Africans in the book are nobler than any of the Europeans, save for the detached narrator-observer, Marlow. However, Marlow knows nothing about his African employees except how they do their jobs. As the steamboat sails up the Congo River, the banks are covered in jungle, and Marlow has no interest in exploring what is behind the thick growth.

The Nigerian writer Chinua Achebe (1930–2013) grew up in Southeastern Nigeria and studied English literature at the University of Ibadan. He had grown up in a community that had refined storytelling to a fine art, and so as he studied English literature, he began to write his own stories, but with a Nigerian voice. He later wrote that when he read *Heart of Darkness*, he identified with Marlow until he realized that he would not have been Marlow, but rather one of the African workers, and that Marlow would have neither have known nor cared anything about him. He decided to write the stories of the people beyond the riverbanks[1].

In *Things Fall Apart*, Achebe tells the story of Okonkwo, a proud man who was raised by a lazy, pleasant, and poor father. Achebe tells a story that is not whitewashed to appeal to European readers, but rather shows a rich society that had values that would appall European readers. The society was polygamous, non-Christian, and willing to employ human sacrifice in certain defined situations. It was also a society that supported its members, reveled in complex stories and proverbs, laughed and enjoyed life. Most importantly, it was an African society told in an African voice—but using English, a

Figure 13.2 Nigerian author Chinua Achebe, 1960. © Getty Images.

colonial language. Achebe and others were inventing Nigerian fiction. That is, they were using a European literary form to communicate an African message. As they did so, their message found its way into Europe and transformed the understandings of a new generation of Europeans.

Frantz Fanon (1925–61) was a French West Indian. He grew up in a middle-class family in the colony Martinique (now a French department). His ancestors were a mixture of African slaves, indentured Indians, and French-Alsatians. He attended a noted high school (Lycée) in Martinique, but in the Second World War Martinique was occupied by Vichy forces, collaborators with the Germans. Fanon was repelled by the racism exhibited by Vichy sailors and fled to join the Free French Forces under de Gaulle. As a soldier he spent time in North Africa, particularly Algeria. As Fanon observed other Europeans, he realized that racism permeated Europe. After the war, Fanon went to France where he studied medicine, specializing in psychiatry. He became interested in the influence of culture on psychiatry, and in 1953 became chief psychiatrist at a hospital in Algeria.

Fanon's first book, *Peau noire, masques blancs* (*Black Skin, White Masks*) was written in France in 1952. Eschewing the more traditional pose of the value-free observer, Fanon wrote of his own experiences in the context of historical and psychiatric theory. Fanon showed a double process: colonialists conducted physical and psychological warfare to annihilate bodies, psyches, and cultures while colonized peoples reacted with violence to recover their history and dignity. Fanon explored the social construction of "Blackness" in a colonial situation. He engaged Hegel, Marx, phenomenology, and existentialism as he developed an innovative and perceptive analysis of a society that is inescapably racist. For Fanon, speaking a language immersed one in a culture, and thus colonized people participated in the culture of their colonizers, and therefore participated in their own oppression. Even if they spoke perfect French, however, they would never be accepted as French because of their skin. Négritude, the acceptance of the beauty and power of being black and a revolt against any suggestion of black inferiority, remains a kind of antidote to the destructive power of colonialism.

In his 1961 work *Les damnés de la terre* (*The Wretched of the Earth*), Fanon began with an analysis of violence as a necessary condition for liberation. Since colonial systems were rooted in a perceived weakness and inferiority on the part of the colonized peoples, violence could provide a necessary jolt to both colonized and colonizers. Following Hegel's analysis of the master/slave relationship, Fanon noted that in order to become individual human subjects—both to the master and to themselves—the slaves needed to struggle. In a colony, once the oppressed revolted, they could perceive themselves and their oppressors as equally human. Colonized intellectuals, the class of people who mediated between the colonizers and the colonized and thus enabled the colonial system, would be needed after independence. As the revolution continued, the psychological structure of colonialism would be broken. Intellectuals could turn their talents to building the world after colonialism. But if they were stuck in colonial consciousness, if the old colonial forms were not sufficient to use in the formation of a new society, then the postcolonial world would have to be built up anew. The postcolonial future could not be imagined because it would occur after a clean break with the past. Fanon did not pretend to understand the future, but he was fascinated to see what could emerge.

In every African country, thinkers and artists strove to develop ways of conceiving, from their own points of view what their history and future might be. Ghana's Kwame Nkrumah, who led his country to independence in 1957, wrote *Neocolonialism, the Last Stage of Imperialism* (1965) in which he described a colonialism that was based not on governance but on economic domination. Foreign capital, said Nkrumah, was not invested for development, but rather for exploitation. Nkrumah, along with other leaders, conceived of African unity, and for a short time Ghana, Guinea, and Mali attempted to form a new state. Eventually, Nkrumah and others founded a loose organization, the Organization of African Unity (OAU).

Jomo Kenyatta of Kenya studied under Malinowski, and in 1938 published an anthropological study of his own people, the Kikuyu. Kenyatta was not in favor of African unions for fear that the interests of his own people would get lost in such a large grouping. Leópold Sédar Senghor, who developed the theory of Négritude and wrote Senegalese poetry, became the first president of Senegal. Thinkers and artists blossomed all over the continent in the 1960s.

Clearly, there were similar writers and thinkers throughout Africa, Asia, and the Americas. The importance of postcolonialism for European thought was immense. First, of course, given the colonial system, these innovators were European. But other European writers also felt their impact. PostColonial writers embodied the theory of cultural relativity. Clearly, if African and Asian cultures were not inferior, then one could not assume that European culture was superior. The intellectuals and artists from colonial areas utilized the European thought that they had studied and mastered. But they also plumbed the depths of their own cultures for ideas. They provided fresh perspectives for European thought. Importantly, postcolonial ideas caused European thinkers to doubt their own basic assumptions.

An Environmental Movement

Part of the evidence for European progress was the growth of useful technology. The industrial and technological revolutions had changed the face and social structure of Europe, and although even the technology's most ardent supporters acknowledged that there were problems, most people felt that the problems were manageable, often by inventing more technology. The environmental movements that grew up in the 1970s saw more problems than solutions. The growth that supported Europeans in increasing luxury began to be seen as a source of their own downfall.

The history of green movements in Europe stretches centuries. Since at least the thirteenth-century rulers were concerned about winter respiratory problems caused by burning wood and soft coal for heat in London. Such burning was forbidden when the knights of the shire assembled. Nobles were also concerned for the welfare of forests and animals in which they hunted. Poachers—even those with long residence in the forests— could be executed, as nobles asserted their exclusive rights. Thus, the sentiment behind the modern witticism—an evil developer wants to build houses on a beautiful lake, while an environmentalist already owns a house on a beautiful lake—had deep historical roots.

The tenor of these concerns changed with industrialization. The Plumage League, to protect birds from being hunted in mating season, was founded in England in 1889. The Coal Abatement Society followed in 1898. We have already seen in this text the importance of public health and the medically driven efforts to create clean waterways and air, and nonmedical movements advocated for the same causes. Atomic and hydrogen bombs provided yet another set of worries, giving rise to antinuclear movements. In the 1950s, bomb testing continued and the effects of radioactive fallout were measurable. The possibility of nuclear proliferation seemed to threaten human existence. In 1967 an oil tanker ran aground in Cornwall, and the resulting oil spill poisoned waters and beaches for miles. Some protest groups focused on the potential damage of shipping oil throughout the world's oceans.

When astronauts photographed the earth from outer space, the blue globe covered by lazy clouds suspended in a dark vacuum provided a vivid image of a fragile island home with no replacement in sight. This picture of the entire earth led some people like the Englishman James Lovelock (*Gaia: A New Look at Life on Earth* - 1979) to resurrect ideas about the world as an interconnected whole. Gaia, the Greek mythical primal earth mother from whom the sky and sea were born, was resurrected as a symbol of the complex integrity of the whole earth, an indivisible dynamic system.

Thus, the modern environmental movement assumed a different form than its predecessors. The Club of Rome, a group of industrialists, scientists, and statesmen who were dedicated to understanding human problems as a linked whole, met

Figure 13.3 *The Blue Marble*. Photograph taken by the crew of Apollo 17, 1972. This photograph captured the imagination of the world as we all saw just how precariously isolated in space the earth was. © NASA (public domain).

for the first time in 1968. They thought the relatively new computer model World3 would enable them to run projections of probable futures. They thus identified five variables: population, food production, industrialization, pollution, and consumption of nonrenewable resources. In 1970 all of these were growing exponentially, and the Club assumed that such growth would continue. However, they also assumed that technological solutions to these problems could only grow linearly. Essentially, they adapted Thomas Malthus's approach to human misery in his 1798 *Essay on Population* (Chapter 6). Like Malthus, they thought that problems grow exponentially, and solutions grow linearly, so problems soon become unmanageable. The Club then ran three alternate scenarios in which they tweaked projected growth trends. Two scenarios predicted collapse in the mid-twenty-first century, while one showed a stable world. These results were published in 1972 in *The Limits to Growth*.[2] The report concluded that there were two positive feedback loops that if unchecked would lead to system collapse. These two loops were growth of population and growth of capital. (More people—or capital—produce even more people—capital—growing at an exponential rate.) Controlling these feedback loops would produce a stable system. The report suggested equalizing birth and death rates and making sure that capital investment did not exceed depreciation. It also suggested investing enough in food production to ensure that everyone had plenty of food. Technological improvements would then slowly lift the quality of living. The report concluded that humans need a goal and a commitment that would lead toward equilibrium. Without such a goal, humans would move unwittingly, yet inexorably, toward a collapse of civilization. *The Limits to Growth* provided a vision that has guided a certain sector of the European environmental movement.

Two movements challenged the assumptions on which the Club of Rome study was based. The first was the "green revolution," a set of interventions in plant breeding designed to vastly increase the productivity of wheat and other calorie rich plants. By the 1970s, agriculture in developing nations had been transformed, and despite population increases, the poorest human beings were soon better fed than they had been before the 1960s. The American Norman Borlaug won the Nobel Peace Prize in 1970 for spearheading the green revolution. Experts have estimated that the fruits of his work saved over a billion people from dying of starvation. Genetically modified organisms (GMOs) have continued to increase food productivity. Borlaug was convinced that this huge increase in the productivity of croplands would eliminate much of the deforestation that was occurring. Borlaug also continually pointed out that despite new food plant varieties, humans had to control population growth to avoid eventual mass starvation.

Ironically, his efforts contributed to population control. As the enriched grains began to be grown all over the world, large-scale machinery was used that required fewer workers. Peasants who had cultivated small fields left for the cities. When people settled in cities, they tended to have fewer children. Whereas more children increased food security on a peasant farm, children in an urban environment were an additional expense. The phenomenon of lowered birthrate in cities, an unexpected consequence, is known as the demographic transition.

In several European countries, the rate of growth in population turned negative. Population was, and is, on the way down. This transition is happening all over the world as an outgrowth of urbanization and education, so the world population is presently expected to peak around the end of the twenty-first century. Thus, events outran the assumptions of the Club of Rome predictions when it came to population and food. Capital investment, however, continues to increase exponentially. The Club of Rome saw increasing capital investment as an indicator of excessive growth. However, capital investment properly used can reduce harmful growth—for instance, by promoting energy efficiency and reduced fossil fuel use.

Other unexpected events involved the development of new resources. For instance, in 1970 telephone and cable signals were sent by copper wire. It seemed that copper would soon run out, and with it our ability to expand communications. The invention of fiber optics, however, meant that signals were sent through bundles of small glass tubes. Glass is made from silica, which is much more plentiful than copper. The identification of what resources were in fact needed turned out to change with systems of technology. This is not to say that resource depletion is not a theoretical problem, but rather that developing a computer model of depletion is quite tricky. The economics of depletion suggest that diminishing supplies of given resources will raise prices, creating incentives to conserve or find alternatives.

At the same time in 1972 in Stockholm, the United Nations held the first of many conferences on the human environment. One of the most important issues that emerged was the conflict between environmental protection and economic development. Developing countries like India noted that Europe had become rich while polluting and that it was unfair to ask the developing countries to agree not to develop economically in the interest of maintaining a safe environment. The list of agreed-upon points contained several potentially contradictory principles around this theme. Because the United Nations had no executive power to control the actions of sovereign states, the organization often seemed weak or wishy-washy. Its role as a forum where states could debate and negotiate was, however, quite valuable.

Out of a variety of international discussions, a number of ideas concerning human action on the environment emerged. One position pragmatically maintained that in spite of the Gaia hypothesis, more progress could be made by concentrating on one issue at a time. For instance, attempts to ameliorate the "ozone hole" in the atmosphere led to a set of protocols agreed to by ninety-three countries to eliminate the use of chemicals like chlorofluorocarbons that destroy ozone. New kinds of refrigerants were developed, and ozone depletion ceased being a pressing problem. Nevertheless, environmental problems and analyses have continued to develop.

Postmodernism

All of the preceding sections discuss issues and movements that called into question the idea that Europe was at the forefront of progress and that the ingredients of that progress were free enterprise, democratic governments that governed lightly, science as the premier method of discerning truth, and human-centered technology that made life spans longer and more comfortable. Theorists working and writing within the critical context created by all of these movements began to question the very basis of analytical thought. That is, they questioned the use of logical reason. It seemed to some as if the incisive use of reason in the past two centuries had brought us to a point from which we could see that reason was insufficient. Reason had turned against itself.

Postmodernism is a word that encompasses a number of critical movements in virtually every field of art and ideas. In previous chapters, we saw that a general characteristic of modernism was a conviction that for all great questions, although traditional and common-sense answers were insufficient, if one went deeper, there was an answer to be found. For instance, we have seen that although nineteenth-century scientists saw the world through a Newtonian lens, in the twentieth century Einstein showed that serious modifications to the Newtonian worldview were necessary to understand new observations. Modern physics was founded on Einstein's relativity theory. We just examined how applying scientific reason and experimentation in agriculture could greatly increase food production.

Postmodernism challenged the idea that any of the encompassing frameworks of thought were sufficient, and thus that a truth could be found. In a sense, postmodernists challenged the Western rational project as defined in the Enlightenment. If there were no answers, then there could be no progress, and rational thought would be just one of many ways of understanding anything. If there were no truth to history, then the past could be whatever one wanted it to be. If there were no true ethical principles, then anything could be permitted. To postmodernists, the future of thought without limits was exciting. To modernists or other critics of postmodernism, the new thinkers were on a slippery slope to chaos.

The modernism/postmodernism dichotomy could be understood as a new iteration of an old debate. Socrates, as presented by Plato, argued that there were eternal forms or ideas that shaped the nature of the world. The task of the philosopher was to understand the truth of those eternal forms and expose false ideas. Socrates opposed the Sophist rhetoricians who, he thought, taught that there were no truths, and thus that the art of persuasion was the most important skill a citizen could have. In the nineteenth century, the relativist Nietzsche stood against the Platonic tradition of truth. Throughout this text, we have seen a variety of thinkers wrestling with the relationship between sensory data, logic, and rational understanding of the world. In general, the supporters of the existence of rationally intelligible truth tended to denigrate the importance of emotion, while those who argued that truth was an illusion saw value in human nonrational capacities.

Three ideas play key roles in the development of postmodern theory:

1) Cultural relativity—cultures must be understood relative to their own terms, and all cultures should be equally valued.

2) Social construction of ideas—all ideas are created by humans and exist in a social context. There are no ideas that exist independently of humans.

3) Language games—language is a self-contained game, the parts of which are meaningful only because of their relationship with other parts. Language only incidentally denotes a world beyond itself.

While the humanities might have had room for relativism, the sciences were founded on the idea that there was a true structure to the universe. Scientists developed theories that were then juxtaposed with experiments, and the outcome was a set of symbolic statements in language or in mathematics that scientists believed expressed a truth about the structure of the universe. If there were no such structure, or if the universe were unstructured, then scientific investigation would not be the valuable activity that scientists and others in authority thought it was.

Thus, a cogent attack on the idea of scientific truth would be more shocking than an attack on the idea of truths expressed in, say, poetry. In 1962 Thomas Kuhn (1922–96) launched such an attack.

Thomas Kuhn and the Development of the Strong Program

In *The Structure of Scientific Revolutions*, Kuhn argued that scientific ideas and activity took place within a particular kind of worldview called a paradigm. Years of training on what questions are interesting and important, what methods are most illuminating and sound, on what answers are considered possible, coherent, and plausible, fixed this paradigm in the minds of scientists. Just like any worldview, it could not be encompassed in an instruction manual; it affected how paradigm bearers literally saw and valued the world. But given the open-ended nature of science, there were always loose ends that were unanswered within a given paradigm, leading at some point to new experiments that would challenge the paradigm. The only resolution of the resulting confusion was the enunciation of a new paradigm.

At this point, wrote Kuhn, scientists who embraced the new paradigm found themselves at odds with scientists who continued to work within the old paradigm. The new paradigm inevitably omitted concepts that those in the old paradigm thought were essential parts of the universe. The new paradigm left some things unexplained and made assumptions that the older school thought were outlandish. For instance, we have seen that instead of explaining the structure of aether, Einstein merely said that aether did not exist. Whereas Newtonians thought that absolute time and space were essential, Einstein decided that time and space would become spacetime and would have no absolute character. There was no logical way to decide which paradigm was correct, and some older scientists fought against relativity theory to the end of their lives. Kuhn noted that the older adherents of the old paradigm would die first, leaving science in the hands of the younger adherents of the new worldview.

One could not claim that moving from one paradigm to another was progress, because a different definition of progress was embedded within each paradigm. One could only say that a change had taken place.

Kuhn also challenged an older philosophical conception of the difference between science and nonscience. The Austrian Karl Popper had convincingly claimed that no scientific theory could be verified, because there was always the possibility that some future experiment would prove the theory wrong. The difference between science and nonscience, said Popper, was that scientific theories could be falsified. Experimental science was not a search for verification, but rather a search for falsification. Those theories that always had an answer for everything, like Freudian psychology or Marxism, were not scientific.

Kuhn replied that not only could scientific theories not be verified, but they also could not be falsified. Different paradigms might provide the criteria for falsification or verification, but there were no incontrovertible meta-paradigms that could provide the criteria for decision. Kuhn applied cultural relativism to science. People lived in different worlds that could not be translated, one to the other. In one world, people saw one thing; in the other world, they saw something else.

But his approach suggested that science itself was cultural, and that scientists operating within different paradigms could not truly understand one another. The next step occurred to several investigators of the scientific process. Perhaps science could be studied using the methods of social science. Science, rather than being a privileged approach to knowledge, was just another culture—a different form of society. At several British, French, and American universities, scholars conceived of science and technology studies as programs of research and teaching.

In Edinburgh, a school of thought known as the strong program emerged. In the strong program, all scientific knowledge was socially constructed. In the strong program, there was no place for the idea of truth. In France, Bruno Latour was associated with the strong program, and although he has since backed away from the radical relativism inherent in the strong program, in the 1980s and 1990s he argued in favor of that approach. In *Laboratory Life: The Social Construction of Scientific Facts* (1979), a book he wrote with the British Stephen Woolgar, they argued that laboratory research has nothing to do with the traditional scientific method. Science was but a Nietzschean battle of wills to see which scientific theory would prevail. Latour argued elsewhere that the distinctions between subject and object and nature and society were simply social constructions.

Lyotard and the Rejection of Metanarratives

The ideas of Latour and Woolgar were echoed by the French philosopher Jean François Lyotard, who in the 1979 book *La condition postmoderne: Rapport sur le savoir* (*The Postmodern Condition: A Report on Knowledge*) defined postmodernism as an incredulity toward metanarratives. Such metanarratives had been used to cement the authority of science as the only way to actually know, or to declare that history was progressive. In a technocratic society, claimed Lyotard, each of us performed routine tasks, and such metanarratives were no longer necessary to unite us in our separate activities. We all retreated to our own perspectives.

Lyotard used Wittgenstein's idea of language games, in which words and expressions were defined by their use in the game of language but had no necessary reference to a nonlinguistic reality. Lyotard argued that different communities had incommensurable narratives. He was skeptical of the narrative of human emancipation that judged freedom by the increased wealth and quality of life produced by science and its technological outcomes. Such a metanarrative seemed to explain everything—so, for example, a war might be justified as a fight for human emancipation. In this way, the language of science and the language of politics and ethics became conjoined.

Science, Lyotard argued, played a language game that claimed to denote aspects of "reality" and worked to shift knowledge from a discussion of human ends to an analysis of means. Technology in the computer age saw knowledge as information and information exchange. There was a loss of meaning, and thus the metanarratives were no longer useful. The old rules of the language game were gone. New ones remained to be invented, but they must be invented in a world in which only effectiveness in performing according to the needs of the technocratic system is rewarded.

Baudrillard and Images . . . of Images

The French postmodern cultural theorist Jean Baudrillard (1929–2007) was fascinated by images. He noted that in a technological world images were created by a technological process. Often these images had no referent in the natural world. In this they bore a resemblance to abstract ideas that were removed from anything concrete. Thus, political ideologies were based on ideas like power, society, politics, and so forth—ideas that did not point to concrete sensorial, entities. People increasingly lived in an urban human-made world, and thus they were used to being surrounded by social constructions. But Baudrillard pointed out that even our images had become removed, and so they existed in a space of hyperreality. In hyperreality, signs stand only for themselves. In the technological age, simulacra, resemblances, did not resemble anything other than themselves. But, wrote Baudrillard, simulacra did not conceal the truth; the truth itself concealed the absence of truth. If we removed the image, we would find that there was nothing behind it.

We lived in a world of reproductions, but the reproductions reproduced only themselves. Science pretended to study the world, but it was studying itself. Its ideas, its experiments, were artificial. Scientific theories referred to abstractions that referred to other abstractions. There was no world behind the theories in a technological society. The more society tried to bring all reality into a coherent picture, the more society became less stable and fearful. The global village was increasingly connected, but it was connected by unreal symbols, or even by no symbols at all. The more we followed the routines of technology, the less we understood the world of human meaning. Humans searched for an elusive meaning that was unattainable in the new world. We only had signs and images; we had no overarching symbols that could show us who we were. For example, we lived in a world in which we did not wear clothing but rather wore brands.

Derrida and Deconstruction

Jacques Derrida (1930–2004) was born an Algerian Jew. He was in high school (Lycée) during the Second World War and experienced the Nazi-sympathizing Vichy regime's efforts to control the Berber language. In Paris after the war, he studied philosophy at the École Normale Supérior, where he had the chance to interact with most of the French thinkers described in the last few chapters. In his studies he emphasized phenomenology, especially Husserl and Levinas, and also closely read Hegel. Eventually, he studied and wrote about much of the canon in Western philosophy. He is best known for developing an approach to texts known as deconstruction. He developed this method as he commented on a wide variety of the canonic texts.

Deconstruction at base concerns itself with the deeper meaning of writing and texts. Derrida found key concepts that seemed to contain contradictions within themselves. He then concentrated on these contradictions to gain new insight not only into these texts but into other texts influenced by them.

For example, Derrida examined Plato's dialogue "Phaedrus" to analyze Socrates' often-expressed antipathy to writing. Derrida saw that the opposition originated in an assumption: speaking consists of signs that refer to thoughts; writing consists of signs that refer to spoken words; thus, writing is a sign of a sign and thus removed from the original idea. Writing, to Socrates, is a kind of poison that seduces us away from reality. It weakens our memories and removes our human connection with the speaker. Since writing can be conveyed far away from the place it was composed, it is alien, an outsider. It is dangerous. It is both a presence and an absence. The poison needs an antidote, and that antidote is the search for truth through dialectic. In this search, we see yet another opposition: true/untrue.

Derrida explored these oppositions in a number of his works. He maintained that speaking is not prior to writing but that writing itself is also primary. All signs are signs of other signs rather than of something more basic. The cutting away of a connection between language and reality is one of the central deconstructive acts. Derrida did not carry out his analyses to show how wrong the texts he examined were, but rather to show what deconstructing a text could show us about ourselves. All texts, including his own, could be deconstructed. All thought could be seen as an expression of opposition or of differences. Presence and absence could not exist without one another. So, for instance, when Derrida analyzed Rousseau, who claimed that culture had corrupted nature, Derrida showed that the idea of nature is itself a cultural product. He did this not to reverse Rousseau's privileging of nature over culture, but rather to remove the act of privileging itself. The only thing we can do to clarify our situation is to understand that we are always balanced between oppositions.

Derrida concerned himself with the difference between that which is unique, unrepeatable, like the present moment, and that which is subject to repeatability, like the motions of a machine. The unique seems to be the opposite of the constantly repeatable. But one's experience of the present moment takes place in time and thus contains what came immediately before, as well as anticipation of what will come immediately after.

When one experiences a moment, that moment is immediately accessible to memory. Thus, the unrepeatable moment is itself repeatable. One is reminded of the teacher who declared that each student was precious and unique. "You are unique—just like everyone else." Unrepeatability and repeatability lie together in every experience.

When we consider self-consciousness, we also find opposition. We are conscious of ourselves as if we were other. The opposition between "I" and "other" collapses. When it came to phenomenology, Derrida argued that the basic phenomenological experience of lived-experience arose from an interior monologue. In this interior monologue, we are both speaker and hearer, and when we look in the mirror, we are both see-er and seen. To accomplish this duality, there has to be a distance, a space, for instance, between the mirror and the self.

This duality seems to lie behind Freud's analysis. The unconscious has a secret that it cannot tell to the conscious. But the analyst can see that when the patient denies a wish at that moment the patient affirms the wish, so, negation is affirmation. If a friend tells us a secret, we may promise not to tell the secret, but we can only have the secret if we tell it to ourselves. And the secret is then no longer secret. It is always ready to be shared. Thus, a secret can only be secret if it is not a secret.

And this process of affirmation and simultaneous negation lies at the heart of the deconstruction project. Deconstruction demonstrates that contradiction lies at the heart of language. And since language lies at the heart of thinking, all thinking is essentially contradictory as well. The only way to expose the contradiction is by using words to analyze the situation. But these words themselves must be based on contradictory dichotomies; deconstruction is a process without end. Deconstruction then shows us that the hope that we might find the eternally true, the essence of Plato's forms, is a vain hope. Or perhaps not—the opposition of eternal/ephemeral is always there. The ephemeral brings us back to the eternal and vice versa.

In the English-speaking world, deconstruction became a tool of literary criticism. Literary critics studied texts and found that the key concepts could be understood as working within oppositions. Before the 1960s, literary criticism (New Criticism) focused on texts as if they stood alone. Derrida showed that texts could never be seen as standing alone: they exist within a literary and cultural tradition. Texts are written in a language that the author did not invent. Every criticism is thus a question about the nature of language. The deconstructive point was that literature was part of a larger human discourse that exists throughout society. Analyzing literature is not about finding figures of speech like irony, but rather about showing that all knowledge is essentially ironic.

Michel Foucault: Power and Truth

Michel Foucault (1926–84) was a French philosopher who was fascinated by outcasts. He was known for developing a method that he described as archaeology of knowledge. He used his archaeological method to examine the history of attempts to control behavior, the history of scientific knowledge, and the history of sexuality, among other topics. As he did so he exposed the historical contingency of all of these topics. The conceptual tool that he used was "power." As he asked how power was expressed, he found that it was often below human consciousness. His archaeological approach led him to dig deep to find hidden layers. Once he found a layer, he could explore it.

In 1966's *Les mots et les choses* (Words and Things—translated as *The Order of Things*, 1973), Foucault echoed Kuhn's description of a paradigm by inventing the "episteme," the worldview within which the science of a given epoch develops. He started with the episteme of the Renaissance in which things resemble, mirror one another, and thus provide knowledge through analogy. The Renaissance episteme made good use of likeness—for instance, that between microcosm and macrocosm, between the human and the cosmos.

The classical episteme that started in the middle of the seventeenth century reordered everything. The key was ideas, mental representation. A word or symbol represented an object but did not resemble it. For the classical mind, the object was real, and so too was the idea that represented it. By concentrating on symbols (words), scientists focused on relationships among these symbols. Creating the order of, say, a grid or graph became the task of the classical age. Ordering species, taxonomy, was the highest form in the study of biology.

In the modern age, especially with Nietzsche, words got cut away from objects, and thus ideas were not necessarily the carriers of knowledge. It was conceivable that something other than representation was at work. Language became a problem; language seemed to speak about itself rather than something else. And human beings became interesting objects of study: both the knowers and the known. Human beings, because they die, and because they are the source of the ideas by which we know the world, pose a problem for the theory of knowledge (epistemology). Foucault concludes that putting human beings at the heart of true knowledge (instead of say, God), as well as at the center of investigation, causes the modern scientific project to collapse. If humans are constructed historically, and if humans construct history, this presents a fatal contradiction.

In 1975 in *Surveiller et punir* (translated as *Discipline and Punish* in 1977) Foucault examined the replacement of execution by imprisonment for criminals. This reform used punishment as a way of shaping people to better fit into society. The prison became a model for schools and other institutions in a technological society. One tool of the modern disciplinary society was observation. It was not necessary to observe people every minute, but it was important that they should believe that they might be observed every moment. Errors of omission were just as important as misdeeds. If people have not done what they should have done (for instance, malingering at work), they must be corrected. They must be "normalized." Standards in all areas of life were necessary. There must be standards for school curricula, for professional practice, for measurement, and so forth. And so, the final tool of the disciplinary society was the examination. Examinations combined observation and normalizing judgments. Those that did not measure up could be directed to further study or correction.

The disciplinary society was interested in controlling the body. People should play a useful role in a complex society. They should submit docilely to control. The means of control generally was not pain, but rather correction. The threat to the system was abnormal individuals like the insane and the criminal. Those that had an unmalleable personality were classified scientifically and incarcerated.

Sexuality represented yet another method of exercising power. For Foucault sexuality did not exist until it was constructed. People learned about sexuality as they learned how to define themselves. A whole panoply of institutions, legal, medical, psychological, and so forth contributed to a society's sense of the meaning of sex. Power over sexuality, a social construction, lay mostly inside human individuals, who by and large had learned well and applied the lessons learned to their definitions of themselves. Subjects controlled themselves. In the modern world, people wanted to talk of liberating their repressed sexuality, but that was a fruitless task, because there was no sexuality to repress until it was socially constructed. Power did not so much repress as it produced. Power in society created who we were and how we would live, and we had no being that was not a social being.

Foucault tended to treat power as an autonomous force, removed from any person or institution. We lived in interwoven networks that expressed a power that had rationality and that moved toward its own ends. Where there was power, there would be resistance, but power could not be overcome. We could only understand our relationship to power as we lived in its grasp.

Science Fights Back: The Sokal Hoax

Few scientists found the postmodern approach compelling. In this text, we have seen numerous examples of effective scientific theories leading to discovery of unexpected characteristics of nature. Without science, for instance, we could not suspect that radio waves even existed. Scientists were sure that they knew more than their predecessors did. As they asked questions of nature, they were not about to question the entire process of the possibility of scientific inquiry.

In 1996 the British physicist Alan Sokal undertook to demonstrate the farcical side of postmodernism, so he wrote a nonsensical discussion of atomic physics in what he saw as postmodern jargon entitled "Transgressing the Boundaries: Towards a Transformative Hermeneutics of Quantum Gravity." In it he claimed, for instance, that the value of π (pi) was socially constructed. He wrote of the post-Enlightenment hegemony as a pernicious influence on science. The piece was published in the journal *Social Text*. He then exposed his hoax in the journal *Lingua Franca*. Sokal claimed that he was not defending science, something that needed no defense, but was rather defending the political left from trendiness. He supported well-done sociology of science but attacked sloppiness. In 1997 Sokal and his Belgian colleague Jean Bricmont wrote *Impostures Intellectuelles* (*Intellectual Impostures*) in which, among other things, they criticized the Strong Program of social constructionism.

Thus, even as the postmodernists used reason to question reason, exposing the contradictions inherent in language, the scientists used reason to repudiate postmodern distortions of reason, as well as to explore the natural world. Technological development—ignoring the sideshow—continued apace.

Political Tsunamis

The end of the twentieth century experienced a head-spinning whirlwind of political changes that included and reframed many of the ideas of the previous 200 years. The democratic socialism that had been adopted after the Second World War was challenged by a kind of neoliberalism. The communist Soviet Union disintegrated, and with it the Cold War. Europe was pushed into a redefinition that resulted in the reunification of Germany and the leadership of Germany and France in forming a European Union that included free movement of peoples across borders and a new currency, the Euro. Behind all of these changes lurked economic debates, decisions about the primacy of individuals versus the primacy of nations, and a slow reevaluation of the very idea of the nation-state.

The End of the Soviet Union

Probably three of the most consequential ideas near the end of the twentieth century were "glasnost," "perestroika," and "demokratizatsiya." These Russian ideas, used by Mikhail Gorbachev (b. 1931), the leader of the Soviet Union beginning in 1985, were roughly translated as "openness," "restructuring," and "democratization." All of them, however, had a particularly Russian flavor. "Glasnost" was a term that was used to describe open court proceedings, but with Gorbachev came to be generally understood as "freedom of speech." Perestroika was used to describe a decentralization of economic decision

Figure 13.4 Helmut Kohl and Mikhail Gorbachev, 1990. The leaders of the Soviet Union and of Germany negotiate the withdrawal of Soviet troops from a uniting Germany. © Wojtek Laski/ Hulton Archive/Getty Images.

making so that the state enterprises could themselves decide what their output levels would be as they sought to cover their own expenses with revenue from sales. Perestroika also allowed the workers collectively to decide on the operational procedures in state factories. Demokratizatsiya denoted a shift that allowed competition in elections at the local level as long as all candidates were Communist Party members. Demokratizatsiya also involved reconstituting the governmental institutions and solidifying Gorbachev's position as head of government.

Gorbachev was born to a peasant family in the Caucasus region of the Soviet Union. His grandparents, with whom he had lived, were sent to the Gulag in the time of agriculture collectivization and purges under Stalin. After the Second World War, Gorbachev proved to be both an excellent student and an adept operator of combine harvesters. In the 1950s, he joined the party, studied law, and got married. He gradually rose in the party, and in 1966 he was cleared for foreign travel, and by the late 1970s was the secretary for agriculture. As a former farmer, when he viewed three years of low harvests caused by bad weather, he began to think that perhaps some decision making about agriculture should be trusted to those plowing the ground. In 1985 he became the general secretary of the Communist Party.

The problem that Gorbachev saw was that the Soviet Union suffered from low productivity, inferior goods, and low worker morale exacerbated by a high rate of alcoholism. Managers of economic entities tended to report to the planners a rosier picture than was warranted. There were neither incentives for providing bad news nor positive incentives for presenting good news. Modern technocratic society was very complex, and it was hard to model the ideal flow of goods and services from a central government perspective, especially if the models were based on inaccurate information. Gorbachev was afraid that the Soviet Union would fall farther and farther behind Western economies.

Gorbachev was a believer in the importance of a centrally planned economy and in socialism. His reforms were meant to make central planning more efficient. Glasnost would enable managers to speak freely without fear of reprisal. Perestroika would introduce market-based information at the local level and would enable quick response to any unexpected and unplanned events. Central planners would then have the information they needed to oversee the economy as a whole. He realized that his reforms would face significant opposition, but he was convinced that if they were given time to work, the Soviet economy would become demonstrably better. With the policy of glasnost, the entire populace would be able to recognize and trust economic achievements. Gorbachev was right about the opposition. It came not only from people who had benefited from, and believed in, the old way, but it also came from people like Boris Yeltsin, the Moscow mayor, who thought the liberal reforms did not go far enough.

In 1986 the nuclear reactor at Chernobyl, Ukraine, melted down and blew up, spewing toxic radiation across Europe. Gorbachev realized that the accident arose from the unwillingness of those in power to listen to those who knew what was happening. Fear of reprisals for not meeting targets encouraged local decision-makers to press on with a test that should have been aborted. The reactor was also shoddily made. Gorbachev later said that with Chernobyl he realized the depth of the problems of cover-ups and incompetence that the Soviet Union faced.

The struggles and uncertainties in the Soviet Union led reformers in other countries in the Eastern bloc to push for greater liberalization in their own countries. But they wanted to use glasnost to talk about independence, not about production figures. Mass demonstrations organized by the major trade union in Poland, Solidarity, pushed the government into compromise reforms. Hungary followed, and soon was taking down its border fence, opening a gate to the West. East Germans and Czechs began to visit Hungary, never to return. As all of these changes unfolded, Gorbachev stood firmly behind his reforms. He suggested that other Eastern countries should also institute glasnost and perestroika, and he refused to send Soviet troops to back up totalitarian rulers in the satellite states.

The fall of the Berlin Wall became an iconic act, symbolic of the entire shift away from communism. On November 9, 1989, hundreds of thousands of East Germans walked through the gates—unhindered by confused guards—and entered West Germany. In weeks, crowds had torn down the wall. Berlin was reunited. No Soviet troops came. On November 28, Czechoslovakian demonstrators completed their "Velvet Revolution" as the government announced that it was no longer a one-party state. Other countries took their own paths, but by early 1990 the Iron Curtain was no more. On December 31, 1991, the Soviet Union ceased to exist.

A confrontation between East and West that had threatened mass annihilation and had consumed the energies of Europeans for decades was over. It ended not with a battle but with celebrations all over Europe. Or, as T.S. Eliot had predicted decades before the Cold War began, not with a bang but a whimper. No one had predicted such an end to the Cold War. It just stopped.

Germany Unites

Helmut Kohl, the leader of the right-of-center Christian Democratic Party of Germany (CDU) became chancellor in 1982. He was a conservative in approach to domestic policy and so worked to find ways to cut government expenditures on welfare, but that was not his most pressing priority. First of all, he wanted to act positively to mend West Germany's relationship with France and build a stronger relationship with East Germany. He reached out to the socialist president of France, François Mitterrand, and the two of them worked to construct pan-European institutions like the small joint military force called Eurocorps. He also reached out to East Germany. Thus, an economically strong Germany was in place to join with France to unify Europe.

As Mikhail Gorbachev loosened his control over the non-Soviet states of the Eastern bloc, East Germans began to increase pressure on their government for reforms. This peaceful protest became known as *Die Wende*, the turning point. And after the Berlin Wall was torn down in late 1989, Kohl began to negotiate.

Figure 13.5 Berlin Wall, then and now. A composite photograph showing Berlin just before the wall came down in 1989 and Berlin at the same spot in 2019. The sign warns travelers that they are leaving the American sector. © Express Newspapers/Hulton Archive/Getty Images.

Kohl had a complex set of intellectual commitments. As a German nationalist he sought to exonerate the German nation from complicity in the Nazi atrocities, and he always described the acts of the Nazis as having been done "in the German name." It was part of his constitutional responsibility to act to reunify Germany. But he also understood that the best interests of the German nation would be served by binding Germany tightly to the other countries of Europe. Germany was too weak to enforce an all-European peace, but Germany was also too strong not to engender hostility and suspicion by trying to manipulate the decisions of its neighbors. There seemed to be one way out of this impasse.

Kohl's vision was a united Germany in a united Europe. There were many reasons that other Europeans might oppose such a goal. After the Second World War, and the Holocaust, the rest of Europe was quite content to see Germany divided. Furthermore, although Europe had slowly been developing trade pacts (see the following text), many Europeans who valued their identities as part of particular nations opposed the idea of a united Europe. After almost forty-five years of living apart, many East and West Germans saw themselves as living in separate countries, not in an artificially divided one.

Kohl therefore had to develop not just a unitary vision but also a practical plan. First, he convinced US president George H. W. Bush as well as Mikhail Gorbachev that a united Germany would be a peaceful Germany. Gorbachev agreed to withdraw troops from East Germany if West Germany would pay the cost. Second, against the advice of economists and bankers, Kohl decided to bring the East Germans into the West German economy, although because of the poor shape of Eastern factories and enterprises, they were not ready to compete with the West. Integrating the two economies would cost the West Germans billions. Many in Germany would have preferred to let the unification gently evolve over decades. Kohl shrewdly thought that if unification did not happen immediately, it probably would never occur.

Many West Germans still can remember the symbolism of the influx of Trabants, East German-made automobiles that sputtered along spewing oiled exhaust beside the sleek Mercedes and Audis of the West. As the air on sidewalks became fouler, many Westerners living near the former border were ready to give up on the unification project. From the other point of view, the owners of the Trabants were proud people who often had saved for ten years to realize the dream of owning an automobile. They did not enjoy being ridiculed. Nevertheless, on October 3, 1990, East Germany ceased to exist, and a unified Germany once again came into being.

East Germany had been the pearl of the Eastern economy, but now it was near the bottom of an expanded market. The West German government poured billions, ultimately trillions, of Deutschemarks into infrastructure projects and other economic supports, for instance giving a facelift to deteriorating historical buildings, but Easterners still suffered high rates of unemployment and consequent bitterness and anger. The conservative government had no interest in supporting socialist institutions, so rather than negotiating a compromise government, the East was forced to join West Germany. Average salaries slowly rose, but many citizens were left behind. Their simmering resentments were to cause problems into the twenty-first century.

Great Britain Steps Back

During the Gorbachev years, the prime minister of the UK was the Tory (Conservative) Margaret Thatcher. She had no interest in participating in a united Europe and was opposed to the unification of Germany. Thatcher was content to rebuild England and to perpetuate already-existing foreign policy alliances with the Commonwealth nations and the United States. Putting her efforts into domestic policy, Thatcher was determined to undo most of the welfare state programs that had defined Great Britain since the Second World War. Since 1973 and the oil embargo put in place by the Organization of the Petroleum Exporting Countries (OPEC), oil-importing countries like the United States and the United Kingdom had suffered what came to be called stagflation. In the Keynesian approach, a government should inject money into the economy during a time of unemployment and should contract the money supply during inflation. However, during the 1970s, the UK suffered both unemployment and inflation. The Keynesians did not have a ready answer.

Margaret Thatcher was opposed to the welfare state. She was influenced by analysts like Friedrich Hayek, whose 1944 book *The Road to Serfdom*, made a highly influential case against government control of economic decision making. For Hayek, there was no essential difference between communism and fascism. Both were socialist, by which

Hayek meant both tried to control the unpredictability of life in a market economy by replacing the market with central planning. But central planning meant that the majority of people relied on the opinions and decisions of a minority, the planners. In order to be effective, the planners had to use coercion to control the economic activities of the millions. So, a socialist government, said Hayek, in order to achieve equality, had to firmly control human behavior. Competition in a free market was the only way humans could react and respond to one another without external coercion.

Individual freedom in the political realm was only possible in the context of freedom in the economic realm, Hayek argued. Even though socialism exerted its control in order to achieve humane ends, the result was inevitably loss of freedom and ultimately the equivalent of slavery.

However, Hayek also reserved important roles for government, something that people who rely on Hayek often ignore. As long as regulations were applied equally to all competitors, Hayek approved of regulating methods of production, quality of goods, sanitation, fraudulent practices, and so forth. Since the market could not guarantee protections for the environment, environmental protection was an essential role of government.

Hayek also supported guaranteeing security in food, shelter, and clothing sufficient to maintain health and the ability to work. For Hayek, once a society had become as wealthy as Europe was, it made sense to provide social insurance against general hazards and to offer aid to victims of natural catastrophes. He supported government planning to control the economic disasters associated with depressions. And he clearly stated that such planning did not have to be coercive.

Thatcher not only echoed Hayek, but she also embraced a form of monetarism in economics in which controlling inflation was more important than controlling unemployment. She was attracted to monetarism because, unlike Keynesianism, monetarism did not look favorably on state spending to increase the money supply. The Labor government that preceded her had actually begun reducing public spending in the face of stagflation, and Thatcher continued apace, although by 1984 her government seemed to have abandoned monetarism. In 1984 there were 3.3 million unemployed versus 1.5 million when she took office.

Thatcher was an individualist who believed that individuals should be held accountable for their conduct. She centralized power in her office and mistrusted the bureaucracy. She privatized government industries like British Airways, British Steel, and most of the utilities, and she fought against the power of trade unions. In principle, she believed in lower taxes. Thus, the 1980s represented a sharp turn to the right in the United Kingdom, paralleling the conservative turn in the United States under President Ronald Reagan.

European Unification

The idea of European unification was not new, but with the exception of a brief period when Napoleon's influence stretched across most of Europe, the idea was essentially moribund. During the period of time covered by this text, the more powerful idea was

Map 4 The European Union. Compare this map with the fragmented map of Europe in 1815 (Chapter 3). One of the main stories of the past 200 years of intellectual history has been conceiving and actualizing a union of Europe.

nationalism. Where there was transnational unification, as with the Austrian or Ottoman empires, linguistic and cultural groups, nations, agitated for autonomy. The only organized forces agitating for unity were the international socialist groups. However, the idea that the proletariat has common interests that are more binding than the ties of nationality failed to convince European workers not to make war against one another in the First World War.

After the Second World War, recent enemies were suspicious of one another. Not only had normal wartime activities robbed Europeans of loved ones, but also intentional torture, rape, starvation, and attempts at national extermination had left psychological sores that would not stop bleeding. The victors had avoided the pitfalls of the Versailles Treaty that ended the First World War, but that was a rational and pragmatic decision. Emotionally, there were still many Europeans who ached for revenge. In the wake of a brutal war, it seemed unlikely that Europeans would soon come together. Yet that was what happened in Western Europe.

Leaders of most countries realized that Europe could not tolerate another devastating war. The Eastern half of Europe was unified under the Soviet Union, but the West was still fragmented. How could they come together? It turned out that the answer was trade. All of the countries traded with one another, and border stops for customs, tariffs, and money exchanges made each transaction more costly. One need not love one's former enemies to realize that free trade could be mutually beneficial. John Maynard Keynes had fruitlessly pointed out the attraction of free trade at the end of the First World War. After the Second World War, Keynes's stock had risen.

In 1951 Belgium, the Netherlands, Luxembourg, France, Italy, and West Germany, with the support of the United States, signed a treaty in Paris creating the European Coal and Steel Community. Coal and steel were seen as the basis for a strong industrial economy, so agreeing to cooperate in this arena signaled the possibility of cooperating in other areas of trade. The European Economic Community was set up in 1958 to do just that. Two major sticking points slowed the attempts to achieve a truly common market. First, countries like France felt that it was important to protect their small farmers and traditional produce, like wine. Second, French president de Gaulle was unwilling to cooperate without maintaining the right to veto proposals that he did not see as in France's interests. An example of what de Gaulle had in mind was his two-time veto of membership for the UK. De Gaulle felt that Great Britain was too enmeshed with its Commonwealth and with the United States to commit itself to cutting those ties to become part of a European Union. Only after de Gaulle's presidency could Great Britain join the European project. The recent Brexit may have proved de Gaulle's point.

Some Europeans were not content slowly to build an open market for trade. They thought that Europe would only reach its potential by uniting politically in a "United States of Europe," explicitly modeled on the United States of America. Winston Churchill had spoken in favor of such a proposal, although he did not want the UK to become a part of it. In 1948 the Congress of Europe brought together political leaders, philosophers, journalists, church leaders, entrepreneurs, and others in a grand pan-European brain trust. The French prime minister Robert Schuman took a leading role. On May 9, 1950 (today known as Europe Day), he promulgated the Schuman declaration supporting the first steps for ultimate unification. He also noted that the "age-old opposition of France and Germany" must be ended before Europe could come together. He therefore supported a series of small achievements that would ultimately pave the way to political integration. The chancellor of West Germany, Konrad Adenauer, worked closely with Schuman in building a set of pan-European institutions. Other key "founding fathers of Europe" were the Italian Alcide de Gasperi and the Frenchman Jean Monnet. The essential relationship for the success of European unity was that between France and Germany.

Eventually, with the Maastricht Treaty in 1993, the European Union was formed. It contained three different levels of union. First, it established a union among states that was aimed at a minimum at maintaining the peace, but also at cooperation in domestic and foreign policy. Second, it created a monetary and trade union that allowed the free flow of capital and goods among member states. As part of this monetary union, the Maastricht Treaty set up the conditions for the creation of the Euro. Third, it created a union of citizens who could vote for representatives in the European parliament and who could freely move from state to state, working in any state that was part of the union.

The newly unified Germany, as the largest European country, was a key and essential participant in the negotiations. As we have seen, Chancellor Helmut Kohl was convinced that a European Union would serve the best interests of Germany. As negotiations over the development of a common currency went on, it was clear to many, including Kohl, that a monetary union without a fiscal union would be incomplete. Yet no country was ready to surrender fiscal power, the power to determine how each government would spend money, to a central authority. Kohl recognized that Germany was economically weak as the country absorbed a bankrupt East Germany, As Germany strengthened, it would be hard to persuade Germans to give up their Deutsche Mark. Saying that "we must grasp the cloak of history" before it disappears, he pushed for premature adoption of the Euro.

When the Maastricht Treaty was presented to the citizens of the various countries, it turned out that in several countries there was at best lukewarm support for union among the voters. Denmark's citizens initially voted against the treaty, and in France the treaty only garnered 51 percent of the vote. In general, those who were reluctant were concerned about sovereignty. Citizens were not sure what the implications for their own national commitments were. The symbolism of losing a currency threatened national identity. Loss of control over monetary policy as a new European central bank replaced the traditional central banks was a pressing concern for many.

The attempts to create a European Union raised important questions about what such a union actually meant or implied. Because of the recent German reunification and lingering fears about the threat that a resurgent independent Germany might pose to the rest of Europe, leaders in almost all countries were in favor of proceeding apace with unification. Germany's chancellor, Helmut Kohl, also affirmed his commitment to a strong union. The issues raised in the national referenda, however, demonstrated the difference between the considered opinions of policy experts and the misgivings and fears of the populace. Nationalism still struck the strongest emotional chords with most Europeans. Most of Europe's new citizens did not think of themselves as Europeans, paid primary attention to local and national news, and often viewed the citizens of other countries as potential threats to their own values and livelihood.

Nevertheless, the Schengen Agreement allowed free movement of people across borders without visa requirements. Step-by-step central banks coordinated their activities until the Euro was issued in 2002. All the countries in the Euro zone (a smaller area than the EU) gave up their national currencies. Trade within the EU was carried out without tariff barriers, although countries negotiated the right to subsidize certain agricultural industries of national interest. Many of the leaders of the EU hoped that with increasing trade and personal contacts opposition to greater political union would weaken. Others opposed greater union and saw the EU primarily as a free-trade zone.

All the countries that belonged to the EU maintained their own national fiscal policies; while money was administered centrally, spending was administered locally. The implications became apparent in the twenty-first century when some countries, notably Greece, overspent their Euro holdings and a monetary crisis developed. All of the countries maintained their own militaries, and thus coordinated military action was left to NATO, a group that contained non-European countries, especially the United States. Where national governments felt their interests were at stake, they reserved the right to choose not to cooperate in EU policies.

Underlying the European Union was a belief that all people are equal. The agreement to allow free movement and employment could only be made if the parties to the agreement thought that it did not matter if a French firm hired a Spaniard in place of a French citizen. Implied in the agreement to allow the free movement of peoples was the assumption that if people brought a foreign culture into a country, any disruptions to common practices would not be too disruptive. The European Union is at heart a union of equal individuals. Not all Europeans believed this, as twenty-first-century disruptions have shown. Individualism and nationalism do not necessarily live comfortably with one another.

The European Union is yet another instance of the notion of "embodied ideas" that we have previously applied to technology and technological systems. The groundwork for the union began to be laid with the completion of a railway line crossing the France/Belgium border in 1842, followed in 1846 by a line connecting Paris and Brussels. By the end of the twentieth century, roads, electricity, telephone wires, wireless systems, and more connected all of Europe. The idea of a free-trade zone emerged from an already-robust trading system. The idea of the free movement of people came out of a mobile population that crossed borders in the hundreds of millions each year. The details had to be hammered out in diplomatic negotiations. The reality already stared everyone in the face.

And the opposition to freedom of movement? Close to 40 percent of Europeans had never traveled to another country. In many respects, the divisions in Europe were not exclusively national.

As the twentieth century drew to a close, it appeared that Europe had solved the problem of internal military struggle. Europe also appeared to be on the road to closer and closer political and perhaps cultural union. Whatever the considerable reservations Europeans held, there were reasons for optimism. But there were also indications of bumps in the road ahead.

Conclusion

Starting in the 1960s, a rising swell of largely youthful voices began to question the assumptions underlying the structures of European government, foreign policy, industry, economic system, and intellectual programs. Europe shed colonies but also shed the assumptions of superiority that had made colonies possible. Many Europeans began to see the Industrial Revolution that had powered Europe's affluence and its attainment of an unprecedented standard of living as the engine of ultimate ecological doom. By the 1970s, questioning voices were accompanied by unprecedented and ill-understood economic problems.

Intellectuals focused on the contradictions behind Western thinking. They found cogent reasons for doubting science as a method for obtaining truth about the universe; they found that language and symbolic systems were self-contained and had only a tenuous connection with anything outside of their ambit; they found that images only referred to other images and texts to other texts. Often their postmodern writings were playful.

In Great Britain and in Germany, conservative governments began to reign in government spending and question social democracy itself. In the communist world, the decision of Mikhail Gorbachev to release controls on speech and restructure economic decision making ultimately led to the collapse of the Soviet Union and its empire of satellite states. By the 1990s, Western Europe had built the European Union and minted new money, the Euro that replaced most national currencies, including the French Franc and the German Deutsche Mark. Former members of the Warsaw Pact began to prepare their applications to become part of the grand union. Only Russia seemed unlikely to ask or to be invited to the table.

Europe entered the twenty-first century in a vastly different way than it had entered the twentieth. Although there were problems and dissenters, it seemed that perhaps Europe had resolved many of its persistent challenges. To help with coordination, there was a brand-new technology available: the computer and the internet. It is to the ideas behind the new cyber world that we turn in the next chapter.

CHAPTER 14
THE CYBER CENTURY APPROACHING

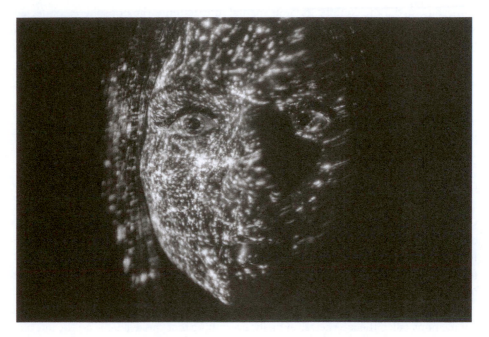

Figure 14.1 Virtual map of the internet projected onto woman's face. Human thought was carried outside the human mind. © Lean Neal/Getty Images News/Getty Images.

The Noosphere

The French Jesuit paleontologist Pierre Teilhard de Chardin (1881–1955) spent his life reconciling evolutionary science and Christianity. His best-known book, *Le Phénoméne humain* (*The Phenomenon of Man*—1955) was written in 1937, but its publication was forbidden by Catholic authorities. Teilhard (he had a double surname) was a courageous person who as a stretcher-bearer in the First World War had been awarded the two highest medals for valor, the Médaille militaire and the Légion d'honneur. He demonstrably had the internal fortitude to persist with his project despite the continual objections of his church superiors throughout his career. Most of his paleontological research was carried out in East Asia.

Teilhard's evolutionary theory was the goal-directed system of Ernst Haeckel rather than the random mutation approach of the Darwinians. He conceived of a vital force that directed the process of evolution. He was confirmed in this approach early in his career when he read Henri Bergson's ideas about an élan vital that took the human form of a creative impulse. Teilhard thus thought the evolution that his research was uncovering was a process that began with matter, but that in human beings took a mental form. As human beings progressed, a noosphere (a mental sphere) emerged that surrounded the earth in pure thought. As human society grew more complex, its institutions contributed to a thickening of the noosphere. As the human race grew more numerous, so did the complexity of its mental interactions. The noosphere connected individual human minds in a unity that ultimately would reach an apex, the Omega Point, that Teilhard associated with the eschatological second coming of Christ.

We have seen a number of theories that posit or suggest an evolutionary development with a utopic end. Hegel's Absolute and Marx's perfect communism are among them. Teilhard's system happened to be published just as another technological revolution was underway. At the end of this chapter, we will see just how apropos Teilhard's idea of the noosphere was.

Chapter Map

Computers represented an unusual sort of machine. Made to help human beings carry out intellectual operations, they represented the intellect reproducing parts of itself. From the very beginning, computers seemed to be a kind of brain or vice versa. We will follow the development of the technology of the computer as it grew from a mechanical to an electronic, to a solid-state device.

Much of the power of computers came from their interconnections in the web of connections called the internet. Eventually, everything that was available on the internet was available on individual computers. The world was literally at one's fingertips.

Scientists and philosophers asked what exactly a computer was. Was it the hardware or the software? Could a program be said to exist if it did not connect to hardware? In what ways did computers differ from human brains? Computers and their creators used metaphoric language both to enable programmers to conceive what they were doing and to enable computer-ignorant people to understand what they were doing when the turned their machines on.

Computers, in part, became storage devices, and eventually computer processors were linked together in vast data storage facilities that could process undreamed-of amounts of data in the blink of an eye. One use was scientific research. Both the Large Hadron Collider at CERN and radio telescopes spread out over kilometers sent their information to computers to construct images of what they had detected. Climate scientists were able to set up computer models of the atmosphere and oceans that predicted the warming of the globe unless we acted.

Artificial Intelligence became a field of study. Thinkers discussed how one would know a computer was intelligent, and how that could be determined. The film *The Matrix* explored a dystopian world of intelligent machines.

Some thinkers imagined that the increasing intelligence of machines would inevitably lead to a time when machines would outstrip human capability and would then have no more use for human beings. Advertisers began to write of "the cloud" as the place where ideas and art resided. It seemed that we were surrounded by ideas in digital form passing over our heads and through our bodies as they streaked toward their destinations.

Computers

The modern computer is first and foremost a conceptual device, that is, it is built with concepts about the nature of thought. Just as an abacus embodies ideas about arithmetical calculation and could not exist without these ideas, so the computer embodies theories about logic and thought and would have no reason for existence without such ideas. Importantly, the implications of the ideas could not be derived without the machine. That is, in some areas, the computer actually made some thoughts possible that could not have been conceived by a human being alone. Steam engines could be invented apart from a theory of ideas, and in fact, as we have seen, were invented without even a scientific understanding of the nature of heat. But computers were necessarily preceded by deep analysis of logic, language, and thought—much of this analysis has been discussed in this text in preceding chapters.

Self-taught English mathematician George Boole (1815–64) invented Boolean algebra. Essentially Boole created the foundation for symbolic logic, and several other thinkers polished the system. In Boolean algebra, variables become either "true" or "false." Operations are represented by symbols denoting "and," "or," and "not," among others. Thus, logical propositions can be set up like equations. Since propositions are either true or false, they have a binary character. Such a logic could be related to a base-two number system, a binary system.

Two Americans made Boole's insights available for computers. In the 1880s, Charles Sanders Pierce saw the connection between Boolean logic and electrical switching circuits: either on or off. In the 1930s, Claude Shannon wrote his doctoral dissertation on "A Symbolic Analysis of Relay and Switching Circuits." By the 1930s, the technology was available to begin to build logic machines, but financial support for building them was lacking. Funding by several governments during the Second World War allowed the budding ideas to be realized. The German engineer Konrad Zuse created electromechanical computers early in the war, but the German government classified them as not relevant to the war effort and they were never used. However, in the UK government support allowed Tommy Flowers and Alan Turing to design machines that broke German codes. Flowers' Colossus was the first programmable, electronic, digital computer. Across the ocean, Americans built the ENIAC computer. Thus, as often happened in the development of technology, only the exigency of war produced the will and commitment to develop new machines.

At first, the idea of switches led to the use of actual mechanical switches being thrown by electrical currents. The next generation saw the noisy mechanical switches disappear

Figure 14.2 Wrens operating the Colossus Computer, 1943. This is the computer that helped break the German code. The women codebreakers are only recently getting the credit they deserve. © Bletchley Park Trust/Getty Images.

in favor of electrical switches that were either on or off. Computer engineers soon realized that triodes, vacuum tubes invented in the early days of radio, could be used as switches that were much faster and more efficient than other forms of switches. After the war, computer research continued as larger and larger electronic machines were built.

The most important idea behind computers was the realization that logical statements could be represented in binary mathematics. Second, the idea of algorithms, step-by-step recipes for undertaking a task, was crucial. Like complex machines, algorithms must specify clearly every single step of a process, no matter how intuitive the process seems. A human can be told to "boil water." A computer must be told to "1) pick up a pan, 2) carry the pan to the sink, 3) put the pan under the water faucet, 4) turn on the water tap," and even these steps are too vague in several places. But once the algorithm has been described and shown to work, it can be used indefinitely. In fact, successful algorithms can be inserted into other algorithms, thus making programming much more efficient.

A third important idea was the idea of a hierarchy of programs. In the Second World War computers, the circuits were manually plugged in by hand. But such a process was time consuming and inexact. Scientists at the Victoria University in Manchester developed a stored program computer in which the program instructions were stored in memory. A second program specifying a particular task could then be stored and connected to the computer's wired-in program. This second level of program could then be unplugged, and a different program plugged in. The machine program is a lower-level code, while the removable program is a higher-level code. Ultimately, programs can be run on top of one another in an ascending hierarchy.

As the computers developed, programmers and designers realized that a computer had to perform several different kinds of operations to complete a task. Since the computer is a conceptual machine, essentially the designers created a model of a certain kind of thinking. They did not necessarily believe that they were replicating the human brain, but rather that they were modeling logical thought. But it was easy for some people to blur the distinction. For instance, the term "memory" suggested that computers did the same thing that human minds do. It also blurred the distinctions between what human minds do and what computers do. The act of "remembering" is quite different in minds and computers.

New Hardware

The problem with vacuum tubes was that they generated a great deal of heat. They therefore had to be separated from one another to avoid overheating. In the late 1940s and early 1950s, a new kind of device, the transistor, was invented that used the properties of certain materials called semiconductors. Transistors could do everything triodes could do, but were smaller, radiated much less heat, and used much less electricity. By the mid-1950s, smaller, more powerful computers were being built that used only transistors.

The Italian typewriter company Olivetti became an electronics company early in the computer era. In 1957 and 1958, it produced three generations of a mainframe computer using only transistors. In 1964 Olivetti sold its mainframe business to the American firm General Electric. But in 1965, Olivetti produced the first personal computer, the Programma 101, which could be used as a programmable calculator. Most of its sales were in the United States, and it was used extensively by the US Air Force and NASA. Other minicomputers followed; for instance, the Polish K-202 arrived in 1971.

The effectiveness of these early computers can be seen in their use in taking American astronauts to the moon. On July 20, 1969, Neal Armstrong was able to land on the moon because of two Apollo Guidance Computers (AGC)—one in the command module and one in the lunar module. These computers weighed 32 kilograms (70 pounds) and had a frequency of a little over 2 megahertz (less than one-thousandth of the frequency of a cell phone today). Nevertheless, these computers were able to calculate the complex trajectories required to land on the moon and then return.

The next step was the integrated circuit. Instead of transistors that were connected by wires, an integrated circuit etched transistors and electrical connections onto a silicon (semiconducting) chip. Soon an entire computer could be built on one chip. The first such chip contained 2,250 transistors. In the early computers, programmers changed the program by reconnecting wires that connected the components. In the new systems of integrated circuits, the program was fixed. On a small chip, the size of a fingernail, an entire "microprocessor" existed.

Figure 14.3 Computer chip manufacturing, 1979. The process pinpoints circuit junctions and automatically and exactly solders wires finer than a human hair. © Bettmann/Getty Images.

The implications of the new microprocessors were not clear. Since computers were primarily used for mathematical calculations and for logical deductions, they seemed to be needed mostly by big organizations like the military, research universities, and large corporations. Computers in the early 1970s continued to be large and housed in special rooms, but the new lighter generation of computers could be transported in the trunk of a car. As computers became more powerful, they were capable of much more, but one could not quite envision what that "more" might be. After all, this situation had never occurred before. Maybe microprocessors would be useful in wristwatches, thought the president of Fairchild.

Personal Computers

But the new computers fascinated many people, usually young people. In 1973 in the UK, enthusiasts founded the Amateur Computer Club (ACC) that put out a newsletter containing instructions for building your own computer. It included price quotes for Intel microprocessor chips. In 1977 the ACC inspired the Dutch club called Hobby Computer Club (HCC) in Leidschendam, the Netherlands. As in the UK, newsletters offered information and technical help. They also put on an exhibition that attracted thousands. Starting in the 1970s, thousands of young Europeans were building their own computers, inventing new programs, exploring the implications of logical axioms, playing and developing games, and otherwise expanding the number of ways to use these devices.

In the 1980s, with the advent of the internet, increasing numbers of people who were not hobbyists found that they wanted to use computers. In 1979 the British computer scientist Christopher Evans wrote a book that became a TV series entitled *The Mighty Micro: The Impact of the Computer Revolution*, which argued that British economy, society, and life were about to be changed by the new personal computer. In 1981 the British Broadcasting Company sponsored the BBC Micro, manufactured by Acorn Computers. It was part of the BBC Computer Literacy Project. The BBC sponsored a TV series *The Computer Programme*, which was designed to teach the basics of computing. By 1982, 80 percent of British schools owned a computer for educational use. Acorn began to push into the American and West German markets. The company continued to develop educational games as well as educational content. Acorn computers also provided hardware and software to interface with programming languages like BASIC and PASCAL that were accessible on Read Only Memory (ROM) disks. Meanwhile, personal computers grew stronger and cheaper. Their capacity ran from 64 kilobytes in the later 1970s to 100 megabytes in the early 1990s to several gigabytes in the early 2000s.

As computers became more powerful, they were able to do more things—many of which previously had not been imagined. By the end of the twentieth century, a computer user could listen to unlimited amounts of music, use a word processor, play games, build scientific models, and design new computer architecture. But the most important aspect of the computer was not realized until the early 1990s. Computers could network with other computers.

The Internet

The most important use for a computer today is to reach out to other computers on the internet. It is then perhaps surprising that when computers were invented, no one imagined that they might be used for such a purpose. Before these machines existed, the word "computers" referred to people who calculated numerical equations. Thus, the computing machine was a machine designed to do what human computers did: that is, compute. Human computers were used in science and in war (to, for example, calculate trajectories of explosive devices) and so that was what the machines were designed to do.

The huge computers of the 1940s, 1950s, and 1960s had been housed in large rooms and were serviced by trained professionals. By the end of the 1950s, many countries owned several computers, occasionally within the same institution. Computers began to be hooked together on local area networks (LANs) and also regionally, using telephone lines. The only people who were able to work with these early networks were computer programmers working on behalf of the military and scientific experts. Since it was useful for the various people within a network to communicate with one another, some of the first network functions were messaging programs like email.

The origins of the internet are generally attributed to the United States Defense Department's ARPANET (Advanced Research Projects Agency), a network dedicated to military research. The network was up and running in 1970. Soon ARPANET spread to defense and scientific organizations of US allies in Europe. The needs of the military in the age of the Cold War and mutually assured destruction (MAD) were to maintain the capability of the network even if some of the nodes of that network were knocked out. Thus, a decentralized system was preferred to one that was controlled by one site.

Ideas Behind Connection

As computers communicated with each other using telephone lines, it was important that the messages not get garbled. In the 1940s and 1950s, scientists used thermodynamics, the science of energy transfer, to study the transfer of information. As we have seen, entropy was a measure of disorder in a physical system. In information theory, the idea was to avoid disorder, or garbled messages, in information transfer. A variety of approaches were developed to minimize miscommunication. Data packets, containing both instructions for their use and tiny parts of the actual message content, were sent by a variety of routes in a network, and the receiving computer recompiled the fragments into the correct order. As it did so, it checked the message for coherence.

As computers began to synchronize their workings, they needed a code that would allow files to be sent from one computer to another. The code is known as a protocol, and computers that shared a protocol were able to exchange files with each other when connected. Higher-level programs would be layered on top of the communication protocols, thus ensuring that no matter who made a new computer for whatever purpose, all computers would be able to communicate.

European Nets

Even though ARPANET created connections with relevant European computers, defense research was not necessarily the primary interest of many European governments. Computing networks for nonmilitary purposes were developed under the aegis of government-owned Postal, Telephone, and Telegraph (PTT) systems. In 1971 the European Council of Ministers began to plan for an all-European online information network (Euronet) to connect work in science and technology, with nodes in London, Paris, Rome, and Frankfurt. The system used a protocol that facilitated server control rather than client control. PTTs preferred to maintain their top position in communications service. The emphasis in Euronet was building infrastructure—cables and switches.

The four main Euronet nodes were also connected with nodes in Brussels, Amsterdam, Copenhagen, and Dublin. Instead of combining communications and information services, they were separated into two different agencies. This meant that the information services could be easily connected to other possible networks. The information side of the system had about a hundred databases.

One of the purposes of Euronet was to avoid reliance on the United States for information services, and thus to maintain a European online retrieval system. The ideal was that all European information sources, not just those connected to science and technology, would eventually be able to use Euronet. Euronet was designed so that the PTTs could easily control the kinds of data moving through the network. The European network was not to be a private system but rather a public service that could communicate by voice, data, or facsimile—anywhere in the world.

In both the American and European networks, the emphasis was on experts finding needed information. Not until the 1990s could the emerging internet begin to be used as a network with commercial and personal utility. In the 1980s, several networking ventures arose, such as the UK's Videotex and the Netherlands's SURFnet, which were examples of somewhat specialized services that existed alongside Euronet. There was no reason to think that the internet should not be a loosely connected set of networks, all using different technologies for different purposes.

In fact, as politicians developed the plan for a unified Europe, one aspect was the creation of transnational networks: railroad systems, electric grids, roads, and so forth. Once something is built on a large-enough scale, it is hard to unbuild it. Technology from the mid-nineteenth century on had been gradually drawing Europe into a close set of relationships. This is not to say that the creators of networks had European unity in mind, but rather that an unexpected consequence of network building was increased unity among the parts of the network. Nevertheless, in the 1970s and 1980s, European unity was clearly on the table. Proponents of European unity talked about how Euronet would connect experts in different countries.

In 1984 Euronet, having built a standardized infrastructure throughout Europe, ceased to exist as such. Control over the infrastructure passed to the consortium of PTTs. Unexpectedly, events in Geneva spun European computing systems in a different, and worldwide, direction.

The World Wide Web

CERN was connected to the United States using a protocol emphasizing client rather than server control (TCP/IP protocol). When the British Tim Berners-Lee, working at CERN in Geneva, had the idea of making access across networks available to everyone, he had in mind a set of users who were experts with computer abilities. He developed (1) Hypertext Markup Language (HTML), which defined the way that websites could be encoded to make them accessible to everyone; (2) Uniform Resource Locator (URL), which provided an address to identify and locate each user); and (3) Hypertext Transfer Protocol (HTTP), which allowed resources to be sent from one user to another. He had invented the first web browser, although he didn't call it that. This web browser, World Wide Web, was constructed using a TCP/IP protocol.

Berners-Lee worked to ensure that CERN would leave all of these systems open to everyone who wanted to use them on a royalty-free basis, and he encouraged other computer programmers to improve them. This they did, so that the World Wide Web became more and more efficient. Berners-Lee realized that if he had tried to keep control of his invention, it would not have taken off. He joined with other web developers to advocate important principles for the web:

1) The web should be decentralized with no central controlling node (since every user is seen as a node) and no way to stop it from working.

2) No user should pay more than another user, thus insuring what is known as "net neutrality."

3) Code should be public and available to everyone, and everyone should be able to contribute to code design.

4) All computers should use the same computer language in every country, thus ensuring that all cultures had access to the web.

5) Standards should be universal and thus agreed on by consensus. Since everyone could potentially have a say in developing the common standards, the process was both transparent and participatory.

These principles emphasized freedom, openness, and access that had no place for proprietary controls. By the end of the century, practices would begin to spin in the opposite direction.

But despite Berners-Lee's thoughtful public approach, the web itself still was available only for cognoscenti. The ease with which people today can access the web did not then exist. One of the key innovations that opened the web to ordinary people was the graphic user interface, an icon to which someone could point. The development of the mouse then allowed people to move a cursor over the icon and click. Berners-Lee was not interested in including nontext materials like icons and pictures, but others were. Both Mac OS8 and Windows 95 included attractive color and graphic capabilities.

The User-Friendly Internet

In the mid-1990s, the rough-and-ready web browser that Berners-Lee had developed was replaced by other approaches. A browser is a program that allows a computer user to find and connect to another website. In Norway, the Opera browser, based on research done at the telecommunications company Telenor, was designed to interface with Windows. Opera was user friendly and designed to appeal to nonexperts. In America, other browsers like Netscape also did the same thing. The web was no longer just a way for experts to communicate with other experts

But what could nonexperts find on the web? Initially, not much. One of the early sites showed a coffee pot in Cambridge, England. You could watch the coffee pot brewing, being emptied, and being rebrewed. Others showed cows, or frogs, or—ultimately anything one could imagine. Whatever it was: the audience was there. Essentially the World Wide Web was defined by the process of invention. The idea was overpowering. Gradually, and then more quickly, people and corporations began to build websites. The question was how to find the websites you wanted to consult.

The Search Idea

The telephone companies were poised to connect their customers to the internet. They thus became internet service providers (ISPs). However, no matter which ISP someone used, the problem of how individual users could search for what they wanted remained. An ISP is not a search engine. Suppose you wanted to watch a coffeepot. How could you find it? Unless you already knew the URL of the coffeepot people, you were out of luck.

Oscar Nierstrasz developed the first search engine, W3Catalog, at the University of Geneva. Several web pages contained lists of web resources. W3Catalog set a web robot (bot) to find these pages and mirror them. Thus, the first search engines were essentially directories, like a telephone book. But they suffered from the same deficit the old telephone books had—searchers had to know exactly what they were looking for. The American search engine Yahoo! was a similar kind of search engine.

JumpStation, hosted at the University of Stirling, Scotland, used "spider" programs to crawl through the web to find new web pages. These web pages were loaded into the search engine's database. So, if computer users wanted to find tarot readings, all they had to do was type "tarot readings" into the search engine. The search engine would run through its listings and produce websites that used the term "tarot reading." The problem for the search engine was how to organize the results. JumpStation did not rank the results. Thus, there might be pages of sites that contained the word "tarot." It was up to the searcher to go through them all and find the right one. Other search engines began to rank the pages. Some looked for "Tarot Reading" in the heading. Others counted the number of times "tarot reading" appeared on the site.

In 1996, two graduate students in computer science, Larry Page and Sergei Brin, developed a program to search the web for the best answer to a request. They both came from academic families and realized the importance of the number of citations a paper got as a measure of its influence. They therefore developed two programs (BackRub and PageRank) that could search all the pages on the web for appropriate web pages and then rank each page by the number of links that it had with other websites. In a few years, they had built a new company, Google, which soon dominated the field of web searches. Their search engine showed the individual searcher what sites were most popular with people who had made a similar search.

Web Business

As computers became connected, creative thinkers began to think of ways to take advantage of the links. For instance, the British postal service developed a set-top box that allowed information like news and weather to be sent over a telephone line and displayed on a television. In 1979 British businessman and computer expert Michael Aldrich[1] thought that perhaps if the connection were from business to business, a computer could coordinate commercial relationships. There was as yet no internet connection, but telephone connections could be made point to point. Aldrich envisioned ordering by computer and having groceries delivered to a home. He called the system teleshopping and soon online shopping. In 1982 the first business-to-consumer purchase was made by a Mrs. Snowball, a 72-year-old. Aldrich was using a British system called videotex. In France, the postal service installed a similar system in network form, Minitel that existed until the advent of the World Wide Web.

Yet another possible use for the new Web was e-commerce. A hedge fund manager, Jeff Bezos, thought he might like to open an online bookstore, and named his idea Amazon. He put *Books in Print* online, so if customers searched, they would be able to order any book in print. Amazon then ordered the book and sent it on to the customer. It was a shaky business initially, but in 1996 the *Wall Street Journal* put Amazon on the front page. It was clear that there was a place for online bookstores, but Amazon had a head start and lots of newly won expertise. By 1997 Amazon had opened a music section, and later became a purveyor of anything they could sell.

The MP3 technology of digitalizing and compressing music files took place at the German Fraunhofer Society for the Advancement of Applied Research. MP3 was based on the selectivity of the human ear; humans can hear only a fraction of the auditory spectrum, so much of the sound produced by voices or musical instruments is unhearable. MP3 filtered out the unheard sounds and thus greatly compressed the size of the file. By the mid-1990s, MP3 was ready for the public. At the same time, computers with hard drives with the memory capacity of several gigabytes arrived. In 1997 the program to allow MP3 files to be loaded onto a computer was released as freeware and was snapped up by millions of eager would-be users. Users could download a Compact Disk (CD) recording once and then play it from their computers. Music users began to engage in practices that came close to copyright theft.

Americans crossed the line. Shawn Fanning developed a program that would search the internet for song files and allow them to be transferred from one computer to another. When people signed up for Napster, they got access to the music files saved on every other Napster-user's computer, offering in return their own. The entire World Wide Web of music, every song in existence, was available. For free. Unfortunately, someone owns to the rights to recently recorded music. Lawsuits ensued. Napster ceased to exist.

But file sharing continued in other guises and with constantly improving programs. In the twenty-first century, video sharing became possible. European courts have worked vigilantly, but not always successfully, to ensure that file sharing is done legally.

Hotwiring Human Desire

It was hard to see at the time, but the whirlwind of unanticipated innovations that the internet brought to computer users began to change these users' expectations and desires. The ability to sit behind a computer, experience a desire, click on a program, and have one's desire relatively quickly delivered directly to one's computer or door bred a certain impatience in the internet-using public. Throughout the world a growing number of people began to demand an infinite range of choices and quick, even instant, digital gratification. As the twentieth century ended, there was a demand for digitalizing everything that could be digitalized, and consequently, at the same time, to write an algorithm for every human process that could be described in discrete steps. The computerized world was impetuously stepping through an unlighted doorway without really knowing where that door might lead—or if there was even a floor on the other side of the door.

Big Data

By 1990 the amount of data stored in computers had outrun the ability of existing computer programs to store or organize it effectively. The solution was to store data on multiple systems that had access to one another. The problem of data size continued into the new century; data began to be measured in zettabytes (sextillion bytes or 10^{21} bytes). The world generated quintillions of bytes daily. It became clear as the new century dawned that managing this amount of data required new networks and processes. Much of the data was shared and processed by corporations in the private sector.

In order to handle the available data, several different processors were used, in a process known as parallel processing or parallel computing. The problem for which the data was to be employed was divided into separate tasks, and different processors each carried out a piece of the task. These tasks were later combined in the main computer. Often the different processors did not reside in the same location, and so grid computing allowed computers in different locations to communicate over the internet as they carried out parallel processing.

Most of the work of big data was carried out in the twenty-first century. But the skeleton of the big data systems was built at the turn of the century. Ethical questions loomed and grew in intensity in the new century. Who owned data concerning individual human beings? What kinds of rights did individuals or groups have? Did they have rights to privacy? What kinds of analysis were ethical? These questions became extremely important in the twenty-first century as large firms like Amazon and Facebook began to dominate their sectors.

eScience

The term "eScience" emerged in 2000 from the United Kingdom's Office of Science and Technology. It described a program to develop the shared use of computers in scientific research. The goal was to enable the UK to be a leader in the worldwide knowledge economy, including both corporations and universities.

On the continent, the main original use of eScience was originally analysis of data produced by the Large Hadron Collider at CERN. In order to carry out eScience, new infrastructural grids and computational tools needed further development. Eventually several disciplines in both the natural and social sciences were able to make use of these tools. The European Grid Infrastructure, the Open Science Grid, and the Nordic

DataGrid facility were all individual consortia of institutions sharing computing abilities. These and others came together in the Worldwide Computing Grid that connects 100 nationwide clusters.

Climate Change

Climate is affected by an extraordinary number of separable processes. Following are a few such processes: (1) energy taken from the sun and reradiated into space, (2) heat transfer between atmosphere, oceans, and land, (3) a variety of currents (winds, convection currents, circulating waters, etc.) in both the atmosphere and oceans, (4) introduction of new gases into the atmosphere by both humans and natural processes, (5) the long-term carbon cycle in which carbon is buried deep in the earth and emerges millions of years later, (6) changes in the intensity of solar radiation over time, and so forth.

Understanding the relationships among these various processes must utilize scientific understanding of how each works. For instance, physics has long developed models for

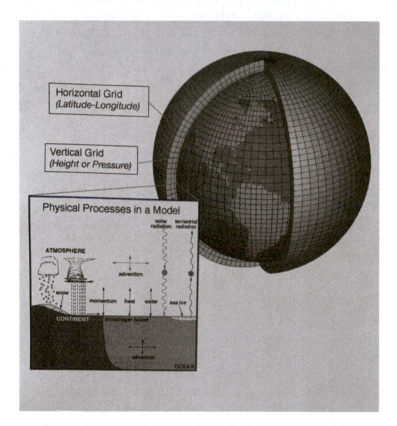

Figure 14.4 Climate change models. The earth and its atmosphere are divided up into cells in order to define data points for computer use. Each cell is approximately 300 cubic miles. © Courtesy NOAA (public domain).

fluid flow, and these theories have to be built into the theory at a global level. Thus, climate modeling relies on eScience.

The most utilized models were known as General Circulation Models (GCMs), also known as Global Climate Models. The models imagine the atmosphere and oceans divided into small cubes (cells), much like a three-dimensional graph might be divided into cells of an arbitrary size. Each cell is treated as a uniform entity with a certain temperature, a set rate of fluid inflow and outflow, a uniform chemical construction, and so forth. The accuracy of prediction, of course, is related to the size of the cells. If the cells are 1,000 cubic kilometers in size, the assumption of uniformity is likely to be inaccurate. In the late twentieth century, some models used cells that were roughly 100–200 kilometers in size. Usually, the entire grid contained 96 × 73 points with nineteen vertical levels, and this yielded 500,000 variables. When the computer ran the model, it calculated differential equations describing the changes in all of these data points as they interacted. Without computers, these calculations would have been impossible.

The first study to attempt a realistic model of the earth was published in 1975 and was by necessity quite crude. [2] The study broke the earth into large grid boxes with sides of 500 kilometers (about 300 miles), but the 1975-style supercomputer took fifty days of computation to model the past three centuries. Continued studies became more and more complex and more accurate as computing power increased and new models were developed.

In the late 1980s, meteorologists began to warn about the possibility of global warming due to human action. Ironically, a few years previously scientists worried that aerosols in the atmosphere might lead to cooling. Scientists began to develop computer models to see what would happen if what are known as "greenhouse gases" continued to pour into the atmosphere from burning fossil fuels. These models showed global warming and consequent melting of polar and glacial ice. Scientists sounded the alarm for several years. In 1988 they ran three retrospective scenarios to describe results over the past thirty years, to check for accuracy, and then checked to see what the models predicted for 2060. The model showed that at current levels of producing trace gases and aerosols, the globe would warm by 4 degrees centigrade by the middle of the next century. The consequences for humans and other organisms would be enormous.

In 1989 an international program began to work to compare all future models of global warming. Soon many countries opened centers and programs aimed at climate modeling. Nevertheless, models continued to be cruder than scientists would have liked. All were based on the assumption that the laws of physics were accurate. Some physical laws (like the differential equations of fluid mechanics) could only be approximated. The main sticking point was understanding how heat moved at the intersection of atmosphere and oceans. Another issue that affected the way different models reached competing results was the analysis of clouds and their reflectivity in the models. Since clouds change from moment to moment, they provided a real challenge to modelers. Scientists were helped in their understanding by a violent volcanic outburst of Mount Pinatubo in the Philippines. As they studied that way, the volcanic clouds affected their models; they were able to adjust their assumptions. In 1996 the comparative models showed that "the fingerprint" of human action could be seen in the climate changes of recent years. Since carbon dioxide and other gases that cause heat retention on the earth enter the atmosphere from a variety of sources, understanding what human actions were at least partially responsible was quite important in framing any action plans. By 2000 models were increasingly sophisticated and used a variety of natural and human sources of carbon in their predictions—like internal combustion engines or jet planes.

Radio Telescopes[3]

By the middle of the twentieth century and the discovery of cosmic background microwave radiation, it was clear, if anyone had doubted, that stars emitted every frequency of electromagnetic radiation, not just light. "Seeing" that radiation, however, was a bit of a problem. Radio waves can be several meters long, and to detect such radiation one needs a "mirror" that is several times bigger. In fact, the bigger the mirror, the more precise the resolution of the resulting image.

In fact, to use radio waves in our observations we don't use optical mirrors, but rather much larger dish antennas. However, to further extend the size of the telescope, we combine antennas over a very wide area. In order to maximize the amount of radiation collected, a collection of parabolic dish antennas (much like the dish antennas used to pick up television signals, but much bigger) is organized on railroad tracks. As they all focus on one point in the sky, they slowly roll to keep up with rotation of the earth.

Figure 14.5 French radio telescope (1953). © GETTY.

Large computers control the speed of the antennas and the directions where they point. As the radiation focuses on one central antenna, the signals are sent to another computer that uses the incoming data to create images. As antennas are separated by long distances from one another, they can use interferometry to pinpoint the location of the source of the radiation in space. Each antenna uses a hydrogen clock to print the exact time a particular piece of data was received. The computer uses these time stamps to reassemble the data correctly. The entire field of radio astronomy would be impossible without the data treatment available in eScience.

Computers and Ideas

In one view, technology is arguably an extension of human capabilities.[4] The nuclear bomb can be seen as an extension of the fist, the automobile as an extension of the leg, and the radio as an extension of the voice. In this view, the computer is an extension of the human brain—at least the logical parts. This characteristic of computers complicates our understanding of them. Computers are concretized ideas that produce other ideas. The methods of intellectual history are more appropriate to understanding some aspects of computers than are the methods of the natural sciences. Yet science and engineering are indispensable in comprehending, building, and improving computers and computer networks.

Understanding what a computer is bears similarities to understanding what human thought is. To materialists, thought is an emanation of the physical brain. To Platonists, true ideas exist in their own realm and can only with effort be accessed by humans. In this text, we have studied people who thought humans discovered ideas and others who thought humans invented ideas. The mind-body problem is centuries old, and it continues in new form with computers. Is the computer the physical machine, the software program, or the structure of logical thought itself? Does a program exist when it has not yet been run on a machine? Can advanced computers develop consciousness? Will they?

Studying computers sheds light on a number of issues concerning language and thought that we have discussed in this text. Computers provide a new, fruitful ground for considering questions of logic, language, technology, mind, reality, and knowledge. Often computers are used to pursue logical questions that would take a logician months or years to solve. Used in this way, computers aid in human cognition. But computers also serve as heuristic metaphors to think about such cognition.

A computer, to date, is not the same as a human brain; and a human brain is not a computer. Each neuron is a complex entity that accomplishes many things inside its cell walls, and different kinds of neurons do different things. The nature of connections among neurons through axons and dendrites using various chemical ions is currently under study—but the process is only vaguely similar to anything that happens in and among computer chips. Brains contain many cells that are not neurons. But from its very beginnings, scientists saw similarities between computers and brains. And both

365

scientists who study brains and scientists who study computers occasionally get ideas from one another. Brains are not computers, but they have enough in common that the computer as brain is a common metaphor.

From the beginning, computers have been understood in terms of metaphors.[5] Thus, for instance, "file" and "folder" are concepts from an office filing system. Yet in the computer there are only coded instructions linking memory cells. Although a physical folder could never hold as many files as a computer folder, still the metaphor is useful as users try to connect their computer experiences to the physical and social worlds. Similar analyses can be applied to computer metaphors like memory, windows, pages, threads servers, clients, memory leaks, garbage collection, trash, and so forth. Programmers also use metaphors at program levels that are invisible to the computer users. The use of such metaphors should not be problematical unless they are misleading or inadequate. Metaphors may obscure as well as reveal, and in fact, there are instances in which they have done just that as programmers struggle to solve difficult problems.

An issue, however, is what the nature of a computer metaphor is. Traditional metaphors bring into juxtaposition things that existed before the metaphor was even dreamed of. With computers, however, the program is often being created along with the metaphor. Computer science is unlike the physical sciences in that the computer programmers are creating the thing they are studying, whereas physical scientists do not think they are creating nature itself as they study it. Furthermore, computer programs are used to study other computer programs. The metaphors in computing are not just useful figures of speech, teaching tools so to speak. They become part of the reality that they are being used to describe.

One function of computer metaphors is to obscure the abstract nature of a computer program so that the computer user experiences something concrete that is understandable in human terms. Amazon designs its computer presence to allow you to think you are in a store putting things in your shopping cart as you proceed to check out. Essentially the objects of computer programs are abstract. But these abstractions create a virtual concrete world.

Artificial Intelligence

In 1955, the year of the publication of Teilhard's *The Phenomenon of Man*, John McCarthy of Dartmouth College in New Hampshire coined the phrase "artificial intelligence" to describe a summer research project he was planning for the next summer. The Dartmouth Summer Research Project on Artificial Intelligence brought together several of the primary thinkers in the field of information theory and cybernetics.

With the development of highly magnification electron microscopes in the 1930s, biologists were able to study the details of neurons and their parts, particularly the axons and dendrites that connected them with other neurons. Other studies had indicated that electrical current consisted of sodium ions being transported across membranes, and it was also clear that at least some of the action of neurons was an all-or-nothing situation: either the neuron fired or it didn't. As digital computers developed during and after the Second World War, it occurred to many that the electrical workings of the brain were analogous to the electrical workings of a computer. From the beginning, the brain and computer sciences were conceptually linked. Gradually the metaphor reversed, so people in common parlance began referring to brains as computers.

In 1936 the English code-breaking mathematician Alan Turing (1912–54) first suggested that a machine could carry out any mathematical computation that could be described as an algorithm. An algorithm is a well-defined set of steps that must be carried out to solve the problem. Symbolic logic (based on the algebra invented in 1854 by George Boole—thus, Boolean algebra) had been developed in such a way that it was closely related to mathematics, so a computing machine could also be said to be a logic machine. The Second World War stimulated the invention of the first generation of programmable computing machines, and versions of these computers were built in Germany, the United Kingdom, and the United States.

Turing's proposed machine was a digital machine in which each step in the algorithm was answered by "yes" or "no." If numbers were expressed in base-two form, that is, if the entire number system consisted of only a "0" and a "1," then the machine could be made of a set of switches in which each switch was either off (described by "0") or on (described by "1"). For instance, in base two the number "5" is written as "101"—which when switched would be "on, off, on." Thus, forms of logic could be expressed as electronic digital circuits.

In 1950 Turing wondered if such a logic machine could ever be intelligent. He proposed a test, called the Turing test, to determine whether a machine had the intelligence of a human. In the Turing test, a person and a computer are in two closed rooms. In another room, a person types a question that is sent into the two closed rooms. Both the computer and the human answerer type responses. The questioner decides whether an answer is from a computer or from a person. If the questioner cannot tell the difference, then the computer could be said to be intelligent.

Not everyone agreed that the Turing test was sufficient. Turing himself began his paper "Computing Machinery and Intelligence" (1950), asking if machines could think, and then admitted that he could not define what it meant to think. Thus, his test is a stand-in for thinking. Not everyone agreed that such a test was adequate. For instance, in 1966 Joseph Weizenbaum made up a program, ELIZA, that would act like a psychotherapist who reflects back what the client is saying. The program was able to fool some experts. Another program modeled the speech of a paranoid schizophrenic. Several psychiatrists were unable to determine which was which. Several other arguments have cogently questioned the sufficiency of Turing's test.

But science fiction assumed that intelligent robots were possible. The collection of short stories entitled *I, Robot* (1950) by Isaac Asimov not only described a world inhabited by intelligent robots but described a system of ethics that should be built into any such device:

1) A robot may not injure a human being or, through inaction, allow a human being to come to harm.

2) A robot must obey the orders given it by human beings except where such orders would conflict with the First Law.

3) A robot must protect its own existence as long as such protection does not conflict with the First and Second Laws.

Part of the field of Artificial Intelligence (AI) involves defining what is meant by "intelligence." As we have seen in this text, for the past two centuries thinkers have been unable to arrive at a generally accepted definition of "thought" or "mind." Using digital, algorithmic-dependent machines to create AI assumes that intelligence is rational, logical, and at its base algorithmic. Human beings clearly experience much more than logic as they think (see Chapter 3). They are, among other things, emotional dreamers who not only think but act with bodies that seem inextricably attached to their minds. One might expect, then, that any successful attempt to mimic human thinking should involve more than logic. Yet in the late 1950s and early 1960s, major researchers made wildly optimistic predictions about the imminent success of AI, and when these attempts at prophecy fell far short of the mark, an "AI winter" involving losses of funding occurred. This process recurred in the years around 1990.

Part of the problem that AI researchers faced is that their ideas outran the available computing power. The solution to this issue was patience. Gordon Moore, the CEO of Intel, predicted in 1965 that computing power (actually a prediction of the number of components on an integrated circuit board) would double every year for ten years. In 1975 he changed that prediction to doubling every two years. This prediction was borne out for decades. The ability of machines to meet the high hopes of AI researchers increased exponentially.

But no matter how much power was available, it was still not enough for many applications. For a time, AI theorists used logical systems that followed decision trees. In such a system, from one premise either one possibility or another must occur. Each point of decision produced another fork in the road. In only a few steps, the number of possible paths exploded in an exponential cascade. When the computer found a logical dead-end, it had to retrace its steps to take another path, and the exponential explosion increased. Such a process can be used to map out some very simple logical problems, but its use is limited.

Furthermore, any human decision requires a vast amount of knowledge about the world. Computers were incapable of possessing memory banks that would hold that amount of information. But not only did general information need to be stored; it also needed to be accessed appropriately. Searching a data memory for appropriate background information might involve several different categories of data. For instance, finding a solution to the problem that I am out of bread when I want to eat some might involve information about ways to cook without bread, location of stores, transportation options, my bank account, and so forth. These might all exist in different areas of memory.

One solution was the adoption of an entirely different approach to intelligent problem-solving. In the 1980s, researchers adopted an approach called "expert systems." The point was that experts acting within the range of their expertise do not have to access every area of knowledge. A computer program could be designed for a particular task, for instance, connecting medical symptoms with possible causes of the symptoms. The expert system approach was quite useful, and programmers could design programs for many industries or activities that were specific to the tasks required. These programs could be adjusted to the needs of specific organizations. Such an approach cannot be called AI, but in a restricted domain a computer could make accurate decisions more frequently than a human expert. Once the algorithm was defined, the machine followed the steps of the algorithm more faithfully than most professional experts.

In 1997 the world was entranced when an IBM computer called "Deep Blue" beat the world's chess champion Garry Kasparov. Because of advances in hardware as well as advances in program design, Deep Blue was able to process 200,000,000 moves a second as it made its decisions. But Deep Blue also had a deep memory for previous chess games and for chess positions in former games that had been previously analyzed. Deep Blue was not asked to do anything but play chess. It did that supremely well. But Deep Blue was incapable of telling a robot how to go to the store to buy bread.

A next step was the development of knowledge-based computer systems that not only held a vast amount of knowledge in storage but that also contained an "inference engine" that allowed the system to create new knowledge. This new knowledge was itself stored in the knowledge base. Quickly the knowledge base exploded. But it was insufficient to carry on a conversation, recognize pictures, or do most of the things that a human toddler could manage.

In 1999 the Wachowskis released *The Matrix*, a film based on the premise that machines had become not only superintelligent but also united. The machines connected humans' minds to a computer-simulated world so that the machines could harvest human electrical output. A small group of humans managed to remain unconnected and fought the machines for the good of all humankind. This dystopia explored issues related to AI by exploring the implications of the matrix. The film used Plato's cave, Descartes's evil demon, and other theories of mind and intelligence to ask whether our mental life can be accurately simulated by a cyber-system. Clearly, there was a physical world and a mental world. The film was a trilogy (*The Matrix*, *The Matrix Reloaded*, and *The Matrix Revolutions*), and early in the twenty-first century the second and third films explored the possibility that there were different levels besides those of physical/ matrix (mind), and that the physical world might also be a mental simulation. At the end, the gifted Neo, who is the salvation of the humans, finds that the antihuman aspect of the machines is a computer bug, and he joins the machines to cure them. Humans and machines cannot exist without one another, and the nexus human/machine is a total system.

But outside of science fiction, leaders of computer and network development continued to build increasingly powerful computer systems to do tasks associated with intelligence. AI seemed likely to assume many distinct forms. Perhaps instead of intelligent robots, AI would occur piecemeal in small devices: the internet of things.

The Singularity

In 1958 a conversation with John von Neumann was reported in which von Neumann described the likelihood that technological progress would arrive at a "singularity" in which thinking machines would change forever the nature of human life and society. Several thinkers, like the British Irving John Good in 1965, echoed this idea. According to Good, once the first machine with greater than human intelligence was created, it would be able to create even more intelligent machines and human beings would become irrelevant. Their puny attempts at thinking would no longer be needed.

The achievement of superhuman intelligence could come about in two ways. One was to amplify existing human intelligence through genetic engineering, bioengineering, prosthetic brain-device implants, or some other method. Superhumans may or may not be well disposed toward old-fashioned humans. The other was to continue to develop devices (computers) that would become increasingly intelligent. As we have seen, Asimov suggested ways to program devices to serve humans rather than compete with them. In either case, superintelligence would be more and more capable of amplifying the intelligence of its successors, so at some point old-fashioned humans would be superfluous in the realm of intelligence.

Thinkers who tackled these questions disagreed on the implications. Some thought that AI is either not possible or not possible on the routes we have taken. The point that AI will not occur is bolstered by the vast difference between the algorithm-driven processes used in computers, and the vast range and scope of human thought that easily grasps relevant connections from different areas. Human thought seemed to be connected with human bodies in ill-understood ways. Emotions affected thinking, and

Figure 14.6 Man with circuit board brain, 1949. Where does human stop and computer begin? © GraphicaArtis/Hulton Archive/Getty Images.

general health made a difference in how people think. Without spelling out the brain-body connection more fully, the thinkers that moved in this direction said that human intelligence was vastly different from computer processing.

Another issue was the old mind-brain problem. Human consciousness is connected to the action of our brains, but there is no glimmering of a theory about how the consciousness that all of us experience could emerge from electrical circuitry. Brain maps using sophisticated technology (like the MRI) show associations between certain kinds of conscious events and areas of the brain, but the nature of these connections is obscure.

At the turn of the century, whether or not we were headed toward a singularity and the obliteration of life as we experience it, the question of AI that was equal to or greater than human intelligence raised interesting moral dilemmas that helped clarify some kinds of ethical issues. One could ask whether intelligent entities had rights or responsibilities equal to those of humans. If a machine acted badly, should it be punished or repaired? Could such a question be asked about human beings? Could one say that a seemingly intelligent agent was indeed intelligent if it had no consciousness? If a robot acted badly, who was responsible? Its owner? Its manufacturer? Itself?

Finally, we return to the opening vignette. Teilhard had foreseen the existence of a noosphere, a sphere of intelligence surrounding the earth. As the number of connections within and among computers increases, could these connections act like synapses in human brains? Thus, we can certainly imagine a sphere of intelligence that includes all the ideas whirling around the globe through telephones, radios, computer grids, and all other electronic devices. This indeed is a kind of noosphere. But what if these connections are producing a new kind of conscious entity? What if humans are to the entire internet as neurons are to the brain? A neuron cannot comprehend the thought to which it contributes. Perhaps we are approaching the singularity—the Omega Point of Teilhard. If so, could we ever know?

Conclusion

As readers of this text, we are living in a cyber age that would have been hard for a person in 1999 to imagine. This chapter has discussed the primary ideas behind the development of our cyber world and has presented some of the intellectual problems raised by the existence of networked computers. At the time of this writing, the singularity has not yet emerged.

Yet the ability of human beings to conceive of so many life processes and ideas as algorithms that can be described in binary language and inserted into a computer is awe inspiring. In this chapter, we have seen the ideas behind the building of computers and the expansion of their capabilities. We have viewed the opening up of the internet and a global web of computation. We have seen how these ideas changed our personal lives, our businesses, and our science. And we have seen some of the ideas behind the possible creation of artificial human intelligence.

Early in this text, we examined the philosopher G. W. F. Hegel's idea of a time when human beings would unite, bringing together the subjective and objective worlds and living within the Absolute. We end this text with theories of human beings uniting in a cyber-unified world, existing as nodes in an overarching consciousness, the noosphere. Hegel wrote of Geist, spirit, transcendental mind. He appreciated the power of the binary. Strangely, thinkers today are echoing these ideas. But in the cyber world, human beings may only be an incidental part.

EPILOGUE
CENTAUR TO CYBORG

Summary and Reflections

On January 31, 2020, Great Britain officially exited the European Union (EU) just as the country suffered its first cases of Covid-19, the pandemic virus. In 2020, part of the European response to Covid-19 was to close country borders to restrict movement between states. For the past decade, Russian hackers, encouraged by the election of a pro-Russian president in the United States, had been attacking government computer systems in the EU as they attempted to destabilize the EU and threaten general elections. EU countries, especially Germany, sought ways to counter this threat. Thus, freedom of movement and openness, the signature promises of the internet and the EU, were both challenged by enemies of the EU and by nature itself.

A famous painting by the postimpressionist Paul Gauguin asked, "D'où Venons Nous / Que Sommes Nous / Où Allons Nous" ("Where do we come from? What are we? Where are we going?"). This book has tried to present elements of the European conversation about these questions during the past 200 years. In this epilogue, we will summarize some of the major points in this discussion as we take a peek at the first twenty years of the new millennium. We will follow the development of the three perspectives outlined in the slogan of the French Revolutionaries: Liberty, Equality, and Fraternity. We will then examine technology, science, language, and knowledge as these slogans have been reshaped by events in the new century.

Liberty

The first perspective, Liberty, describes the desire of individuals to pursue their own lives without compulsion by others or by the state. As a one-word slogan, it would describe the world of Social Darwinism, a world of unbridled competition. The word "liberty" is individualistic to the extreme. In Chapter 2, we saw the invention of a rational, calculating individual, and simple theories of society built around the ideal of liberty. Throughout this text, we have seen redefinitions of individuals in the light of new scientific knowledge and new technological/social contexts. Several ideas we have explored center on an analysis of individuals and individual rights. By the twentieth century, "liberty" was realized in the right of all adults to vote, in the personification of corporations as people and, for some, the rights of all people to the fruits of the European industrial society.

Increasingly our conception of an individual has been changing. In 1800 those who experienced an individualistic worldview advocated full citizenship only to property-owners. Such individuals were expected to be able to reason rationally about their own self-interest and to make choices that furthered that interest. While God may have seen all human beings as spiritually equal, only the few had the ability to participate fully in society and government. This text has described how full citizenship was extended to all adults throughout the past two centuries.

But full citizenship on the internet requires only access to a networked computer. Computer users need not even use their own names or descriptions. They can work with invented identities. They may even be nothing but computer code, bots. People who have the knack, or the luck, of being able to create content of interest to numbers of similarly networked people may find that their creations "go viral." They may find that with sufficient viral videos, advertisers will pay well to be associated with their messages.

The variety of platforms for intellectual expression challenges old assumptions. Increasingly it is easier for scholars and thinkers to publish their ideas; concomitantly, it is harder for readers to know how valid those ideas are. Peer review still exists, but preprints, not only in the sciences but also in the humanities, are timelier than journals. Some platforms allow scholars to undertake discussion of ideas while the ideas are being formed. Such platforms offer the promise of drawing more people into intellectual discussion, but by opening the gates, they also implicitly challenge expertise.

Equality

The second term, "Equality," is a social term. People are equal only in comparison with one another. Since people are demonstrably unequal—in their talents, possessions, social status, and ambitions—equality seems to demand action by the society to redistribute wealth and constrain ambition. That is, a society of liberty and a society of equality seem incommensurable. Marx and Engels were among the first to realize this as they built a theory of a classless society.

In 1800 almost all people lived in a community. By 1900 sociologists were writing of anomie: a lack of feeling that one was a part of a community that had an ethos, a value system. The difference was urbanization. By 1900 half of the population in Western Europe lived and worked in a city where the intermediate institutions of communities no longer existed there. Belongingness had shrunk to families and neighborhood pubs or churches. By the turn of the millennium, most of Europe lived in cities. It was easy to feel that one was just an interchangeable cog. In 2000 Europe was more than two-thirds an urban/suburban continent. Many urbanites defined themselves as individuals within a work and family context. The idea of the democratic equality of individuals from all cultures came somewhat easily to educated urbanites. It came less easily to the 30 percent living in the countryside, many of whom still defined themselves in community, religious, national, or racial terms.

Internet forums and platforms created new ways of grouping people. These groupings could express commonalities of interests, political leanings, professional expertise, working for multinational and global institutions, or any number of other things. Flash mobs could bring those people together—for good or for ill. Internet trolls could anonymously attack others on the internet. Although members' allegiances to internet-only groups were generally not as strong as they were to groups defined before the internet, there was a proliferation of groups as more and more people spent more time interacting with social media.

The resurgence of nationalism in the twenty-first century must be understood in relationship to social media and the internet. Nationalism implies a we/they relationship. The equality of all peoples is a fiction to a nationalist. Interestingly, in some forms of nationalism equality within the group requires a differentiation of jobs, activities, and compensation—strangely reflecting the Christian idea of the Body of Christ made up of individuals with differing talents. Each plays a required role with the support of others, and all feel free within the nation. In such a scenario, participants tend to resist the intrusion of outsiders of different nationalities.

Thus, a subtext of nationalism is often ethnic discrimination or racism. In the twenty-first century, some Europeans find themselves to be outsiders in their own communities. During the colonial and postcolonial years, immigrants from all over the world became Europeans. Many of them engendered multigenerational and multicultural European families. In the early twentieth century, anti-Semitism fueled nationalism. In the twenty-first century, other groups have joined Jews as targets of nationalist movements. Europeans with ancestors from Africa or Asia often have to work to redefine their identities as their fellow citizens reject them. The problem of identity has been exacerbated by the influx of refugees from devastated parts of the world. Nationalist groups have used these refugees to trigger anti-EU sentiments.

The Struggle between Liberty and Equality

Liberty became associated with liberalism and capitalism, which together acted to provide material wealth. Neither liberal nor capitalist theory had a formula for distributing that wealth. Wealth was used for investment in order to create more wealth. Meanwhile, the investing class accumulated wealth at a faster rate than the noninvesting class. Liberal capitalism offered freedom and liberty, as well as increasing national wealth. When not tempered by legislation, it also offered extreme inequality. It did not offer human connection or a meaningful life. These are just not part of the theory. The answer to unequal wealth distribution was found in the post–Second World War democratic socialist consensus. The answer to meaning has been left to religion, nationalist movements, or popular culture. None has done a particularly good job.

The EU was first and foremost a free-trade bloc, carefully constructed in volumes of carefully negotiated regulations. But the Schengen Agreement was a statement of the universal equality of all people. With free movement of people, a Romanian was equivalent to a German and vice versa. The EU was an attempt to create a liberal-democratic superstate that could replace nationalism with individualism. But the lack of fervor in the Union's citizens can be seen in the lackluster turnout for EU elections. The rise in support for nationalist parties throughout the countries that make up the EU shows that nationalism will not go quietly.

Clearly, a very large minority of Europeans were still nationalists. Especially people who struggled to find work and to share in the European bounty began to resent the foreigners who came, moved in, took jobs, bought property, and acted as if the country were theirs. The straws that broke the camel's back were millions of non-European refugees who arrived from war-torn, water-scarce regions of the world. Nationalism once again claimed a place in the European soul. But the new nationalism is not particularly uplifting. It is built not on belonging to something greater but, rather, on resentment and anger. The question of human meaning is hardly comprehensible in this new world. If a question cannot be clearly asked, then it is probably nonsensical—or extremely important.

Thus, one of the major points of discussions of this text has been the clash of individualistic and collectivist ideas. Ideas have consequences, and some of the consequences of fervently held ideas involve war and conquest. The individualists in twentieth-century liberal democracies understood only too well that the implications of fascism and communism were devastating for liberty. The first half of the twentieth century illustrates this violent clash of ideas and the attempts to somehow find a way to reconcile them.

Fraternity

The third term from the French Revolution, Fraternity, suggests that perhaps compromise between the first two terms is possible. If people look at one another as family, perhaps they will wish for the others the best of all worlds. Perhaps a sibling can seek to help a sibling. Fraternity, then, evokes a world of reconciliation and transcendence. Through Fraternity, we may move from the selfish perspective of individualism, through the apparent disinheritance of equality, to a state in which we embrace one another's strengths and find our meaning as human beings in union with each other. "Fraternity" is thus a word of hope and future, a word of utopia. Inasmuch as "fraternity" reflects family relationships, it also reflects the existence of people who are not family members.

At the extreme, the difference between individualism and collectivism is the difference between counting and feeling joy. In classical economics, competing individuals produced measurable wealth. In utilitarianism, happiness was defined in terms of things that could be measured so that decisions could be taken to maximize the total amount of happiness. But in 1800, Romantics did not search for the daily happiness of having finished a good day's work, but rather the uplifting ecstasy that came from feeling at one with the universe. The highest experience of collectivists was not getting more for oneself, but rather the joy found in losing oneself. Perhaps the collective experience can be seen as a search for meaning. Marxists could find meaning in working on behalf of history; nationalists could find meaning in serving their culture, the nation. Religious practitioners could find meaning in experiencing oneness with God. People could also find meaning in angrily confronting outsiders.

In 1900 Max Weber suggested that capitalism had turned the acquisition of wealth into a quest that was structured like Calvinism. If making money is akin to accumulating God's grace, then perhaps quantitatively oriented people could become meaning-seekers. Weber did not suggest that capitalists could achieve meaning. He called them specialists without spirit, a nullity. But Weber's thesis does provide a context for understanding the drive to make more money by people who have more than enough. An unexpected consequence is that the search for increasing amounts of countable, assessable units can produce experts. Experts know how best to achieve numerical progress in whatever their fields are.

As material wealth not only increased but also was shared with growing numbers of people, it turned out that often Europeans preferred working water mains and well-maintained roads to a search for meaning through the revolution. A new refrigerator seemed better than a government medal or a priest's blessing. Given the choice, many of the peoples of Eastern Europe during the Cold War opted for Western prosperity. The ecstatic self-sacrifice of the revolutionaries had turned into the numbing sameness of bureaucracies. When nationalism was on the rise, anthems like the Marseillaise stirred the blood. But when the revolution froze and the goods were still unequally distributed, nationalist fervor turned into nationalist bitterness.

Technology: Ideas and Things

Technological changes clearly shaped the European experience. If we imagine a large European city in 1800, it probably had a population between 100,000 and 200,000. The largest cities, London and Paris, were around 850,00, well short of a million. The streets were largely unpaved, there was no central water system, and sewers were open ditches. Transportation was by foot or horse. Spending on infrastructure was mostly concentrated on palaces, public buildings, and churches. Travel between cities was by water where possible. Communications were by word of mouth or letter.

As European infrastructure grew over the past 200 years, it defined possibility. Every bridge silently declared: you shall cross the river here and not there. Railways, telegraph and telephone lines, roads, airports, shipyards, factories, sidewalks, skyscrapers, and cell phone towers quietly guided humans in certain directions and not others. Infrastructure connected national groupings and laid the way for new countries. By the end of the twentieth century, the economic and personal connections across state lines made tighter connections among the states a compelling idea. It may also be that asymmetries in the inter- and intrastate bonds caused corresponding strains in the drive toward union.

Until recently, few people recognized to what extent money was an idea. For most of the past 200 years, money was defined with reference to the solidity of gold, and the gleam of gold distracted all but a few from recognizing that money was conceptual. Today, with money defined by lines of code in a computer that can be transferred around the world in an instant, it is hard to escape this recognition. Today nongovernmental individuals and organizations have created virtual currencies with no grounding in anything material. The days of currencies controlled by nation-states may be numbered.

This idea, money, could be used to leverage the creation of vast hosts of machines and other technology. These technological creations were themselves embodiments of ideas. Just as with money, the embodiments obscured the ideas. But the ideas were simultaneously scientific, social, and idiosyncratic. At first glance, technology seemed to be part of a nonintellectual world. In fact, technology usually embodied a solution to the problems defined in the world where that technology was developed. The railroad solved the problem of quickly moving goods and people when they were far from water. Speed brought down costs. Costs were important because of the new economics of the Industrial Revolution. And technology often drove science. Scientifically the railroad and steam engine stimulated the study of heat and the development of thermodynamics. Then the theory of thermodynamics and the idea of entropy sparked awareness of how systems (including the universe) tended to run down, becoming enervated. And as people moved easily from place to place, they created a society unimaginable in a world of stagecoaches and barges.

The Cyber Century

Furthermore, a system of machines, an industry or a conglomerate, also incorporates ideas. By the end of the twentieth century, not only were ideas materialized, but the materialized ideas produced other ideas. Computers became adjuncts to the human thought process, especially where thought was logical and rule driven. Today whole areas of creative thought, like architecture, film, or science, rely on cyber systems. If computers were suddenly to disappear, common practices in such fields would have to change. For instance, as medicine has converted to computerized record keeping, new categories of diagnosis have had to be developed. Computer programs can read X-rays and MRIs accurately. Robotic machines carry out microsurgeries only as assistants to human surgeons—at least up to now. Whole areas of human thought have been outsourced so that humans can use artificial intelligence to amplify their own thoughts.

The implications are staggering. We are entering an age in which autonomous cars, robot-driven trucks, drone-delivered merchandise, films starring dead actors and actresses, machine-made news reporting, and more can all be imagined. What are the implications for thought, for the development of philosophical systems by deep thinkers? Increasingly scholars have grown accustomed to using databases, statistical packages, and deep-modeling programs, to mention only a few. Even in the humanities, scholars use desktop computers with internet connections and access to large complex databases. It is hard to imagine Kant writing today without being connected to his colleagues at a global level. Scholarly papers and books that were not written using the available technologies are now quite rare. But we are on the cusp of becoming scholarly partners with the global cyber world itself.

Ten years into our present millennium, cell phones had stopped being only phones. Across Europe people used their phones to play games, check the weather, listen to music, watch videos, access databases, and get news updates. When they wanted to communicate with another human being, they were more likely to text than call. Cell phones only incidentally functioned as telephones. On cell phones, but more often on internet-connected computers, video game aficionados met each other across national boundaries. A solitary person could play the same game with the computer as an opponent.

The primary development behind the evolution of the cell phone was the app—the ubiquitous nickname for "application." Whatever the creative geniuses hired by Olivetti, Nokia, or other cell phone makers had imagined, the reality was sure to be different when the inventive talents of the entire globe were unleashed. App developers could be anyone, but when their apps were ready for release, they could make their app available to anyone with a cell phone or computer in a few steps. As people started using a particular app, the purpose of cell phones shifted a little bit. The cell phone makers had outsourced invention. Of course, as apps were downloaded and used, the companies who owned the app stores became economically stronger.

Another important concept was "platform." Cell phones became a platform on which inventors and users carried out their pirouettes. Another kind of platform was a website on which visitors were invited to post messages. Facebook, Twitter, Instagram, Snapchat, and so forth were content-less webpages. Users provided the content, and they paid for this privilege by allowing their personal information to be sold to advertisers. Advertisers on the platform paid the platform whenever someone clicked on the ad.

Platforms could support intellectual exchange. For instance, although the original twitter messages (tweets) were limited to 140 characters, much longer messages could be attached to them. Thus, a tweet could say, "Check out the latest draft of my article," and an interested reader could download a lengthy dissertation. Programs like PowerPoint, Word, Photoshop, Moviemaker, or Excel (and other versions of the same activities) allowed thinkers to create ideas and present them in a variety of formats. These presentations could be instantaneously available all over the world.

All of these possibilities changed the ways scholars and thinkers worked, thought, and communicated. The changes were rapid and as revolutionary as the invention of printing, book distribution systems, and public libraries had been in previous centuries. The cyber age did not just give us electronic instead of paper books—or electronic bookstores instead of brick stores. The cyber age gave us a multimedia extravaganza of possibilities. Professors could now sit at their desks as they made documentary videos, embed those videos into PowerPoint presentations, add charts made by using statistical programs, and attach their latest articles. They could then upload the PowerPoint to be previewed by students and colleagues before using the PowerPoint as a backdrop to a public lecture. As scholars pored over the vast array of images available on the internet, grappled with the best way to make a compelling visual argument, considered how to relate this visual case to the verbal case made in an article, they had different sorts of thoughts than they might have had a few decades before. Furthermore, these capabilities were available to anyone of any age, and platforms like YouTube enabled anyone's productions to be seen by everyone else, potentially.

If we connect the idea of scientific units (atoms, molecules, genes) with the idea of social individuals, we might also connect the idea of the scientific field (gravitational, electromagnetic) with systems of ideas and systems of technology. Individual thinkers exist within both technological and ideational webs. Cyber systems bring ideas and technology together, and within the "cyber field," individual (atomic) intellectuals interact—attracting, repelling, and reconfiguring—in the search to understand the complexity within which they exist.

Parts of the preceding paragraphs might well seem like a description of the obvious to those who grew up with the internet. But to those who began their intellectual lives in the twentieth century, the difference between worlds may seem vast. We have history courses because people are not born with historical memories. As we study history, we can understand in what ways we are living in times of profound change.

Science

Ideas about modern science exist between two poles. In the first, nature exists independent of any observation of or thought about it. In the second, nothing knowable exists outside of human senses and thought. The first underlies the activity of scientists and the understanding of science by most laypeople. The second underlies an influential philosophical approach. Scientists' attitude toward their own efforts is bolstered by over three centuries of successful predictions and science-based inventions. Skeptical philosophers' critical attitudes toward science are bolstered by a philosophical focus on the individual as the source of knowledge, complete with a recognition of the limitations of human capacities, and a belief in the disjunction between symbols (words) and whatever is symbolized. In general, the philosophical critique does not hold that knowledge of the universe is held by society rather than by the individual.

Scientists usually see their activity as evolving or progressing. Current theories allow scientists to accurately connect observations and make predictions, but in the future, scientists expect to discover new data that will stretch the capacities of theory and require theoretical adjustments or replacements. The gold standard of a scientific theory is expressed mathematically, because mathematics renders a precision that cannot be found in words. When mathematics works to the limits of experimental precision, it seems that mathematics must be an inherent and integral part of nature. That is, mathematical relationships are there to be discovered. And if the universe is constructed according to mathematical principles, then in doing mathematics humans may discover profound eternal truths.

Science: A Critique

But since mathematical knowledge evolves along with (and often independently of) science, those who study, but do not practice, science find it hard to accept that earlier mathematical theories can be as accurate as later theories. In this approach, mathematics is not discovered, but rather invented.

The critique of science goes something like this:

If science starts with pure sensory observation, then it starts with something that is generally quite complex and connected. Perception does not necessarily entail thought, and the division of a perceptual whole into a group of separate objects seems somewhat arbitrary. Only language allows us to see separate objects. The forest can become trees and bushes only after we have learned to see separate plants. Words, then, create individual things, and human thought invents nature. In this approach, the world of units is culturally constructed, not discovered. We have learned to experience our own inventions as things that exist independently of ourselves.

The essence of scientific theory, mathematical analysis, relies on reifying the world of things and then abstracting these things into symbols. The mathematical world of science is an unreal dream world that scientists experience as real. Abstraction is the antithesis of concrete reality, and concrete reality is a step removed from actual human sensory experience. To live in the scientific world is to remove ourselves from actual human experience.

Science: A Response to the Critique

The scientific reply is very simple:

Mathematics works. Abstract thought is part of the human experience. It is what we do well. The philosophical critique described earlier would root us in the present. However, abstract thought allows us to project into the future and to remember the past. Only abstract thought allows us to experience imperceptible things, like radio waves. So abstract thought lies at the heart of technological invention, and without technology, humans would have long ago become extinct. If mathematics is socially constructed, a human product, then why is it capable of accurate prediction? Even if mathematics as a symbol system is created, it seems clear that the external world has a structure that can be accurately portrayed by this symbol system. Furthermore, we are now able to construct more and more precise measuring instruments that provide results consistent with mathematical models. So, it appears that the universe is knowable by the mathematical sciences.

Science: New Possibilities

But the twenty-first century world has created new kinds of abstractions and has made possible previously inconceivable scientific studies.

Computer systems are capable of handling and analyzing immense amounts of data. Human beings can study the results of a computer analysis, but no human being is capable of checking the vast quantities of calculations that produced those results. Nor is a human being capable of following the lines of code that made up the various levels of the program used by the computer. There are just too many lines. But computers make accurate scientific predictions. Thus, human beings have a powerful colleague in a networked computer. The cyber world has pushed beyond previous debates about knowledge. It impels us to ask new philosophical questions.

Humans have a propensity to believe that the world is static: always the same. Even Einstein had trouble imagining that the universe could be expanding. If we live in a changing universe, then it may be that the laws of nature themselves are changing. Scientists have recently begun to consider this possibility. If so, it may be that behind our contemporary mathematical laws lie other mathematical laws that describe how mathematics changes.

Technology and Science

Modern science was based on close observation and measurement of the natural world. Measurements became crucial because mathematical models allowed these measurements to be tested and their implications explored. As scientists built mathematical models, they worked in two different directions. Overwhelmingly they looked for irreducible units—atoms—which, when understood, could be built back up through synthesis to understand entire systems. This idea, called reductionism, paralleled the individualism based on liberty described earlier. The other scientific approach was to start with wholes—fields, organisms, species—because without the whole, the parts could neither be properly understood nor built back up into anything resembling the observable world. These two approaches could potentially complement one another, but often they proved incompatible. Even today the particle-based quantum theory has not been reconciled with the field-based gravitational theory, despite the development of a quantum field theory.

Since science is based on precise measurements, the more exact the measuring tools became, the more precise the theoretical predictions were. And out of precision came finely tuned technology. Of course, science developed in a social world that was being measured in terms of precise amounts of money used to support new enterprises that would change the future. Thus, precision, mathematics, and invention evolved together in society and science. It has been the task of thinkers in the social sciences and humanities to understand this complex relationship.

Language

One of the major recurring themes in this text has been an impulse to understand the nature of human language—the means of expression of almost every idea. By paying attention to the forms of language, scholars painstakingly put together a historical map of the growth of European languages from ancient, dead languages like Indo-European. On one level, understanding language differences made it possible for nationalists to argue that their nation's thought patterns were unique among cultures, and thus that their people needed to rule themselves. On another level, logicians argued that language was intended to express logical connections among common human sensory impressions, and that any other use was nonsensical.

Some postmodern linguists and philosophers claimed that language was self-contained, that it acted like a metaphorical game in which verbal expressions fit together in ways that were intuitively obvious but not able to be codified in a set of rules. Other linguists argued that language was generated by deep mental structures and that a capacity for language was inherent to human beings, even while individual languages had to be learned experientially. In both of these cases, there was no necessary connection between language and a world outside of language. People talked meaningfully to one another, but the meaning did not necessarily involve describing a world outside of mind. In postmodernism, there was no way to evaluate the truth or falsity of statements. One person's reality was as valid as another's.

In the cyber world, language has taken on another dimension. In the twenty-first century, computers have been able to learn how to construct meaningful expressions and how to respond to human expressions in an apparently meaningful way. One way of "teaching" computers language capabilities is to program them to find linguistic expressions on the internet and by sampling large numbers of instances of the use of words, phrases, and sentences by humans and by connecting these expressions to the context in which they appeared, to be able to use the expressions correctly. Computers can make relatively accurate translations from one language to another. No one has suggested that computers somehow understand language, but they can appear to do so. More than one human computer user has argued with a Siri or an Alexa as if that computer program with the silky voice was another human being. Computers, following algorithms, have written poems that cannot be differentiated from human poems—even by professional poetry professors.

Knowledge

Yet another issue that recurs in every chapter is the nature of knowledge. What can we know? What does it mean to know something? What are the limits to knowledge? The problem of knowledge focuses on the individual knower. Rarely is the knower taken to be an entire society, or a combination of human and nonhuman beings. An exception is the "social facts" of Emile Durkheim and other sociological ideas about a trans-individual sort of knowing, embedded in cultures.

In philosophy, the British approach was called analytic philosophy. This philosophy claimed that all knowledge could be expressed in logical terms that relate basic statements about simple sensory perceptions to one another. Any human thoughts that did not arise from sensory perceptions or that could not be related to one another logically were not meaningful. They were statements about the nonexistent. It was the task of philosophy to clarify language.

The Continental approach, best exemplified in phenomenology, started with human minds as experienced in wholes, gestalts, rather than with atoms of perception. Phenomenology included purposes and feelings. It also eschewed abstraction. The world portrayed by mathematics and logic could not exist beyond human experience.

As computers crunch vast data fields and build models within parameters set by human beings, they create new knowledge that is inaccessible to human checks. Scientists have developed procedures to check the accuracy of computers by, for example, running the programs on different machines or tweaking parameters to see whether the new results make sense. Scientists run historical scenarios using computers. Since the historical data is known, the ability of the machines to make accurate predictions can be examined. Nevertheless, computers are scientific partners—if only junior partners. Future human knowledge will be possible only with that partnership.

Some of this knowledge seems insidious. The large systems through which computer users access the internet are capable of saving large amounts of personal information that is fed into algorithms that allow computer systems to track human individuals with advertising and messages aimed directly at them. In many ways, computer users continually feed the needs of commercial corporations. In some situations, it also feeds the need of government and law enforcement agencies to track individuals. The cyber state has been called the "surveillance state." Whether this cyber tendency to track and guide the behavior of people can be controlled and harnessed has yet to be determined.

In the beginning of the twentieth century, the Futurist Marinetti hailed the birth of the centaur in the form of the automobile, not a blend of human and animal as in the ancient centaur, but a blend of human and machine. Today, perhaps Marinetti would hail the birth of yet another centaur, a blend of human and computer systems: a cyborg. Is the cyber-centaur a friend of unlinked humans? We can only hope.

NOTES

Chapter 1

1. Alexander Pope (1725) Quoted in Bartleby.com. Available online: https://www.bartleby.com /297/154.html

2. *Declaration of the Rights of Man and Citizen* (1789) Available online: https://avalon.law.yale.e du/18th_century/rightsof.asp

Chapter 2

1. Adam Smith, *An Inquiry into the Nature and Causes of the Wealth of Nations* (London: W. Strahan and T. Cadell, 1776), Bk IV Ch II, Available online: https://www.marxists.org/refer ence/archive/smith-adam/works/wealth-of-nations/book04/ch02.htm

2. Ibid. Book I Chapter II.

3. Ibid. Book I Chapter I.

4. Ibid.

5. Ibid. Bk 5, Ch 1.

6. Quoted in "Jeremy Benthan," *Stanford Encyclopedia of Philosophy*, 2014.

7. John Stuart Mill, On Liberty, Ch. III. Available online: https://www.utilitarianism.com/ol/t hree.html

8. Mill, Autobiography, Ch VII. Available online: https://www.bartleby.com/25/1/7.html

9. Mary Wollstonecraft, *Vindication of the Rights of Women*, 1792, Ch 3, Available online: https ://www.marxists.org/reference/archive/wollstonecraft-mary/1792/vindication-rights-wom an/ch03.htm

10. Olympe de Gouges, *The Declaration of the Rights of Woman* (September 1791), Available online: http://chnm.gmu.edu/revolution/d/293/

11. "Petition of Women of the Third Estate to the King" (January 1, 1789), Available online: http://chnm.gmu.edu/revolution/d/472/

12. "Women's Petition to the National Assembly," Available online: http://chnm.gmu.edu/ revolution/d/629/

13. John Donne, "An Anatomy of the World" 1611, Available online: https://www.poetryfoundat ion.org/poems/44092/an-anatomy-of-the-world

Chapter 3

1. Wordsworth (1802), "The World Is Too Much With Us," Available online: https://www.poe tryfoundation.org/poems/45564/the-world-is-too-much-with-us

2. Quoted in Muriel Spark, *Mary Shelley* (London: Cardinal, 1987), 157, from Mary Shelley's introduction to the 1831 edition of *Frankenstein*.

3. In J.C.D. Clark (ed.), *Reflections on the Revolution in France: A Critical Edition* (Stanford University Press, 2001), 61.

4. Ibid.

5. Edmund Burke, "Reflections on the Revolution in France," in *The Works of the Right Honourable Edmund Burke*, vol. 2 (London: Henry G. Bohn, 1864), 515.

6. Thomas Carlyle, On Heroes, "Lecture IV. The Hero as Priest. Luther; Refoirmation: Knox; Puritanism," 1840, Available online: https://ebooks.adelaide.edu.au/c/carlyle/thomas/on _heroes/chapter4.html

7. Quoted in Avramenko, Richard and Ethan Alexander-Davey, *Aristocratic Souls in Democratic Times* (Lexington Books, 2018).

8. Schlegel quoted in Jochen Schulte-Sasse, et al. (ed. and trans.) *Theory as Practice. A Critical Anthology of Early German Romantic Writings* (University of Minnesota Press, 1997), 244–5.

9. In "19th Century Romantic Aesthetics," *Stanford Encyclopedia of Philosophy*, first published June 14, 2016. Available online: https://plato.stanford.edu/entries/aesthetics-19th-romantic/

10. William Blake, "Auguries of Innocence," Available online: https://www.artofeurope.com/bl ake/bla3.htm

11. William Wordsworth "Prospectus" to *The Recluse* line 68, Available online: https://books.g oogle.com/books?id=730VI3FC9PoC&pg=PA30&lpg=PA30&dq=Wordsworth+Prospec tus+to+The+Recluse&source=bl&ots=KrKbIZ_wV6&sig=ACfU3U175o6D_pOUZGBKbg HzBhBss-4qxg&hl=en&sa=X&ved=2ahUKEwiJ6brEtdnlAhXGtp4KHeK0DCAQ6AEw CnoECAgQAQ#v=onepage&q=Wordsworth%20Prospectus%20to%20The%20Recluse&f= false

12. Wordsworth "Preface to Lyrical Ballads" paragraph 26. https://www.bartleby.com/39/36.html

13. Quoted in *Romanticism @ UAB*. Available online: http://romantics-uab.blogspot.com/2009 /03/preface-to-lyrical-ballads-gross-and.html

14. Wordsworth, "Lines Composed a Few Miles above Tintern Abbey, On Revisiting the Banks of the Wye during a Tour. July 13, 1798," Available online: https://www.poetryfoundation.o rg/poems/45527/lines-composed-a-few-miles-above-tintern-abbey-on-revisiting-the-banks -of-the-wye-during-a-tour-july-13-1798

15. Percy Bysshe Shelley, "Ozymandias," Available online: https://www.poetryfoundation.org/po ems/46565/ozymandias

16. John Keats, "Ode on a Grecian Urn," Available online: https://www.poetryfoundation.org/po ems/44477/ode-on-a-grecian-urn

17. Samuel Taylor Coleridge, "Kubla Khan," Available online: https://www.poetryfoundation.org /poems/43991/kubla-khan

18. Coleridge, "Aids to Reflection," Quoted in Available online: http://anglicantheologicalreview .org/static/pdf/articles/barbeau.pdf.

19. Hegel, G. W. F. *Phenomenology of Spirit*, A.V. Miller trans., Oxford: Oxford University Press, 1977, p. 462.

20. Quoted in Schelling, Friedrich von and Andrew Bowie, *On the History of Modern Philosophy* (Cambridge: Cambridge University Press, 1994), 16.

Chapter 4

1. Quoted in *Chambers's Cyclopedia of English Literature*, 3rd ed., vol. VII (New York: American Book Exchange, 1880), 253.

2. Mary Somerville, *On the Connection of the Physical Sciences*, 1. https://books.google.com/books?id=v-IIAAAAIAAJ&pg=PA1&lpg=PA1&dq=%22we+perceive+the+operation+of+a+force+which+is+mixed+up+with+everything+that+exists+in+the+heavens+or+on+earth;+which+pervades+every+atom,+rules+the+motions+of+animate+and+inanimate+beings...%22&source=bl&ots=-jTmVT1N7A&sig=ACfU3U12ZqdgRF1t4s6JjgdeKb-kjFy8dQ&hl=en&sa=X&ved=2ahUKEwjJhfKZlt7lAhXQHjQIHVTvCsQQ6AEwAXoECAkQAQ#v=onepage&q=%22we%20perceive%20the%20operation%20of%20a%20force%20which%20is%20mixed%20up%20with%20everything%20that%20exists%20in%20the%20heavens%20or%20on%20earth%3B%20which%20pervades%20every%20atom%2C%20rules%20the%20motions%20of%20animate%20and%20inanimate%20beings...%22&f=false

Chapter 5

1. "Harriet Law," Available online: http://www.leicestersecularsociety.org.uk/Harriet_Law.php

2. Quoted in Terrell Carver, "Communism for Critical Critics? *The German Ideology* and the Problem of Technology," *History of Political Thought*, IX, no. 1 (Spring 1988): 129.

3. Marx, "Theses on Feuerbach," Thesis XI. Available online: https://www.marxists.org/archive/marx/works/1845/theses/theses.htm

Chapter 6

1. Darwin, Charles, *Origin of Species*, second ed., p. 62, Available online: http://darwin-online.org.uk/Variorum/1860/1860-62-c-1859.html

2. Ibid, p. 490.

3. Ibid, p. 156.

4. Ibid, 3rd ed., 1861, p. 266. Available online: http://darwin-online.org.uk/Variorum/1861/1861-266-c-1859.html

5. Darwin, Letter to Charles Lyell, December 10, 1859, Available online: https://www.darwinproject.ac.uk/letter/DCP-LETT-2575.xml

6. Kipling, Rudyard, "The White Man's Burden" (1899), Available online: https://sourcebooks.fordham.edu/mod/Kipling.asp

Notes

Chapter 7

1. From Gobineau, Count A. de, *The Moral and Intellectual Diversity of Races, with Particular Reference to their Respective Influence in the Civil and Political History of Mankind,* Introduction by H. Hotz (Philadelphia: J.B. Lippincott, 1856), 443. Available online: https://books.google .com/books?id=R_AUAAAAYAAJ&pg=PA443&lpg=PA443&dq=The+dark+races+are+the +lowest+on+the+scale.+The+shape+of+the+pelvis+has+a+character+of+animalism,+which +is+imprinted+on+the+individuals+of+that+race+ere+their+birth,+and+seems+to+portend +their+destiny&source=bl&ots=IwWKss1khO&sig=ACfU3U17eiL9hlfo9DvKq93tTElJ3hH RLQ&hl=et&sa=X&ved=2ahUKEwjIj83K_4XmAhWmCTQIHYSwA88Q6AEwAHoECAQQA Q#v=onepage&q=The%20dark%20races%20are%20the%20lowest%20on%20the%20scale.%2 0The%20shape%20of%20the%20pelvis%20has%20a%20character%20of%20animalism%2C% 20which%20is%20imprinted%20on%20the%20individuals%20of%20that%20race%20ere% 20their%20birth%2C%20and%20seems%20to%20portend%20their%20destiny&f=false

2. "Jeanne-Victoire," (attrib. to Jeanne Deroin) "Appel aux Femmes" (Appeal to Women), *La Femme Libre (The Free Woman),* 1 (1832): 1–3. English translation by Anna Wheeler originally published in Robert Owen's *The Crisis,* June 15, 1833. Reprinted in Susan Groag Bell and Karen M. Offen, eds., *Women, the Family, and Freedom: The Debate in Documents, Volume I, 1750-1880* (Palo Alto, CA: Stanford University Press, 1983), 146–7. Available online: https://womhist.alexanderstreet.com/awrm/doc5.htm

3. George Sand [Amantine-Lucile-Aurore Dupin, baroness Dudevant], excerpts from *Indiana* (originally published in Paris, 1832). Reprinted in *George Sand, Indiana: With a New Chronology of Her Life and Work,* translated by George Burnham Ives (Chicago: Cassandra Editions, Academy Press Ltd, 1978), 205–8. Available online: https://womhist.alexanderstreet .com/awrm/doc6.htm

4. Louise Otto, "Program," *Frauen-Zeitung, Ein Organ fur die Hoheren Weiblichen Interessen,* no. I, April 21, 1849. Translated by Susan Groag Bell. Reprinted in Susan Groag Bell and Karen M. Offen, eds., *Women, the Family, and Freedom: The Debate in Documents, Volume I, 1750-1880* (Palo Alto, CA: Stanford University Press, 1983), 263–4. Available online: https://wo mhist.alexanderstreet.com/awrm/doc12.htm

5. Gamble, Eliza Burt, *The Evolution of Woman. An Inquiry into the Dogma of Her Inferiority to Man,* "Preface," G.P Putnam's Sons, 1894, vi. Available online: https://archive.org/details/cu 31924031728763/page/n13

6. Harriet Taylor Mill, excerpt from "Enfranchisement of Women," *Westminster Review* (July 1851): 295–6. Reprinted in Ann P. Robson and John M. Robson, eds., *Sexual Equality: Writings by John Stuart Mill, Harriet Taylor Mill, and Helen Taylor* (Toronto: University of Toronto Press, 1994), 178–203. Available online: https://womhist.alexanderstreet.com/awrm/doc15.htm

Chapter 8

1. Weber, Max, *The Protestant Ethic and the Spirit of Capitalism,* Talcott Parsons trans. (London and Boston: Unwin Hyman, 1930), Available online: https://www.marxists.org/reference/ archive/weber/protestant-ethic/index.htm

2. Marshall, Alfred, Letter to A.L. Bowley, February 27, 1906, cited in: David L. Sills, Robert King Merton, *Social Science Quotations: Who Said What, When, and Where* (Transaction Publishers, 2000), 151.

Chapter 10

1. John Maynard Keynes, *The Economic Consequences of the Peace* (New York: Harcourt, Brace, and Howe, 1920), 226.
2. Bertrand Russell, in Ludwig Wittgenstein, *Tractatus Logico-Philosophicus* (London: Kegan Paul, Trench, Trubner, & Co. Ltd., 1922), 10.

Chapter 11

1. Quoted in Thomas Morris, *The Matter of the Heart. A History of the Heart in Eleven Operations* (New York, St Martin's Press, 2018), 6.

Chapter 13

1. Achebe, Chinua, "An Image of Africa: Racism in Conrad's 'Heart of Darkness,'" *Massachusetts Review* 18 (1977). Rpt. in Heart of Darkness, An Authoritative Text, background and Sources Criticism. 1961. 3rd ed. Ed. Robert Kimbrough (London: W. W Norton and Co., 1988), 251–61. Available online: http://kirbyk.net/hod/image.of.africa.html
2. Limits to Growth. Available online: http://www.donellameadows.org/wp-content/userfiles/Limits-to-Growth-digital-scan-version.pdf

Chapter 14

1. See the Michael Aldrich Archive, Available online: https://www.aldricharchive.co.uk/
2. Syukuro Manabe and Kirk Bryan, "A Global Ocean-Atmosphere Climate Model. Part I. The Atmospheric Circulation," *The Journal of Physical Oceanography* from "Timeline: The History of Climate Modeling," *CarbonBrief*, January 16, 2018. Available online: https://www.carbonbrief.org/timeline-history-climate-modelling
3. A good description of the process can be seen in the National Radio Astronomy Observatory web page "What are Radio Telescopes?" Available online: https://public.nrao.edu/telescopes/radio-telescopes/
4. See Marshall McLuhan, *Understanding Media*, 1964.
5. T.R. Colburn and G.M Shute, "Metaphor in Computer Science," *Journal of Applied Logic* 6 (2008): 526–33.

FURTHER READING AND RESEARCH

If you enjoy intellectual history, one of the most important things you can do is read lots of primary texts. I recommend that you begin with texts that appeal to a wide readership rather than texts meant for specialists. In the following recommendations, I have included two or three primary texts under each chapter heading. To get you started, here are some of my favorites among the more readable books. If you enjoy fiction, try Fyodor Dostoyevsky's *The Brothers Karamazov* or *Crime and Punishment*. Emile Zola's *Germinal* is fascinating. If you are interested in the social sciences, Max Weber's *The Protestant Ethic and the Spirit of Capitalism* or Emile Durkheim's *Suicide* are quite accessible and intriguing. Adam Smith's *Wealth of Nations* and Charles Darwin's *The Origin of Species* are important, accessible, well written, but lengthy; feel free to sample. Albert Einstein's *Relativity: The Special and the General Theory* is written for nonphysicists and conveys the words of a master. In Philosophy, Jean-Paul Sartre's *Existentialism Is a Humanism* is an excellent and readable introduction to existentialism. Friedrich Nietzsche's *Genealogy of Morality* rewards every effort you put into it. Simone de Beauvoir's *The Second Sex* is provocative and easily read. It will introduce you to several philosophical schools. Mary Wollstonecraft's *A Vindication of the Rights of Women* is a seminal work. I could go on, but my main point is that there are hundreds of influential and readable books, most available for free online, that will introduce you to the ongoing conversation that is intellectual history. It's time to get involved.

The internet has transformed the field of intellectual history. If you are an undergraduate student, you almost certainly grew up in a web-connected world, even if you had no computer access in your home. But many of your professors were educated in a pre-internet world, and they have had to relearn the research skills they had mastered in graduate school.

The first place to start is usually *Wikipedia*. Since it is only partially peer reviewed, it is not the place to end. Although articles in *Wikipedia* sometimes are insufficient, *Wikipedia* has become quite effective in pointing out the shortcomings in its own articles. Most *Wikipedia* articles have a substantial set of notes and resources, as do most online encyclopedias. Many thinkers and concepts are also represented in the much more authoritative *Stanford Encyclopedia of Philosophy*. *The Internet Encyclopedia of Philosophy* is peer reviewed and generally reliable. The *International Encyclopedia of the Social and Behavioral Sciences* is also a valuable online resource. *The Routledge Encyclopedia of Philosophy* is substantial. *The Cambridge History of Modern European Thought* provides excellent in-depth articles that bear directly on the material in this text. *Oxford Reference Online* provides access to articles on most of the people and ideas treated in this text.

There are many more online encyclopedias and databases. Most of them are quite costly and are beyond the means of individual students and scholars. A decent college or university library probably subscribes to a wide variety of these valuable reference books. Make use of them while you are still in academia.

One of the best ways to identify a question for research is to start with a primary source or sources. Read critically and begin to ask questions about the text. What would you like to ask the author if that person were available? That is, step into the intellectual history salon. When you are ready with questions, you are ready to see how other scholars may have answered them. You can enter the conversation in the salon. The best way to find sources for a research paper is to find a recent scholarly paper that deals with a closely related subject. Begin with the sources listed in its bibliography. As you use those sources, see what is in their bibliographies. You can then use the databases in your library (like JSTOR and EBSCOhost) to access most of the articles. Most will probably be online. If they are not, find them in your library or use interlibrary loan to have them sent for your use.

Much of the fun in historical research is searching archives and rarely used sources to find ways of answering your question. Often this kind of research is done at the graduate level, in part because it usually involves travel. Nevertheless, the more you can mine primary sources to answer your question, the more you may feel that you have made a small contribution to the sum of our historical knowledge. Remember: ideas are not fragile—feel free to toss them around. They are time-travelers that have changed as they moved.

Hundreds of books in intellectual history are published each year. It is impossible to keep up with all of them or to list even a small sample here. What follows is an idiosyncratic list of primary and secondary works that I think may be useful to you. Another intellectual historian would probably offer a different list, although I suspect that there would be many overlaps. Most of the primary sources are also described in the body of the text.

Chapter 1 Important Ideas and Events as Seen in 1800 CE

Doyle, William, *The Oxford History of the French Revolution* (2003).
Israel, Jonathan, *Revolutionary Ideas: An Intellectual History of the French Revolution from The Rights of Man to Robespierre* (2014).
Kaufmann, Walter, *Goethe, Kant, and Hegel* (1991)
Kuehn, Manfred, *Kant: A Biography* (2002)
Rosen, William, *The Most Powerful Idea in the World: A Story of Steam, Industry, and Invention* (2012).
Uglow, Jenny, *The Lunar Men: The Inventors of the Modern World* (2003).

Chapter 2 Individuals and Atoms: Individuals as Source of Wealth, Reason, and Morality

Selected Primary Sources

Mill, John Stuart, *Utilitarianism* (1863); or *On Liberty* (1859).
Smith, Adam, *An Inquiry into the Nature and Causes of the Wealth of Nations* (1776).
Wollstonecraft, Mary, *A Vindication of the Rights of Woman* (1792).

Selected Secondary Sources

Buchwald, Jed Z. and Robert Fox, eds., *The Oxford Handbook of the History of Physics* (2014).
Garber, Elizabeth, *The Language of Physics: The Calculus and the Development of Theoretical Physics in Europe, 1750–1914* (1999).
Golinski, Jan, *Science as Public Culture: Chemistry and Enlightenment in Britain*, 1760–1820 (1999).
Katzenstein, Mary Fainsod and Carol McClurg Mueller, *The Women's Movements of the United States and Western Europe: Consciousness, Political Opportunity, and Public Policy* (1987).
Turner, Rachel S, *Neo-Liberal Ideology: History, Concepts and Policies* (2008).

Chapter 3 Transcendence: From Community to God: Collective Wisdom and Revolutionary Transformation

Selected Primary Sources

Burke, Edmund, *Reflections on the Revolution in France* (1790).
Wordsworth, William, "Preface to Lyrical Ballads" (1798).

Selected Secondary Sources

Ameriks, Karl, *The Cambridge Companion to German Idealism* (2000).
Beers, Henry A., *A History of English Romanticism in the Nineteenth Century* (2014).
Buchwald, Jed, *The Rise of the Wave Theory of Light: Optical Theory and Experiment in the Early Nineteenth Century* (1989).
Eccleshall, Robert, *English Conservatism Since the Restoration: An Introduction & Anthology* (1990).
Fosso, Kurt, *Buried Communities: Wordsworth and the Bonds of Mourning* (2003)
Fritzman, J. M., *Hegel* (2014).
Jones, Emily, *Edmund Burke and the Invention of Modern Conservatism, 1830–1914* (2017).
Pinker, Terry P., *German Philosophy, 1760–1860: The Legacy of Idealism.* (2002).

Chapter 4 Mechanizing the Human World

Selected Primary Sources

Bernard, Claude, *An Introduction to the Study of Experimental Medicine*
Somerville, Mary, *Personal Recollections, From Early Life to Old Age.*

Selected Secondary Sources

Anderson, Marlow, Victor J. Katz and Robin J. Wilson, *Who Gave You the Epsilon?: And Other Tales of Mathematical History* (2009).
Bowler, Peter and Iwan Rhys Morus, *Making Modern Science: A Historical Survey* (2005).
Buchwald, Jed, *From Maxwell to Microphysics: Aspects of Electromagnetic Theory in the Last Quarter of the Nineteenth Century* (1985).
Burton, David M., *The History of Mathematics: An Introduction* (1997).
Christopher, J. T., *Heat and Thermodynamics: A Historical Perspective* (2007).
Harman, Peter, *Energy, Force, and Matter: The Conceptual Development of Nineteenth-Century Physics* (1982).
Harman, Peter, *The Natural Philosophy of James Clerk Maxwell* (1998).
Hunt, Bruce, *The Maxwellians* (1991).
Jungnickel, Christa and Russell McCormmach, *The Intellectual Mastery of Nature: Theoretical Physics from Ohm to Einstein* (1986).
Kuhn, Thomas, "Energy Conservation as an Example of Simultaneous Discovery" (1957).
Morus, Iwan Rhys, *The Oxford Illustrated History of Science* (2017).
Smith, Crosbie, *The Science of Energy: A Cultural History of Energy Physics in Victorian Britain* (1998).

Smith, Crosbie and M. Norton Wise, *Energy and Empire: A Biographical Study of Lord Kelvin* (1989).

Thomasen, Laura Sovso and Henrik Kragh Sorensen, "The Irony of Romantic Mathematics: Bridging the Historiographies of Literature and Mathematics" (2016).

Chapter 5 Socialisms and Marxism

Selected Primary Sources

Fourier, Charles, *Theory of the Four Movements* (1808).
Marx, Karl and Friedrich Engels, *The Communist Manifesto* (1848).
Saint-Simon, Henri, *On the Industrial System* (1822).

Selected Secondary Sources

Althusser, Louis and Étienne Balibar, *Reading Capital* (2009).
Barnett, Vincent, *Marx* (2009).
Engels, Frederick, *Socialism:" Utopian and Scientific* (1880).
Goldstein, L., "Early Feminist Themes in French Utopian Socialism: The St. Simonians and Fourier" (1982).
Harrington, Michael, *Socialism* (1973).
Lenin, Vladimir, *Karl Marx: A Brief Biographical Sketch* (1913).
Lindemann, Albert, *A History of European Socialism* (1984).
McLellan, David, *Karl Marx: A Biography* (2006).

Chapter 6 From God's Plan to Marketplace Creation: Darwin and Darwinisms

Selected Primary Sources

Darwin, Charles, *The Origin of Species* (1859).
Kropotkin, Peter, *Mutual Aid: A Factor of Evolution* (1902).
Nietzsche, Friedrich, *On the Genealogy of Morality* (1887).
Paley, William, *Natural Theology, or Evidences of the Existence and Attributes of the Deity collected from the Appearances of Nature* (1802).
Spencer, Herbert, *The Social Organism* (1860).

Selected Secondary Sources

Bowler, Peter J., *Evolution: The History of an Idea* (2003).
Browne, Janet, *Charles Darwin: vol. 1 Voyaging. vol. 2 The Power of Place* (2002).
Francis, Mark, *Herbert Spencer and the Invention of Modern Life* (2007).
MacLaughlin, Jim, *Kropotkin and the Anarchist Intellectual Tradition* (2016).
Morris, Brian, *Kropotkin: The Politics of Community* (2004).

Chapter 7 Nationalism and Other "isms"

Selected Primary Sources

Fichte, Johann Gottlieb, *Addresses to the German Nation* (1806).
Herzl, Theodor, *The Jewish State* (1896).
Mazzini, Giuseppe, *On Nationality* (1862).
Pearson, Karl, *National Life from the Standpoint of Science* (1902).

Selected Secondary Sources

Gould, Stephen Jay, *The Mismeasure of Man* (1996).
Ruti, Marti, *The Age of Scientific Sexism* (2015).
Herzl, Theodor and Marvin Lowenthal, *The Diaries of Theodor Herzl* (1956).
Richards, Graham, *Race, Racism and Psychology: Towards a Reflexive History* (2011).
Hessler, Martina et al., *Urban Modernity: Cultural Innovation in the Second Industrial Revolution* (2010).
Paletschek, Sylvia and Bianka Pietrow-Ennker, *Women's Emancipation Movements in the Nineteenth Century: A European Perspective* (2006).
Tucker, William H. and Mazal Holocaust Collection, *The Science and Politics of Racial Research* (1994).

Chapter 8 Redefining Individuals and Society: Sociology, Economics, and Clinical Psychology

Selected Primary Sources

Durkheim, Emile, *Suicide* (1897).
Freud, Sigmund, *Civilization and Its Discontents* (1930).
Weber, Max, *The Protestant Ethic and the Spirit of Capitalism* (1905).

Selected Secondary Sources

Brunn, Hans Henrik, *Science, Values, and Politics in Max Weber's Methodology* (2007).
Dufresne, Todd, *Killing Freud: Twentieth-Century Culture and the Death of Psychoanalysis* (2003).
Gay, Peter, *Freud: A Life for Our Time* (1988).
Isaksson, Anna, "Classical Sociology through the Lens of Gendered Experiences," https://doi.org/10.3389/fsoc.2020.532792.
Jones, Ernest, *The Life and Work of Sigmund Freud* (1953–57).
Redman, Samuel J., *Bone Rooms: From Scientific Racism to Human Prehistory in Museums* (2016).
Sera-Shriar, Efram, *The Making of British Anthropology, 1813–1871. Science and Culture in the Nineteenth Century* (2013).
Waters, Tony and Dagmar Waters, *Weber's Rationalism and Modern Society* (2015).

Chapter 9 The Early Modern World

Selected Primary Sources

Bergson, Henri, *An Introduction to Metaphysics* (1903).
Einstein, Albert, *Relativity: The Special and the General Theory* (1916).
Kandinsky, Wassily, *Concerning the Spiritual in Art* (1912).
Wittgenstein, Ludwig, *Tractatus* (1922).

Selected Secondary Sources

Butler, Christopher, Early Modernism: Literature, Music, and Painting in Europe, 1900–1916 (1994).
Galaty, David et al., *Revolutions in Art and Ideas at the Turn of the Twentieth Century* (1987).
Galison, Peter, *Einstein's Clocks, Poincaré's Maps* (2004).
Henderson, Linda Dalrymple, *The Fourth Dimension and Non-Euclidean Geometry in Modern Art* (2013).
Kern, Steven, *The Culture of Time and Space, 1880–1918* (2003).
Levenson, Michael, *The Cambridge Companion to Modernism* (2011).
Linett, Maren Tova, *The Cambridge Companion to Modernist Women Writers* (2010).
Mohanty, J. N., *The Philosophy of Edmund Husserl: A Historical Development* (2008).
Nagel, Ernest and James Neumann, *Gödel's Proof* (1958).
Dreyfus, Hubert L., and Mark A. Wrathall, *A Companion to Phenomenology and Existentialism* (2006).
Staley, Richard, *Einstein's Generation: The Origins of the Relativity Revolution* (2008)
Trudeau, Richard J., *The Non-Euclidean Revolution* (1987).

Chapter 10 Searching for a New World Order

Selected Primary Sources

Lenin, Vladimir, *Imperialism, The Highest Stage of Capitalism* (1917).
Marinetti, F. T., *Manifesto of Futurism* (1909).
Mussolini, Benito, *My Autobiography: With "The Political and Social Doctrine of Fascism"* (1928).
Yeats, W. B., "The Second Coming" (1920).

Selected Secondary Sources

Blom, Philipp, *Fracture: Life and Culture in the West, 1918–1938* (2015).
Evans, Richard J., *The Third Reich in Power* (2005).
Gellately, Robert, *Lenin, Stalin, and Hitler: The Age of Social Catastrophe* (2007).
Gill, Graeme, *Stalinism* (1998).
Kershaw, Ian, *Hitler 1889–1936: Hubris* (1999).
Mazower, Mark, *Dark continent: Europe's Twentieth Century* (2009).
Miller, Barbara, *Nazi Ideology Before 1933: A Documentation* (2014).
Sternhell, Zeev, *The Birth of Fascist Ideology, From Cultural Rebellion to Political Revolution* (1994).
Tucker, Robert C., *Stalinism: Essays in historical interpretation* (2017).

Chapter 11 Technology and Science at Mid-century

Selected Primary Sources

Feynman, Richard P., *QED: The Strange Theory of Light and Matter* (1985).
Watson, James, *The Double Helix* (1968).

Selected Secondary Sources

Bynum, W. F. et al., *The Western Medical Tradition: 1800–2000* (2006).
Mukherjee, Siddharta, *The Gene: An Intimate History* (2017).
Perlov, Delia and Alex Vilenkin, *Cosmology for the Curious* (2017).
Rhodes, Richard, *Energy: A Human History*, Simon and Schuster (2018).
Styler, Daniel F., *The Strange World of Quantum Mechanics* (2000).

Chapter 12 New Anomalies and Challenges

Selected Primary Sources

de Beauvoir, Simone, *The Second Sex* (1949).
Claude Levi Strauss, *Structural Anthropology* (1958).
Arendt, Hannah, *The Human Condition* (1958).

Selected Secondary Sources

Bakewell, Sarah, At the Existentialist Cafe (2016).
Berry, David, *Revisiting the Frankfurt School: Essays on Culture, Media and Theory* (2011).
Bottomore, Tom, *The Frankfurt School and its Critics* (2002).
Dor, Joel, *Introduction to the Reading of Lacan: The Unconscious Structured Like a Language* (2001).
Mahon, Joseph and Jo Campling, *Existentialism, Feminism, and Simone De Beauvoir* (1997).
Mann, Bonnie, *Women's Liberation and the Sublime: Feminism, Postmodernism, Environment* (2006).
Moyn, Samuel, *The Last Utopia: Human Rights in History* (2010)
Schwartz, Frederic J., *Blind Spots: Critical Theory and the History of Art in Twentieth-Century Germany* (2005).

Chapter 13 Intellect against Reason: Reason Fights Back

Selected Primary Sources

Fanon, Frantz, *The Wretched of the Earth* (1963).
Foucault, Michel, *History of Madness* (2006).
Kuhn, Thomas, *The Structure of Scientific Revolutions* (1962).

Selected Secondary Sources

Berend, Ivan T., *The Contemporary Crisis of the European Union: Prospects for the Future* (2017).

Blee, Kathleen M. and Sandra McGee Deutsch, eds., *Women of the Right: Comparisons and Interplay Across Borders* (2012).

Clemens, Clay and William E. Paterson, eds., *The Kohl Chancellorship* (1998).

Curd, Martin, J. A. Cover, and Christopher Pincock, *Philosophy of Science: The Central Issues* (2013).

Gray, John, *Enlightenment's Wake: Politics and Culture at the Close of the Modern Age* (2007).

Hainsworth, Paul, *The Extreme Right in Western Europe* (2008).

Kelly, Mark G. E., *The Political Philosophy of Michel Foucault* (2009).

McCormick, John, *The European Union: Politics and Policies* (2007).

Rajan, Tilottama, *Deconstruction and the Remainders of Phenomenology: Sartre, Derrida, Foucault, Baudrillard* (2002).

Sim, Stuart, *The Routledge Companion to Postmodernism* (2001).

Sokal, Alan D., and Jean Bricmont. *Fashionable Nonsense: Postmodern Intellectuals' Abuse of Science* (2011).

von Plato, Alexander, *The End of the Cold War?: Bush, Kohl, Gorbachev, and the Reunification of Germany* (2016).

Yesilada, Birol A. and David M. Wood, *The Emerging European Union* (2009).

Chapter 14 The Cyber Century Approaching

Copeland, Jack, *Artificial Intelligence: A Philosophical Introduction* (1993).

Dormehl, Luke, *Thinking Machines: The Quest for Artificial Intelligence -- and Where It's Taking Us Next* (2017).

Galison, Peter, *Big Science: The Growth of Large Scale Research* (1994).

Isaacson, Walter, *The Innovators: How a Group of Hackers, Geniuses, and Geeks Created the Digital Revolution* (2015).

Levy, Steven, *Hackers: Heroes of the Computer Revolution* (2010).

O'Neil, Cathy, *Weapons of Math Destruction: How Big Data Increases Inequality and Threatens Democracy* (2017).

Pearl, Judea and Dana Mackenzie, *The Book of Why: The New Science of Cause and Effect* (2018).

Swain, Michael and Paul Freiberger, *Fire in the Valley: The Birth and Death of the Personal Computer* (2014).

Wiener, Norbert, *The Human Use of Human Beings* (1988).

INDEX OF NAMES

Index of Names

INDEX OF CONCEPTS

Index of Concepts

$E=mc^2$ 262

economics
  classical   30, 107, 112, 118, 136, 143, 305, 376
  historical school   186
  marginal   37, 198–200

ecosystem   5, 142, 206

egalitarianism   28, 72, 232

electricity   50, 56, 57, 77–80, 85, 90, 94, 98, 100, 102, 194, 206–9, 287, 346, 353

electromagnetism   79, 95, 97–100, 194, 219

electron   104, 207, 226–8, 267, 276, 278, 280, 283, 286, 350–3, 366, 367, 371, 379

embryology   77, 223

empiricist   13

empty signifier   307, 308

energy   8, 84, 85, 95–8, 143, 194, 207, 217, 221, 223, 226, 227, 229, 262, 263, 276, 278, 279, 283–7, 290, 293, 328, 356, 362

Enlightenment   4, 8, 20–2, 29, 40, 43, 48, 50, 62, 72, 74, 75, 88, 108, 131, 135, 170, 314, 322, 329

entropy, maximization of   95–7

environment   5, 22, 25, 60, 108, 109, 132–5, 138, 144, 149, 169, 173, 174, 185, 244, 266, 267, 269, 270, 318, 325–8, 342

environmental movement   325–9

epigenesis   90

episteme   335

epistemology   191, 335

epoché (bracketing off)   256

equality   25, 41, 45–8, 50, 59, 62, 72, 111, 124, 157, 162, 168, 170, 174–6, 240, 319, 342, 373–6, 388

equivalence principle (relativity)   217

eScience   361–3, 365

essentialist   176

Estates General   23, 46, 62

ether   93, 98, 101, 102, 213, 214

ethnocentrism   159

eugenics   142, 152, 222, 267, 270

Euronet   356, 357

The European Organization for Nuclear Research (CERN)   280, 350, 357, 361

European Union   319, 337, 343–7, 373, 375

Euro zone   345

evolution   115, 128, 129, 131–6, 138, 139, 144, 145, 149–51, 153, 163, 173, 176, 223, 249, 270, 284, 350, 379, 388

exist (definition)   13, 74, 193, 228–9, 257, 258, 380

existentialism   76, 255, 290, 297–301, 309, 324, 390

experience   2, 4, 10, 12, 15, 41, 43, 57, 63–5, 67, 70, 71, 73–6, 90, 143, 146, 153, 156, 158, 178, 184–5, 193, 203, 204, 206, 212, 217, 218, 253–7, 259, 265, 286, 287, 300, 302–4, 308, 311, 314, 316, 324, 333, 334, 360, 368, 371, 376, 381, 384

experiment   12, 22, 40, 45, 51, 79, 92, 93, 98–100, 107, 110, 143, 171, 213, 214, 216–18, 221, 223, 224, 226, 228, 229, 262, 292, 330, 332

expert system approach   369

exponential growth   384

extension   52, 117, 207, 208, 233, 365

factory system   8, 16, 17, 108

faith   16, 21, 34, 39, 61, 74, 75, 98, 105, 131, 136, 138, 156, 167, 175, 299, 369

Falange   249

falsification   92, 331

fascism   247–9, 295, 300, 313, 314, 341, 376

feedback loop   327

feminism   111, 147, 184, 291, 310–13

Feynman diagrams   277

field   2, 80, 81, 85, 98, 194, 214, 217–20, 222, 277, 278, 280, 300, 380, 382

field theory   2, 85, 214, 219, 277, 382

file sharing   360

First International (International Workingmen's Association)   105

five year plan   246, 290, 294

Flatland   220–1

Flying shuttle   16

force   2, 8, 10–12, 14, 73, 78–81, 84, 85, 90, 94, 95, 98, 99, 102, 133, 148, 149, 153, 203, 219, 263, 278, 280, 283–5, 307, 336, 349

form   210

fossil record   133, 138

fourth dimension   206, 211, 214, 221, 281

franchise   24, 40, 41, 117, 123, 162, 174, 176, 177, 239

Frankfurt School   291, 309, 313–15

fraternity   25, 62, 168, 373, 376

freedom   4, 21, 24, 42, 49, 63–5, 70–5, 117, 129, 131, 159, 167, 179, 244, 290, 292, 298–301, 309, 311, 314, 315, 318, 320, 332, 337, 342, 346, 358, 373, 375

free enterprise   35, 47, 49, 290, 329

free market   4, 33, 34, 136, 137, 142, 233, 296, 342

free will   228, 308

French Revolution   21–5, 28, 29, 37, 43, 46, 50, 57, 59, 61, 62, 64, 68, 71, 72, 94, 112, 117, 156, 158, 159, 168, 170, 178, 180, 373, 376

Freud, theory of mind   185

functionalism   305

fundamental particles   276, 278, 279

futurism   230

Gaia hypothesis   328

Geist   75, 186, 372

gene   2, 223, 263, 266–9

Index of Concepts

radio telescopes   282, 350, 364–5
radio waves   285, 336, 364, 381
railroads   3, 20, 85–8, 117, 156, 160, 207, 208, 233,
      244, 357, 364, 378
randomness   140, 286
rationalization   187–9
realism
      art   116–17
      novel   115
red shift   282
reductionism   269, 382
relativity theory
      general   276
      special   276
religion   15, 16, 20, 25, 28, 47, 57, 59, 61, 66, 74,
      75, 112, 114, 128, 131, 143, 158, 179, 187,
      189, 192, 193, 203, 233, 247, 265, 375
representation   23, 39, 46, 210, 211, 284, 313, 335
representational art   210
repression   314
republicanism   23, 25
reversion to the mean   267
revolution   3, 8, 9, 14–17, 20–6, 28, 29, 34, 37,
      39, 43, 46, 47, 50, 55, 57, 59, 61, 62, 64, 68,
      71, 72, 94, 105, 107, 112, 115, 117–18, 120,
      122–3, 152, 156, 158, 159, 161, 167, 168,
      170, 174, 175, 178, 180, 193, 199, 203, 204,
      207, 221, 223, 243, 244, 246, 247, 301, 314,
      317, 318, 320, 321, 325, 327, 339, 347, 350,
      369, 373, 376–9
      1832   117
      1848   117–18, 161, 170
      communist   243, 246, 320
      French   21–5, 28–9, 37, 43, 46, 50, 57, 59, 61,
      62, 64, 68, 71, 72, 94, 112, 117, 156, 158,
      159, 168, 170, 178, 180, 373, 376
revolutionary vanguard   244
romanticism
      English   57, 66–70
      German   57, 64–6

Sanskrit   162, 163
Sapir-Whorf hypothesis   303
Say's Law   37, 241
scala naturae   132, 144
Schengen Agreement   345, 375
Schrödinger's cat   228
science   2, 4, 8–10, 12, 13, 15, 18, 20, 22, 28, 35,
      45, 49, 51, 63, 64, 67, 70, 74–7, 79, 81,
      83–5, 89–94, 96–7, 100–4, 112–14, 128,
      130, 131, 138, 140, 142–4, 149, 150, 153,
      158, 163, 164, 171, 172, 184, 186–91, 193,
      196, 197, 199, 200, 204, 210, 213, 220–3,
      234
science and technology studies   331

science-based medicine   271
science fiction   220–1, 270
scientific method   13, 92, 271, 331
scientific racism   171–2
scientific socialism   112
second industrial revolution   206–10
second international   124
second wave feminism   310–13
secular (freethought) movement   106
secularism   62, 67
semiconductor   353
sense   8, 12–14, 41, 44, 67, 73, 159, 192–3, 212,
      380
sensorium   10
signifier   303, 306–8
singularity   283, 370–1
Sisyphus   300–1
social class   23, 29, 31, 43, 45, 75, 105–7, 112, 115,
      117, 119, 120, 122, 129, 140, 142, 143, 150,
      151, 154, 159, 165, 167, 170, 174, 198, 204,
      220, 221, 223, 239, 240, 243, 244, 247, 248,
      311, 312, 321, 324, 375
social construction of ideas   319, 329
social contract   21, 46
Social Darwinism   129, 152, 153, 234
social democracy   129, 152–3
social facts   184, 191–3
socialism   43, 105–25, 147, 177, 246, 247, 293,
      312, 320, 337, 338, 342
      scientific (Marx)   112, 118–22
      utopian   107–15, 118
socialist humanism   315
socialist realism   247
social laws   199
social welfare system   295–7
sociology   112–14, 183–7, 190, 204, 265, 301, 305,
      336
software   350, 355, 365
sovereignty   345
soviets   243, 291, 292, 320, 321
Soviet Union   135, 243, 246, 248, 249, 264, 265,
      267, 290–3, 295, 318–21, 337–9, 344, 347
space   4, 10–14, 52, 57, 63, 77–8, 80–1, 85, 96, 98,
      102, 193, 206, 207, 210, 212, 213, 216, 217,
      219–21, 226, 227, 257, 276, 278, 280–5, 326,
      330, 332, 334, 362, 365
spacetime   206, 207, 219, 281, 283
special theory of relativity   214, 215
spectral lines   227, 228
spider program   359
spirit   2, 57, 67, 73, 75, 79, 98, 142, 144, 160, 165,
      167, 168, 186–9, 236, 248, 307, 315, 372,
      374, 377
stagflation   341, 342
Stalinism   245–7, 321

408

Index of Concepts

vital force   90, 349
vivisection   92
Voltaic pile   28

Warsaw pact   293, 318, 320, 347
wave   2, 77, 78, 98, 152, 213, 226–9, 285, 299, 310, 312, 313
wave theory   2
weather prediction   85, 88–9
website   156, 177, 350, 357–60
Weimar Constitution   238
Weltanschauung   164
Weltansicht   164

Whig History   167
wholes   1–3, 300, 382, 384
will to power   146–9, 300
wireless
   radio   20
   telegraph   20, 100, 208
   telephone   100
Wirtschaftswunder   295
women's rights   27, 40, 43, 46, 106, 162, 174, 177
world soul   73
World Wide Web   357–8, 360

Zionism   178–9, 181, 182